# DIGITAL DEFLATION

## The Productivity Revolution and How It Will Ignite the Economy

**GRAHAM Y. TANAKA**

**McGraw-Hill**

New York   Chicago   San Francisco
Lisbon   London   Madrid   Mexico City
Milan   New Delhi   San Juan   Seoul

*The **McGraw·Hill** Companies*

1 2 3 4 5 6 7 8 9 0   DOC/DOC   0 9 8 7 6 5 4 3

ISBN 0-07-137617-8

McGraw-Hill books are available at special discounts to use as premiums and sales promotions, or for use in corporate training programs. For more information, please write to the Director of Special Sales, Professional Publishing, McGraw-Hill, Two Penn Plaza, New York, NY 10121-2298. Or contact your local bookstore.

 This book is printed on recycled, acid-free paper containing a minimum of 50% recycled, de-inked fiber.

Library of Congress Cataloging-in-Publication Data

Tanaka, Graham Y.
  Digital deflation : the productivity revolution and how it will ignite the economy / by Graham Tanaka.
      p. cm.
  Includes bibliographical references.
  ISBN 0-07-137617-8 (alk. paper)
  1. Technological innovations—Economic aspects—United States.   2. Industrial productivity—Effect of technological innovations on—United States.   3. Digital divide—Economic aspects—United States.   4. United States—Economic policy—2001–   I. Title.
HD45 .T36 2003
330.973—dc21
                                        2003012929

# DEDICATION

This book is dedicated to my mom, Yuri, and in memory of my dad, Yasuo Clifford, who always encouraged me to do my best and who gave me the guidance and education to achieve my goals. I would also like to dedicate this book to my wife, Molly, and my kids, Spencer and Russell, who were patient and accommodating on those countless weekends and evenings I spent researching and writing *Digital Deflation*.

# C O N T E N T S

**Preface**  xii

**Introduction**  xiv

CHAPTER 1

## MYSTERIES, PUZZLES, AND PARADOXES OF THE NEW ECONOMY  1

The New Economy of the 1990s  1
Was the New Economy of the 1990s Real?  3
Why Were the 1990s So Great?  5
Is There Too Much Optimism or Too Much Pessimism?  7
Are We Heading for Deflation Like Japan in the '90s or the U.S. in the '30s?  9
Can the Future Be What It Used to Be?  10

CHAPTER 2

## SOLVING THE MYSTERY:  MISSING PRODUCTIVITY AND THE GREAT INFLATION MISMEASURE  11

Demographics:  Baby Boomers, Working Women, and the Super
  Bull Market  11
Three Hits and a Miss  15
Where's the Missing Productivity?  15
The Boskin Reports on the CPI  19
"Faster, Better, Cheaper"—The Parable of the Pink Caddy  21
The Intel–Microsoft Double Helix and John the Barber's PC  23
The Consumer Knows Best  24
How the Government Counts Quality Improvement  26
Solving the Mystery of the New Economy  28

CHAPTER 3

## THE THEORY OF DIGITAL DEFLATION: FASTER, BETTER, CHEAPER  31

Digital Deflation Is a *Good* Thing  31
Digital Deflation Defined  32
The Digital Drivers  35

The "Next Big Thing"  39
Is the Digital Revolution Better Than the Industrial Revolution?  40
The Laws of Digital Deflation  41
How Big Is Digital Deflation?  43
What's Missing from the GDP Deflator?  47
The Lost Components  49

CHAPTER 4

# WHY THE OLD MODELS DIDN'T WORK IN THE 1970s AND 1980s  53

Economic Models Work Best in Times of Stability and Few Surprises  53
The 1950s and 1960s: Existing Economic Models Worked Well  54
The Late 1960s/Early 1970s: Models Break Down with the Rise
    in Inflation  55
Internal Disruption from Wage-Price Controls  56
External Disruption from OPEC Oil Price Increases  59
The Late 1970s: Hyperinflation  59
The Demise of the Keynesian Dynasty  60
Monetarism Takes the Lead  60
The 1980s: Volcker to the Rescue  62
The Early 1980s: Enter the Supply-Siders  64
The Late 1980s: Market Price Rule Predictors  67
Demographics—Why the Traditional Models Didn't Work  69
Demographic Forces Turn Positive in the 1980s and 1990s  71

CHAPTER 5

# WHY ECONOMISTS HAVE DIFFICULTY EXPLAINING THE NEW ECONOMY  74

The Amazing 1990s—Strong Growth and *Low* Inflation  74
Information Technology, Productivity, and the New Economy  77
Overstated Inflation and Undermeasured Productivity  78
Was the Internet Driving the New Economy?  80
Digital Deflation—Why the Old Models Didn't Work in the 1990s  80
Productivity from Digital Deflation Is About Quality, Not Quantity  83
What the Government Didn't See…  86
…Consumers and Investors Could See  87
The Year 2000 Lockdown  88
The Wealth Effect—A Rising New Force in the New Economy  92

Is There a Corporate Wealth Effect?   95
Investor-Consumers   95
New Models Needed   96

**CHAPTER 6**

## REDEFINING THE NEW ECONOMY   98

New Forces in the New Economy   98
What Is the New Economy?   99
Digital Deflation Redefines the New Economy   100
Old Economy Companies in the New Economy   103
The Importance of R&D   106
The Old Economy Will Lose Share and Profits to the New Economy   107
How the New Economy Lifts Productivity   108
Structural Productivity Gains   109
When Did the Government Start to Measure Digital Deflation?   110
How Did Computer Quality Improvement Boost Productivity in the
    Late 1990s?   112
Massive Implications for Productivity Across the Economy   114
Software Quality Improvements Are Elusive but Real   115
Communication Services Are Getting Faster, Better, Cheaper   117
The Huge Healthcare Quality Mismeasure   119
The Service Sector Is Grossly Undermeasured   120
The Service Sector Supply Chain   122
Solving the Mystery of Rising Capital Spending and Declining
    Productivity   124
The "Productivity Revolution" Is Under Way   126
Disaggregation into the New Economy and the Old Economy   128

**CHAPTER 7**

## NEW MODELS FOR THE NEW ECONOMY   129

Better Models, Better Forecasting   129

**I. DEMOGRAPHIC MODELS   130**

A Demographic Foundation for the New Economy   130
The Demographic–Inflation Model   131
The Demographic–Stock Market Model   135
The Demographic–Productivity Model   135
Demographic–Productivity Model Adjusted for Unmeasured
    Digital Deflation   136

Demographic–GDP Models    137
The Stock Market and Real GDP    137
The Stock Market and Corporate Profits    139
"Potential Productivity"    139

II. PRODUCTIVITY MODELS    140

The Capital Spending–Productivity Model Revisited    140
How Long Has the Government Undermeasured Productivity?    142
Productivity and Profit Margin Model    143
The 120% Profit–Productivity Rule of Thumb    145
The Over 3.0% Productivity Growth Rule    146
The New Economy Productivity–Profit Enigma    146
Are Quality Gains Empty Calories?    148
The Fed's Productivity and Capital Decomposition Model    151
New Models for Predicting Information Technology's Contribution to
    GDP and Productivity    153

III. DIGITAL DEFLATION MODELS    156

Estimating the Undermeasurement of Digital Deflation    157
The "GDP Deflator-Digital Deflation" Model    159
Computer and Semiconductor Digital Deflation "Lost" As Intermediate
    Goods    161
IT Industries Not Yet Measured for Quality Improvement, Including
    Computer Services, Software, and Communications    163
Non-IT Industries Not Yet Measured for Quality Improvement, Including
    Healthcare, Financial Services, and the Military    167
The Quality Improvement Quotient    172
The "CPI-Digital Deflation" Model    173

IV. WEALTH MODELS    177

Household Tangible and Net Financial Assets    177
The Wealth Effect    181
The Consumer Wealth Effect    181
The Realized Capital Gains Wealth Effect    185
The Corporate Wealth Effect    186

**CHAPTER 8**

## THE WEALTH IN OUR FUTURE    191

The 2020 Vision    191
A Wide Range of Possible Outcomes    193

Value Created from Digitally Driven Quality Improvement   194
Two More Decades of Value Creation   196
Value to Wealth: The New Economy's Virtuous Circle   198
Measuring Wealth   200
Adjusting Wealth for Digital Deflation   202
A Strong Demographic Foundation for Generating Wealth   203
The Digital Deflation Wealth Multipliers   206
The Key to Wealth Is Low Inflation   207
A "Near Zero Experience"   208
Picturing Zero Inflation Will Be Difficult for Many   209
The GDP Deflator Adjusted for Digital Deflation   210
The CPI Adjusted for Digital Deflation   212
Why the CPI and GDP Deflator Will Diverge   213
Which Is the Right Inflation Rate?   214
Four Scenarios for the Wealth In Our Future   215
Fair Value P/E's and Wealth   217

**CHAPTER 9**

## THE NEW ECONOMY STOCK MARKET   218

The Importance of Equities   218
A "New Economy Stock Market Model"   219
Inflation, Interest Rates, and Fair Value P/E's   224
P/E Ratio Forecasts for the Next Two Decades   228
Higher Productivity and Profit Margins in the Next Two Decades   229
New Economy Stock Market Projections   236
Two More Decades of Wealth Creation   236
A New Economy Wealth Model   239
Growth in Equity-Like Assets   240
How Digital Deflation Helps Homeowners Build Wealth   242
Digital Deflation Helps Tangible Assets by Driving Interest Rates
   Lower   243
The Enormous Upside Potential for Wealth Creation in the
   United States   244
On the Upside   245
On the Downside   247
Most Likely Scenario   248
The Surprising Importance of the Real Bond Rate   248
Stocks, Wealth, and the New Economy   252

**CHAPTER 10**

## MONETARY POLICY: NEW "SPEED LIMITS" FOR THE FED   255

The Fed's Challenge   255
A Tale of Two Economies   256
Avoiding a Repeat of the 1920s and 1930s   260
Learning from the 1920s and 1930s   265
Counting Quality Improvement Will Make the Fed's Job Easier   266
New Speed Limits for the Fed   268
Running Out of Room at the Fed   273
Lessons from Japan's Deflationary Slump   275
Productivity Gains in a Deflationary Economy   278
The Past and Future Fed   281

**CHAPTER 11**

## FISCAL POLICY AND BETTER DATA IN A DIGITALLY DEFLATING WORLD   283

Wealth and Poverty in the New Economy   283
Wage Earners Will Earn More   286
The New Economy, Unemployment, and Crime   288
The "Politics Of Need"   290
Better Data for the New Economy   292
The New Economy and Budget Surpluses   294
The Dark Side of Demographics   295

**CHAPTER 12**

## WISE INVESTING IN THE NEW ECONOMY   299

Real-World Investing   299
Real-World Results   301
Did the Internet Boom Spike the Punch?   304
Investing Wisely in the New Economy   306
Pointers for Investing in a Resurging New Economy   307
The Prelude to a New Era of Prosperity   312

**CHAPTER 13**

## DIGITAL DEMOCRACY: GLOBALIZATION OF THE NEW ECONOMY   315

New Economy Entrepreneurship   315
Digital Democracy   316
Counting Digital Deflation and Productivity Properly   319
Japan and China Can Create Enormous Wealth   320
Europe Must Recognize Digital Deflation to Optimize It   322
Cowboy Capitalism and Wealth Creation   326
The Soviet Experiment   327
Digital Deflation and the Dollar   328
Global Prosperity Will Lift All Boats   330


**CHAPTER 14**

## THREATS AND OPPORTUNITIES:  MAKING THE WORLD A BETTER PLACE   331

Making the Digital Revolution Better Than the Industrial Revolution   331
The Politics of Better Data   333
Fixing the Third Rail   335
Better Healthcare from Better Data   338
Moving Faster with the Fed   339
How Much Does the Fed Know?   340
One Foot on the Brakes and One Foot on the Gas   343
Capital, Labor, and Technology   344
Managing Booms and Bubbles   346
Quality Improvement and Degradation   347
Making the World a Better Place   348


**EPILOGUE**

## CLOSER TO DEFLATION THAN YOU THINK   355

## FIRESIDE CHAT INTERVIEWS WITH CREATORS OF DIGITAL DEFLATION   357

Interview with Gordon Moore (Intel)   357
Interview with Richard S. Hill (Novellus)   363
Interview with Doug J. Dunn (ASML Holding N.V.)   367
Interview with Michael Dell (Dell, Inc.)   374

Interview with Irwin Jacobs   376
Interview with Stephen Fodor   381

**APPENDIX A: Tanaka Capital Management
P/E Conversion Table   392**

**APPENDIX B: Household Tangible, Net Financial, and Equity-
Like Assets as Percentage of Net Worth   393**

**APPENDIX C: Decades of Growth in Equity-Like Assets   394**

**APPENDIX D: Wealth Model Using 3.00% Real Rate   395**

**References   396**

**Index   407**

**Acknowledgements   417**

# PREFACE

## INVESTING IN THE NEW MILLENNIUM

This book reveals the fundamental drivers of the New Economy in the 1990s and sets the stage for a clearer understanding of the economic and investment environment of the next 10–20 years. By introducing some new theories and by challenging or tweaking some old ones, readers will be shown how to make some sense out of these confusing times. When the "good times" were happening, there was perhaps less urgency to understand exactly why they were happening. Now there is a greater need to know, and real answers will be offered. Perhaps even more importantly, it will be shown how rapidly advancing technologies may create economic conditions over the next two decades that could be almost as favorable as the 1990s—if appropriate fiscal and monetary policies are pursued. Investors will learn what to watch for so that they can make important adjustments to their portfolios based on whether the proper policy decisions are made during the next few years.

Many of the inflation, interest rate, and stock market theories presented in this book are brand new to the public. As most of the scenarios described are long term in nature, they should be particularly helpful for investors faced with the daunting task of planning for their retirement over the next ten to twenty years. After the sharp stock market downturn in the first few years of the new millennium, some investors are questioning the value of investing in common stocks. Anxiety levels may remain high due to the absence of clear explanations for how the New Economy of the 1990s arrived so mysteriously, setting records for growth and creating prosperity, only to suddenly disappear.

The process for developing the Theory of Digital Deflation started with unrelated theories on Demographics and productivity well before anyone was talking about the New Economy. As luck would have it, however, these theories established an absolutely critical foundation for researching and understanding Digital Deflation and how it uniquely drives the New Economy. With the benefit of growing Digital Deflation over the next two decades, the U.S. economy can attain higher growth without inflation, creating proportionately more real value and vastly more wealth than ever in the history of mankind.

There will be threats and challenges to overcome. Our fiscal and monetary policymakers will need to open their minds to using new theories and models to set the appropriate policies for the New Economy. Investors and corporate managers will have to learn new tricks to win in a brave new world where some rules will change and some won't, but most assuredly, the New Economy will take share from the Old. It is hoped that this book will help all investors, large and small, as we may possibly be standing at the doorstep of the next multi-year bull market.

Graham Y. Tanaka

# INTRODUCTION

I have organized the book into four chapter groupings plus the "Fireside Chat" interviews section, so readers can read the book at his or her own pace. The first three chapters present the basic concept of Digital Deflation and how I realized its existence.

The second grouping, Chapters 4 through 7, reviews why economists have had so much trouble predicting the economy using the Old Economic models. New theories and models are offered to help explain what really drove the "New Economy" of the 1990s.

Chapters 8 and 9 describe why many of the favorable forces that fueled the '90s are poised to return—and how the stock market can generate significant wealth for investors over the next one to two decades.

The last five chapters (Chapters 10–14) discuss the key implications for a future world of increasing Digital Deflation, starting with all-important monetary policy in Chapter 10 and fiscal policy in Chapter 11. There is a chapter dedicated to investors, a chapter providing a global perspective, and one that highlights the threats and opportunities ahead.

Finally, there is a collection of informal interviews with leading lights of the Digital Revolution. They provide personal insights on the unique contributions of their advancing technologies to our economy, in the past, as well as for the next several years.

# 1

## CHAPTER

# Mysteries, Puzzles, and Paradoxes of the New Economy

The trouble with our times is that the future is not what it used to be.
*Paul Valery (1871–1945)*

*What drove the U.S. economy in the 1990s, and will those same conditions ever be seen again? How did the U.S. economy set a record for the longest expansion ever, while at the same time, surprisingly, the rate of inflation declined in half? Why did productivity gains suddenly accelerate in the late 1990s after decades of disappointment? Despite the economic downturn and the stock market's sharp declines in the early 2000s, the achievements of the New Economy of the 1990s were very real. Is there any chance that they will reemerge any time soon? Or are we at risk of suffering the kind of deflationary slump that Japan experienced in the 1990s, or the U.S. itself experienced in the 1930s? Conversely, could we face a return to the hyperinflation, stagnation, and budget deficits of the 1970s and early 1980s?*

### THE NEW ECONOMY OF THE 1990s

Even now, with the benefit of a few years of historical perspective, the American economy of the 1990s remains full of mysteries, puzzles, and paradoxes.

How could the U.S. economy expand so vigorously for a record 10 years, while at the same time, inflation and interest rates declined in half to 40-year lows? These concurrent trends flew in the face of de-

1

cades of economic experience and thought, which held that sooner or later, more dollars and a strong gross domestic product (GDP) *had* to translate into more inflation. And how could the unemployment rate move to record lows without reigniting inflation? Real wages did rise for the first time since the early 1970s, but somehow, that didn't seem to result in higher prices from so-called cost-push inflation.

If the decline in inflation in the 1990s was related to labor productivity gains, why did it take until the late 1990s for growth in productivity to move up after two and one-half decades of disappointment? Inflation, in fact, had already started to decline a full 15 years *before* the rise in productivity gains in the late 1990s.

The American consumer of the 1990s was also a puzzle. We know that consumers are rational, they are careful when it comes to spending, and they can be quick to lose faith in a shaky economy. So why did they appear to spend beyond their means through the late 1990s? And why did they then maintain their confidence and continue to spend well into the Post '90s era of economic slowdown, recession, extensive layoffs, and stock market declines?

The corporate sector staged its own mystery in the 1990s. Companies were able to rebuild their profit margins and grow their earnings vigorously. How could they do this despite fierce global competition and the lack of pricing flexibility domestically? Many investors are curious to know when, if ever, corporate earnings will get back to prior peak levels.

As for the stock market, investors continue to struggle over what part of the 1990s was real. How could the U.S. stock and bond markets move to such lofty levels in the face of high real interest rates? What then really caused the Post '90s stock market collapse? Most importantly, what are the market's prospects for the future?

As the New Economy took hold during the decade of the 1990s, even our governments pleasantly surprised us—for a while. Federal, state, and local budget deficits suddenly became surpluses only to disappear just as suddenly in the Post '90s economic slowdown. To what extent were these budget surpluses related to the New Economy, and will we ever see surpluses again?

There were also global anomalies in the 1990s. The U.S. economy grew much faster than the "rest of the world." Yet, inflation in the United States plunged to levels well below those of most other industrialized countries. Is this why American households enjoyed a significantly greater surge in wealth than households in other countries?

Were these trends enough to explain why the dollar was so strong in that decade, despite a dramatic expansion in the U.S. trade deficit?

While many attribute the strong economic growth and the vast creation of wealth in the 1990s to something called a *New Economy,* economists have had difficulty agreeing on a definition of this New Economy and on what created it in the first place. If the New Economy was the result of a surge in capital spending on information technology (IT), why didn't it show up earlier—in the 1970s or 1980s, for example, when IT spending grew even more vigorously in percentage terms than in the 1990s? Was it because IT spending reached some sort of critical mass, with IT capital spending rising to more than 4% of GDP and "IT-producing industries" rising to almost 8% of the economy by the end of the 1990s? Or was the New Economy merely the result of a temporary, late-decade surge in spending to combat the dreaded Y2K millennium bug?

Some have suggested that it was the Internet and the dot-com phenomenon that powered the New Economy of the late 1990s. If that was the case, does the bursting of the Dot-com Bubble mean that we've seen the end of the New Economy?

Looking ahead over the next decade or two, many investors, corporate managers, and policymakers are anxious to know what the prospects are for the economy and the stock market. They want to know whether the "good times" of the New Economy of the 1990s can return in the foreseeable future.

Some pessimists are predicting a replay of the 1970s, characterized by sluggish growth, high inflation, high interest rates and lower price–earnings (P/E) ratios on common stocks. Optimists, on the other hand, point to record low inflation, low interest rates, strong growth in labor productivity, and continuing innovation in technology, healthcare, and other fields, suggesting better times ahead. So *which will it be?*

This book will attempt to answer these and other questions, with a particular emphasis on looking forward. First, we need to validate that there was a New Economy in the 1990s before we can understand what drove it—and whether it can return.

## WAS THE NEW ECONOMY OF THE 1990s REAL?

After the Y2K spending spike and "nonevent," the bursting of the Dot-com Bubble, the 1929-like decline in the Nasdaq, and the abrupt and persistent downturn in IT capital spending, it is understandable that much of the general public has begun to doubt the existence of a New Economy. Many corporate managers, economists, and policymakers feel the same way. We've seen the broader stock market averages drop by close to 50%. This includes three successive years of stock market declines, which hasn't happened since 1939–1941. So, many investors feel disillusioned or upset.

It will be no surprise then if we see more analogies made between the 1990s and the 1920s and 1930s. A few have even referred to the 1990s as a "hoax"—a kind of fraud built on a flimsy foundation of aggressive accounting, management malfeasance, and deceptive investment banking metrics that included price-revenue multiples, clicks, page-views, and EBITDA (earnings before interest, taxes, depreciation, and amortization) multiples.

In this book, I hope to demonstrate that the New Economy of the 1990s was not a hoax. In fact, the fundamental forces generating economic growth and creating enormous wealth in the 1990s were very real. We will see that, by far, the crowning achievement of the 1990s economy was the decline in inflation. In terms of wealth creation, everything else followed.

Figuratively speaking, the dramatic decline in inflation was the horse that pulled the cart. Inflation declined from 4.8% in 1989 to 2.2% in 1999 on the Consumer Price Index (CPI), and from 3.8% to 1.4% on the broader GDP Deflator. Lower inflation drove interest rates down almost in half, with 3-month Treasury bill yields declining from 8.1% to 4.6% in the same time period.

Was this important? Absolutely. Lower inflation and lower interest rates helped lift P/E ratios in the stock market from 16.2 times next 12 months' earnings at the beginning of the decade to 24.9 times earnings by the end of the decade. The stock market generated a total return of 19.0% per year from 1990 to 1999—almost twice as high as the 10% per year average of the prior 75 years.

Due to the appreciation of both common stocks and home values, American household net worth doubled, rising by an astounding $22 trillion to $42 trillion by the end of the decade (1999). Even after the stock market declines in 2000 and 2001, household net worth remained at a lofty $40 trillion, due largely to a $2 trillion rise in home values. For the overall economy, perhaps President Clinton's Council of Economic Advisers said it best in its January 2001 Economic Report to the President: "When productivity growth and GDP growth both accelerate sharply, when unemployment and inflation fall to their lowest levels in 30 years, when poverty starts to fall again after years of worsening, and when incomes accelerate across the board, clearly a significant change has occurred."

The New Economy was certainly very real. But, unfortunately, the president's economists could not explain very convincingly *why* or *how* these economic milestones were achieved—or whether they could be repeated. They could not explain many of the surprises, contradictions, and paradoxes that appeared during the record 10-year expansion that extended through the year 2000. This shortage of explanations, of course, has made it extremely difficult for prognosticators to predict with any degree of certainty the economy and the stock market of the future.

## WHY WERE THE 1990s SO GREAT?

Many observers believe that the surge in prosperity in the 1990s was a direct result of well-executed Federal Reserve monetary policies. Some believe that the enormous creation of wealth was a result of the Clinton administration's fiscal policies, while others believe that the boom resulted from the earlier policies of the Reagan administration.* Much of the credit has been given to a fiscally responsible Congress, with "budget rules" that required spending cuts or tax revenue increases to offset new spending increases. A few point to the absence of a jolt from the OPEC oil cartel. As noted above—many Americans identify the IT revolution and the explosion of the Internet as the primary drivers for the booming economy and the rising stock market. In 2000, Bob McTeer, president of the Dallas Federal Reserve, commented, "In the New Economy, knowledge is more important to economic success than money or machinery. Modern tools facilitate the application of brainpower, not muscle or machine power, opening all sectors of the economy to productivity gains."[1]

While there is some validity to each of the above explanations, it turns out that there are more fundamental forces at play, particularly in regard to inflation and productivity. Those larger forces are what this book is about.

---

* It will be seen that the New Economy is largely a nonpolitical phenomenon, and its return will be best achieved with the cooperation of all political parties.

Economists, including those at the Federal Reserve, stress the importance of growth in labor productivity if the economy is to continue to grow in the future with low inflation. Simply put, strong gains in labor productivity (real output per person-hour) allow companies to raise worker compensation, cover other cost increases, and improve profit margins without having to raise prices—thereby producing lower inflation for the consumer. In essence, strong growth in productivity is a very fundamental building block in the wealth-creation process. Producing more output for the same labor input creates real value at little additional cost, except for the cost of capital. In addition, if the labor force isn't growing, then the existing labor force needs to produce more if the economy is to continue to grow at all.

As suggested above, some economists cite the surge in IT capital spending as the primary driver for achieving higher labor productivity gains in the late 1990s. In the 1990s, nominal business spending on IT did grow at a fairly rapid 8.7% per year—considerably faster than the 5.4% per year growth in nominal GDP. However, based on published data, over the last 50 years, the relationship between business capital spending and productivity growth has been quite fuzzy.

What many people don't realize is that IT capital spending grew even more rapidly in the 1970s and 1980s (13.9% and 14.8% per year, respectively). Yet productivity growth plunged in those two decades to a relatively dismal 1.6% per year. And to make matters more puzzling, this disappointing growth in productivity followed two decades of vigorous productivity gains of 2.8% per year in the 1950s, and 2.9% per year in the 1960s when IT was in its infancy.

The 1970s and 1980s, in fact, presented a real challenge for economists. Information technology was supposed to enhance the worker's ability to produce more goods and services, yet reported productivity gains slowed during two decades of heavy IT spending and the proliferation of computers to the corporate desktop. This was one of the most perplexing puzzles of that era. The so-called productivity paradox of rising capital spending and declining productivity led one economist, Robert Solow, to quip in 1987: "You can see the computer age everywhere but in the productivity statistics." Surely productivity growth didn't decline in the 1970s and 1980s *because* technology investments were accelerating.

By the late 1990s, just as surprisingly for those searching for productivity gains, productivity growth finally did rebound: from a 1.5% per year average rate in the first 5 years of the 1990s to a 2.1% average during the last half of the decade. Many economists single out this modest rise in productivity growth as the main reason for the extra-long economic expansion. On the basis of the reported numbers, though, that appears to be a bit of a stretch because the productivity numbers didn't rise by very much. In reality, it was only in the year 2000, the 10th and final year of the economic expansion, that productivity growth finally climbed to a very respectable 3.0%. (This incidentally was a year that IT capital spending surged by 16.7%, driven by a spike in spending for Internet and telecom infrastructure build-outs.)

For economists, however, the real surprise came in the recession year of 2001. Despite a recession and a decline in IT capital spending of 8.4% in nominal terms and 3.7% in real terms, growth in productivity remained at 1.9%, a relatively high rate for a recession year.

Even skeptics of "structural" productivity gains and of the New Economy were particularly impressed that productivity growth could remain high during an entire economic cycle, particularly during a recession. It was apparent that an unusual rise in productivity growth was under way—for whatever reason or reasons. It was equally apparent that productivity gains had once again become delinked from growth in IT capital spending; this time with growth in labor productivity remaining high while IT capital spending declined sharply.

This only deepened the mystery of what was driving the New Economy. If it wasn't IT capital spending, what was it?

## IS THERE TOO MUCH OPTIMISM OR TOO MUCH PESSIMISM?

The economic and stock market booms of the 1990s were highly unusual if not miraculous even when viewed within the long-term context of American economic history. Yet few economists or investment strategists can agree about how difficult or how likely it would be to repeat the decade's record-setting expansion and wealth creation. Rarely have there been such widely diverging economic views about our economic future. Much of this can be explained by the lack of understanding of what was really driving the economy.

It might have been expected that warnings should have been issued earlier—about how the massive creation of wealth, jobs, and a better quality of life cannot be repeated in the first decade of the 21st century. It seems that there should be some immutable economic law of gravity which would pull the United States, its economy, its stock market, and its currency back to earth. After the Post '90s recession and the stock market downturns of 2000, 2001, and 2002, it was only a matter of time for more bleak prognostications to be made.

Yet, based on recent history or perhaps an innate awareness of what is going on around them, many Americans still seem to feel that much of the good times of the 1990s will reassert themselves sometime in the new decade of the 2000s. But they aren't sure why. Most consumers and investors sense that technology will in some way help the economy and improve their lives. They see the benefits of the ongoing Digital Revolution and newly developed digital technologies all around them in faster, better, cheaper, and lighter laptop computers and wireless Internet access appliances. They see DVD player/recorders, CD burners, digital cameras, new software and electronic games and even self-tuning autos all getting better and becoming more affordable every year. They can benefit from faster and more convenient Internet access to information for shopping and for ordering online. But what does this mean for our economic future?

Indirectly, consumers benefit enormously from lower prices and better service due to Internet-based supply chain management. In healthcare services, they can see the benefits of new technologies in new drugs with better efficacy and dosing regimens or in surgical procedures with improved outcomes and recovery times. In government services, they see digital technologies in faster licensing and better access to information on government Web sites. Even in defense, the public sees the benefits of technology vividly in the images of smart bombs and missiles flying into windows of military installations during the 1990–1991 Persian Gulf War and in the infrared tracking of enemy personnel in the 2002 Afghanistan conflict. Are American consumers and investors merely being too optimistic—or are they on to something?

In the late 1990s, the economy accelerated as it matured, yet inflation did not rear its ugly head as some had feared. Powered by rising corporate profits and declining inflation and interest rates, the stock market surged to new highs, and the average American gained new-found wealth. To what extent was the New Economy of the 1990s fleeting or ephemeral and will any or all of those positive forces and trends ever reappear? Did the stock market bubble at the turn of the century toll the death knell of the New Economy or will the New Economy return?

## ARE WE HEADING FOR DEFLATION LIKE JAPAN IN THE '90s OR THE U.S. IN THE '30s?

One thing that's strange about the present day economy is that people are credibly arguing both ends of the inflation–deflation spectrum. Most economists (notably including policymakers at the Federal Reserve) continue to argue that inflation is the real threat. A small minority point to the miserable state of the Japanese economy, mired in a deep deflationary trap, and they suggest that this is where our economy is headed.

The popular belief is that Japan is not like the United States and that "Japan has its own problems." True, it is well documented that Japan has not been able to transition smoothly out of a post–World War II "super economy" status into an economy more efficiently structured with free and open markets, to better serve its own consumers, savers, and investors. Also well known are the problems associated with Japan's banking system and its mountains of bad loans, as well as its not-so-transparent accounting standards. However, much can be learned from how the world's second-largest economy could unwittingly slide into a deflationary slump that has lasted over 7 years.

Could the United States fall into a similar deflationary spiral? One has to at least ask: If inflation in the United States could decline to the low single digits during a record-long economic expansion, why couldn't the United States also enter into outright deflation if the economy slipped into a prolonged recession? With inflation already running as low as 1% to 2%, it doesn't take much to drop below zero. This possibility, of course, makes it even more critical that we understand why the United States has been able to enjoy such low inflation in recent years and whether inflation in the United States will move higher or lower over the next few years.

Most people believe that the United States will never again experience anything like the Depression of the 1930s, largely because our economic data are better, our systems of controls are better, and our policymakers are smart enough to avoid making the same mistakes again. Yet, during the last three decades economists and policymakers have repeatedly been surprised—first by an extended period of hyperinflation, then by disinflation, and finally by the uniquely prosperous period in the 1990s of strong economic growth with simultaneously low inflation. It is troublesome that as we proceed into the

21st century, there is still so much that we don't know about the economy.

## CAN THE FUTURE BE WHAT IT USED TO BE?

Everybody, every investor, wage earner, corporate manager, small business owner, policymaker, and consumer would benefit if the next decade can be even half as prosperous as the 1990s. Across the country, there is a yearning for a return to the "good times" of the 1990s, but at the same time there is a palpable feeling of anxiety that we may not return to those conditions anytime soon.

It has long been recognized that changes in fiscal and monetary policy can dramatically alter the health of an economy and the wealth of a nation. Yet, sound policy decisions are heavily dependent on good data. Throughout the book, there will be references to the accuracy of our economic data and the appropriateness of fiscal and monetary policy before, during, and immediately after the New Economy expansion of the 1990s. Getting the numbers right is not simply an academic exercise. With new perspectives and better data, we will reach some very different conclusions about how to manage the economy of the future.

We will have to understand why the United States has been able to enjoy such low inflation in recent years. We will have to understand the strange patterns of productivity growth that have bedeviled the economists over the past decade or more. The Theory of Digital Deflation, introduced and elaborated upon in the next few chapters, will go a long way toward explaining both.

If we are to get solidly back on track to prosperity, some very important fiscal and monetary decisions will have to be made properly in Washington, D.C. It will help immensely to first understand the New Economy before we proceed to judge the correctness of those policy decisions. Only then can policymakers, managers, and investors understand and develop reasonable expectations for whether the enormous potential for growth and wealth creation from a resurging New Economy can be realized during the next two decades. Indeed, if we do things right, the potential is there for the future to be as good as it used to be.

## NOTES

1. "The New Paradigm," *1999 Annual Report of the Federal Reserve Bank of Dallas*, Robert D. McTeer, Jr., et al.

# 2

## CHAPTER

# Solving the Mystery: Missing Productivity and the Great Inflation Mismeasure

Pluck out the heart of my mystery.
*Hamlet, William Shakespeare (1564–1616)*

*The arrival of Baby Boomers and Working Women into the workforce changed the economy in ways economists had never seen before, first creating record-high inflation in the 1970s and early 1980s, then disinflation in the 1980s, and eventually the need for greater productivity gains if the economy was going to grow at all. Remarkably, in the 1990s, reported inflation continued to decline, and late in the decade, productivity growth finally began to climb. Could these trends be related, and could they help solve the mystery of the New Economy?\**

### DEMOGRAPHICS: BABY BOOMERS, WORKING WOMEN, AND THE SUPER BULL MARKET

The opportunity to unravel the mystery of the New Economy grew out of a series of research projects going back over several years—and a healthy dose of good luck. As is often the case, the search originally began with a far more narrow focus: the search for the "missing" pro-

---

\* Although the term *New Economy* has fallen into disrepute as a result of the dot-com implosion and stock market decline, I believe that there were new and unique elements to the economy of that period—elements which are still with us. I will continue to use this term, but *redefined* with a new meaning to reflect new theories presented in this book.

ductivity gains that many economists had been seeking since the 1970s and 1980s. By the end of the 1990s, I realized that I was looking at a much larger phenomenon—a set of major economic forces that were driving the New Economy.

The critical foundation for this discovery process was laid back in 1982 with my study relating changes in the labor force to changes in the rate of inflation and common stock returns. The study, "Demographics and the Stock Market,"[1] was the result of an effort to understand two things: first, why inflation had been raging for 15 years, from 1966 to 1981; and second, why the Dow Jones Industrial Average couldn't seem to break through the 1000-point barrier during those painful years.

This study proved to be surprisingly successful in predicting the soaring stock market of the 1980s and 1990s and very useful in positioning investors for a decline in interest rates and an extended bull market. Although I certainly had no such idea back in the early 1980s, this study also provided the foundation for understanding the New Economy in the 1990s. Why? Because it was critically important to first understand how the subtle but powerful demographic or population-based changes in the labor force were influencing the overall economy.

The long-term effects of labor-force growth on inflation, productivity, interest rates, and the stock market have been enormous over the years. But *enormous* doesn't necessarily translate into *obvious*, and most economists have not studied the effects of once-a-generation changes in the labor force on the economy. In fact, these effects are almost imperceptible unless they are viewed over years, and even decades, as seen in Exhibit 2-1, an updated three-part graph from the original 1982 demographic study.

The shaded portion of the bottom graph in Exhibit 2-1 shows that the youngest and least experienced segment of the labor force grew by 3% to 4% per year during the same 15 years (1966–1981) that inflation surged toward double digits. Baby Boomers and Working Women were piling into the workforce in record numbers, and this large-scale expansion of the least experienced portion of the workforce would have been a strain for any economy. The "Politics of Need"* of that era was to create jobs. Indeed, Washington responded

---

* I define the *Politics of Need* as what must be done in a political context to address the changing socioeconomic needs of a society. I will return to this theme in Chapter 11.

## E X H I B I T   2-1

Demographics and the Stock Market

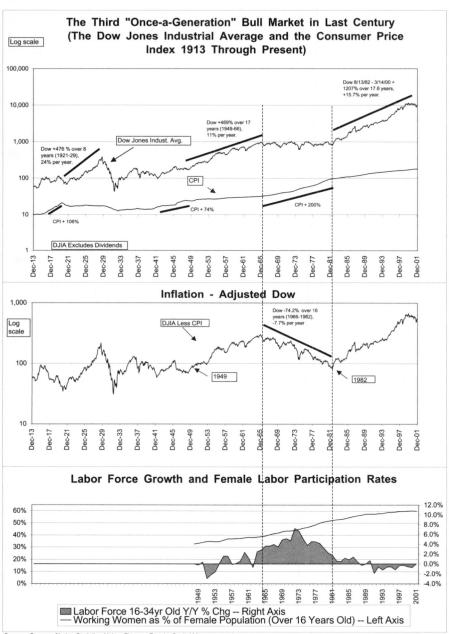

Sources: Bureau of Labor Statistics; Yahoo Finance; Tanaka Capital Management, Inc.

with stimulative fiscal programs and expansionary monetary policies.

The miracle was that jobs were created, but the unintended by-product was rising inflation. With plentiful labor, it was easier and cheaper for companies to hire new workers than to invest in new capital equipment. Labor was substituted for capital, and labor productivity growth declined, putting upward pressure on inflation.

In addition, on the demand side of the economy, Baby Boomers and Working Women were entering their prime years for household formation, with a rising propensity to consume rather than to save. With the country in a demographic mode to spend, and with policies tilted toward stimulus, the result was a superheated economy and a surge in inflation.

Along with high inflation came double-digit interest rates, a burgeoning budget deficit, and a stock market which did well just to remain flat. The flat stock market and the rapid rise in inflation can be seen in the top graph in Exhibit 2-1. This graph shows how the 1966–1981 era was the third major period of rising inflation coincident with a flat stock market in the 20th century.

For investors, the real damage was that during those 15 years, the stock market declined by 70% in real terms, when adjusted for the ravages of double-digit inflation. This can be seen more clearly in the middle graph, which presents the inflation-adjusted Dow Jones Industrial Average. It reached its modern-day low in June of 1982. This sad plunge took real stock market values—stated in inflation-adjusted terms—back an entire generation in time to 1949 levels.

Observing these trends allowed the development of the following hypothesis: What if growth in the labor force and the rise in inflation were more than just a coincidence? If the demographic surge in the youngest segment of the workforce had actually *caused* a dramatic rise in inflation over a very long 15-year period, this potentially had huge implications for inflation and the stock market over the next 15 to 20 years. Why? Because we knew with relative certainty how many young people in the United States would be leaving school and entering the workforce during each of the next 18 to 20 years, and therefore we knew that the trend was toward very little growth in the workforce. In addition, the accelerated trend of working women was likely to slow. Female labor participation rates had jumped from 39% of working-age women in 1965 to 52% in 1981 (as shown by the rising line on the bottom graph in Exhibit 2-1).

## THREE HITS AND A MISS

With the Baby Boomers and Working Women already having been absorbed into the workforce by the early 1980s, the demographic pressures on the economy would become decidedly more favorable going forward. So the next question was: Could prospective changes in the growth rate of the youngest and least experienced segment of the workforce actually be used to *predict* inflation and returns on common stocks?

I performed further analysis, correlating growth in the labor force with inflation and other economic indicators. This resulted in a follow-up report in 1983, which presented very bullish projections for the economy and the stock market over the next 10 years (1984–1993). This study, "Demographics, Productivity & the Return on Common Stocks,"[2] confirmed that there were indeed strong historical correlations between the average annual rate of growth in the youngest segment of the workforce versus inflation, labor productivity growth, and the real returns on common stocks. These relationships between growth in the labor force and the various indicators of the economy formed the basis of a new Demographic Theory of Economics.

With very good data from the Bureau of Labor on the age distribution of the American youth, it was clear that the annual growth rate of the youngest portion of the U.S. labor force would approach zero, and even turn slightly negative over the next 10 years. What this meant was that with little growth in the workforce, the *only* way for the U.S. economy to grow would be for the existing (nongrowing) workforce to produce more goods and services. This, of course, was clearly a recipe calling for an increase in labor productivity, or output per person-hour, a bullish sign both for the economy and for investors. Instead of using labor to fuel growth, as was the pattern in the late 1960s and the 1970s, there would be a fundamental need in the 1980s and 1990s to substitute capital for increasingly scarce labor.

From a policy perspective, a shortage of labor and the need for higher productivity growth meant that the government had to make a dramatic shift to a new "Politics of Need"—away from fiscal policies primarily focused on consumption and job growth, and toward policies that encouraged savings and investment. Our political representatives responded appropriately. Income tax rates were reduced, interest deductibility for consumer loans was eliminated, and eventually capital gains tax rates were trimmed.

The impending labor shortage and the need for higher productivity growth also called for changes in monetary policy. In the ensuing years, monetary policy needed to be aimed at bringing about lower inflation and lower interest rates, to facilitate the raising of capital for increased capital spending and improved labor productivity gains for the static workforce. Again, our policymakers, specifically the Federal Reserve, responded appropriately.

Based on these demographic studies and their models, my long-term projections were for a significant drop in inflation—from 5.9% in 1983 to an average of 3.0% per year over the next 10 years, through 1993. In addition, the demographic models projected a surge in labor productivity growth—from 2.1% in 1983 to an average of 3.0% per year through 1993—and a significant increase in inflation-adjusted returns on common stocks, from about 5.7% per year from 1981 to 1983 to an average of 11.3% per year in the 1984–1993 decade.

These projections are shown in Exhibit 2-2, along with what actually happened. The graphs are most easily understood if you start at the bottom and work your way up the page.

In all four of these graphs, each of the vertical bars represents a five-year average, with the exception of the 1981–1983 transition period. The solid line connecting the dots reflects the forward-looking projections that I made in the 1983 study, and the hollow bars represent the actual results in the ensuing years (1983–1993).

When these 1983–1993 projections were made, they were unusual, in the sense that economists had not previously correlated inflation in the overall economy with growth in the labor force. Similarly, investment strategists had not correlated stock market returns inversely with growth in the labor force. These forecasts from the Demographic Theory of Economics also differed significantly from prevailing views, because they projected that inflation would fall by 50%, and that real annual common stock returns would double. At the time, these estimates generated reactions ranging from friendly skepticism to good-humored ridicule.

Intuitively it made sense, and the data seemed to confirm that a surge in the labor force would lead to a rise in inflation, lower productivity growth, and lower inflation-adjusted returns on stocks. But there was a second piece of the hypothesis that had yet to be tested. Would the opposite hold true during the second half of a full cycle of accelerating and then decelerating growth in the workforce? When growth in the labor force slowed after the Baby Boomers were ab-

**E X H I B I T  2-2**

## How Changes in the Labor Force Affect Inflation, Productivity, and Real Returns on Common Stocks

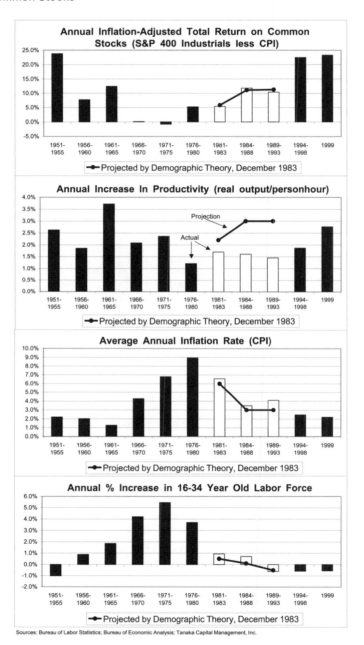

Sources: Bureau of Labor Statistics; Bureau of Economic Analysis; Tanaka Capital Management, Inc.

sorbed into the economy, would inflation really decline? Would productivity growth rise, and would real returns on common stocks reach double-digit annual rates?

The graphs in Exhibit 2-2 show what actually happened in the ensuing 18 years—that is, from 1983 to the end of the 1990s. Indeed, the pendulum of labor force growth *did* swing back, taking the Demographic Theory through a complete labor force cycle—and fully validating the thesis.

As predicted in 1983, the annual growth in the youngest segment of the labor force in the 1983–1993 period approximated zero. (Again, this was not exactly rocket science, as we pretty much knew in 1983 how many kids were how old.) The inflation rate also declined significantly as projected by the Demographic Theory models, although the rate as reported for the CPI averaged about 0.5% to 1.0% above my projections. Real returns on common stocks were almost exactly as projected, nicely validating the thesis that more moderate growth in the youngest segment of the labor force can lead to lower inflation and higher real returns on stocks.

It was only my projections for gains in labor productivity (the third graph from the bottom in Exhibit 2-2) that were significantly off target. The Demographic Models had predicted 3.0% per year productivity growth, whereas the productivity growth reported by the government averaged only 1.5% per year. That was pretty far off—so much so that I felt challenged to pursue this disparity.

## WHERE'S THE MISSING PRODUCTIVITY?

Could it be that the government's reported productivity numbers were wrong? After all, hadn't economists been lamenting for years that productivity gains should have been stronger given the dramatic rise in capital spending, particularly for IT?

But if there was an error, where was it? Productivity growth was calculated by dividing the growth in real GDP by the number of labor hours per person in a given period. If the result of this simple calculation was wrong, it could only mean that either real GDP or labor hours were being measured incorrectly. In light of how carefully both GDP and labor hours were measured by the federal government, any suggestion that either of these numbers was wrong would surely be met with more than skepticism and good-humored ridicule. Nevertheless, I began a search for what appeared to be this "missing" productivity.

In the late 1990s, the economic expansion grew legs, productivity growth finally began to accelerate, and economists started talking about a New Economy. But they could not put their finger on exactly what was causing the economy to do things it had not done before, including the extended period of strong economic growth, the simultaneous decline in the rate of inflation, and—most notable, from my point of view—the late arrival of rising productivity growth. Something was happening here, and given the importance of inflation, interest rates, and productivity to policymakers, business managers, and investors, it was becoming even more important to understand what was really driving this New Economy. If the government was undermeasuring productivity growth, that might also help explain what was fueling the New Economy.

It was the realization that the Demographic Theory had been so well validated through a full labor cycle—except for the productivity numbers—that provided the first clue to understanding the New Economy. Maybe productivity growth really was being undermeasured. Another clue was provided by the Boskin Reports on the CPI.

## THE BOSKIN REPORTS ON THE CPI

The next clue came from the government itself. In December 1996, the government published a study focusing on the accuracy of the CPI. Commissioned by the Senate Finance Committee, and directed by economist Michael J. Boskin, this blue-ribbon panel of economists reached several dramatic conclusions. Most importantly, their study pointed to a 1.3% per year overstatement of the inflation rate, as "measured" by the CPI in the years prior to 1996, and a 1.1% overstatement in 1996 (following a formula change made during 1996). The commission identified four areas that were contributing to an upward bias in the CPI, including product substitution by consumers, substituting different retail outlets, new products, and quality change in products. The upward bias for quality change alone on the CPI was estimated to be approximately 0.6% per year.

From the investor's point of view, the discovery of a 1 percentage-point overstatement of reported inflation was a potentially *huge* development. If true, it would mean that interest rates might possibly be a full 1% too high. That may sound small, but with interest rates already in the low single digits, it was very significant. It would mean that P/E ratios could be revised upward several multiple points. It would mean that the Federal Reserve could allow the economy to expand at a faster rate if inflation were truly 1% lower.

Surprisingly, very little resulted from this report, at least from the perspective of the capital markets and investors. It seemed to sink under the waves, leaving not much of a trace behind. Some observers have suggested that politics may have interfered, in light of the fact that the Bureau of Labor Statistics (BLS) initially resisted many of the commission's findings.

However, giving due credit to the BLS, in the years immediately following the original Boskin report in 1996, the statistical agency made several important changes to the CPI measurement process. This was captured in a follow-up report published in February 2000, "Update of Boskin Commission's Estimate of Bias." This study found that between 1996 and 2000, the Bureau of Labor Statistics made seven changes to improve its measurement methods for the CPI. Yet, the update report estimated that the CPI was still overstating inflation—but now the overstatement amounted to "only" 0.7% to 0.9% per year.

What much of the public does not realize is that this meant that from 1996 to 1999, the BLS had been able to make corrections resulting in a very significant 0.4% to 0.6% point reduction per year in the CPI. (This was simply the difference between the 1.3% overstatement estimated in the 1996 report and the more recently estimated overstatement of 0.7% to 0.9% per year in the 2000 report.) For anyone trying to understand the New Economy of the late 1990s, this was a critically important finding. The difference between the 1996 and 2000 Boskin Commission estimates of CPI overstatements was, in effect, a *permanent reduction in reported inflation* of 0.4% to 0.6%, for every year going forward.

By simply measuring inflation more accurately, the BLS had indirectly and unknowingly made an invaluable contribution to the economic boom of the late 1990s. This half percent "permanent" reduction in measured inflation allowed the Federal Reserve to let the economy grow faster in the late 1990s, without rekindling fears of inflation. Lower inflation and interest rates meant more growth, jobs, and wealth creation. The agency should be recognized for this achievement.

Somewhat surprisingly, in response to the Boskin Commission's update report, the Commissioner of the BLS, made the following observation:

> The measurement issues considered by the [Boskin] Advisory Commission are complex and there is considerable uncertainty attached to the magnitude of many bias components. This is particularly true of bias resulting from quality change and the introduction of new goods. Because of this uncertainty, we do not believe that it is currently possible to produce reliable estimates of bias in the CPI.

This, of course, was an honest and straightforward acknowledgment that even after the BLS had made numerous procedural changes, the CPI was *still* not highly reliable as a true measure of inflation for the consumer. The government admitted, explicitly, that it had little confidence in its ability to measure quality change and the impact of new products. From the investor's point of view, of course, these issues raised the possibility of additional permanent downward revisions to the CPI. It also provided another important clue for solving the mystery of the New Economy. Could it be that the government was really overstating inflation by another 0.7% to 0.9% per year, at least for the Consumer Price Index?

The quality change (or "quality improvement") aspect of the overstatement of the CPI was particularly intriguing, and looked very promising for further research. Consumers certainly understood that large numbers of electronic products, for example, were rapidly improving in quality every year. In fact, it seemed that every time you bought a digital product, a newly improved and more feature-rich version was introduced a few weeks later at the same price! Consumers had quickly learned to manage through this ongoing challenge of "buyer's remorse." They long ago understood and accepted that digital products always get faster, better, and cheaper.

So was the government undermeasuring these rapid improvements in the performance of digital products and thereby overstating inflation? In other words, was the consumer getting more value per dollar spent that was not being measured properly by the government? It was time to look into how much more value the consumer was actually buying each year—and whether the government was actually measuring this quality improvement.

## "FASTER, BETTER, CHEAPER"—THE PARABLE OF THE PINK CADDY

How much quality improvement was there? Was it significant enough for the government to measure?

To begin to answer these questions, let's look at the example of the cell phone. It has become quite pervasive throughout society, and illustrates just how far digital technologies have advanced in improving the quality of products—and how far they might advance in the future. I call this story the "Parable of the Pink Caddy."

In October 1983, Motorola and AT&T unveiled the first mobile telephone. Paul Blaylock, now at Nextel Communications, related his experience with this first mobile phone—which was best depicted as *mobile* because it could hardly have been described as *portable*. Blaylock at the time was the chief financial analyst for the Illinois Commerce Commission, and received an invitation to attend "a special event," which turned out to be the unveiling of the mobile phone.

"Motorola and AT&T popped the trunk on a pink Caddy—there was a 29-pound 'unit' bolted into the trunk," recalls Blaylock. "That was the first cell phone. The 'heat sinks' around it took up a large portion of the enormous trunk. From it ran a thick cord into the interior, and to one of the largest handsets I had ever seen. There were also two large five-foot dual antennas mounted on the back of the car. That day, we witnessed a modern miracle—one of the first public demos in the United States of a real phone call from a car."

After the initial demonstration of a call from the car to a landline telephone, the AT&T vice president in charge took questions from the media.

> *Question 1:* How much do you anticipate this "mobile phone" will cost?
> *Answer:* Approximately $4000.
> *Question 2:* How much do you guess it will cost per minute?
> *Answer:* Approximately 75 cents to $1.00 per minute, once initial networks are built, which will probably require several years.
> *Question 3:* How many do you expect to be in service in the year 2000?
> *Answer:* Approximately 750,000.

A month later, as part of its breakup agreement, AT&T relinquished its rights to cellular frequencies, and a federal judge approved the transfer of cellular services to the Baby Bells. Cellular telephones caught on quickly, and soon were being produced by the millions, using analog technology. The first mobile phones were still bulky—although no longer weighing in at 29 pounds! And they were also expensive. Nevertheless, they were functional, and more and more business executives began connecting by mobile phone. As both cell phone service providers and the handsets themselves increasingly turned to digital technologies, costs dropped dramatically. Functions and performance were enhanced, and cell phones became a mainstream consumer item.

Today, more than *400 million* cell phones are sold each year, worldwide. (Recall AT&T's 1983 prediction that some 750,000 might be in service in the United States by the year 2000!) Most cost well under $100, and many pricing plans provide large amounts of airtime for $40 to $60 a month. They weigh only a few ounces—and, mercifully, you don't have to buy a Cadillac to haul them around and cool them off.

For many consumers, the convenience, time-saving, and safety benefits of a mobile phone are worth multiples of the cost of the service. And very soon, cell phones as we know them will again obsolete themselves. They will increasingly become true "convergence devices," as companies add new features that not only allow the owner to talk in a more secure digital mode, but also connect to the Internet, send and receive e-mails, retrieve games, grab stock quotes, check the weather, get directions to a restaurant, capture and send pictures, shop online, act as a personal digital assistant (PDA), and record and play music.

Currently and prospectively, these are valuable enhancements. They add tremendous value to a product or service that is either staying level or is actually dropping in price. So the question naturally became, how many of these kinds of advances in product quality— and equivalent price "reductions"—was the government actually measuring?

## THE INTEL–MICROSOFT DOUBLE HELIX AND JOHN THE BARBER'S PC

In a search for other widely used consumer electronic items that have been rapidly and continuously improving in quality and performance, the personal computer was an obvious candidate.

It was back in the early 1990s that Andy Grove, then chairman of Intel, used the image of a double helix—two lines spiraling in parallel, like a DNA sequence—to illustrate how Intel and Microsoft depended on each other to continue to develop faster and better microprocessors and software, in order to keep improving the performance of personal computers. Intel and Microsoft both realized early on that in order to grow, they would have to use the constantly advancing semiconductor technologies to improve their products and stimulate demand. They found that they could offer significantly more performance with each design cycle at the same price—and sell more units.

To the consumer, the benefits of constantly improving digital technologies were obvious, as reflected in a true story that I'll call "John the Barber's PC."

In the first quarter of 2001, John the Barber bought himself a new personal computer, and he was quite proud of it. He could recite the key performance attributes right there as he was cutting your hair. In fact, he could tell you feature by feature exactly how much more performance he got from his new model than he had from the old model he bought a little more than 3 years earlier. He also pointed out that his new, turbocharged machine cost less than its predecessor.

These advancements in product quality are quantified in Exhibit 2-3. Calculating the compound annual growth rates revealed that all key performance attributes of John's PC system had been improved at annual rates in the *high 40% range*, or greater. In addition, the price had declined by *4.9%* per year!

Was the government measuring *any* of this?

## THE CONSUMER KNOWS BEST

The cases of the cell phone and the PC demonstrate that consumers are clearly benefiting from rapidly advancing digital products. Moreover, consumers are quite aware of what is going on in the marketplace—in many cases, well before an economist's theory appears to explain that marketplace. In fact, to me as a consumer, a "kick the tires" approach to assessing the increasing real value of technology-based products contributed importantly to understanding what is really driving the New Economy.

A light went on when I realized that the commonality of just about *all* products and services demonstrating large advancements in performance for the same or lower prices was that they were driven by constantly improving digital technologies. That's how they were getting faster, better, and cheaper. This was true not only of cell phones and PCs, but also Nintendo handheld Game Boys, Sony Playstations, household appliances, digital cameras, autos, aircraft, defense equipment, medical products—and services, such as retail-

**E X H I B I T  2-3**

Faster, Better, Cheaper PCs

| Personal Computer Key Performance Attributes | Fall 1997 Model | March 2001 Model | Annual Performance Improvement |
|---|---|---|---|
| Processor | 200 Mg Hz Pentium MMX | 1.3 Gig Hertz Pentium 4 | 69.0%/year faster clock cycle |
| Hard Drive | 2 Gigabytes | 40 Gigabytes | 129.7%/year |
| Main Memory | 32 Megabytes DRAM 100 Mg Mz speed | 128 Megabytes RDRAM 400 Mg Hz speed cd | 47.8%/year more memory; 47.8%/year faster |
| Input Device | 12x CD Drive | 16x DVD/CD | Invaluable new feature |
| Monitor | 17" with 4MB & 1x AGP Graphics | 19" with 32 MB & 4x AGP Graphics | Higher resolution; 47.8%/year faster motion & graphics |
| Printer | Epson 200 Color Inkjet 2.5 ppm black, 720x360 dpi | HP 970 Color Inkjet 12 ppm black, 2400x1200 dpi | 55.5%/year speed; 95.8%/year resolution |
| System Price | $2,500 delivered | $2,100 delivered | 4.9%/year cheaper |

Source: Tanaka Capital Management, Inc.

ing, education, online banking, Internet access, and so on. A profound shift was taking place. As the Digital Revolution percolated throughout the economy, all *kinds* of things were getting faster, better, and cheaper.

In fact, the basic digital technologies were becoming so powerful that some—for example, self-tuning automobile engines—were beginning to deliver vastly more value and functionality to the consumer than the incremental cost of the underlying digital components. It is well known from Moore's Law that semiconductors double the number of transistors on a piece of silicon every 18 to 24 months. But it wasn't just semiconductors that were improving by leaps and bounds each year. Software, magnetic memory, optical transmission, and even displays were getting better at double-digit rates per year.

And what was *really* exciting was that leading companies at the forefront of developing these technologies could all show research and development roadmaps suggesting that these technologies will *continue to advance at similar double-digit rates of performance gains for at least 10 to 15 years into the future.* The key, critical question again posed itself: For how many technology-driven products and services was the government measuring these rapid improvements in quality and value? Were these improvements in quality being reflected annually in GDP accounts?

If they weren't, what were the consequences?

## HOW THE GOVERNMENT COUNTS QUALITY IMPROVEMENT

Many calls to economists and analysts at the government's statistical agencies revealed that they have been hard at work trying to measure quality improvement for the U.S. economy starting well before the first Boskin report.

The classical approach for decades had been to measure improving product quality only by counting the incremental cost of adding new components, such as the cost of an additional bathroom in the average new home, or the cost of antilock brakes in a car. The government then would simply adjust the price index or deflator to reflect the increased cost of the new feature, so that the product's higher selling price would reflect the new feature's higher component cost, and not appear to be inflationary just because the end product price went up.

But it became clear that these traditional "cost-based" methods had great difficulty adjusting for the incremental value being added by digital components, because (as in the case of John the Barber's PC) the underlying digital technologies offered double-digit performance gains every year, at the same or lower costs than the prior models. Ironically, because there was no increase in costs for these tech-based goods, there was also no "measured" increase in value or quality. If the government continued to use traditional cost-based measurement techniques, it would be unable to report an increase in the value of John the Barber's PC.

Fortunately, the story doesn't stop there. Recognizing the difficulty in measuring and adjusting inflation indices for the rapid improvement in the value of technology-based products at no additional cost, the U.S. statistical agencies were the first in the world to employ "hedonic" models to estimate product quality improvement in computers. *Hedonic models* measure the implied value to consumers of each individual new feature in a product by examining, for example, 50 different configurations of PCs, and determining how much more people are willing to pay for an extra 10 gigabytes of hard-drive capacity, or another gigahertz of processing power. In other words, the value of the extra 10 gigabytes is imputed by comparing the prices of PCs equipped with the extra 10 gigabytes versus those configured without it.

After considerable research, the U.S. government started to incorporate hedonic data, beginning in the late 1980s at the Bureau of Economic Analysis, with price deflators for the measurement of quality improvement in mainframe computers. Shortly thereafter, in 1990, the Bureau of Labor Statistics began in its inflation indices to utilize hedonics to measure quality improvement for all computers "made for final sale" (meaning excluding computers sold as components of larger end products).

The hedonic modeling process requires an enormous effort to gather data on different configurations for each digital product. But with strong correlations validating the hedonic approach, the federal agencies pressed on. By the end of the 1990s, they had added other digital product categories to the hedonic process, most notably semiconductors made for final sale.

While it was reassuring to learn that the government was using hedonics to measure the improvement in computers and semiconductors, as well as a few very small consumer items such as camcorders and video cassette recorders, it was a little surprising to find that no other large categories of products and services were measured hedonically for improving quality. Virtually every government pricing analyst covering fields like software, autos, healthcare commodities (pharmaceuticals), healthcare services, financial services, etc., admitted that they were not measuring the improvement in quality if there was not an associated component cost increase. Several analysts expressed their desire to measure more, but cited limited resources.

It became increasingly evident that the potential for the undermeasurement of quality improvement across the economy was enormous. This was expressed in a conversation with a government economist in 2001. "The vast majority of IT [information technology] does not have adjustments for quality," he told me. "There are thousands of IT products. Think about telecom. [The category of] computers is a drop in the bucket. . . . In order to readjust to the challenges of IT, which is much more quantitative in nature and much more sophisticated, you can't use the same type of method you would use to track the price of watermelon."

## SOLVING THE MYSTERY OF THE NEW ECONOMY

As we solve the mystery of the New Economy, it is important to understand the rather curious way that economists account for quality improvement. If a consumer bought a new PC with 25% better performance but at the same price as last year's model, that PC would be counted by economists as having had the *equivalent* of a 25% reduction in price. It would be measured as "deflationary," in the sense that getting more performance for the same price was equivalent to buying the same PC at a lower price.

Deflationary. Now things are getting interesting! This is not how most people—especially those with any awareness of the 1930s—think of deflation. This deflation is not being caused by a severe recession or a depression leading to price-cutting and a downward spiral in wages. Rather, it is the fortuitous result of advancing digital technologies that create greater performance and greater value for consumers at the same or lower prices. It turns out that economists have no choice but to convert these faster and better products into the equivalent of products with lower prices, thereby creating "deflation."

If the government is not counting quality improvement in a number of information technology-driven products and services across the economy, this means logically that there is an equally enormous potential for the undercounting of deflation, and therefore the overstatement of inflation. In effect, by not counting annual quality improvement, the government is not measuring enough equivalent "deflation" in the economy.

A second very curious aspect of this translation of quality improvement from digitally driven products into the economic equivalent of deflation is that in addition to helping to reduce the rate of inflation in the overall economy, these improvements in quality are also directly increasing real output and real productivity gains, as reported by the government. By making the appropriate downward adjustments to the GDP Deflator for rapidly advancing digital technologies, the government would be properly counting the greater real value of the new digitally driven products actually being sold in the marketplace. The result would be the reporting of lower inflation in the GDP Deflator *and higher output* in the form of higher real GDP.

Since there is typically no increase in the number of hours worked to make these advancing digital products, this boost to real output also translates into a boost to productivity growth, or real output per person-hour. Importantly, this counting of more real output and higher productivity growth is not merely an artificial result of economic accounting for quality improvement. It is a *more accurate reflection of the greater real value being delivered to consumers*, at the same or lower prices with every technology product design cycle.

Eureka! In the context of modern economics, this is a rare phenomenon, indeed. The rapid and constant improvement in digital technologies is itself creating both lower measured inflation *and* higher real output simultaneously. It is *real*, in the sense that higher-value products are being delivered to consumers at the same or lower prices. It is *growing*, because information technology is continuing to grow as a percentage of the economy. It is *improving the quality of life*, which is perfectly obvious to the consumers who happily snap up DVD players, digital cameras, video game consoles, incredibly powerful (and more affordable) laptops, and convergence cell phones.

Most important, it helps explain the New Economy. *The overstatement of inflation and the missing productivity are one and the same.* It is ironic that the proper measurement of the rapidly and constantly improving performance and quality of technology-driven products would help correct the overstatement of inflation, as well as help "find" the long-missing productivity growth that economists have been seeking for years. Technology-driven productivity growth has been there all along. We just haven't measured it yet.

The government currently reports quality improvement in little more than computers made for final sale. However, our statistical experts have pointed us (and themselves) in the right direction. As the government gets further into the process of more accurately counting quality improvement for more products and services, we will see that actual inflation is considerably lower than what has been reported, and growth in real output and productivity are considerably higher than what the government has been reporting. The public will learn of this in the form of gradual revisions to the real GDP and inflation data over the next several years.

In the end, there will be a massive, cumulative overhaul and retrospective restatement of the economic data—a restatement that I believe will show that fiscal, monetary, and corporate decision making have been suboptimal for years, because they have been based on suboptimal data. The implications of these suboptimal decisions will be discussed in later chapters.

Nevertheless, it is our good fortune that rapidly and constantly improving digital technologies appeared on the economic scene and gained critical mass just in time to provide the lift in real output and productivity growth, and a reduction in inflation, that were much needed by an economy approaching zero growth in its workforce. It is likely that without the benefits of a growing and increasingly pervasive Digital Revolution, the economies of the United States and the rest of the industrialized world would have been wallowing in much more sluggish growth and in higher inflation in the 1990s.

Indeed, the delivery of constantly improving value in products and services in that mysterious and wonderful decade of the 1990s created significant wealth. Whether similar amounts of value and wealth can be created in the next one to two decades will depend, to a great extent, on how well we understand and measure the ways in which rapidly and constantly advancing digital technologies will continue to drive and shape our economy.

## NOTES

1. Tanaka, Graham Y., "Demographics and the Stock Market," *MT&A Outlook*, July 1982.

2. Tanaka, Graham Y., "Demographics, Productivity & the Return on Common Stocks," *MT&A Outlook*, December 1983.

# 3 CHAPTER

## The Theory of Digital Deflation: Faster, Better, Cheaper

Everything that can be invented has been invented.
—*Charles H. Duell, Commissioner, U.S. Office of Patents, 1899*

*The Theory of Digital Deflation evolved partly to help explain an intriguing economic development of the 1990s: the New Economy. It also grew out of a need to understand how rapidly advancing technologies improve products for consumers—and, in the process, create fortunes for some companies and despair for others. Several key digital technologies promise to advance at double-digit rates for one to two decades into the future. They will drive innovation, resulting in new and improved products and services, many of which cannot even be identified today. Faster, better, and cheaper products will contribute to a phenomenon called Digital Deflation—a phenomenon that we can appreciate only if we can understand and properly quantify the rapidly improving quality of digitally driven products and services. Ultimately, as the government counts this quality improvement more accurately, the Digital Revolution may prove to have more beneficial impact on the human condition than the Industrial Revolution a century earlier.*

### DIGITAL DEFLATION IS A *GOOD* THING

Most people realize, intuitively, that technology has been contributing something very special and very important to the economy and to our society in recent years. At the same time, most people find it difficult to *explain* that contribution, at least in economic terms. Just how does using a handheld RIM Blackberry, or working on a laptop with wireless Internet access, or firing up a cell phone with position location, or shopping on the Internet actually add value for the consumer, the economy, or society as a whole?

And if they do add value, don't we need to figure out *how much* value? Are we properly measuring the total value of technology-driven products and services?

These are the kinds of questions every business manager, economist, government policymaker, and indeed, every investor should ask. In answering these questions, we will find that rapidly advancing technologies are creating a kind of "good deflation," far different from the deflation of the 1930s.

The Theory of Digital Deflation evolved as a way of understanding and demystifying an economy in the 1990s that appeared to be defying gravity. There was also a need to understand, at the company or "microeconomic" level, how rapidly improving technologies make products and services faster, better, and cheaper for consumers, and for how long into the future advancements could be made before they hit some sort of technological wall. (If technological innovation is in some sense the Golden Goose, you'd like to know the projected lifespan of that goose.) The reward, of course, was that certain companies that truly understood how to leverage new technological advancements and drive the price-performance curve would tend to succeed and take market share away from those that didn't.

It was the convergence of these macroeconomic and microeconomic pursuits that helped crystallize the Theory of Digital Deflation.

## DIGITAL DEFLATION DEFINED

Digital Deflation is an economic concept that converts the improvement in performance and quality of a product or service—the result of rapid and recurring advancements in digitally driven technologies—into an annual percentage increase in real economic value for the consumer. In "big picture" terms, Digital Deflation attempts to quantify, on an annual basis, the ongoing advances of the Digital Revolution in terms of its value creation for the economy and the aggregate benefits to society.

The term *digital* in Digital Deflation is the fairly standard reference to technologies that use data converted into ones and zeroes so they can be stored and processed by simple "on/off" switches in magnetic, semiconductor, optical, and other media. My use of the term *deflation* is more unusual. Most of us understand deflation to represent a condition where prices are going down—the opposite of inflation. As discussed in the last chapter, deflation can also reflect the curious but increasingly common occurrence of product quality going up while prices remain stable. As in the examples of PCs and cell phones, a 30% to 40% per year improvement in performance for new models at the same price as the previous year's models is equal to buying at a discount. You pay a lower price per megahertz of processing speed or you get a speakerphone thrown in for free. Appropriately, economists translate rising product quality at the same price into the economic equivalent of deflation, and hence, the term *Digital Deflation*. Digital Deflation can be measured in either weak or strong forms. In its weakest, most basic form, Digital Deflation measures the percentage improvement in quality or value to the consumer of a digitally driven product or service, based on the sum of the weighted average annual improvement in the Key Performance Attributes of that product or service (the characteristics of a product or service most important to a consumer in determining value).

In its strongest form or definition, Digital Deflation measures the percentage improvement in the total utilitarian value to the consumer of any product or service improved by digital technologies, at a constant price, with consideration given to (1) the cost and time to shop and purchase, (2) the total cost of ownership, and (3) any incremental value added through the post-purchase development of new uses.

The Key Performance Attributes used in measuring quality improvement for most digitally intensive products would include (for example) speed, memory, weight, size, functionality, and image resolution. And although the relative importance of Key Performance Attributes vary from one consumer to another, and from one product to another, average component "weights" can be estimated, given large enough sample sizes. The increased value of a rapidly improving digital component can be worth multiples of the incremental cost of that component, depending on the perceived value of the Key Performance Attribute relative to the overall value of the product or service.

It should be stressed that Digital Deflation is a form of "good" deflation, in that it reflects the increase in real economic value of better-performing, higher-quality digital products and services being delivered to the consumer at the same or lower prices. It is very different in origin and economic impact from the kind of destructive deflation caused by a tightening of monetary policy (e.g., the United States in the 1930s), by ill-conceived and highly restrictive government policies (e.g., the Smoot-Hawley Tariff from the same era) or by structural inefficiencies and rigidities (e.g., Japan in the 1990s).

Digital Deflation is also very different from what might be called cost-cutting deflation, such as that experienced by the United States in the 1980s—a period of leveraged buyouts, consolidations, and rationalizations of overhead and other costs. These are essentially nonrepeating, one-shot reductions in costs. Digital Deflation, by contrast, is a recurring phenomenon. It benefits from the rapid and virtually continuous advancements in digital technologies, as reflected in enhancements to end products and services with each successive product design cycle or service upgrade. In addition, the benefits of Digital Deflation can be seen in many nondigital technologies and in many products and services that may be only indirectly driven by digital advances.

The drug industry can be used to help illustrate this broader application of a variety of technologies to continuously improve product category performance. While the underlying technologies for drug discovery and improving drug efficacy and safety—such as combinatorial chemistry, mass screening, and genetic research—are not primarily driven by digital technologies, they are nevertheless heavy beneficiaries of rapid and recurring advances in digital instruments, supercomputers, data-storage devices, and analytical software tools that get faster, better, and cheaper every year.

Why does this matter? According to most reports, drug prices are "highly inflationary." But in these reports, significant improvements in the efficacy and safety profile of new and enhanced pharmaceuticals are not being taken into account. If drug prices were adjusted for quality improvement, they would not appear to be so inflationary. (In fact, they might appear to be getting cheaper.) So, relatively far from the high-tech realm of computers, we find other examples in which the performance of products and services is being enhanced. The key commonality is that digital technologies are improving the value to the consumer of many non-IT products on an ongoing basis and at rapid rates, and only a few of these enhancements are being measured by the government.

## THE DIGITAL DRIVERS

"Any sufficiently advanced technology," science fiction author and futurist Arthur C. Clarke once wrote, "will be indistinguishable from magic."

Nowhere is this more true than in the realm of digital technologies. They are "magical," in the sense that they are constantly being invented, obsoleted, and reinvented. They are equally magical in their ability to generate double-digit rates of improvements in products and services every year.

Underneath all this magic are several key digital technologies. But the best known and most important is a very specific kind of magic that has become an increasingly pervasive driver of the Digital Revolution: the semiconductor. These integrated circuits, etched on flat chips of silicon, began with humble origins, but quickly became amazingly complex. Today, they resemble miniature club sandwiches, with several interconnecting layers of conducting circuits separated by insulating layers. Like clockwork, over the years, they have been getting smaller and smaller, allowing the packing of more tiny transistors (or switches) closer together, thereby improving speed, processing power, and storage capacity with each design cycle.

What is truly amazing is that the rate of growth in the number of transistors has been incredibly constant for over 35 years. In 1965, Gordon Moore, then director of research at Fairchild Semiconductor, published an article in *Electronics* magazine in which he estimated that, based on early trends, the number of transistors on an integrated circuit (semiconductor) would double every year over the following 10 years. "The complexity for minimum component costs," Moore wrote, "has increased at a rate of roughly a factor of two per year. . . . Certainly over the short term this rate can be expected to continue, if not to increase. Over the longer term, the rate of increase is a bit more uncertain, although there is no reason to believe it will not remain nearly constant for at least 10 years. That means by 1975, the number of components per integrated circuit for minimum cost will be 65,000."[1]

Since the mid-1960s, when Fairchild was laying down 60 transistors per chip, the rate of improvement in semiconductors has in fact stabilized, in a range of doubling the number of transistors every 18–24 months (41–56% per year). This trend has become known as Moore's Law. By the year 2000, Moore's modest startup, Intel, was producing

**E X H I B I T   3-1**

Moore's Law in Action

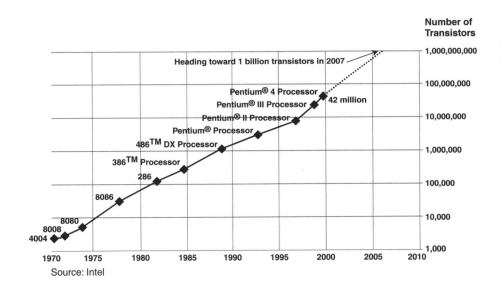

Source: Intel

Pentium 4 microprocessors with 42 million transistors per chip. Exhibit 3-1, Moore's Law in Action, shows how microprocessors have been on a remarkably steady path of growth in transistors. And it is well known in Silicon Valley that the improvement in speed, processing power, and storage capacity of semiconductor chips is directly related to the number of transistors that can be packed onto a piece of silicon.

Of greater interest, for our purposes, is the fact that the designers and manufacturers of semiconductor manufacturing equipment can identify technology roadmaps projecting advances at least 10 to 15 years out into the future. Intel, for example, predicts that microprocessors will contain 1 billion transistors by the year 2007, implying a compound rate of 57% more transistors each year, or very close to the high end of the 41–56% per year growth in transistors projected by Moore's Law.

Again, does this matter? Yes. This underlying 41–56% per year improvement in semiconductor functionality is rippling throughout the economy, year in and year out. More than any other digital driver, this remarkably steady, almost metronomic beat—an average of 48% per year improvement in semiconductor performance—creates *real value*, and is setting the pace for converting the ingenuity and creativity of the Digital Revolution into faster, better, and cheaper goods and services for consumers worldwide.

Other digital drivers that have contributed significantly to the Digital Revolution include magnetic storage, software, and—more recently—optical technologies. Magnetic tape has been around for decades, and many people take for granted the ever faster, better, and cheaper benefits of magnetic storage. For decades, though, hard drives (the most common form of magnetic storage) have been doubling every year the amount of data that they can hold. This is almost *twice* the rate of improvement in semiconductors. As one government economist put it, "The hard drive makes Moore's Law look like it's standing still!"

These improvements, too, are likely to continue, although perhaps at closer to a 60% per year rate over the near term due to cyclical pressures on the industry. As engineers and researchers scramble to keep advancing the state of the art with new recording heads—consumers will continue to reap the benefits of dramatic annual increases in the hard-drive capacity on their PCs.

What else? Software, too, has emerged as a fundamental technology helping to drive the Digital Revolution. Software has been getting better and better, in all its variations—from operating system and network management software to applications like balancing your checkbook, ordering flowers online, or moving an image more realistically on a Sony Playstation. And yet, like other technology drivers cited above, the impact of software on our economy has been grossly overlooked. The Department of Commerce only began to measure software as a separate product in GDP accounts in October 1999. Interviews with the managements of several software companies reveal that in the next several years, they too will continue to make significant advancements in "features and functions" which, in many cases, will keep pace with the advances in hardware.

Other digital technologies continue to improve at rapid rates. In fact, the fastest-improving technology has been in the area of long-haul transmission of data over optical fibers. In recent years, the speed of fiber-optic transmission of data has *doubled every 9 months*, or the equivalent of 133% per year.

This rate of improvement is likely to slow in the future, mainly for practical reasons. So much fiber was put in place in the 1998–2001 period that long-haul capacity far outstripped the ability of the telecommunications industry to sign up customers and deploy broadband capacity in the short-haul metro markets and in the so-called last mile to the home or office. When the market again catches up with the technology, it's reasonable to expect that the pace of optical technology innovation will again accelerate.

Advancements will be made in other key technologies, including display technologies from liquid crystal on silicon to organic light emitting displays (OLEDs). Color displays will become commonplace, and large flat panel displays will become increasingly affordable. In addition, we will have the benefit of many new technologies that currently are only in their infancy. Nanotechnology, for example, will permit the manipulation of individual molecules and atoms to make semiconductors and other devices one-thousandth as big as current devices.

Exhibit 3-2 presents a conversion graph showing how fast four-key digital technologies are likely to improve in performance, or to

**E X H I B I T  3-2**

Digital Driver "Price Performance" Curve*

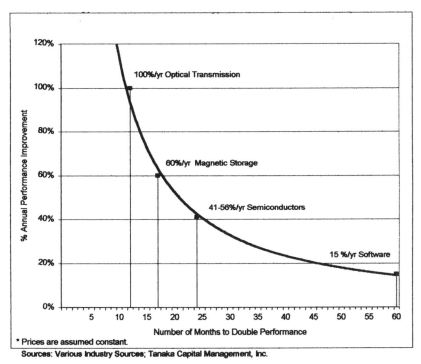

Sources: Various Industry Sources; Tanaka Capital Management, Inc.

generate quality improvement, annually. It assumes constant average selling prices per unit from one year to the next. Keep in mind that this price–performance curve reflects just a few of the basic drivers of the ongoing Digital Revolution.

## THE NEXT BIG THING

Every couple of years, there is a great hue and cry across the land that an important high-technology product has matured, and that this signals the impending and certain closing of the digital frontier. This happened with mainframes, which many times were projected to disappear, and yet are still thriving. Distributed data processing died and came back to life as networked servers and PCs. Personal computers, of course, were supposed to have peaked out several times during the 1980s and '90s, but kept growing.

Although a few digital products and services are able to leverage new technologies and develop new uses, the truth is that most make way for truly faster, better, and cheaper alternatives. Minicomputers, in fact, did disappear, but they were in large part the victim of powerful, high-function PCs and workstations. This is the price of doing business in the midst of the constantly improving and evolving Digital Revolution, which—as it defines winners and losers—creates more real value for consumers, and more Digital Deflation for the economy.

The Internet is perhaps one relatively new phenomenon that really is almost "indistinguishable from magic." The Internet happened because a number of bright and motivated individuals, working independently on different building blocks, were able to harness several rapidly advancing digital technologies to create a brand-new communications platform. The happy result is that people who don't know each other can communicate, exchange information, and transact business. You can research, buy, or sell almost anything on the Net, and new uses are being invented every day.

My purpose in citing this list of supposedly magic inventions is to underscore the fact that we should not be surprised by the invention of the Internet or any other revolutionary technology-based products and services. They make sense within the context of the steady drumbeat of digital technologies advancing at strong double-digit rates every year. Given an environment that is conducive to innovation, entrepreneurship, and capital investment, there will surely be more Internets in the future. Simply put, given the right economic environment, innovation will happen.

In broader terms, assuming a healthy economy, the Digital Revolution will continue to grow and prosper for years, and probably *decades*, into the future. While candidates for the "next big thing" are incubating in research labs around the world, we will be enjoying the benefits of faster, better, and cheaper consumer electronic devices, convergence personal digital assistant–cell phone appliances, digital imaging, and ubiquitous wireless Internet access. A few years down the road, the next big thing may well be personalized medicine, custom-designed drugs, and individually tailored dietary programs, all based on each person's genetic makeup.

Are these views too optimistic? Consider the following quotes, which illustrate how hazardous it has been to predict the demise, or even the limitations, of technology:

"I think there is a world market for maybe five computers."
—*Thomas Watson, Chairman of IBM, 1943*

"Computers in the future may weigh no more than 1.5 tons."
—*Popular Mechanics, 1949*

"But what . . . is it good for?"
—*Engineer at the Advanced Computing Systems Division of IBM*
*commenting on the microchip, 1968*

"There is no reason anyone would want a computer in their home."
—*Ken Olson, Chairman and Founder, Digital Equipment Corp., 1977*

"640K ought to be enough for anybody."
—*Bill Gates, 1981*

## IS THE DIGITAL REVOLUTION BETTER THAN THE INDUSTRIAL REVOLUTION?

As we proceed further into the 21st century, the rapidly evolving Digital Revolution will be perceived by many to be more powerful than the Industrial Revolution that preceded it a century ago. Let's consider the facts.

The Industrial Revolution was driven by a variety of unrelated inventions that were developed over a period of several decades. Their contributions to society were immense, but once they were developed and introduced to markets worldwide, these basic inventions of the Industrial Revolution proved to be somewhat limited, in terms of further incremental contributions to efficiency and productivity growth. In many cases, they were bounded by the laws of physics.

For example, steam engines could only become so efficient before they would "hit the wall," as defined by the laws of thermodynamics and the steam cycle. Electricity could only be generated, distributed, and stored so efficiently. There were also clear limits to the capabilities of the combustion engine. Although it found its way into a succession of new applications, such as autos, airplanes, and production lines, once those were more or less perfected, that was it. Combustion engines could not, and did not, become 20% more efficient in year 2, and in year 3, and so on.

The Digital Revolution, as I have tried to demonstrate, is a completely different phenomenon. It is driven by technologies that have been improving their performance at double-digit rates annually for over 30 years, and are likely to continue to do so without hitting the wall on manufacturing processes for at least the next 15 to 20 years. It has already started to obsolete entire industries, and to spawn brand-new ones, as digital replaces analog in industry after industry in both the goods-producing and service sectors.

## THE LAWS OF DIGITAL DEFLATION

When examined closely, the Digital Revolution along with its primary economic benefit, Digital Deflation, demonstrate identifiable characteristics that have been surprisingly consistent over time, in a variety of applications and industries. In effect, they are the "laws" of Digital Deflation. Some are borrowed from the Old Economy, but they take on new meaning in the New Economy. Although they are the result of advances in science and technology, by their impact they are laws of an economic nature. They give structure and meaning to the thesis that the Digital Revolution is producing faster, better, and cheaper products and services that consumers appreciate—even if these benefits are not yet fully acknowledged in the economic reports of the government. I have identified a dozen such rules:

1. *Rapid and recurring advances* in the underlying digital technologies will create improvement in the price and performance (price–performance) of digital products and services at relatively steady, generally double-digit rates annually, and also with every product design cycle.
2. The rate of improvement in the price–performance or quality of each digital product or service will reflect the sum of the weighted rates of improvement in the key performance attrib-

utes of each product or service. Relative weights reflect the average consumer's utilitarian or *perceived value, rather than the cost* of the components (digital or otherwise).

3. Acting as *digital performance multipliers,* advancing digital technologies can increase the value of the final product or service by several times more than the incremental cost of the digital components. For example, by doubling the storage capacity of an MP3 music player, the newest version of semiconductor flash memory can virtually double the value of the MP3 player to the consumer, even though the incremental cost of the newest chip is close to zero.

4. Most of the underlying technologies can be expected to deliver more value and create more Digital Deflation for the economy at the same rapid rates for the *next 10 years, and possibly for 20 years or more.*

5. *All participants in the supply chain* contributing to the delivery of a rapidly improving digitally driven product or service are themselves helping to create Digital Deflation at the same rate of improvement as the final end product. The electronics retailer and the help desk operator are integrally involved in the delivery of the digitally deflating product.

6. Over the years, large amounts of Digital Deflation are being generated across the economy, due to the *power of compounding at rapid double-digit rates* each and every year—e.g., semiconductors increasing the number of transistors at 41–56% per year, magnetic storage increasing the aerial bit density by 60% to 100% per year, and software-improving features and functions by about 15% per year. This means that over time, the cumulative undermeasurement of quality improvement from advancing digital technologies can be enormous for the aggregate economy.

7. The *elasticity of demand is very powerful* in digitally driven products and services, because the percentage improvement in performance and quality is so large with each new digital product design cycle. With typically 10% to 40% more performance and value offered yearly at the same price for digitally driven products and services, unit demand tends to grow considerably faster than it does for the nondigitally driven products.

8. For digital products and services, low labor and other variable costs, as well as high R&D costs, can create *powerful economies of*

*scale.* This means that the next unit sold will typically carry high incremental profit margins, as fixed costs are spread over more units. Incidentally, this is one reason that high-tech stocks can be quite volatile. Profitability will often rise (or fall) much faster than revenues.

9. Digital *product life cycles are typically very short*, reflecting the rapid, double-digit annual rate of improvement in digital technologies.

10. For the overall economy, rapidly advancing digital technologies are *increasing real output and productivity gains—and reducing inflation simultaneously* (the essence of Digital Deflation).

11. By boosting productivity growth and lowering inflation simultaneously, Digital Deflation *raises the ideal or "potential GDP" growth rate, lifts the "potential productivity" growth rate, moderates the business cycle, and reduces the optimal unemployment rate* that can be sustained without an increase in inflation.

12. Digital Deflation *will only get larger* as the New Economy grows to command a greater share of the overall economy, and as digital technologies begin to be leveraged by an increasing number of noninformation technology industries.

## HOW BIG IS DIGITAL DEFLATION?

To judge the benefits and estimate the impact of Digital Deflation on the economy, you must first ask, "How big is information technology?"

Unfortunately, there is no simple answer. The lack of a clear definition of information technology has contributed to the difficulty in figuring out what has really been driving the New Economy. For example, in GDP accounts for 2001, IT represented only 4.2% of final sales of goods and services, much lower than the 8% IT number that is often quoted by economists. This is because gross domestic product only reports IT as Information Processing Equipment and Software in the corporate capital-spending category Business Fixed Investment. Most of the countless IT-based products and services which are purchased by consumers and the government (as opposed to the corporate sector) are not broken out, and therefore they are hard to identify as IT.

What we *can* say with confidence is that business spending on information processing equipment and software has consistently grown faster than the overall economy. It expanded from 3.2% of GDP in

1989 to 4.3% of GDP by 1999. The steady 50-year growth trend can be seen in Exhibit 3-3.

Keep in mind that computers represent the only major category in GDP accounts to reflect significant downward price adjustments for performance and quality improvement. Accordingly, it is the only category to be reflecting Digital Deflation to a significant degree in the GDP accounts.* As seen in Exhibit 3-3, corporate spending on Computers and Peripheral Equipment reached "only" 1% of GDP in the late 1990s—up significantly from 0.7% of GDP in the early 1990s. (I put the word *only* in quotes because 1% of the U.S. GDP is a very huge number, indeed.)

It is important to realize that even at a small 1% of GDP, given the very rapid 20% to 30% rate of annual improvement estimated by the government for computers in the late 1990s, the government has already been counting quality improvement and Digital Deflation at the rate of 20% to 30% per year, times 1% of GDP, or about 0.2% to 0.3% per year reduction in the overall GDP Deflator.

Said slightly differently: The U.S. government is already including about 0.2% to 0.3% per year of deflation in the actual GDP Deflator, *just from the estimated annual quality improvement in computers made for final sale.* This contribution of deflation toward the overall GDP Deflator can be seen in Exhibit 3-4, where the GDP Deflator is divided into its contribution of *deflation* from Information Processing Equipment and Software, and *inflation* from all other (i.e., noninformation processing) industries.

In the upper graph, the thin solid line represents the deflator for the Information Processing and Software category of GDP, and includes the subcategories of computers and peripherals, software, communications equipment, instruments, photocopy machines, and office & accounting equipment. This graph clearly shows information technology to have been deflationary since 1982, as estimated by the government and as actually included in GDP accounts. Note that the estimated annual rate of deflation has been increasing (that is, going deeper into the negative) since the early 1990s. The right side of the graph shows how the blended average rates of deflation for the Information Processing categories pulled down the overall GDP Deflator at an increasing rate during the decade.

---

* Quality adjustments are made for semiconductors, but are only applied to the minuscule amount made for final sale to consumers. There are also modest adjustments made for quality improvement in portions of software, communications equipment, and a handful of consumer electronics items.

**EXHIBIT 3-3**

How Big Is Information Technology?

| | GDP Nominal $Bil. | [1] GDP Info.Proc. Eqt.& Software From Bus. Fixed Inv. Nominal $ Bil. | % GDP | [2] GDP Computers & Peripheral Equipment Nominal $ Bil. | % GDP | [3] Gross Product Originating IT Producing Industries Nominal $ Bil. | % GDP |
|---|---|---|---|---|---|---|---|
| 1949 | $267.7 | $1.6 | 0.6% | - | - | - | - |
| 1959 | 507.4 | 4.0 | 0.8% | - | - | - | - |
| 1969 | 985.3 | 14.6 | 1.5% | - | - | - | - |
| 1979 | 2,566.4 | 58.6 | 2.3% | - | - | - | - |
| 1989 | 5,489.1 | 173.0 | 3.2% | $43.1 | 0.8% | - | - |
| 1990 | 5,803.2 | 176.1 | 3.0% | 38.6 | 0.7% | $318.0 | 5.5% |
| 1991 | 5,986.2 | 181.4 | 3.0% | 37.7 | 0.6% | 330.2 | 5.5% |
| 1992 | 6,318.9 | 197.5 | 3.1% | 43.6 | 0.7% | 353.2 | 5.6% |
| 1993 | 6,642.3 | 215.0 | 3.2% | 47.2 | 0.7% | 386.2 | 5.8% |
| 1994 | 7,054.3 | 233.7 | 3.3% | 51.3 | 0.7% | 426.0 | 6.0% |
| 1995 | 7,400.5 | 262.0 | 3.5% | 64.6 | 0.9% | 471.1 | 6.4% |
| 1996 | 7,813.2 | 287.3 | 3.7% | 70.9 | 0.9% | 522.0 | 6.7% |
| 1997 | 8,318.4 | 325.2 | 3.9% | 79.6 | 1.0% | 588.4 | 7.1% |
| 1998 | 8,781.5 | 363.4 | 4.1% | 84.2 | 1.0% | 646.9 | 7.4% |
| 1999 | 9,268.6 | 399.7 | 4.3% | 90.8 | 1.0% | 718.2 | 7.7% |
| 2000 | 9,872.9 | 466.5 | 4.7% | 109.3 | 1.1% | 796.6 | 8.1% |
| 2001 | 10,208.1 | 427.1 | 4.2% | 87.7 | 0.9% | N.A. | N.A. |

[1] GDP Accounts

[2] Computer & Peripheral Equipment, Communications & Other, with Software added in November 2000

[3] Information Technology from Gross Product Originating

Sources: Department of Commerce; Bureau of Economic Analysis; Tanaka Capital Management, Inc.

It also can be seen that the GDP Deflator line has been separating from and dropping below the deflator for the noninformation processing industries. If it weren't for the Digital Deflation being counted in computers—and hence reflected in the overall deflator for Information Processing Equipment & Software—the GDP Deflator would have been 0.2% to 0.3% higher per year than what was actually reported in the 1990s.

The bottom graph in Exhibit 3-4 presents the individual deflators for the three subcategories Computer & Peripherals, Software, and

**E X H I B I T   3-4**

Information Processing and Non-Information Processing Categories of the GDP Deflator

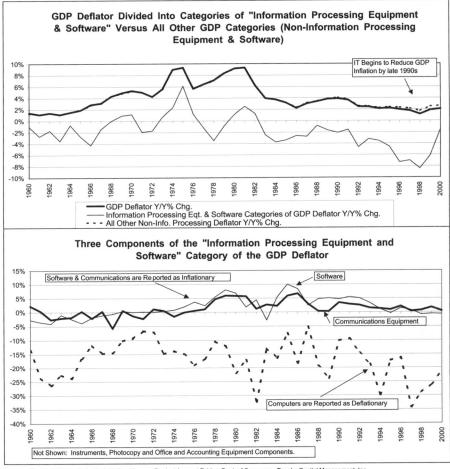

Sources: Bureau of Economic Analysis National Income Product Account Tables; Dept. of Commerce; Tanaka Capital Management, Inc.

Communications Equipment. It can be clearly seen that on a net basis, only the Computers & Peripherals category was estimated by the government to have been showing quality-adjusted price declines. Deflators for Software and Communications Equipment were measured by the government to be above zero and therefore inflationary. Again, note how Computers & Peripherals were estimated by the government to have become increasingly deflationary in the second half of the 1990s. This reflected accelerating economies of scale, faster advances in computer performance in the later years of the decade, and an industry shift toward the "direct sales" model embraced by Dell, Gateway, and others. Faster growth brought on faster advances.

It was the higher rates of performance improvement, as well as the increasing importance of IT as a percent of GDP, that resulted in greater "good" deflation being created by computers in the late 1990s than in the early 1990s. This higher level of Digital Deflation translated into (1) higher rates of growth in real output, and (2) higher growth in productivity in the overall economy. The 0.2 to 0.3 percentage point's contribution of Digital Deflation and productivity growth to the economy also represented half of the 0.5% "productivity surge" that made economists jubilant in the late 1990s. Productivity gains rose from an average of 1.6% per year in the early 1990s to 2.1% per year in the late 1990s.

Don't let this flurry of numbers distract you from the central point: As these charts demonstrate, our economy has been going through a fundamental shift in a positive direction, and the government is only just beginning to count it.

## WHAT'S MISSING FROM THE GDP DEFLATOR?

The government is already taking into account about 0.2% to 0.3% per year of Digital Deflation in the U.S. economy by counting the performance and quality improvement of computers made for final sale. But what about the Digital Deflation in the computers and semiconductors that are *not* counted as final sales in GDP because they are merely components in larger final products (e.g., computers in cars, missiles, and aircraft; or semiconductors in machinery, tools, autos, trucks, and consumer electronics)? What about all the other areas of information technology that are not being counted for quality improvement in the GDP data, such as the whole universe of software, communications equipment, and computer services?

The answers, once again, came from the government's own data. In 1998, the Department of Commerce published a study, "The Emerging Digital Economy," that was designed to explain how the Internet was affecting the U.S. economy. That first study was followed by the "Emerging Digital Economy II" in 1999 and "Digital Economy 2000" in June 2000. These reports provided much more comprehensive estimates of the size and impact of information technology by analyzing the government's data for "Gross Product Originating by Industry" (GPO).

GPO theoretically equals GDP in aggregate, but differs in that it measures the income or *value added by each industry and subindustry*. In other words: Whereas GDP measures only final goods and services sold to the ultimate purchaser, GPO measures the value generated by manufacturers of components—such as semiconductors and computers—that end up as parts of larger final products.

By estimating the size of each of the "Information Technology-Producing Industries" within the GPO industry accounts, the Department of Commerce estimated that IT totaled approximately 8.1% of the economy in 2000 versus 7.7% of the economy in 1999 and 5.5% of the economy in 1990. This is the source of economists' references to IT being 8.0% of the economy (see Exhibit 3-3, section [3]).

Projecting out to the end of the next two decades, I estimate that information technology (using this broader definition from the Department of Commerce) could rise to about 11.9% of the economy by 2010, and 16.1% of the economy by 2020, up from 8.1% in 2000. This would happen if IT continued to grow at about the same growth rate relative to the overall economy that was demonstrated from 1990 to 1998. (The hypergrowth years of 1999 and 2000 were excluded from the relative growth rate estimate to avoid including the pre-Y2K IT spending spike in 1999 and the Dot-com and Telecom Bubbles of 2000.) Recall that with near–zero growth in the labor force, a higher mix of GDP growth needs to come from IT spending and productivity growth, as seen in the 1990s.

The implications are critically important: If information technology expands from 8.1% of the economy to 11.9% in 2010 and 16.1% in 2020, *the opportunity for the creation of more quality improvement and more Digital Deflation could double in the next two decades.*

This realization is enormously positive for the economy. But from my point of view, what is even more exciting is that these Digital Economy reports for the first time provided hard data—allowing estimates to be made of the dollar value of shipments of semiconductors and computers *not* made for final sale (i.e., semiconductors and computers sold as components), as well as their respective amounts of quality improvement. An analysis of these data revealed undeniable "smoking gun" evidence that there are large amounts of quality improvement—and therefore large amounts of Digital Deflation—not being counted for two additional fast-growing parts of the economy today.

In these reports, the inclusion of hedonic, quality-adjusted deflators for semiconductors and computers sold as components, in addition to the already published quality-adjusted deflators for computers made for final sale, resulted in a reduction in the GPO Deflator of 0.60% per year on average in the 1996–2000 five-year period. This was an astounding amount of good deflation generated from just three IT-producing industries.

The interpretation of these results can be tricky. For the GDP Deflator, quality-adjusted deflators for semiconductors and for computers sold as components are only theoretical. They are not being counted in GDP accounts because they are not sold as final goods, so their good deflation never shows up in the GDP Deflator!

Nevertheless, they are *real*, and they are among the largest components of good deflation that have been missing from some of the most important government-generated economic data.

## THE LOST COMPONENTS

For an economist interested in Digital Deflation, there are two ways to handle the uncounted quality improvement and good deflation from semiconductors and computers sold as components. The first is to assume that the GDP Deflator is unquestionably correct, in which case an adjustment for greater deflation from IT-producing industries should be accompanied by an offsetting upward adjustment in the amount of inflation in non-IT producing industries. In other words, if you assume that the GDP Deflator and therefore the GPO Deflator are 100% accurate, you would have to assume that there is more inflation in the non-IT economy than is being counted. For example, in 2000, the overall GPO Deflator was 2.28%, and the weighted contribution of *deflation* from IT-producing industries was −0.51%. This implies that the weighted contribution of *inflation* from non-IT-producing industries was 2.79%.

This line of thinking is depicted in Exhibit 3-5, which presents the GPO Deflator divided into IT and Non-IT categories for the decade of the 1990s and the year 2000.

The second way to handle the uncounted quality improvement and good deflation from semiconductors and computers sold as components is to assume that the government has fairly correctly counted

## EXHIBIT 3-5

IT and Non-IT Categories of the GPO Deflator

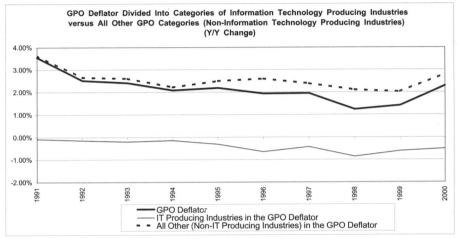

GPO Deflator Divided Into Categories of Information Technology Producing Industries versus All Other GPO Categories (Non-Information Technology Producing Industries) (Y/Y Change)

——— GPO Deflator
——— IT Producing Industries in the GPO Deflator
– – – All Other (Non-IT Producing Industries) in the GPO Deflator

Sources: Bureau of Economic Analysis National Income Product Account Tables; Dept. of Commerce; Tanaka Capital Management, Inc.

inflation in the non-IT-producing industries (e.g., food, clothing, housing, and autos), for which it has decades of experience in counting inflation. Logically then, the *undercounting* of quality improvement and good deflation in semiconductors and computers sold as components would have to mean that the GPO and GDP Deflators are *overstating* inflation in the overall economy.

I believe that this is the correct interpretation. It is far more likely that the government has been undercounting deflation in the many new and rapidly changing industries in the IT-producing economy, and has been overstating inflation in the GDP Deflator, than it is that the government has been significantly undercounting inflation in the many old and well-established non-IT industries.

The table in Exhibit 3-6 gives an idea of just how much Digital Deflation is not yet being counted and reported in the GDP Deflator. The third column shows how much Digital Deflation has been counted by the government in the GDP Deflator for computers made for final sale. The fourth column shows the Digital Deflation that has been generated by semiconductors and computers made as components, as well as computers made for final sale and a small amount for communications hardware. These GPO Deflators were calculated from the raw

**E X H I B I T   3-6**

Uncounted Digital Deflation from Semiconductors and Computers Sold As Components

| Year | Reported GDP Deflator | GPO Deflator | Digital Deflation Counted in GDP Deflator in Info-Proc. Deflator | Digital Deflation Measured in GPO Deflator in IT-Producing Industries | Uncounted Digital Deflation in GDP Deflator from Semiconductors & Computers Sold as Components & Other IT Components |
|------|------|------|------|------|------|
| 1991 | 3.6% | 3.6% | -0.05% | -0.08% | -0.03% |
| 1992 | 2.4% | 2.5% | -0.15% | -0.14% | 0.00% |
| 1993 | 2.4% | 2.4% | -0.11% | -0.19% | -0.09% |
| 1994 | 2.1% | 2.1% | -0.12% | -0.14% | -0.03% |
| 1995 | 2.2% | 2.2% | -0.16% | -0.31% | -0.15% |
| 1996 | 1.9% | 1.9% | -0.27% | -0.65% | -0.38% |
| 1997 | 1.9% | 1.9% | -0.27% | -0.43% | -0.15% |
| 1998 | 1.2% | 1.2% | -0.37% | -0.87% | -0.50% |
| 1999 | 1.4% | 1.4% | -0.29% | -0.62% | -0.33% |
| 2000 | 2.1% | 2.3% | -0.14% | -0.51% | -0.37% |
| 2001 | 2.4% | N.A. | -0.21% | N.A. | N.A. |

NOTE: Numbers may not add due to rounding.

Sources: Department of Commerce; Tanaka Capital Management, Inc.

data in the above-mentioned Digital Economy reports, which did include hedonic quality adjustments for those four categories.

The difference in the last column reflects the Digital Deflation that has been generated at the component level but has been "lost" in GDP accounts. Again, in the case of components, the government can't apply a quality-adjusted deflator because it can only apply deflators to final products sold in GDP accounts. So this quality improvement is lost forever. And except for the semiconductors that end up in computers made for final sale, it never gets converted into a deflator equivalent to the annual improvement in quality. The semiconductors loaded in an auto, for example, are never adjusted for the quality enhancement of each of the semiconductors, so the real quality improvement is never reflected in the overall GDP Deflator.

As in the case of computers made for final sale, the uncounted Digital Deflation in these industries at the component level accelerated rapidly during the 1990s. The uncounted Digital Deflation rose from an average of only 0.06% per year from 1991 to 1995 to an average of 0.35 % per year in the 1996–2000 five-year period. As a result, the late 1990s were actually *far less inflationary* than the government reported. In the year 2000 alone, the GDP Deflator was overstated by 0.37% just from the undercounting of quality improvement in semiconductors and computers sold as components. This hints at a proverbial tip of the iceberg—in other words, a *colossal* overstatement of inflation—considering that it comes from not counting Digital Deflation in just two of the many IT-producing industries.

Though unintended, by specifying the size and magnitude of the quality improvement for two IT industries, the Digital Economy reports helped to confirm the thesis that there are large amounts of uncounted Digital Deflation in the economy today. But for the scores of other IT industries that make up the rest of the 8% of GDP that is IT, the government does not yet have estimates of the annual percentage rates of quality improvement. To me, it became quite clear that estimates were needed for the annual improvement in performance for software, computer services, communications equipment, and a host of other IT products and services. And yes, what about the many non-IT industries, such as pharmaceuticals or outpatient surgery, that are utilizing digital and other technologies to continually enhance the performance and real value of their products and services to the consumer?

Estimates of uncounted quality improvement and Digital Deflation across the economy are provided in Chapters 6 and 7, which show how additional IT and non-IT industries are generating enormous amounts of quality improvement every year due to constantly and rapidly improving digital technologies. Because the government is not yet counting the vast majority of the Digital Deflation being created annually, there remains a very large opportunity to count this good deflation properly, ushering in an era of even lower inflation and higher productivity growth than that of the 1990s.

The implications for fiscal and monetary policy, interest rates, stock valuations, and wealth creation are potentially staggering.

## NOTES

1. Moore, Gordon E., "Cramming More Components onto Integrated Circuits," *Electronics*, April 19, 1965.

# 4

# Why the Old Models Didn't Work in the 1970s and 1980s

If the only tool you have is a hammer, everything begins to look like a nail.
*Mark Twain (1835–1910)*

*During the 1970s, 1980s, and 1990s, a variety of economic theories and models went in and out of favor, as economists and policymakers alike tried to adjust to dramatically changing economic conditions and the shifting needs of society. Keynesian, Phillips Curve, Monetarist, Supply-Side, and Price-Rule theories were applied with varying degrees of success, but none could describe or predict with consistency how inflation could explode in the 1970s and early 1980s, and then die off in the late 1980s and 1990s. We need to understand the shortcomings of these traditional economic models before we can truly appreciate why they are having an even tougher time making accurate predictions in a world of increasing Digital Deflation.*

## ECONOMIC MODELS WORK BEST IN TIMES OF STABILITY AND FEW SURPRISES

To be useful in the real world, economic models must be able to (1) describe existing conditions and (2) help economists, policymakers, corporate planners, investors, and others predict the future direction of the economy under a variety of different assumptions or scenarios. Typically, economists use fairly standard economic models to explain what's happening today and to forecast out into the future (generally 1 or 2 years at most).

Both the information that is plugged into these models and the results that come out of them are generally macroeconomic numbers—in other words, streams of data that portray the causes and effects of economic activity. The models themselves are typically variations of simple formulas such as Y = C + I + G + X. Often, they are *if/then* propositions, expressed quantitatively. For example, one model might conclude that if the Federal Reserve decided to print more money and accelerate the growth in the supply of money in the hands of the public by 2% more per year, then inflation might increase by 2% per year over the next 12 months. Another model might predict that if the government decided to pump prime the economy either by increasing government expenditures by 5% or by reducing taxes by 4%, then output or real GDP growth should increase by 2% per year over the next 3 years.

As it turns out, economic modeling works pretty well, as long as the following four conditions are met:

1. The economic models are able to measure the impact of the most important underlying forces on the economy of that era.
2. There are no significant temporary disruptions or windfalls from either internal or external sources to distort the economy.
3. There are no major long-term societal shifts that have a significant impact on the economy (such as changing demographics or consumer preferences).
4. The data used as input for the models are reasonably accurate.

It's when these conditions are *not* met that the traditional models get into trouble.

## THE 1950s AND 1960s: EXISTING ECONOMIC MODELS WORKED WELL

In the postwar 1950s and 1960s, Americans returned to normalcy. In particular, they went about the business of raising families. Birth rates soared and the resulting Baby Boomers poured into the local school systems, straining education budgets and forcing a wave of school construction projects across the country. But aside from these kinds of indirect effects, this tidal wave of kids was not a major factor in the economy. They were still too young to work and too young to act directly as consumers in the marketplace.

Not so for the *parents* of the Baby Boomers, of course, who had to work extra hard to support their growing families. They were highly motivated and highly productive. As a result, in the 1950s and 1960s, the U.S. economy enjoyed an extended period of economic expansion and prosperity. Concurrently, corporate America embarked upon an era of major rebuilding and capital investment. The results were predictable: Productivity soared, and inflation remained very low. With the absence of major external shocks to the economic system, it was a great era of prosperity for America.

From 1952 to 1967 inflation averaged only 1.5% per year. Even today, that low level of inflation for that many years seems unbelievable. Over that 16-year period (1952–1967), real growth in the economy averaged an impressive 3.8% per year, productivity gains averaged a whopping 2.4%, corporate profits averaged a strong 10.6% of GNP, 3-month Treasury Bills yielded an average of only 2.8%, and the stock market surged to new highs. It was a great time to be a consumer—and an investor.

It was also a great time to be an economist modeling the U.S. economy. The 1950s and 1960s were as stable as they were prosperous, and this combination of stability and prosperity could be understood and explained easily within the context of classical economic theories. Models could be adjusted for the politically influenced, presidential election–based four-year credit cycle, within which government spending was boosted and Federal Reserve monetary policy was made more stimulative during election years. Of course, the economy would have to be reigned in a year or two after the elections, which would be accomplished through tighter monetary policy by the Federal Reserve. This added more cyclicality to the economy, but the economists *knew that*. With these adjustments, models could be put into "cruise control" and tweaked modestly from one period to the next.

## LATE 1960s/EARLY 1970s: MODELS BREAK DOWN WITH THE RISE IN INFLATION

By 1968 things changed in a big way. Inflation jumped up to 4.3% on the Consumer Price Index (CPI). And that was just the beginning. Inflation rose further to 5.8% by 1970 and showed no signs of abating. Businesses large and small scrambled to deal with waves of cost increases, and consumers felt the squeeze as prices rose by leaps and bounds. The government was having a great deal of difficulty controlling this unwelcome surge in inflation or even understanding it.

Economists were at a loss to explain exactly where this inflation was coming from. Tried-and-true economic models broke down as inflation continued to exceed expectations, and there simply weren't a lot of new theories that could explain what was going on. Perhaps the most compelling explanation came from the Keynesians, who believed that the persistent inflation that started in the late 1960s and continued into the early 1970s was the result of wartime fiscal spending (the Vietnam War), layered on top of President Johnson's Great Society spending (sometimes referred to as the "guns-and-butter" theory).

Appealing, but let's examine what happened. For decades, Keynesian economic theories worked pretty well, and in fact, most contemporary economists have a little bit of John Maynard Keynes in them. Keynes's theories postulate that a government's fiscal policies can be employed to counterbalance the ups and downs of economic cycles. During a weak economy, the government can spend more or reduce taxes to stimulate demand in the private sector, thereby pump priming the overall economy. When the economy overheats, the government can cut back on spending or raise tax rates to slow the economy down. The Keynesian thesis was eminently logical and particularly appealing to fiscal policymakers who liked the idea that they could manage the economy.

It turned out that managing the economy was not that easy. For example: Federal government expenditures were cranked up from 15% to 17% of the GDP in the prosperous 1950s and early 1960s to 18% to 19% of GDP in the 1967–1974 period before being elevated in 1975 to a whole new level of 21.2%. The economy seemed to respond well at first, growing by 4.8% in real terms in 1968. But then it sputtered, suffering outright recessions in 1970 and 1973 to 1974 despite elevated government spending.

Keynesian theories worked well to explain the initial rise in GDP growth, but could not explain the economy's transformation into a new world of ever-rising inflation and stop–start economic cycles that were to become symptomatic of the seventies. The fiscal and monetary timeline in Exhibit 4-1 shows how recessions have historically produced budget deficits and how stimulative monetary policies have led to cyclical increases in inflation.

## INTERNAL DISRUPTION FROM WAGE–PRICE CONTROLS

President Richard M. Nixon assumed office in 1969, after inflation already had started to rise. Although not of its own making, inflation

# EXHIBIT 4-1

Fiscal and Monetary Timeline

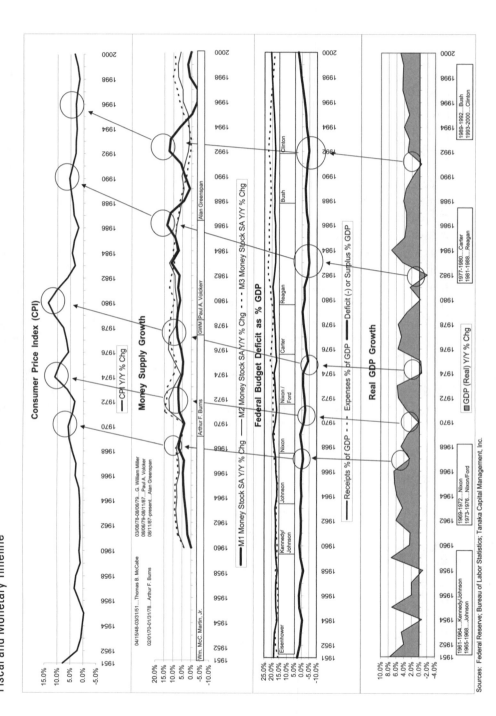

Sources: Federal Reserve; Bureau of Labor Statistics; Tanaka Capital Management, Inc.

soon became a consuming focus for the new administration. Nixon and his advisers became so frustrated and believed so strongly they could directly manage the economy, that wage and price controls were imposed in August 1971. The vast majority of business people, economists, and professional investors recommended against freezing wages and controlling prices, but the White House went ahead with radical economic surgery.

With the benefit of hindsight, the surgery didn't make any sense. One of the most conservative presidents in decades imposed an antifree market, Soviet-style, centralized planning model upon the already stressed U.S. economy. Price controls effectively gummed up the economy so much that it could not respond in a predictable fashion to *any* stimulus or depressant. The corporate sector had to absorb inflationary cost increases and couldn't pass on these higher costs via end product price increases. True, under price controls, reported inflation did come down temporarily (to 3.3% in 1972). But this simply masked the true level of inflation, like sweeping dust under the rug. The U.S. economy *appeared* to be continuing to grow, but in fact, as profit margins became severely squeezed, it was truly an era of profitless prosperity.

Economic forecasting was placed "on hold" for two to three years as distortions were introduced throughout the economic system.

Now the question became, could economists model *anything*? If not, how could the Federal Reserve and fiscal policymakers figure out what to do next—or what effects a particular policy change would have? And what was to be done about the inflation problem, still spiraling out of control?

Today, we know that imposing price controls to limit inflation was a classic case of treating the symptom, rather than the disease. The problem was that back then inflation was believed to be the primary disease, and it wasn't. Something or some things were causing inflation to bubble up, but no one knew *which* things. No one knew whether this particular wave of inflation was similar to, or entirely different from, prior episodes.

Even now, it seems a little scary to think how this was similar to the fundamental lack of understanding that contributed to the Great Depression of the 1930s. Policymakers in the 1920s and 1930s had far less economic information than we do today. Without the benefit of national income accounts, gross domestic product, and other key economic data that we take for granted today, policymakers back then wrongly imposed the Smoot-Hawley Tariff on foreign trade, and the money supply was reduced by a staggering 25%. In the 1970s, whatever the underlying cause of inflation, the imposition of wage and price controls only obfuscated true economic conditions and made economic modeling and forecasting virtually impossible to carry out with any accuracy.

## EXTERNAL DISRUPTION FROM OPEC OIL PRICE INCREASES

In 1973, to make matters even worse, oil-importing countries like the United States were forced to absorb the first round of OPEC price increases. This imposed a major exogenous shock to the U.S. economy. Dramatic increases in oil prices further fueled inflation fears and added to the feeling of helplessness on the part of policymakers. But how much of the inflation was being caused by OPEC, directly or indirectly, and how much was coming from other sources? No one knew. And how could economists even measure the true rate of inflation, when prices were being artificially held down by price controls, even as energy and petroleum-based chemical costs were skyrocketing? Again, no one knew.

If inflation numbers were not accurate, economists could not accurately measure growth in the "real" economy. Fiscal policymakers, in turn, had difficulty determining if their policies were stimulative or restrictive, and monetary policymakers had greater difficulty determining if their policies were reducing inflation or adding to it.

## THE LATE 1970s: HYPERINFLATION

When wage and price controls were finally lifted in April 1974, companies scrambled to raise prices, in many cases by double-digit percentages to make up for the cost increases that had accumulated while their hands were tied. When the rug was lifted, the dust came back out. Predictably, the CPI surged by 11.1% in 1974 and 9.1% in 1975, and consumers revolted against the sharply higher product prices for everything from cars to flooring. Demand slowed, ushering in the painfully long recession of 1974–1975.

Economists once again had their hands full. Trying to model the economy in that period following the removal of wage and price controls proved just as difficult as modeling during the price-control era.

As companies hiked prices to catch up to their cost increases, reported inflation numbers were temporarily a lot higher than true underlying inflation, and the economy became severely stressed.

For Presidents Gerald Ford (August 1974–1976) and Jimmy Carter (1977–1980), inflation proved to be an even greater problem than it had been for President Nixon. Even after enduring a painful recession in 1974 to 1975, inflation only declined to 5.7% on the CPI in 1976. This contributed, of course, to the demise of the Ford administration, which had tried valiantly to use even moral suasion to "whip inflation now." Under President Carter, inflation started to rebound again, surging to 6.5%, 7.6%, and 11.3% in 1977, 1978, and 1979, before reaching a frightfully high level of 13.5% for the CPI by 1980!

But the question still remained. What was really causing this terrible inflationary spiral and how could it be controlled?

## THE DEMISE OF THE KEYNESIAN DYNASTY

By the late 1970s, the United States was long out of Vietnam, the government's guns-and-butter spending was winding down, and federal expenditures had dropped from 21.1% of GDP in 1975 to 19.1% in 1979. According to the Keynesian thesis, the very large (2%) reduction in the government's share of the economy should have resulted in a cooling of the economy and a slowing of inflation.

In fact, the lower level of fiscal stimulus failed to slow the economy, and private spending fueled real GDP growth at fairly robust rates of 5.6%, 4.6%, 5.5% and 3.2% in 1976, 1977, 1978, and 1979, respectively. Also, inflation started to rise again.

For many economists, the Keynesian theories were losing their predictive appeal. Conspicuously silent were the many economists who had been claiming that high levels of government spending and budget deficit financing were causing inflation by squeezing out the private sector. Deficit spending actually declined in the Carter years— from 2.9% to 1.9% of GDP—and yet inflation kept on rising. What was going on?

## MONETARISM TAKES THE LEAD

Of course, the science of economics can always improve. In the late 1960s, Milton Friedman and others at the University of Chicago offered new theories on the role of money in the economy. They demonstrated a strong relationship between growth in the money supply, the pace of the economic growth, and subsequent inflation.

This insight spawned a whole generation of "Monetarist" economists who produced a plethora of models focusing on various definitions of money supply or cash in the hands of the public, checking accounts, savings accounts, etc. Simply put, the Monetarist prescription was to put just enough new money in circulation to match the potential rate of growth of GDP without leading to inflation. If the government printed more currency than was needed by the growing real economy for transactions, it would lead to lower interest rates, too much money chasing too few goods, and an increase in inflation. Alternatively, if it didn't print enough money to meet the needs of the growing economy, it would lead to "tight" monetary conditions, higher interest rates, a slowing economy, and lower inflation.

In the 1970s, economists began to embrace Monetarism, displacing Keynesian theory as the leading economic art form. Even the Federal Reserve became a heavy user of Monetarist theories and models. After all, it was the Fed's role to manage liquidity or the supply of money, and Monetarism gave the Fed an important new tool as well as the confidence that they could better manage the economy and inflation by carefully managing the rate of growth in the money supply.

The embrace of Monetarism by the Fed had some unexpected and generally positive consequences. For the first time, it gave fiscal policymakers, corporate planners, investors, and the public at large a relatively quick indication of what the historically secretive Fed was doing in conducting monetary policy. More importantly, in making the Fed's moves more public, it gave the Fed greater accountability. It got to the point where every week Wall Street would watch with bated breath for the money supply numbers to be published on the broad tape. It seemed that all the world would know or at least have some idea what the Fed was doing on any given Friday when the monetary aggregates came out.

And what of our economists? Economists could tinker with their money supply models, and they were again a happy lot. On the positive side, Monetarist models could predict with reasonable accuracy the direction and level of economic strength 6 to 9 months later as well as the direction of inflation several months down the road. This was good. But on the negative side, inflation was back up to double-digit levels and showed no signs of abating—and the Monetarist models couldn't tell us *why*. Yes, the monetarists could predict how much inflation might rise if money supply growth accelerated from the existing rate of growth by, say, 2%, but they could not say why inflation was at its already high levels. Monetarist theories also could not explain why a certain rate of money-supply growth would be inflationary in one period and not in another.

## THE 1980s: VOLCKER TO THE RESCUE

Late in the summer of 1979, President Carter, under mounting pressure from an angry business community, appointed Paul Volcker as Chairman of the Federal Reserve, a post he would hold until 1987. Inflation was spinning out of control, and strong medicine was required. Chairman Volcker acted quickly to slow down the rate of growth in the money supply aggregates. By October 1979 he had moved the Fed away from its traditional focus of managing and stabilizing interest rates. I reviewed this major shift in policy in a study distributed in March 1982 "The Economy in Transition and High Real Rates": "At that time the Federal Reserve instituted a policy of letting interest rates fluctuate and began concentrating on controlling money growth. Unfortunately, this task was made more difficult by the deregulation of financial markets (NOW accounts, elimination of Regulation Q, etc.) during 1980. The resultant volatility (*of both interest rates and money supply growth*) . . . produced higher real rates."[1]

In February 1980, Volcker's Fed raised the discount rate to 13.0%, the highest level since the Fed started setting the rate in 1914. The Fed's actions severely restricted growth in the money supply, actually *shrinking* the M1 aggregate by 1.6% by April. Predictably, the economy entered a recession in 1980. With the normal lag of several months, inflation hit what proved to be an annual high watermark at 13.5% for all of 1980. In 1981, the Fed restricted money supply growth again—this time so severely that short-term interest rates soared to over 20%, a level that anyone active in the capital markets at that time would never forget. By the fall of 1981, yields on 30-year Treasury Bonds exceeded 14.6%.

Having taken his oath of office in January of 1981, President Reagan (1981–1988) already was well ensconced in the White House. Although he didn't like these high interest rates, there was nothing he could do about them. A Fed chairman inherited from the prior administration was calling the shots. Fed Chairman Volcker "broke the back of inflation,"[2] reducing inflation expectations (as measured by the University of Michigan Consumer Survey) from 12% in early 1980 down to 7% by mid 1982. Reported inflation as measured by the CPI dropped in half: from 13.5% in 1980 to 6.1% in 1982. In 1983, the CPI declined in half again to an astonishing 3.2%.

In the process of grinding down inflation, moreover, Volcker also firmly established the independence of the Federal Reserve. He insulated the Fed from the politics and pressures of the White House and Congress, and he established precedence for resisting the election year pump priming that previous Federal Reserve Boards had felt obliged to carry out.

Between 1979 and 1982, Volcker moved the Fed squarely into the Monetarist camp by focusing more on managing growth of the monetary aggregates. That was a sound strategy in a period when the inflationary spiral had to be broken. However, Volcker and his Fed also realized that no one economic theory or model would work for all seasons. In 1984–1985, the Fed moved to widen its focus and monitor a broader set of economic conditions. This set the stage for a more flexible, multidimensional Federal Reserve Board that has become the hallmark of the modern Fed, including the very successful Greenspan era in the 1990s.

At about this point in time, I corresponded with Chairman Volcker on several issues that were important to me (and presumably to my colleagues in the financial community). These included the unusually high volatility of interest rates, the extraordinarily high level of real interest rates, and whether the Fed should become more accommodative (reduce interest rates further) to get the economy growing again. My concern was that the Federal Reserve had felt so obliged to carry the inflation-fighting torch by itself that it kept interest rates too high for too long.

I felt the risk was that it gave fiscal policymakers the sense that they needed to stimulate the economy, and that the fiscal foot would be stomping on the gas at the same time that the monetary foot was still on the brakes—not a particularly efficient scenario. (This situation of overly tight monetary policy, inviting offsetting stimulative fiscal policy, is a recurring theme that has reappeared again in the early 2000s and will be addressed in later chapters.)

I'm reprinting that private correspondence here with Mr. Volcker's permission, because it reveals Chairman Volcker's insights at that time. Note that he clearly warns about the dangers of targeting or "stabilizing" *only* interest rates, and he emphasizes the importance of sustained economic growth. (See Exhibits 4-2 and 4-3 on pages 65 and 66.

## THE EARLY 1980s: ENTER THE SUPPLY-SIDERS

The economy in the early Reagan years was in a major transition, and so was the science of economics. President Reagan harbored strong beliefs that government had become too big, tax rates were too high, and government regulations were stifling the economy. His timing was right because the public agreed and wanted change. He set out to reduce the size and regulatory roles of government, bringing in a team of "supply-siders," including David Stockman and Richard Darman.

Briefly, the Supply Side school of economics holds that lower tax rates encourage people to work harder and encourage companies to invest, resulting in faster economic growth. Supply Side theories and models in fact did aid economists who were trying to understand the effect of tax cuts on the economy and the resulting benefits to society. It was refreshing to see economic theories reach out to estimate the impact of society on the economy—to explain and predict how people would act differently under a new set of ground rules.

Did the Supply Side approach work? There is no doubt that lower income tax rates encouraged people in the 1980s to work harder at the margin. And there is no doubt that lower capital gains tax rates encouraged people and companies to invest more. From 1981 to 1984, Federal revenues fell from a high of 19.3% of GDP to 17.5% as President Reagan in fact did get tax rates lowered. Initially, the economy entered a recession due to Fed Chairman Volcker's tough anti-inflation monetary policy but then quickly began a remarkable 8-year period of growth from 1983 through the end of Reagan's presidency in 1988 before turning down in the middle of President George Bush's term in 1990. Something was going right.

There was, of course, great debate over the Supply Side "experiment" that continues even to this day. Earlier in Chapter 2, I discussed how in the 1980s, the politics of need in the United States called for a shift in fiscal priorities from policies that created millions of new jobs to policies that helped the existing (nongrowing) workforce become more productive. From the perspective of the Demographic Theory of Economics, supply side economics encouraged investment and sav-

# EXHIBIT 4-2

## October 21, 1985 Letter to Paul A. Volcker from Graham Y. Tanaka

MILBANK TANAKA & ASSOCIATES, INC.
60 East 42nd Street, New York, NY 10165
(212) 687-9722

October 21, 1985

Mr. Paul Volcker
Chairman
The Federal Reserve Board
20 Constitution, N.W
Washington, DC    20551

Dear Mr. Volker,

As an investment counselor and an interested citizen, I would like to congratulate you and the other members of the Federal Reserve Board for courageously confronting the inflation problem almost single-handedly.

I am concerned, however, about one past and one potential future problem and I wonder what (if anything) can be done to address them:

(1) It appears that <u>interest rate volatility</u> may have contributed 145-180 basis points to the "real" rate over the last 15 years. Much of this volatility appears to have occurred as the Fed attempted to stabilize M-1 growth. Since M-1 growth has proven difficult to stabilize would it be worth trying to stabilize rates?

(2) As a direct response to the pain and suffering being born by those who continued to bet on hyper-inflation (farmers, oilmen and domestic basic industries), it seems that Congress is moving inexorably toward legislating bailouts, trade barriers, etc., which will only exacerbate our government debt demands and kill the economy. To use a bridge metaphor, at what point will playing all our (disinflation) trump cards too early risk our losing the game? Isn't there a lot more room now to accomodate and get the economy moving again?

We all appreciate your efforts and offer our best wishes for the future.

Sincerely,

Graham Y. Tanaka, CFA

**E X H I B I T  4-3**

November 4, 1985 Letter to Graham Y. Tanaka from Paul A. Volcker
Published with Permission from Paul A. Volcker

BOARD OF GOVERNORS
OF THE
FEDERAL RESERVE SYSTEM
WASHINGTON, D. C. 20551

November 4, 1985

PAUL A. VOLCKER
CHAIRMAN

Mr. Graham Y. Tanaka
Milbank Tanaka & Associates, Inc.
60 East 42nd Street
New York, New York  10165

Dear Mr. Tanaka:

Thank you for your letter and your kind remarks about our efforts to stem inflation.

As regards your point about interest rate volatility, while quantifications may be difficult, I would not quarrel with your assertion that volatility has been a contributor to the "liquidity" or "risk" premium that has been built into real rates. I believe that as we moved away from the more rigorous monetary targeting of the 1979-82 period, there has been some associated reduction in short-run interest rate variability. To move strongly in the direction of focusing on "stabilizing" interest rates, however, would run a risk of causing economic instability, since quite clearly no interest rate level is right for all economic circumstances. In my view, the approach we've been taking in the past couple of years of basing our actions on an assessment of a broad set of considerations-- including monetary growth, trends in the economy, and condi-tions in domestic and international financial markets--is the best way to cope with the realities of a rapidly changing and uncertain world.

On your second question, I would underscore that, although the monetary authority has a special responsibility in the area of fostering price stability, the Federal Reserve has not pursued that objective without regard to other aspects of the economic situation. We believe that sustained growth is important, not only for domestic reasons but also for the achievement of a healthier world economy, and we have endeav-ored to be reasonably accommodative. A good many of the tensions in the economy can be eased in a lasting way only if we come to grips with the problem of huge federal budget deficits, which have held real rates at high levels, thereby contributing to the distortions of an overvalued dollar and a massive imbalance in our international trade position.

Again, thank you for writing and sharing your thoughts.

Sincerely,

Paul A. Volcker

ing—and greater productivity from the existing workforce—so it was clearly the right policy for the 1980s.

The federal budget deficit rose to record levels, because at the same time that tax revenues were declining as a percentage of the economy, Reagan's "Star Wars" defense initiatives caused a major spike in military spending. Experts predicted that the resulting deficit would be monetized through the printing of more money, and that this ultimately would lead to a resurgence in inflation. But President Reagan was able to cap and reduce the growth in the nondefense part of the federal budget, and the private sector boomed. Short-term interest rates remained high, rising to double digits again in 1984—mainly because federal government borrowing competed with the private sector for available funds, and the Fed refused to print more money to finance the deficit.

From a Monetarist point of view, tight money should have led to a recession, and from a Keynesian point of view, stimulative fiscal policy should have produced a strong economy and inflation. This was an exciting experiment for those who like to debate whether fiscal policy is stronger than monetary policy or vice versa. In this case, it looked like "good hitting overcame good pitching," as the economy grew at very strong rates despite the Fed's high interest rates.

Again, what was surprising in all this was that *inflation remained relatively low*. Obviously, something was contributing to this highly unusual combination of relatively moderate inflation (3%–4%) and strong real GDP growth (3%–4%) per year from 1983 to 1988. Although the Reagan revolution's Supply Side tax cuts deserved some of the credit for stimulating growth in the private sector, it was evident that there must be some other favorable forces contributing to this extended period of prosperity.

But what were they?

## THE LATE 1980s: MARKET PRICE RULE PREDICTORS

In the late 1980s, new "Market Price Rule" theories and models espoused by economists such as Larry Kudlow and Wayne Angell took us further along the road to understanding and predicting the rapidly changing economy. These common sense theories postulated that the commodity and capital markets could tell us where inflation was heading near term. The assumption was that at any given point in time, the commodity and capital markets best represented the collective wisdom, intelligence, and intuition of millions of buyers and sellers in the marketplace, and would offer the most accurate expectation of future inflation.

Today, economists, planners, and Fed policymakers employ variations on these themes to fine-tune their forecasts for inflation. Why? Because Market Price Rule theories address very well one of the two main goals of economic models—to help as predictors of the future, even if it is only for predicting inflation over the very short term. If gold and basic commodity price futures start to rise, for example, then inflation is likely to start to rise near term. If commodity price futures decline, then inflation should also decline within a few months.

In early 1987, commodity prices and interest rate futures started to rise dramatically, and Market Price Rule models indicated that the Fed should tighten the money supply to slow down the economy and avert a rebound in inflation. Unfortunately, these early warning signs were popping up right in the middle of a change of horses, as Alan Greenspan took over the reigns of the Fed on August 11, 1987. His first monetary move was to tighten, causing the October 1987 stock market crash. Right move, wrong timing: With the benefit of hindsight, this tightening move came too late, and therefore struck a more debilitating blow to the stock market than it would have if the Fed had moved earlier, when commodity prices were flashing "inflation." Ironically, after the crash, the Fed had to reverse course to prevent a financial panic. It loosened monetary policy by lowering interest rates in 1988, and the stock market rebounded to precrash levels in less than a year.

The crash of 1987 was a valuable learning experience for the Fed. While it underscored the importance of considering market price indicators for the future direction of inflation, it also demonstrated the fragile and sensitive relationship between changes in Fed policy and stock market values. For beginning Chairman Greenspan, it was also a sobering lesson in *sensing early* the need for making changes in monetary policy, and *acting sooner*, rather than waiting for reams of corroborative economic data to verify an accelerating and inflationary economy.

In the end—as the new chairman discovered to his dismay—a monetary policy that waits too long to react and then has to overcompensate to make up for lost ground adds significantly to the volatility risk premiums in interest rates and in stock prices. Being late and oversteering, of course, raises the cost of capital for both the private and public sectors. It certainly illustrates the importance of obtaining the most accurate and up-to-date data, and underscores the value of incorporating new economic models and theories to understand new forces in the economy.

As with the more traditional Keynesian and Monetarist models in the 1970s and early 1980s, the Supply Side and Market Price Rule theories could address only one of the two main goals of economic modeling. They could predict very well *what* inflation would be doing over the very near term, but they could not explain *why*. By 1989 and 1990, inflation was starting to percolate back up to 4.8% and 5.4%, and again, nobody really knew why. Many suspected that inflation was a direct result of a burgeoning budget deficit.

By then, George Bush was well into his presidency (1989–1992), and he and his team were eager to make their mark. In an effort to reduce the budget deficit, they undertook a major effort to limit the rate of growth in government spending. Bush was able to secure an agreement with the Democrat-controlled Congress to limit spending increases—but only if he consented to tax increases. Although President Bush suffered politically and was ridiculed by the press for violating his campaign pledge for "no more taxes," the spending discipline he was able to secure with Congress did help to reduce the budget deficit. Of course, this fiscal discipline would later prove to have been an important first step toward a decline in interest rates and an increase in capital to finance the nascent stages of the New Economy boom of the 1990s.

## DEMOGRAPHICS—WHY THE TRADITIONAL MODELS DIDN'T WORK

The economic models of the late 1960s, 1970s and early 1980s were doomed from the outset because economists did not understand the important impact of demographics on the economy. Therefore, they could not predict how a demographic surge in the labor force would suppress productivity and boost inflation. In fact, this sea change in demographics was a new force that economists rarely considered as having had a valid role in the science of economics.

With Baby Boomers piling into the workforce, however, American society was undergoing dramatic change. These new forces were so subtle and these trends took so long to develop that they were not being detected on the economists' radar screens. Most economists had been trained on classical Supply/Demand economics, Phillips Curve, Keynesian, and Monetarist theories, and had cut their teeth on four-year, election-based credit cycles—not on changes in the youngest age band of labor force cohorts.

This was a wholly new phenomenon with a whole new set of rules. Time horizons were very different. Demographic changes occur over years and decades, not the quarters or months that are the economist's normal differencing intervals. Even today, although some economists are incorporating population and other demographic trends in their models, most still do not recognize demographics as one of the most important fundamental forces driving the economy. This is most remarkable considering that there are few other primary forces that can have as direct an impact on both capital and labor, traditionally the two most important inputs to the economy.*

In Chapter 2, the Demographic Theory of Economics was offered as a framework for describing the primary underlying force that would change the economy in many ways, as shifts in the mix of labor and capital would fundamentally alter productivity, inflation, and returns on common stocks. In the late 1960s and 1970s, as the Baby Boomers entered the workforce, they flooded the economy with new and inexperienced labor. In addition, more and more women were entering the workforce in all fields and at all levels as it became the norm for female Baby Boomers to actively pursue careers. This unprecedented combination of Baby Boomers and Working Women created an extraordinary demand for jobs.

For American society, the Politics of Need was to create jobs, and that happened as fiscal and monetary policies were altered to become very stimulative. Labor was substituted for capital investment, productivity suffered, inflation soared, interest rates jumped to double-digit levels, corporate profit margins deteriorated, and the stock and bond markets produced zero returns after adjusting for inflation. Although the U.S. economic engine became the job-generating envy of the world, little inflation-adjusted or real wealth was being created, and American society felt anxious and unsettled.

This major new demographic force on the economy actually began to have its first impact in 1965, when growth in the youngest segment of the workforce started to accelerate to a rate of 2% to 3% per year. It was not a coincidence that in 1965 the stock market made its last good run, reaching a high of 994 points on the Dow Jones Indus-

---

* A third new primary economic input will be discussed later in the book—the effect of rapidly improving technologies.

trials in January of 1966. The stock market would have difficulty moving over 1000 on the Dow for the next 15 years as inflation exploded to reach a peak in the early 1980s, creating a long and frustrating drought for investors.

With inflation soaring, American society altered how it worked and played. Households changed how they consumed, saved, and invested. Blessed with jobs, but being paid in dollars that deteriorated in value and purchasing power with every passing month, consumers had to learn new art forms. In a world of inflation, it paid to borrow and spend—and pay back your loans in cheaper dollars. It didn't pay to save because the savings would be eroded in value over time. It also didn't pay to invest in financial assets such as stocks and bonds. The future stream of dividends and interest income would be eroded by inflation with each passing year.

So society borrowed and consumed. If households wanted to invest, it made more sense to invest in tangible assets like real estate. Theoretically, at least, tangible assets would act as a hedge against inflation and become a store of value. In the 1970s and 1980s, investing in real estate tax shelters and oil and gas partnerships became the game, not investing in financial assets.

These inflationary trends were further compounded by the fact that the Baby Boomers and Working Women were forming households and starting families. As they entered their car and house buying years, they became active consumers, taking on debt and further adding to inflation from the consumer demand side (demand–pull inflation). Demographically, they were at the age and points in their lives where there was a significantly higher propensity to consume rather than to save and invest.

From the late 1960s through the early 1980s, demographics had contributed to a new kind of inflation, and had changed the economy dramatically. All of these demographically induced changes were tough on the economists and their economic models. It didn't matter whether you were a Keynesian, a Phillips Curver, a Monetarist, or a Supply Sider. These very new, once-a-generation demographic trends did not fit neatly into any of these models, and you had no effective way of accounting for them.

## DEMOGRAPHIC FORCES TURN POSITIVE IN THE 1980s AND 1990s

By 1982, financial assets had been decimated by a decade and a half of hyperinflation. When things looked bleakest for common stock and bond investors, however, there emerged a glimmer of hope. As it happened, 1982 was the demographic turning point. This was when the demographic pendulum started to swing in the other direction—toward more modest labor force growth, particularly for the youngest age group. If your models picked up on these kinds of factors, then you had reason to look forward to lower inflation and better times ahead.

This glimmer of hope was revealed in a study entitled "Demographics and the Stock Market," which I distributed in 1982:

> Since 1965, the Dow Jones Industrial Average has been in a flat trading pattern.
>
> However, after adjusting for inflation, the Dow has declined over 70%, almost completely offsetting the 360% appreciation from 1949 to 1965. . . . Demographics have played a subtle but significant role in the decline in capital asset values since 1965. . . . Rapid growth in the 20–34 year age group of the labor force coincided with an acceleration of the trend toward working women, creating a fairly dramatic surplus labor situation. This tended to reduce productivity and increase inflation as businesses substituted the relatively more available (and cheaper) labor for investment capital. . . . While the high growth in Working Women may continue over the next several years, growth in the important 20- to 34-year-old segment of the overall labor force should slow dramatically with the aging of the Baby Boom individuals. This will reverse the "cheapening" of investment capital as labor again becomes more scarce (as in the 1950s), capital is substituted for labor, and capital asset values appreciate.[3]

What was really exciting was that the same Demographic Theory that revealed the true underlying source of the hyperinflation in the 1970s and early 1980s could be used to predict an equally dramatic reversal and decline in inflation in the late 1980s and 1990s. With the luxury of knowing how many kids were 14, 15, 16, 17, 18, and 19 years old, it was very easy to predict with a high degree of accuracy how fast the 20- to 34-year-old segment of the workforce would grow each year for the next 20 years.

Looking at the numbers, it was clear that the youngest segment of the workforce would be approaching *zero growth* from the mid-1980s through the 1990s, and well into the 21st century, creating an extended labor-shortage scenario. The good news was that this would provide an opportunity to improve productivity through higher capital investment, as I articulated in a December 1983 study entitled "Demographics, Productivity and the Return on Common Stocks":

Over the next 10 to 15 years, powerful demographic trends are likely to generate strong gains in productivity and the kinds of returns on common stocks that may approximate the 10% to 20% per year inflation-adjusted gains of the 1950s. Ironically, the driving force will be the maturing of the very same Baby Boom individuals who originally contributed to the low productivity, high inflation, and negligible common stock returns of the last 15 years. Recent rapid growth of the young and inexperienced segment of the workforce will give way to faster growth of the group of workers in their thirties and forties—those who will be more productive not just because they are at more responsible periods in their lives, but also because they will have moved up the learning curve, and will be more able to utilize new technological tools than their predecessors.[4]

For economists who had suffered through the 1970s and early 1980s to get their models to properly reflect the era of high inflation, this was a new frustration. By the mid- to late 1980s, their models started to miss in the *other* direction. Inflation started to come in *below* their expectations. Yet many economists persisted in asserting that inflation would come roaring back. Interestingly, the vast majority of investors agreed with the economists. They priced bonds at stubbornly high real interest rates, and sold common stocks down to very low P/E ratios.

After several years of steadily declining inflation, however, both economists and investors began to wonder whether inflation would reappear. My contention was that it would not. Although Volcker's Fed was correctly credited with breaking the back of inflation, what it did was to significantly diminish inflation psychology just as inflation was beginning to settle down on its own anyway due to improving demographics. Although the economists and investors did not appreciate it back then, it would be the beginning of an extended period of steadily improving labor force fundamentals and the unfolding of a dramatic once-in-a-generation super bull market.

## NOTES

1. Tanaka, Graham Y., "The Economy in Transition and High Real Rates," *MT&A Outlook*, March 1982.

2. Levy, David. "The Region: Paul A. Volcker," Federal Reserve Bank of Minneapolis, December 1992.

3. Tanaka, Graham Y., "Demographics and the Stock Market," *MT&A Outlook*, July 1982.

4. Tanaka, Graham Y., "Demographics, Productivity and the Return on Common Stocks," *MT&A Outlook*, December 1983.

# 5

## CHAPTER

# Why Economists Have Difficulty Explaining the New Economy

Baseball is 90% mental, the other half is physical.

—*Yogi Berra*

*The 1990s introduced new challenges for economists and policymakers as they tried to understand a surprising, new kind of economic expansion where inflation declined and the economy got stronger as it aged. A name was put on it, but things didn't seem to add up and none of the old models could explain the so-called New Economy. More important, none could predict whether the New Economy's massive creation of wealth will be repeated in the future.*

## THE AMAZING 1990s—STRONG GROWTH *AND* LOW INFLATION

In the 1990s, the economy initiated what would become a record 10-year expansion, setting records for length as well as strength. The expansion started in the second quarter of 1991 and continued throughout the rest of the decade into the 2000s. What was truly amazing was that inflation seemed to develop a mind of its own, delinking from the strength of the economy. Inflation declined from a peak of 5.4% for the CPI in 1990 to 3.0% in 1992 and then kept on getting weaker, settling in a fairly benign range of 1.6% to 2.9% in the 1993–1999 period.

The decline in inflation occurred even as economic growth accelerated and got stronger and stronger as the decade wore on. In past

cycles, normally after a few years of strong economic growth, inflation would start to rise as the economy would near its capacity limitations. Companies would enjoy great pricing flexibility and profits
would rise providing incentives to add to capacity. This cycle was remarkably different. By 1999, the economy had entered its ninth year
of expansion, and inflation weighed in at only 2.2% on the CPI and
only 1.4% on the GDP Deflator. Companies still had very little pricing
flexibility, yet profits were growing rapidly.

Unlike the 1970s and 1980s, consumers in the 1990s actually began to feel well off as reflected in the vigorous consumer spending
patterns and the various indicators of consumer sentiment. The decade of the 1990s was an exciting decade not just for consumers, but
also for most workers who began to see real wage gains, net of inflation because inflation remained so low. Although many jobs were
lost due to mergers and consolidations, workers usually were able to
find employment fairly quickly as labor became more and more
scarce in the growing economy. For the corporate sector, it was an
opportunity to reduce costs, improve profitability, compete vigorously in the global marketplace, and shore up their balance sheets
from the inflation-ravaged 1970s and early 1980s. For the federal
government, it was an opportunity to pay down debt with the unexpected windfall of hundreds of billions of dollars of surpluses. For
investors in stocks and bonds, it was "heaven" as corporate profits
soared and the economy began to set records for length and
strength—without inflation. This meant lower interest rates and
higher P/E ratios.

These 1990s trends defied the analysis and predictions of most
economists, whether they employed traditional or even the newer
economic theories. Most believed that corporate downsizing was
contributing to this Goldilocks economy. As long as the private sector could continue to become more efficient, the economy could
keep humming at just the right pace, not too hot and not too cold,
and inflation would behave itself. But by the late 1990s, the economy
wasn't just humming. It was absolutely booming, with real GDP
growing at 4.4%, 4.4%, and 4.2% in 1997, 1998, and 1999. Yet inflation
remained subdued at only 2.3%, 1.6%, and 2.2% for the CPI and an
even lower 1.9%, 1.2%, and 1.4% for the GDP Deflator in the same
three years.

In the 1990s political arena, much of the time was spent with a
deadlocked Republican Congress and a Democratic White House that

could agree on one thing: They could see that the public wanted the budget deficit reduced. So federal government spending was limited about as severely as any democratically elected institution could limit itself. Total federal government spending declined from 22% of GDP in the 1980s to around 18% in the late 1990s. What happened of course was that despite this reduction in fiscal stimulus, the overall economy began its greatest surge of growth in modern history. A strong case can be made that this great growth was enabled by the reduction of a "fiscal drag" on the economy allowing the private sector to excel. In any case, the private sector grew significantly faster than the government sector. And in the 1990s, the Keynesian model was again disproved as fiscal spending declined as a percent of the economy and the overall economy went on a tear.

For Phillips Curve enthusiasts, it was worse. They believe that the unemployment rate and the inflation rate are inversely related, and that any fiscal or monetary policy efforts to stimulate the economy eventually would cause unemployment to decline to a certain level below which wage rates would rise, creating a concomitant rise in systemic inflation. That certain level has been called the *non-accelerating inflation rate of unemployment,* or NAIRU. In practice, it's been hard to identify the NAIRU and it has been more useful as a general notion than as an effective economic tool. The Phillips Curve models were wrong in the 1970s because both unemployment and inflation went up. They were wrong in the 1980s because both unemployment and inflation went down. And they were wrong in the 1990s because unemployment dropped to below 4.0%, reaching the lowest rates in over 30 years, yet inflation remained quiescent.

By the late 1990s even the long-reigning Monetarists were standing on shaky ground as the rug had been pulled out from under them. It started with the deregulation of the financial markets and the phasing out of Regulation Q during the 1980s. It continued with the creation of so many new financial instruments and different methods to pay for transactions that money supply growth became more and more difficult to measure and link closely with inflation.

Without Reg Q, the Federal Reserve also lost its ability to sharply brake the economy by raising interest rates. In the past under Reg Q, savings and loans (S&Ls) could not pay over a certain level of interest rates to attract deposits, so when the Fed raised short-term interest rates above that level, depositors would have to scramble to switch their funds out of the S&Ls and into higher-yielding instruments, for example, bank certificates of deposit (CDs). This "disintermediation" or outflow of money out of the S&Ls quickly reduced the availability of construction loans and mortgages. It is all the better that Reg Q was eliminated because it had only become an archaic regulatory contrivance that added far more cyclicality to the economy than was necessary. Its absence in no small way helped to smooth the road for a less bumpy economy in the 1990s.

Throughout the decade of the 1990s even the Demographic Theory was having trouble explaining this rapid growth/low inflation economy. As discussed in Chapter 2, it had successfully predicted a prosperous economy, and it had successfully predicted simultaneously low rates of inflation, but the projected rise in productivity that was supposed to link the two was missing in action. How could the economy keep barreling ahead without reigniting inflation if there was no help from strong productivity gains?

Although the reported productivity data did not indicate it, many economists, including Alan Greenspan, suspected that the strong economy/low inflation scenario had something to do with technology and productivity. Ironically, all economic indicators were acting as if the Demographic Theory was working except for the absence of measured and reported productivity data. Never mind that everywhere you looked in the "real world" it felt like technology and capital spending were stepping in to give productivity and the economy a huge boost. It was just difficult to find this missing productivity, and it was even more difficult to pinpoint the mechanism of action for this economic miracle if it wasn't coming from higher productivity.

## INFORMATION TECHNOLOGY, PRODUCTIVITY, AND THE NEW ECONOMY

It seemed that all throughout the 1990s, economists and policymakers alike had been predicting a great boom in prosperity based on the rising trend in high-technology capital investments and a resulting rise in productivity. The fact that productivity was not being "found" was not because people weren't looking for it. Corporations did step up their capital spending programs with an increasing emphasis on information technology, and of course, the economic boom arrived with a vigor and longevity that surprised even the optimists. President Clinton, who had been elected in 1992, enjoyed reelection to a second term in 1996 as he and his economic advisers demonstrated great skills in riding the unprecedented wave of economic prosperity. The president exhibited an unusually strong understanding of economics and surrounded himself with financial experts and economists who understood Wall Street and the functioning of the capital markets. They also worked hard to respect the independence of the Federal Reserve.

As it turns out, the economy was perilously close at one point to going in the wrong direction, one that could have deferred the start of the New Economy. Early in his first administration, President Clinton labored over the direction he would take in formulating his fiscal and economic policies. He reportedly sat in the White House for days with Treasury Secretary Rubin on one side arguing for fiscal restraint. The secretary reasoned that a reduction in the budget deficit would reduce interest rates, stimulate the economy, and achieve the President's ultimate political goals of full employment and reelection to a second term. On the other side was a prominent Democratic congressman arguing emphatically to increase federal spending because that was why he was elected. It is difficult to estimate how many years of New Economy growth would have been lost if President Clinton had opted to accelerate spending rather than to pursue a path of smaller deficits, lower interest rates, and an expanding private sector.

For the New Economy, it was also critical that the Clinton administration seemed to have a keen appreciation for technology. It did not stand in the way of progress and it sensed the importance of the emerging new phenomenon called the Internet. What didn't arrive until Clinton's second administration was the much-anticipated rise in productivity—or at least productivity as measured and reported by the government.

## OVERSTATED INFLATION AND UNDERMEASURED PRODUCTIVITY

Chapters 2 and 3 provided examples of how and why productivity gains had been generated but not counted in the U.S. economic statistics. With inflation data that had become inaccurate and outmoded by the rapidly changing New Economy, it was not surprising that the Bureau of Labor Statistics reported productivity gains to be *declining* in the 1980s and most of the 1990s. In the 1990s, when capital spending was surging, nonfarm productivity growth was reported by the government to average a disappointing 1.8% versus 2.8%, 2.9%, 2.0%, and 1.4% in the decades of the 1950s, 1960s, 1970s and 1980s, respectively. The low productivity reports defied logic as well as real world experience as capital spending on equipment (excluding structures) grew from 7.4% of nominal GDP in 1990 to an unprecedented 9.9% of GDP by 1999 and 10.5% of GDP in 2000. In an increasingly scarce labor environment, capital was being substituted for labor as had been predicted by the Demographic Theory, but where were the productivity gains?

In the 1990s, information technology capital investments (Information Processing Equipment and Software) were rising even faster than overall equipment capital spending, growing from 3.0% of nominal GDP in 1990 to 4.3% of GDP by 1999 and 4.7% of GDP in 2000. In real terms, Information Processing Equipment and Software grew to an even larger 6.1% of real GDP in 1999 and 7.3% in 2000 (given the chain-linked calculations, these can only be rough approximations). With all this information technology that was supposed to help workers to be more productive, where was the productivity? Where were all the labor savings that were supposed to appear as a result of the capital investments?

Beginning in 1996, in fact, there was a strengthening in reported nonfarm labor productivity growth that continued through the second half of the 1990s. From 1995 to 1999, productivity growth finished in an upward trend at 0.9%, 2.6%, 2.0%, 2.6%, and 2.3% before jumping to 3.3% in 2000. For the second half of the decade, growth in productivity averaged 2.1% versus 1.5% in the first half of the decade, leading many economists, including those at the Fed, to herald a new era of "structurally higher" productivity. There seemed to be no question that technology finally was helping the economy grow, but how and why beginning in 1996?

In the year 2000 edition of the excellent Digital Economy series, the Department of Commerce stated that "Although IT (information technology) industries still account for a relatively small share of the economy's total output—an estimated 8.3% in 2000—they contributed nearly a third of real U.S. economic growth between 1995 and 1999."[1] So even as the government statistics were only reporting a delayed and modest pickup in productivity from the high-tech capital spending boom, the data were at least reflecting high tech's direct contribution to growth in GDP from rapid growth in the *sale* of high-tech equipment.

## WAS THE INTERNET DRIVING THE NEW ECONOMY?

There was no doubt that the economy in the 1990s was something special, and sooner or later the underlying drivers would be discovered—hopefully before the booming economy disappeared! In the meantime, economists and the public in general started to refer to the dynamic and rapidly growing economy as the New Economy. Some believed that the whole economy was being turbocharged by the digital economy and the Internet. Others believed that the Internet single-handedly was driving the economy to new heights. They defined the New Economy as any part of the economy related to the Internet or the rapidly proliferating dot-coms.

There is no question that the Internet had been contributing significantly to the efficiency of the economy particularly in supply chain management and inventory replenishment. There was also no doubt that the Internet would contribute even more in the future. However, by late 1999 and through most of 2000, the Internet movement started to slow, and many of the dot-coms had begun to struggle. Ironically, this was exactly when the government was starting to report that productivity was really breaking out on the upside. Economists were left speechless by the report of an astounding 8.0% annual rate of productivity growth in the fourth quarter of 1999, just as the decade was ending—and just as the dot-coms started to swoon.

With those countervailing trends it was difficult to credit the Internet alone for the high growth/low inflation economic miracle, and most economists realized that the Internet was still too small to exert that much influence on the entire economy. Yet it was difficult to put a finger on exactly what was causing or enabling this record economic expansion with low inflation. What was the mysterious benefactor that was giving anonymously to the economy, and why did it take so long for productivity to show up? There was definitely something "new" about this economy, but the underlying drivers remained elusive.

## DIGITAL DEFLATION—WHY THE OLD MODELS DIDN'T WORK IN THE 1990s

In the 1970s and 1980s, economic models were distorted by the unknown and unmeasured forces of demographics—changes in the labor force which acted to create inflation and then disinflation. In the

1990s, economic models were being distorted by the unknown and unmeasured benefits of Digital Deflation, which was driven by faster, better, and cheaper technology-based products and services. The government has only recently started to measure the effects of quality improvement in computers and semiconductors, but it does not yet fully measure or appreciate the Digital Deflation phenomenon across the whole economy. In the 1990s, this meant that the reported numbers for inflation were overstated and productivity growth understated.

For economists, the inaccurate inflation and productivity numbers made it very difficult to model the effects of productivity gains on the real economy and vice versa, at least not with any accuracy. If the productivity numbers were wrong to begin with, it would be awfully difficult for economists to discover what was driving productivity! It's tough to measure what you can't see. If data so basic as inflation were inaccurately reported, it is no wonder that the economists' models in general didn't work tracking the New Economy of the 1990s.

Interestingly, the underappreciated and undermeasured forces of demographics and Digital Deflation have a lot in common. Both are new and novel forces that took several years to develop and gather steam. They have been powerful in their depth and breadth of impact on the economy. The two have been elusive and not well understood to the casual and academic observer alike, and both have never really been fully recognized—at least not for their impact on inflation and productivity.

They are, however, fundamentally different. While the bulk of the inflationary and disinflationary effects of demographics had been felt in the 1970s, 1980s, and 1990s, the primary benefits of Digital Deflation are still very much ahead of us. While low growth in the labor force will provide a stable foundation of low inflation for years to come, the deflationary and productivity-enhancing benefits of Digital Deflation will only become greater as information technology grows to become an even larger part of the economy and our lives. From a quality of data point of view, what's also fundamentally different is that while the demographic or population data have always been published with fairly good accuracy, the government's methods for measuring the effects of Digital Deflation have been compromised. The government has had enormous difficulty in replacing old methods with new methods to measure the very rapid and high rates of quality improvement in new digital products and services.

If the government has the wrong tools and is not able to, or for some reason does not want to, measure how digital technologies produce faster, better, and cheaper products with each new product design cycle, they, of course, won't be able to measure the greater real value. By not measuring the quality improvements in digital products and services, the government will routinely introduce a bias that shows them to be inflationary rather than to reflect their naturally deflating attributes. With obsolete and inaccurate economic data the public won't be able to understand or fully appreciate the benefits of Digital Deflation, policymakers will make the wrong fiscal and monetary policy decisions, and corporate managers won't be able to optimize on their opportunities.

To be sure, the biggest obstacle to obtaining more accurate data is not the lack of new tools or motivation at the Bureau of Labor Statistics or the Department of Commerce. They have tools such as match-pricing and hedonics, the latter of which has been used quite successfully to measure implicitly how much more consumers are willing to pay for a change in a single product component or characteristic. Rather the obstacles at least for the near term are likely to be those of the past: (1) the lack of sufficient funding and staffing to apply the tools comprehensively and with sufficient frequency and (2) the complexity, subjectivity, and enormity of the undertaking to properly measure quality improvement and equivalent price deflators on technology-driven products. (These obstacles exist as well for measuring the value of continuing quality improvement in non-high-tech products and services.) The good people at the Bureau of Labor Statistics and Department of Commerce are eager to count the quality, and they know how. They are just understaffed and underfinanced for the task.

In the 1990s, despite the inaccurate inflation and productivity data, it was clear to even the casual observer that the Digital Revolution was doing great things for the U.S. economy. Digital technologies were improving the performance of products, and consumers knew they were getting more "bang for the buck." Even if the government wasn't measuring it, consumers knew that the $100 they spent on a new cell phone bought typically 20% to 30% more real value through new and better features and functions than the cell phone they bought one year earlier.

A new, higher-performing product offered at the same price would be the economic equivalent of the same old-quality product at a lower price. Both instances produce deflation. This, of course, is how Digital Deflation is generated product by product across the economy. In this case, the new cell phone offers 20% to 30% more value for the same price which equates to 20% to 30% Digital Deflation. It's been generated even if the government doesn't count it in GDP. It doesn't go away or disappear. The higher values are fully appreciated by the consumer who responds by buying a new cell phone more frequently than if cell phone features and functions didn't change.

The end result is that the Digital Economy is gaining market share versus the Non-Digital Economy because the consumer at the margin sees digital products as offering more and better value by becoming faster, better, and cheaper with each new design cycle. This recurring upgrading of product performance with each design cycle often happens more than once a year as in the case of personal computers. The consumer buys more of the improved quality (digitally deflating) products at the expense of nondigital products, which typically cost more each year due to the constant pressure of wage and raw material cost inflation. For economists, these divergent trends introduce yet another challenge. How do you model an economy where one part is growing rapidly and deflating while another much larger part of the economy is growing slowly, but is generally inflating?

## PRODUCTIVITY FROM DIGITAL DEFLATION IS ABOUT QUALITY, NOT QUANTITY

To really challenge an economist, one need only ask how technology-based quality improvement and Digital Deflation affect productivity growth and how these phenomena should be measured. In the cell phone example, the Digital Deflation Theory would say that a new handset model with a 20% to 30% improvement in performance offered at the same price as the old model should convert to a 20% to 30% improvement in productivity. How? Not from the classical definition of the creation of productivity.

The unusual "productivity" gain from Digital Deflation is not derived from people using technology equipment to produce *more* cell phones per person-hour on a production line. Rather, the growth in productivity that is uniquely generated by Digital Deflation is a result of the same worker producing *more valuable* cell phones in the same hour of work. If the cell phone is 20% to 30% more valuable due to rapid advances in the performance of semiconductors, software, displays, and other digital drivers, then the worker has produced more real GDP by producing a higher value item in the same amount of time. *Higher growth in productivity from Digital Deflation results from higher value units being produced per hour rather than from more units being produced per hour.*

In short, Digital Deflation is about quality, not quantity. That 20% to 30% higher value per new unit is every bit as important in its effect on improving real output per hour of labor as a faster production line producing 20% to 30% more units per hour. Both cases improve labor productivity by 20% to 30%. Of course, there are differences. For one, quality-based improvements in productivity have a very bright future thanks to the Digital Revolution. As pointed out in "The Laws of Digital Deflation" in Chapter 3, many digital technologies will continue to make rapid, double-digit advances in performance each year for the next 20 years. This has huge implications for the future. By contrast, Old Economy production lines will be hard-pressed to make even a fraction of those kinds of process-line speed improvements in the years ahead.

The second major difference is that the proper economic accounting for the creation of *quality*-based productivity gains is to report the improvement in real value produced as a *reduction in the price* of the product. This, of course, is where the deflation is introduced. If you think about it, there is really no other way to account for the effects of Digital Deflation in boosting real output and therefore productivity. It's not as simple as recording more units being produced per hour. Since the price on the new digital product is typically the same as the price on the old model being replaced, it's also not as simple as reporting more dollars of goods being produced per hour of labor. That leaves the method which converts a 20% to 30% higher-value new product offered at the same price into an equivalent dollar-priced product but with a deflator of 20% to 30%. That deflator allows economists to make a calculation converting a cell phone with a $100 nominal dollar value into a phone with a real value of $120 to $130. This cell phone would then contribute $100 to nominal GDP and $120 to $130 to real GDP, with the difference being the Digital Deflation created by the enhanced technologies in the new upgraded model.

The above example may appear at first to be counterintuitive, but this deflator mechanism is the only way to account for quality improvement in products driven by rapidly advancing digital technologies. This is particularly true for those products that are being enhanced two or three times a year to reflect the latest digital technology and software enhancements. It's a process that has been used already by the U.S. government to measure some industries, but its mechanism of action is still novel enough that it has been questioned by many economists and government statisticians, particularly in Europe. The key is that these quality adjustments need to be made across many more product areas and industries than the government has been including in its analysis to date.

This is not to say that digital technologies don't contribute to productivity through the normal process by which technology-based equipment enhances the unit output per hour of production line and service sector workers to help them become more productive. In fact the Digital Revolution really contributes to productivity growth in three important ways:

1. The strong growth in demand for rapidly improving digital consumer and capital goods products and services contributes directly to growth in the *production of information technology* and nominal GDP, leading to labor-based economies of scale and traditional *quantity*-based labor productivity gains.
2. The dramatic growth in the *use of information technology* capital equipment is boosting *quantity*-based gains in productivity for workers who leverage that technology equipment to produce other goods and services.
3. Rapidly improving digital technologies drive dramatic and recurring *improvement in the real value* of the output of goods and services, creating *quality*-based productivity gains. By continuously adjusting the real output for the higher-performing and higher-quality products, there is a one-for-one increase in the growth of labor productivity (output per person-hour). Depending upon the digitally driven product, the rates of annual quality improvement can run as high as 30% to 100% per year.

All three contributors to productivity gains are important and not necessarily easy to measure, but it is the quality-based productivity gains that to the greatest extent are not being counted.

There is a very important point to make about how the amount of the mismeasure from undercounting quality improvement gets larger and larger as digital technologies proliferate into more and more industries, products, and services. The subtle but important point is that even if the government is not fully counting the higher real output from improving product quality, the consumer sees it and buys more at the margin, creating a bigger mismeasure than if he or she didn't perceive the greater deal. Thanks to perceptive consumers, the undercounting of quality improvement and hence Digital Deflation will only get larger over time.

## WHAT THE GOVERNMENT DIDN'T SEE . . .

The government has only recently started to estimate the Digital Deflation quality improvement in computers, in semiconductors, and in a modest fashion a few other items. It's not nearly enough. Software and communications are two glaring areas where very nominal adjustments are made for the continuing improvement in product quality and performance. In the cell phone example, the government picks up the cell phone transaction as $100 on the new model bought this year and $100 spent for the old model last year with no adjustment for cell phone performance or quality improvement between one model and the next. The 20% to 30% higher value in this year's model is not reported, which results in lost GDP and therefore lost productivity. Of course, the higher value is not lost to the consumer. He or she appreciates the better cell phone for the same price, thank you. It's just not appreciated and not counted by the government even though real value was created. (The government does make an adjustment for extra minutes in monthly plans, but cell phone service is grossly underweighted by the use of the industry's relative weighting from 1993 to 1995.)

What happens is that the government is not reporting to the public that added value of output from added quality. This phenomenon of constantly improving digital products is being repeated throughout the economy, product after product and day after day, which reflects the magnitude of the government's mismeasure. The result is that real output and productivity are undermeasured on a grand scale, by an estimated 2.0% per year as will be shown in the next two chapters. This means that inflation is equally overstated because the government has not been adjusting the inflation index downward for all those quality improvements, except for computers, nominal amounts for software, and switches and minuscule amounts for other very small consumer products. In other words it has not been measuring Digital Deflation except to a minor degree. For economists who have been struggling with models to understand the missing productivity, this is where they may want to look.

## ... CONSUMERS AND INVESTORS COULD SEE

In the real world, consumers and investors in the 1990s could see the benefits of Digital Deflation even if the government wasn't counting it. This was one reason why consumer demand exceeded economists' expectations. Consumers could see the real value improvements with each newly announced product.

This perception applies to corporate consumers as well. Top managements are constantly being bombarded with requests to buy a new upgrade to a particular piece of technology equipment or software so that the company could improve worker efficiency and stay ahead of the competition. Requests stream in for the newest enterprise software or Web-enabled database reporting systems, for networked servers with attached storage devices, and for the latest portable convergence product with wireless e-mail, always-on Internet access, and voice and video capabilities. Many of these capital projects come with very short investment payback periods of as little as 6 to 8 months.

Throughout the 1990s as Silicon Valley cranked out more new digital products with more features and functions and at better prices, demand skyrocketed, and technology companies of all types and sizes generated strong double-digit growth in sales and profits. So even though the government wasn't measuring the full value of the digital goods and services being produced in real terms, they were at least recording the high double-digit growth rates in *nominal* dollars of sales. These above-average growth rates attracted investors and many profited handsomely by owning companies that were able to compound their earnings at high growth rates throughout the decade.

Digital technologies were improving the quality of life. The investor knew it, and the consumer knew it. It is unfortunate that many economists suspected it, but couldn't prove it. At the turn of the century, Chairman Greenspan of the Fed was known to have been asking corporate top managements that he met how long they could keep generating the kinds of productivity gains they were producing. It was a great question. Unfortunately, he was only asking about traditional quantity-based productivity gains. What also needed to be asked was at what rate was each company producing quality-based productivity gains coming from rising product quality and Digital Deflation, and would that rate change in the future. Without accurate data, economists, policymakers on "The Hill," policymakers at the Fed, corporate planners, investors, and consumers had to fly by the seat of their pants. If they made the right decisions regarding inflation, it was by real world observation, instinct or luck, not from analyzing outmoded, incomplete, and misleading economic data.

Economists in the 1970s and 1980s had to contend with the new and powerful forces of changing demographics. For economists in the 1990s, it was difficult to measure and model an economy that was benefiting more and more each year from yet another force they had never seen before—Digital Deflation. If new digital technologies were delivering faster and better products at cheaper prices every year, and the government was having difficulty measuring this contribution of higher performance as the economic equivalent of lower prices, it follows that none of the traditional economic models could assimilate what was happening in the real economy from these new technologies.

Remember that real GDP growth is supposed to measure the increase in the real value of goods and services transacted by subtracting the appropriate inflation rate from the measured growth of nominal dollar GDP. If you subtract a bad number, inflation, from a good number, nominal GDP growth, you end up with a bad number, real GDP growth. The corruption of the productivity numbers arises directly from the inaccurate real GDP numbers, since productivity is obtained by dividing output or real GDP by the number of labor hours worked. If the government was measuring most technology-related goods as inflationary when in fact they were deflationary, then of course the traditional economic models wouldn't work.

## THE YEAR 2000 LOCKDOWN

The Year 2000 was a year that many feared with all the publicity over Y2K computer lockdowns and the possible cataclysmic effects on the economy. Ironically, some prognosticators were saying that the Digital Revolution, which had contributed to a record 8 years of economic expansion, would bring about the economy's demise. The fear was that maybe these digital technologies weren't so great after all. Fortunately, the Y2K meltdown never materialized and the public breathed a sigh of relief.

For those who were searching for missing productivity, however, the Y2K threat introduced other major distortions. As the private sector and the government sector both raced to prepare for the Y2K bug, the solution for many was to completely replace their old legacy hardware and software with brand new Y2K-compliant hardware and software. At the same time, they would be installing equipment and software that was probably several design cycles faster, better, and cheaper than the "old stuff." Why risk installing makeshift software fixes that may not work?

In the years preceding the year 2000, capital spending for technology equipment and software surged, growing by 13.2%, 11.7%, and 9.9% for the years 1997, 1998, and 1999. As complete systems of very old equipment and software were replaced by the latest and greatest, it was no surprise that growth in productivity also surged, reaching a high of 8.0% in the final quarter of 1999 (later restated to 7.8%), and settling in at 2.3% for all of 1999. For big-ticket technology providers such as IBM and the mainframe software vendors, this Y2K spending boom introduced a spike in order patterns, with the inevitable decline in orders and shipments beginning in the third quarter of 1999 and extending well into the next decade.

For productivity seekers in 2000, these were exciting times. Although reported productivity growth also declined predictably from the lofty fourth quarter 1999 peak, it remained at a fairly high level at 3.3% for all of 2000. So despite the removal of the temporary Y2K capital expenditure spike and despite the continuing stream of bad data that didn't fully capture the real quality improvements in output, it appeared that the underlying strength of rising productivity growth powered by the Digital Revolution and IT spending was finally beginning to show.

Digital Deflation was also beginning to be picked up in the reported numbers even if it was only partially measured, for computers made for final sale and nominally for some other items. As the computer hardware portion of the Digital Economy was getting larger as a percentage of the overall economy, the dramatic improvements in product performance and quality were finally starting to show up as real growth and as productivity gains that were too large *not* to be noticed.

While the threat of Y2K lockdown got all the attention in late 1999 and in 2000, the real story was that 2000 was the year that measured productivity broke out of its Old Economy mold aided by traditional quantitative productivity gains from rising IT spending, as well as from rising qualitative productivity gains from Digital Deflation.

As alluded to in Chapters 2 and 3, an important reason that Digital Deflation was being counted at all was that by 1987, the Bureau of Labor Statistics (BLS) was finally making quality adjustments for advances in the performance of computers made for final sale. Retroactive adjustments had already been made by the Bureau of Economic Analysis (BEA) to reflect what was in fact Digital Deflation in these computers back to 1959.

In the next few chapters, I will show that except for adjustments for computers made for final sale—and nominal adjustments for semiconductors made for export, prepackaged software, and a few consumer product categories—the BLS has not been capturing gigantic gains in quality and performance in the rest of the economy. Software, communications, medical products and services, and other major consumer products are a few of the biggest areas of mismeasure. It will be seen that the undermeasurement of quality improvement means that the government has been overstating inflation by about 2.0% on the GDP Deflator and by about 1.0% on the CPI.

In later chapters, it will be explained that, unfortunately for investors and employees in the burgeoning New Economy as well as for society as a whole, the Fed armed with reams of incomplete and inaccurate data on inflation, kept its foot on the monetary brakes for far too long in 2000 and 2001. The result of inadvertently tight money was less-than-expected final demand, inventory reductions, profit declines, job cutbacks, and a sharp decline in IT spending. Heaped on top of the post-Y2K capital spending slowdown, these trends exacerbated the dramatic crash in technology and telecommunications stocks that contributed to a decline of over 75% in the Nasdaq and close to a 50% decline in the broader market averages.

Although the Fed suspected that productivity gains were powering the economy, Chairman Greenspan wasn't convinced that the strength in productivity wasn't just temporary. He felt that the economy needed to go through a slowdown to be sure. Waiting for a slowdown or a recession to confirm the existence of "more permanent" productivity gains was one of the few mistakes of Greenspan's Fed. It cost people over two million jobs, it cost the country hundreds of billions of dollars of economic growth, it cost investors trillions of dollars of stock market value, and it curtailed the very capital spending that was producing Digital Deflation.

What went wrong? First, as noted, the Fed was encumbered with incomplete and inaccurate data. Second, tried-and-true economic models seemed to lose their effectiveness in this new economic order. In a sense, the Fed was flying blind. In addition, many previous decades of experience had rewarded the Fed for taking a "gradualist" approach. But, with a rapidly evolving New Economy and with the faster moving hands on technology's clock, perhaps that experience was now working against it.

In the end, there was a lockdown of sorts in 2000, but it wasn't from calendar-related bugs in computer software. Consumers and corporations reacted quickly and decisively to the 50% drop in Nasdaq from March to the late fall of 2000 and "locked down" on their purchases. By November 2000, consumer sentiment had plunged precipitously, retail sales slowed abruptly, and many corporations used their finely honed, Web-enabled technology skills to shut down inventory supply lines. Many managements of New Economy companies referred to this period as "seeing business falling off the table." New digital technologies and the Internet had helped to compress a normal inventory recession from two quarters into a few months. Even the classic two-quarter definition of a recession would have to be revised to reflect the Digital Revolution and the digital compression of response times. With faster communication, shorter supply lines, and leaner inventories, recessions would have to be defined more by the magnitude of a decline in GDP than by the length of the decline. Again, economists will have to adjust their models to reflect the new realities of the New Economy.

In 2000, the Digital Revolution was already making its mark on politics, the economy, and the stock market. A tight Fed and the rapid response of the public to the sharp stock market decline may have inadvertently cost Al Gore an extraordinarily close election. This was particularly ironic given that some believe a tight Fed cost George Bush, senior, the presidential election 8 years earlier. Before President-Elect George W. Bush took his oath of office in January 2001, he held a powwow in Texas with top business leaders to assess the economy. Debate was spirited about whether the U.S. economy was already in a recession. One of the more interesting anecdotes to come out of that session was that some leaders felt their industries were not only in a recession, but that it may have been the first recession in history that had already been discounted by the consumer *before it happened.*

There was no denying it. The consumer was using all that technology had to offer to become better informed and to get the latest information "in a nanosecond." More households had become investors during the 1980s and 1990s, and by 2000, over half of all Americans owned stocks. There was a new thirst for knowledge, especially for things having to do with the economy and the stock market. CNBC, Fox News and CNN had become major sources of important and timely news for more and more of the public during the day, and the Internet provided small investors with many of the tools and data that had previously been available only to large institutional investors.

The SEC accelerated the flow of information in the fourth quarter of 2000 with a new requirement that companies make "full disclosure" of any change in material information broadly to the public rather than to trickle it out through Wall Street analysts or through more limited disclosure as had been common practice in the past. Information was moving lightning fast, no doubt, adding to stock market volatility. These trends toward more demand for faster and better information coupled with newly evolving technologies and ubiquitous Internet access were combining to revolutionize the way people acted and transacted. Surely the economy would be affected.

## THE WEALTH EFFECT—A RISING NEW FORCE IN THE NEW ECONOMY

In the 1990s, a third major new force appeared on the scene to affect the economy in ways that economists had not seen before. Economists already had their hands full dealing with the effects of demographics and Digital Deflation and probably didn't need another challenge! This new force, the "wealth effect," described in popular terms reflects how the rising stock market of the 1990s fueled a rise in consumer spending beyond levels suggested by the normal relationship between growth in income and growth in spending. In broader economic terms, *the wealth effect really describes how individual consumers and corporate consumers alter their spending decisions based on balance sheet considerations and expectations rather than solely on incomes.* To truly appreciate how quickly the wealth effect came on the economic scene and made economic modeling even more difficult, one need only go back to 1996. That was when a few astute economists began to notice that the swings in the stock market might be influencing rather than merely predicting or discounting the real economy.

Prior to 1996, for several decades consumers had spent a very stable 91% of their disposable personal incomes. This was validated even as far back as 1983 in a study I wrote entitled "Disinflation, Consumer Spending and a Healthy Surge in Financial Assets."[2] That study pointed out that:

> For over 30 years the consumer has maintained spending at a remarkably stable proportion of both disposable income and consumer net worth. The consumer does what is rational—he spends what he can afford, which appears to be about 91% of disposable income and 20% of net worth, year in and year out.

This stable relationship between consumer spending and the combination of disposable income and net worth continued well into the 1990s. Somewhere in the mid-1990s, however, evidence began to mount that this relationship was being disrupted. Award-winning economist Ed Hyman of ISI Group, for example, was early in identifying the existence of a wealth effect, which he believes started in 1996. He has published charts showing a strong relationship between the 3-month moving average of the percent change in the Nasdaq and the 3-month moving averages of retail sales and consumer spending.

By 1996, the Federal Reserve began to get anxious that rising stock prices might be creating a potential problem for the real economy. At the end of that year, the economy had entered its fifth year of expansion with inflation still not rising above 2.8% to 2.9% despite predictions and fears that it would move higher with the aging of the economic expansion. With vigorous earnings growth and benign inflation, the stock market reached the high end of historical valuations. For the Fed it also seemed too good to be true. Alan Greenspan, Chairman of the Fed, became worried that the U.S. stock market might be suffering from the same speculative boom–bust that had crippled Japan in the 1980s and 1990s. He gave what came to be known as his "irrational exuberance" speech on December 5, 1996:

> Clearly, sustained low inflation implies less uncertainty about the future, and lower risk premiums imply higher prices of stocks and other earning assets. We can see that in the inverse relationship exhibited by price/earnings ratios and the rate of inflation in the past. But how do

we know when irrational exuberance has unduly escalated asset values, which then become subject to unexpected and prolonged contractions as they have in Japan over the past decade? And how do we factor that assessment into monetary policy? We as central bankers need not be concerned if a collapsing financial asset bubble does not threaten to impair the real economy, its production, jobs, and price stability. Indeed, the sharp stock market break of 1987 had few negative consequences for the economy. But we should not underestimate or become complacent about the complexity of the interactions of asset markets and the economy. Thus, evaluating shifts in balance sheets generally, and in asset prices particularly, must be an integral part of the development of monetary policy.[3]

For investors, this speech was interpreted to mean that the Fed felt that stock prices were too high and that it would raise interest rates soon. This caused a sharp 4% sell-off in stocks that night in the overseas equity markets. However, the U.S. capital markets did not seem to suffer from those comments. Total returns on the S&P 500 averaged an incredible 27.6% *per year* in the 3 calendar years after the irrational exuberance speech. This underscores the difficulty of predicting the stock market, even for the brightest financial minds at the Fed.

What was Chairman Greenspan trying to accomplish, by speaking of irrational exuberance? Historically, the Fed had steered away from commenting on the stock market to avoid any appearance of manipulating or meddling with the markets. However, Greenspan's Fed began to suspect that rising stock market values were spilling over into the real economy in the form of higher consumer spending. Although logical, and although a few economists like Ed Hyman were picking up the signals, it was not easy to prove. This wealth effect theory continued to be hotly debated throughout 2000 and 2001 as consumer spending weakened in late 2000, but then came back and remained surprisingly strong in 2001 despite the first back-to-back 2-year decline in the stock market since the 1973–1974 period.

Greenspan's Fed has been quick to assimilate and factor in new economic influences on the economy, including the wealth effect. Quite deservedly it has been recognized for its open-minded approach to economic modeling. However, at the end of 2000 even the Fed was caught by surprise with the suddenness of the economic slowdown—partly as a result of the sharp 50% decline in Nasdaq. It is clear that economists in general need to model the increasingly important linkage between changes in stock market values and the real economy.

Yes, there is a wealth effect—and a reverse wealth effect as well. It is easy to sense the existence of a wealth effect when the stock market and consumer spending are both in a parallel 9-year uptrend as they were in the 1990s. The theory becomes a lot stronger when it's tested through a full cycle. The sharp Nasdaq downturn in 2000 and the sudden slowdown in retail sales at the end of 2000 and early 2001 were proof positive of the existence of a reverse wealth effect. There should be few doubters left.

## IS THERE A CORPORATE WEALTH EFFECT?

One reason that the Fed and many others were caught by surprise with a recession in 2001 was that the wealth effect and the reverse wealth effect apply to corporate consumers as well as to individual consumers. If business executives charged with the responsibility to run a lean organization see a sudden drop in the stock market, it is now a lot easier to quickly shut down the production lines, throttle back on the supply lines, and defer capital spending plans. Like individual consumer response times, corporate manager response times have been shortened dramatically by advancing digital technologies.

For monetary policymakers, it will become more critical that changes in inventory levels and capital spending plans be monitored more closely than ever. Today's investments in technology inventories and technology capital equipment will lead to tomorrow's Digital Deflation and productivity gains. If both are throttled back in a slowing economy, the creation of beneficial Digital Deflation could also be throttled back.

## INVESTOR-CONSUMERS

I've asked you to look backward in time for the better part of the last two chapters. Let's take a few pages, at this point, to begin to look forward.

Over the next several years, as the Digital Revolution gets back on its feet and returns to grow at an above-average compound rate over time, more and more consumers will become "investor-consumers." Rising stock prices and a new era of prosperity will make more households upwardly mobile, with many moving from the middle class into the upper middle class, and some even moving up-ward into rarified reaches of the upper class of wealth.

As their stock market nest eggs are rebuilt and become larger over the next several years, investor-consumers naturally will again view an increasingly larger proportion of their increase in net worth as "surplus wealth." Over time, more of that surplus will be viewed as spendable wealth versus savings for retirement.

Rising stock market wealth will have an enormous impact on so-ciety and the economy. Some will be able to retire from the full-time workforce earlier than they ever dreamed. For a rising minority, the notion of work will be viewed more as a hobby or a challenge than as a source of income to provide sustenance.

Sociologists and economists will have to put on their thinking caps. Societal change of this order of magnitude will bring many new opportunities and threats to society and to the economy. After the huge stock market disappointments of the early 2000s, what happens to a whole society that is made to be much richer than it expected? The debate about the partial privatization of Social Security will take on greater significance when it is realized that *the least fortunate will be the minority of Americans that don't own stocks.*

Over the next 10 to 20 years, as the Digital Revolution grows to become a bigger piece of a bigger economic pie, the wealth effect is certain to become even stronger. If the new investor-consumer and his or her wealth effect are not properly factored into economists' models, economic forecasting will be even more prone to error. The same can be said for the corporate wealth effect. As the wealth effect grows and evolves over time, there is no doubt that traditional economic rela-tionships and mechanisms of action will change. Over the next 10 to 20 years, modeling the wealth effect will be a challenge. However, it will be a lot easier to meet that challenge if it is better understood. The sudden 2000–2002 economic slowdown should be viewed and appre-ciated as a wake-up call for this increasingly important new force on the economy.

## NEW MODELS NEEDED

By the end of the 1990s and in the early years of the 21st century, it be-came painfully clear that economists and policymakers were having a tough time measuring or even understanding the New Economy. Go-ing forward, they will need better and more complete data, and they will have to call upon modern techniques and analytical tools if they are going to measure the rapidly changing economic landscape.

They will also need new economic models to measure and predict how new digital technologies are going to boost product quality, productivity, and real economic growth and at the same time reduce inflation to minimal levels. Ideally, these new models should attempt to measure how major new forces such as demographics, productivity growth, Digital Deflation, and the wealth effect will drive the economy.

The ultimate goal will be for these and other models to help policymakers and corporate managers to make the right decisions and enable the economy to reach closer to its maximum potential over the long term. Along the way, there will be an opportunity for policymakers to moderate the dramatic swings that have plagued the capital markets and to minimize or virtually eliminate the recessions that have caused so much pain and suffering and destroyed so much wealth worldwide.

## NOTES

1. "Digital Economy 2000," U.S. Department of Commerce, June 2000.
2. Tanaka, Graham Y., "Disinflation, Consumer Spending, and a Healthy Surge in Financial Assets," May 1983.
3. Greenspan, Alan, speech presented at the American Enterprise Institute for Public Policy Research, Washington, D.C., December 5, 1996.

# 6

## CHAPTER

# Redefining the New Economy

It is better to be roughly right than precisely wrong.
*John Maynard Keynes (1883–1946)*

*Everyone has talked about the New Economy, but there is little agreement over what it really means. Digital Deflation helps redefine the New Economy and shows how undermeasured quality improvements from rapidly advancing digital technologies are contributing significantly more to productivity than the government is reporting.*

### NEW FORCES IN THE NEW ECONOMY

The preceding two chapters identified four major new forces on the economy that have made economic forecasting extraordinarily difficult during the last 30 years. These four forces, demographics, productivity growth, Digital Deflation, and the wealth effect, also have been shown to require new economic models as well as better data from the government to measure these new phenomena more accurately. These forces are very different from each other in action and impact, yet they are very interdependent. The good news is that they can all be modeled, and therefore they can be better understood. What is exciting is that if these forces are allowed to play out, there is a real possibility that over the next 10 to 20 years the entire economy can match the record annual rate of growth of the 1990s—with even lower inflation.

What is at stake for investors and for society as a whole is a new era of prosperity. But for this to be realized, it is critical that fiscal and monetary leaders in the United States and in other important economies better understand what is really driving the New Economy and how it is fundamentally different from the Old Economy. Investors will want to take advantage of what a resurging New Economy will have to offer, and corporate managements will need to know how they fit into the picture.

Demographics, productivity growth, Digital Deflation, and the wealth effect are contributing importantly to what people are calling the New Economy and in doing so these forces are helping to define and shape it. Digital Deflation will exert a greater and greater influence on the economy over time as information technology (IT) grows to become a larger part of the economy and everyday life. In the process, it will build upon a strong foundation of moderate labor force growth and potentially create an even larger wealth effect than has been seen to date.

In this chapter, the New Economy will be clearly and concisely defined with the aid of some of the most important distinguishing characteristics of Digital Deflation. Managers, policymakers, and investors will be able to more easily discern which industries and companies are truly contributing to the New Economy versus the Old Economy and who should prosper over the long term.

## WHAT IS THE NEW ECONOMY?

Ask some of your friends how they would define the New Economy and you're likely to get a wide variety of answers. This is especially true after the technology crash of 2000–2002. Some would say that the New Economy took off with the boom in the Internet but crashed and burned along with every dot-com that didn't make it in that first wave in 1999–2001. An increasing number of these people believe that the New Economy is composed of all industries and all things related to the Internet. They are convinced, quite understandably, that the Digital Revolution has come and gone.

There is another group which feels that there never was a New Economy in the first place. A surprising number of economists and businesspeople still hold to this belief. Jack Welch, former chairman of General Electric and one of the most progressive business thinkers of our time, strongly believes that there are no New or Old Economies, just a different way of doing business.

In the vast spectrum of New Economy believers and nonbelievers is a third group of people who believes that there is a New Economy which is utilizing technology's advances to become more efficient and to yield higher productivity. For this perception the country can thank Alan Greenspan, the Federal Reserve, and several private economists for focusing public attention early and often on the importance of productivity to maintain economic growth while holding down inflation.

However, after the 2000–2002 collapse in technology and telecom capital spending, many of these believers in the Digital Revolution are now concerned—at least a bit—that the 1990s' New Economy was only a temporary phenomenon to be enjoyed while it lasted. Understandably, some of these "true believers" are wondering if the New Economy can ever be resurrected to be even a shadow of the 1990s' boom. They also wonder if Nasdaq's meteoric rise throughout the decade of the 1990s was merely an act of irrational exuberance. Others are more optimistic.

The problem is that there has been no widely accepted standard or metric to judge whether a company, an industry, or a section of the economy is Old or New. How can the New Economy of the future be understood, managed, and optimized if we don't know what it is? Should the definition be product related? For example, are New Economy companies only those that produce technology goods and services, leaving all others to be branded as languishing in the Old Economy? This definition would be convenient for the investor who could segregate the economy into the Old and New by looking at the Dow Jones Industrials versus another index that is more tech-laden, such as the Nasdaq composite. Is it more accurate to use an even narrower Internet definition that would limit the New Economy to only those companies directly involved in the Internet? What about an economist's definition which might focus on those parts of the economy that utilize technology to improve productivity?

## DIGITAL DEFLATION REDEFINES THE NEW ECONOMY

It turns out that the Theory of Digital Deflation presents a convenient metric or yardstick to allow investors, policymakers, and economists alike to differentiate between Old and New. Simply put, if a company or industry consistently delivers to the customer higher value products or services per dollar, it is creating Digital Deflation and is part of the New Economy.

While Digital Deflation was first observed from a consumer's point of view as being faster, better, and cheaper personal computers and cell phones, it became apparent that these price and performance improvements were happening frequently and regularly in a number of other products and services across the economy. The common thread was that the performance of these products was driven largely by digital technologies. Some industries had "designed in" higher digital content and used more technology to drive their products than others. Some companies leveraged rapidly evolving digital technologies faster or earlier than their competitors. Both of these groups were finding out pretty quickly that they would be beneficiaries of the next technological advance (faster semiconductors, better features and functions in the software, bigger and cheaper magnetic memory, etc.) ahead of the competition.

So, if some companies or some industries were producing and delivering more of this performance improvement earlier than others, then they were delivering to the consumer more value per dollar than their competitors—and delivering more good deflation to the economy.

For the economy, Digital Deflation represents the combined benefits of performance improvement and price declines that are a natural result of digital technologies improving with each new design cycle. The consumer sees Digital Deflation as faster, better, and cheaper products and services from PCs to cell phones to self-tuning autos. The government is beginning to become more adept at seeing and counting what the consumer sees, but it has a long way to go. It needs to measure more of these constantly improving digital technologies, capture more of these quality improvements in IT and non-IT products and services, and report how more industries with technology-driven products will create more good deflation well into the future.

With better and more accurate data, more economists, policymakers, and investors will be able to appreciate Digital Deflation as a recurring source of *naturally created deflation* that will be generated with each product design cycle. They will then notice that some industries and sectors of the economy will be able to generate more performance improvement than others and that some companies will be able to deliver faster and better-performing products at lower prices than the competition. These digitally driven, faster, and better-performing products at the margin will also be more appealing to the consumer than the nonimproving analog products in the Old Economy. Therein lies an opportunity for a simple and consistent definition of the New Economy and how it differs materially from the Old Economy:

1. The New Economy is that portion of the economy that leverages continuing advances in technology to deliver more value to the consumer per dollar by creating a recurring stream of higher-quality and better-performing products and services at the same or lower prices with each new design cycle. By delivering faster, better, and cheaper products and services that are *naturally deflating*, companies in the New Economy are generating more good deflation by offering more for less with each passing year.

2. The New Economy includes companies delivering IT products such as computers, software, and communications equipment, but also includes companies delivering non-IT products that utilize digital technologies to improve performance or product design. The latter would potentially include manufacturers of a wide variety of products such as pharmaceuticals, autos, aircraft, home appliances, cameras, and toys. In addition, large parts of the service sector are distributing, delivering, selling, servicing, and maintaining digitally driven products that are improving in quality and performance with every new product design or service upgrade. As an integral part of the "supply chain" for delivering digitally deflating products, these service providers are also contributing directly to the New Economy.

3. The key is that all New Economy Companies must be able to deliver product and service performance improvement on top of improvement in a recurring and predictable fashion based on an identifiable technology roadmap for constantly improving digital and nondigital technologies for many years into the future. By continuously improving quality and reducing costs, New Economy Companies can afford to pass on quality improvements and cost reductions to their customers. In the process, they inject quality-based productivity gains and Digital Deflation into the economy, and over time they will gain market share from the Old Economy.

4. The Old Economy is that portion of the economy that tends to be *naturally inflating* over time. Old Economy Companies have in common low digital content in their products or services, physical capacity constraints in their raw material and labor resources, limited opportunities for quantity-based productivity gains, and little or no quality-based productivity gains to offset inflationary pressures from wages, benefits, and commodity

prices. With little benefit from continuously improving digital or other technologies, Old Economy Companies typically produce little, or certainly less, in the way of quality or performance-based product improvements than New Economy Companies. Hence, on a net basis, they generate little or no Digital Deflation. As they must resort to price increases to maintain profitable operations, Old Economy Companies typically inject inflation into the aggregate economy over a full economic cycle.

While Digital Deflation is the sweet reward of faster, better, and cheaper digital products, there are parallels in other nondigital fields. For decades, the pharmaceutical industry has created faster working, better, safer, and cheaper drugs, placing this industry solidly in the New Economy. This is because, although new drug prices have gone up over the years, the performance and safety attributes of new drugs have improved at a rate that offsets much of the increase in average selling prices. These trends are likely to continue well into the future, particularly as commercial products are generated from advances in genomics.

## OLD ECONOMY COMPANIES IN THE NEW ECONOMY

Although most people would place General Electric squarely in the Old Economy camp, Jack Welch would not be happy with that label. In fact, he sees GE as one of the companies that ultimately will benefit the most from new technologies. It is noteworthy that GE has identified $1.6 billion of cost savings equal to 1.2% of revenues that it can achieve annually by the "digitization" of the company and its many processes.

For GE, digitization means using the Internet to reduce costs in many of the companywide make, buy, and sell processes. One of the earliest digitized "buy" processes was the use of the Internet to host live auctions for suppliers to bid on GE's vast purchasing requirements, saving the company several percentage points of costs. The reality is that by utilizing digital technologies, this successful company has already become one of the leading creators and beneficiaries of the Digital Revolution. Through its digitization process as well as many other ongoing programs to leverage technology to reduce costs, GE is probably contributing more solidly to the New Economy than even Mr. Welch realizes.

How does GE do it? This is an example of a management doing what's right based on common sense and a sound corporate philosophy that happens to "travel well" in the rapidly changing Digital Revolution. Over time, one of GE's greatest strengths has been its ability to resist being content to use old business models, old business practices, and old thinking that may have worked well in the past. As large and as diversified as it is, GE has embraced a common culture across its vast organization of adapting to change. It has also developed in-house methodologies and tools to effect that change. This has enabled the company to identify and utilize new digital technologies and practices early and to great advantage in the marketplace. It should not be surprising that GE has been able to achieve quantity-based productivity gains of 4% to 6% per year for several years. This has been achieved by applying "best practices" like Six Sigma, globalization, and the early utilization of the Internet for supply chain management and better customer service.

GE plans to continue to increase its productivity or revenue per employee over the next 5 years at strong single-digit rates per year. This is an astounding goal for a company of GE's size and diversity. GE produces about $130 billion in revenue worldwide, equal to about 1.3% of the U.S. GDP, although much of the revenues are produced outside the United States. If GE can achieve mid- to high single-digit productivity gains, smaller companies with less operating leverage should be able to achieve a good fraction of these quantity-based productivity gains.

GE is also generating significant *quality-based* productivity gains by delivering higher value by saving time for consumers. It is actually focusing on reducing what Silicon Valley has long called the customer's "total cost ownership." This TCO would include the time involved in making the buy decision to the ease of use, reduced downtime, and lower cost of maintenance. While GE management is certainly quite aware of how it is driving its customer service initiatives, it has not yet quantified the real value being created. In fact, very few companies are even aware if they are delivering greater value per dollar to customers. To its credit, GE is at least driving to deliver better service and overall value.

In the end, although Jack Welch may believe there is no New Economy, perhaps it is merely an issue of semantics. GE is clearly driving to deliver productivity gains—and thereby creating more value for its customers and more Digital Deflation to the economy. By this definition, maybe GE is a lot closer to being a New Economy contributor than its management or the public appreciates.

Wal-Mart may be a surprising example of a New Economy Company. It has produced average price declines of about 1% per year for its market basket of goods and services for each of the last 10 years. This kind of recurring deflation is allowing Wal-Mart to gobble up market share and compete more aggressively with each passing year. This pattern is being repeated in other categories by other "big box" retailers, such as Home Depot in building supplies and Staples in office supplies. Yet each of these companies might be Old Economy Companies acting only for a time like New Economy Companies. To be truly contributory to the deflationary New Economy for years to come, they need to demonstrate that they can leverage technology and processes to produce service quality improvements and Digital Deflation on an ongoing and recurring basis.

Everyone knows that the "category killer" retailers are benefiting enormously from economies of scale, but at some point they will not be able to squeeze much more out of suppliers by offering to take more volume. The question is to what extent they can offer more digitally-based products, benefit further from Internet-based supplier and customer interfaces, offer better service to customers—and generally ride the wave of continuously improving digital technologies. Based on Wal-Mart's early results, the odds are pretty good that they will remain in the New Economy for some time.

It should be pointed out that virtually all companies have Old and New Economy products and attributes. In fact, to the extent that companies in Old Economy industries utilize digital and other technologies to continuously improve product quality at only modestly higher prices, they may be delivering more real value per dollar to their customers and creating Digital Deflation for the economy. To the extent that they are leveraging digital technologies to infuse their products and services with as much continuously improving digital content as practical, they could be contributing as much to the New Economy as possible for their particular industries.

As has been demonstrated rather emphatically by both GE and Wal-Mart in their financial results, if companies in historically Old Economy industries are delivering more continuously improving, digitally driven real value than their competitors, they will gain market share and/or increase profit margins. This achievement, of course, will not go unnoticed by investors.

## THE IMPORTANCE OF R&D

Old Economy Companies and Industries typically are not research and development (R&D) intensive which hurts them in three ways relative to New Economy Companies. First, they are unlikely to reap the recurring deflationary benefits of the newest digital components and other technologies coming out of R&D to continuously provide faster, better, and cheaper products to stimulate sales growth.

Second, Old Economy Companies often suffer from diseconomies of scale as they approach their physical limits of productive capacity. They do not have the opportunity to benefit from the potentially huge and virtually unlimited economies of scale that inure to the New Economy Company that can amortize its R&D costs over an infinite number of units sold. In the New Economy, Microsoft has the ability to spread its billions of dollars of R&D costs over hundreds of millions of units sold. This keeps per unit prices low for consumers while allowing Microsoft to continue to invest heavily to develop the "Next Big Thing" in software. Similarly, the incremental profit margin on an additional microprocessor sold by Intel can be huge once the very large R&D costs for developing the latest chip are recouped. The same high incremental margins can be generated for Pfizer on any of its blockbuster drugs once R&D costs are recovered.

The reality is that New Economy Companies typically pass on some of the economies of scale benefits to the consumer via lower prices or by charging the same price for the next generation product that offers better performance. However, if the New Economy Company is offering perceptively superior product quality versus its competition, some of the product quality improvement benefits can flow to the bottom line after R&D costs are recouped.

The third benefit that New Economy Companies tend to enjoy from R&D is the ability to take an immediate first year write-off of R&D expenses, thereby sheltering income equal to the whole amount of R&D from taxes. A more "bricks and mortar" intensive Old Economy Company must depreciate physical assets over longer useful lives than a typical New Economy Company with a higher ratio of R&D to capital spending. From a tax point of view, the New Economy Company with very rapid product design cycles can recoup its R&D investment faster than an Old Economy Company that is undergoing less rapid change and must recoup its capital investment over several years.

## THE OLD ECONOMY WILL LOSE SHARE AND PROFITS TO THE NEW ECONOMY

The Old Economy Company is forced to pass on to the consumer naturally rising labor and other production cost inflation via higher end product prices. The efficient Old Economy Company can do its best to cut costs, close plants, eliminate excess layers of distribution and even utilize some digital technologies like Internet-based supply chain management to reduce operating costs. Most of these cost reductions, however, are ephemeral. Once instituted, it is unlikely that the Old Economy Company can achieve the same percentage cost reductions the next year and the next. Unless these companies can figure out how to design greater digital content into their products and services and create recurring quality improvement and Digital Deflation for their customers, they will be destined to remain in the naturally *in*-flating Old Economy.

Old Economy Companies and Industries will face constant pressure on profit margins from rising wage rates throughout the economy and from a continuing loss of share of the consumer's wallet to New Economy industries. Rising labor costs will encourage both Old and New Economy Companies to seek productivity gains. Arbitrage across the labor markets will raise wage and salary scales for Old and New Economy Companies alike, but the New Economy sector can offer stock options and pay higher wages due to faster growth and the leveraging of fixed costs. This suggests that over the long term, talented labor will naturally migrate from the Old Economy to the New. Labor and manager retention is likely to be a recurring issue for the Old Economy, as it was in the 1990s.

Meanwhile, the Old Economy will lose its share to the New—as consumers will choose an improved, higher-performing, feature-packed New Economy product at the same price over an Old Economy product that doesn't offer any improvement in performance but costs more every year. For example, consumers may be more inclined at the margin to buy or replace a new cell phone, DVD player, or other consumer electronic device sooner than they might buy or replace a new piece of furniture.

Even a New Economy Company in a price-competitive industry can run on a track of offering faster and better products at lower and lower prices and still grow sales and profits rapidly. This has been demonstrated for years quite convincingly by the personal computer industry. Although that industry has been fiercely competitive, it quite obviously has gained significant share *from the rest of the economy*. It has done so by continuously offering more for less and by selling many more units to offset the declines in average selling prices.

## HOW THE NEW ECONOMY LIFTS PRODUCTIVITY

From a macroeconomic point of view, it is critical to understand that New Economy Companies are creating large amounts of Digital Deflation—and therefore large productivity gains—with every product design cycle. They are creating higher real output per person-hour simply by producing more value per dollar on the newly upgraded product. By producing a more valuable, higher performing, digitally enhanced product, the New Economy worker is creating more value (quality) per hour of work. *More value per hour* provides the same boost to productivity as the traditional concept of producing more quantity or *more units per hour*. However, measuring quality-based productivity is very different from measuring quantity-based productivity gains, and in fact, the government is capturing only 10% to 15% of the quality-based productivity gains being generated in the U.S. economy today, as will be shown in the next chapter.

The government has been measuring and making adjustments for some of the quality and performance gains in computers since 1985. However, it has *not* yet been able to completely appreciate the full and direct impact of product quality improvement on productivity gains for the rest of the economy. Quite understandably, government and private economists only get more frustrated going down the well-worn Old Economy path trying to analyze why greater capital investment in computers has not led to more units of output being produced per hour by workers using these computers. It has been difficult to understand why for the 30 years until 1995, reported productivity gains across the economy declined at the same time that capital spending for computers, software, and other high-tech investments had been rising dramatically.

Some hypothesized that workers needed better training to use computers and other new technologies. Others believed that productivity gains would have to decline until PCs proliferated to more desktops and became more user friendly. The long decline in reported productivity numbers seemed to suggest, somewhat counterintuitively, that the rise in high-tech capital spending was somehow *hurting* productivity.

In reality, as noted previously, the reported numbers have been wrong. The government has been measuring only a fraction of the quality or performance improvement occurring across the economy because it has been measuring quality gains for only one industry of significance, computers. The result is that overall inflation has been overstated, and overall productivity has been dramatically understated and misleading for years.

Only in the late 1990s when expenditures for computers and information technology exploded and got to be so much larger as a percent of the economy did reported productivity start to rise. By 2000, with the help of the Y2K computer replacement surge and the Internet boom, total spending on IT grew to 8.3% of GDP from 5.8% in 1990[1]. By then, almost by brute force, quantity- and quality-based productivity gains from computers, as well as quantity-based productivity gains from other investments in IT finally produced a surge in reported productivity. The late 1990s' rise in reported productivity is what prompted the ever-vigilant and perceptive Fed to suspect that something new and different was happening to productivity.

## STRUCTURAL PRODUCTIVITY GAINS

Over the last few years, with Chairman Greenspan leading the charge, the Federal Reserve has suggested that the U.S. economy may be in the midst of a more permanent or "structural" improvement in productivity growth. Fortunately for the U.S. economy, the Fed early on sensed a pickup in productivity growth and has focused on it quite assiduously.

However, the Fed felt that the only way to truly validate the structural productivity thesis was to see how well productivity gains held up when the economy went through a recession or a significant slowdown. The assumption was that if productivity gains declined but remained above historical levels when the economy slowed, then it proved the existence of a more permanent increase in productivity. The rationale for this thinking, of course, was that the Fed and others had been trying to understand the late 1990s' pickup in reported productivity growth within the context of Old Economy metrics.

The Fed suspected but did not yet fully appreciate the extent to which the economic data they were pouring over were incomplete. In addition, they did not yet have an understanding of the concept of Digital Deflation and the naturally deflating New Economy. They were not yet aware of this *different kind of structural productivity growth*—growth coming from the rapid and recurring improvement in the real value of digital products and services.

As described earlier, for several years now quality improvement has been measured for computers made for final sale, so the Digital Deflation thesis should not be viewed as totally "coming out of left field." Yet, it is apparent that the Fed and other economists are not fully aware that a good part of the increase in reported productivity in the late 1990s came via this new source of *quality*-based gains from computers. While economists have been focusing on trying to measure *how many* more units of output were being produced by people using computers, the New Economy has been steadily delivering *higher and higher quality* in each newly designed computer model introduced. It appears that the "quality improvement = deflation" phenomenon is so different from what is taught in classical economics that its favorable and recurring impact on reported inflation and productivity seems to have been completely overlooked.

## WHEN DID THE GOVERNMENT START TO MEASURE DIGITAL DEFLATION?

In December 1985, the Bureau of Economic Analysis (BEA) in the Department of Commerce started to make quality adjustments for mainframe computers based on hedonic regression studies done with significant contributions from IBM. Prior to 1985, the BEA simply had to assume that no improvements were being made in the quality or performance of computers. Before then they hadn't developed the tools and methods for measuring computer performance improvement. In hindsight, today the idea that computers were not being improved seems almost comical. But back then it was pioneering work, and in the world of economic statistics, 1985 marked the beginning of a new era. It required some new tools, such as hedonic regression analysis, and it would take several years to develop and perfect.

Soon after making the shift to measuring computer quality for the first time, the BEA went back and restated the price deflator (the inflation index) for GDP accounts for computers going back to 1959.

The results were astounding. Over the entire 25-year period from 1960 to 1985, the index of quality-adjusted computer prices was reestimated to have declined an average of 18.3% per year. These kinds of large declines in a "deflator" or inflation index were very rare within the realm of modern economics, yet there was very little publicity over this event, and public awareness since then has been nonexistent. One of the reasons was that computers made for final sale were measured to represent only 0.6% of nominal GDP in the early 1980s, so any adjustments made to the inflation index for computer quality improvement weren't perceived to have much effect on the economy.

In 1987, over at the Bureau of Labor Statistics (BLS) in the Department of Labor, studies commenced for measuring quality improvements for *all* computers made for final sale (not just mainframes). By 1990, the BLS was ready to introduce a new quality adjustment for computers for use in the Producer Price Index (PPI). With more comprehensive data being provided by the BLS, the BEA soon converted to using the BLS quality-adjusted data for computer performance improvement and price changes in the calculation of their own GDP Deflator.

So while the government first started measuring quality improvement for mainframe computers for the GDP Deflator beginning in 1985, it was only in 1990 that the BLS began to report computer quality improvement as Digital Deflation in the PPI. Not by coincidence, this was just when the United States began its longest and strongest economic expansion in modern history. Though modest, these first reports reflecting computer quality improvement in GDP accounts enabled a very observant Federal Reserve to allow the economic expansion of the 1990s to proceed faster than would have been the case if they had not counted this "good deflation."

By measuring quality improvement in computers, the statistical agencies of the U.S. government were inadvertently making their first attempt at measuring Digital Deflation. The good people at the Bureau of Economic Analysis and the Bureau of Labor Statistics should be praised for being the first government entities in the modern world to measure the performance improvement in computers—opening the door to understanding and more accurately measuring the New Economy.

For the U.S. government, this was the genesis of the translation of advances in digital technologies and product design cycles into what was the economic equivalent of quality-based productivity gains and good deflation. The precedent has now been established for measuring quality improvement across the economy, and there is much more Digital Deflation to be measured in many other large and rapidly growing industries.

## HOW DID COMPUTER QUALITY IMPROVEMENT BOOST PRODUCTIVITY IN THE LATE 1990s?

Since the annual quality improvement in computers was being reflected as deflation in the calculation of the GDP Deflator for the overall economy, when the government converted from nominal GDP for computers to real GDP, computer deflation had the effect of boosting real GDP and productivity growth. To illustrate the power of computer deflation, imagine if computers were Old Economy products. Imagine that computers did not improve in performance every year and that computer prices were raised by say 5% per annum. Computers would then be inflationary, and when the government converted nominal GDP for computers to real GDP, computer inflation would have the effect of reducing real GDP and productivity growth. Fortunately, computers are improving in performance every design cycle, and they are generating massive amounts of good deflation every year, leading to stronger growth in real GDP and higher productivity.

By the late 1990s, computer quality improvement began to show up as higher reported productivity growth for two reasons:

1. Capital spending for computers and peripheral equipment had been growing so much faster than the rest of the economy that the category grew from a weighting of only 0.68% of GDP in the first half of the 1990s to 0.95% of GDP by the second half of the 1990s.
2. The quality-adjusted deflator measuring performance improvement and price declines in computer and peripheral capital equipment was estimated by the BEA and the BLS to have declined by 12.0% per year in the first half of the 1990s, and to have declined by a much greater 22.6% per year in the last half of the 1990s. Remember, a greater quality improvement is reported as a greater decline in the price deflator.

The effect of roughly a 40% increase in the weighting of computer equipment and almost a doubling of the estimated percentage of annual quality improvement of computer equipment was to increase the contribution of computer equipment to the overall GDP Deflator from 0.08% deflation per year in the first half of the 1990s to 0.21% deflation in the second half of the 1990s. The 0.21% deflation was equal to almost one-quarter of 1 percent lower inflation *for the whole economy*. That 0.21% contribution to deflation also had the equivalent effect of boosting both real GDP and productivity growth by 0.13% per year more in the second half than the first half of the decade. For productivity, the 0.13% increase in annual contribution from computer quality improvement accounted for 24% of the economy's 0.54% rise in average productivity from the 1.54% average of the first half of the 1990s to the 2.08% average in the second half of the 1990s. This was a significant increase from just computers made for final sale, a single sector that represented less than 1.0% of the economy.

Economists at the Fed probably know, and economists elsewhere would be interested to know, that a major reason for the almost *doubling* in the rate of decline of the computer deflator in the last half of the 1990s was that many changes were made to the process of calculating the deflator as the decade unfolded. This was only natural as PCs and networked servers replaced mainframes, and as network-attached storage devices replaced tape drives, etc.

It should be noted, however, that computers did not suddenly start to generate a higher rate of performance improvement in the late 1990s. It's just that the government started to measure quality more accurately. Recall that semiconductors, and therefore computers, have demonstrated remarkably steady rates of performance improvement for over 30 years, very much due to the advances being made in semiconductor manufacturing processes as reflected in Moore's Law, as well as in other digital technologies. But when computers are being upgraded more than once a year and when new computers with new functions are being introduced frequently, it can be very difficult to consistently capture all these changes in quality. By the late 1990s, with more experience and better tools, the statistical agencies were getting more adept at measuring advances in computer performance.

Because this productivity boost was from constantly improving computer performance and from the government obtaining better data, it was hard to see where it was coming from. It was perfectly logical for the Fed to take the approach that any remaining growth in productivity after the removal of cyclical increases in productivity was structural. The only problem was that they still couldn't identify exactly what was causing this new increase in structural productivity.

## MASSIVE IMPLICATIONS FOR PRODUCTIVITY ACROSS THE ECONOMY

It's important to understand that the government's first significant efforts to measure quality have massive implications for productivity growth when viewed in the context of the overall economy. But the universal nature of productivity-boosting quality improvement is not immediately obvious unless you understand the concept of Digital Deflation and you are specifically looking for this kind of growth in productivity. The significance of the data showing just how much deflation is being generated by the annual enhancements in computer performance is exciting stuff. But it pales in comparison to the increases in real output and productivity that will result from measuring the uncounted quality improvement across the entire economy.

Fortunately, this book doesn't need to show the government how to measure a new kind of growth in productivity that is so new that it would be difficult to figure out where or how to start. The BLS is already capturing performance improvement for computers and doing an excellent job of it. However, this book does take on the task of showing that the government's conversion of computer-quality improvement into deflation and higher productivity growth is just a small part of a much larger phenomenon. The basis of this phenomenon is the Digital Revolution that has been percolating throughout the *entire* economy, improving upon existing technologies and inventing new technologies every day to lift product quality and performance— not just in the IT sector, but across virtually every industry in the vast non-IT portion of the economy as well. The result is a rapidly growing economy that is creating more value and more Digital Deflation in every industry that leverages the price–performance curve of constantly improving Digital Drivers.

The continuous and recurring creation of value through improving product performance and quality at lower and lower prices helps make the Digital Revolution fundamentally different from any recent economic periods and even very different from the Industrial Revolution that preceded it 100 years earlier. Being fundamentally different, it will not be easy for the government to measure the economic benefits of this new revolution. Technology's digital drivers can lift the quality and performance of products and services in so many different ways that some may say that it will be impossible to measure quality-enhanced productivity for so many industries. But it can be done starting with conservative estimates and improved upon with further analysis.

When the government commits more funding and resources to the effort and is able to measure quality improvement in other industries besides computers, the aggregate contributions to productivity and to society will be astounding. The uncounted performance and quality improvements for certain industries will be found to be quite large, particularly for software, communications, healthcare, and the service sector in general.

## SOFTWARE QUALITY IMPROVEMENTS ARE ELUSIVE BUT REAL

The government does not reflect quality or performance improvement for the overall software category even though it is a very large sector of the economy. In 2000, software was estimated to comprise 2.3% of GDP and has been growing rapidly. To its credit, the BLS has recently started making a very small annual quality adjustment of about 3.1% to the price deflator for prepackaged software. However, this boxed software represents only about one-third of all purchased software. The BLS hasn't yet been able to measure the improvement in quality and performance of software at a rate that is anywhere near its full rate of gain for a number of reasons:

1. For one, the Bureau of Labor Statistics only started to measure software for investment as a separate GDP account in October 1999, so it is still gaining valuable experience in measuring nominal and real value in the industry.
2. Software is also a very difficult animal to capture. It often comes "bundled" or included in the purchase price of a computer, in which case it is not reported as a sale in the purchased software GDP account. How do you measure firmware or software encoded into the microprocessors or microcontrollers before they are shipped?
3. There is also the issue of which Key Performance Attributes to measure and weight more heavily in assessing quality improvement in software. It's not as simple as counting the number of transistors on a silicon chip. You can't just count the increase in lines of code in a software program to measure the amount of

performance improvement in the latest version of, say, Microsoft Office.

4. Quality improvement is also very difficult to quantify across the wide variety of software on the market. The Key Performance Attributes vary widely from operating system software to applications software, and from prepackaged software for PCs to security software for servers and internet service providers.

5. If a new mainframe computer or four-way server is enhanced by a processor performance boost of 35% over the old model at the same price, is the newly upgraded operating software not 35% more valuable?

Just counting the dollar value of software shipped is often difficult. Imagine how difficult it would be to survey participants in a rapidly changing and fiercely competitive industry such as software to try to gauge the relative value of the latest software upgrade or new revision that each company is shipping. Then try to guess how much qualitative information your surveyors are going to obtain from any software company when you realize that another department of the government has been investigating the largest software company in the world.

Clearly, the U.S. economy would benefit from the establishment of an independent quality-based performance metric for software that is fairly universal across major software categories. Only then would software's contribution from quality improvements to productivity be realized and reflected accurately in real GDP accounts.

The government's new GDP Deflator for software estimated software to have been deflationary by about 0.8% per year when the BLS went back and restated the last 10 years through 2000. However, this index largely reflects only product price changes and the small quality change estimated for prepackaged software. If appropriate adjustments are made for a more realistic 15% annual improvement in features and function of the average software package, the software sector will be found to be contributing significantly to the naturally deflating New Economy. The software sector will be found to be contributing to the economy about half as much Digital Deflation and productivity growth as the BLS is counting for the computer sector today. (This rate of quality and performance improvement is developed in the next chapter.)

## COMMUNICATION SERVICES ARE GETTING FASTER, BETTER, CHEAPER

In 1996, the Bureau of Economic Analysis started making a small 5% "bias adjustment" for quality changes in voice switches. This is a small subcategory at less than 10% of the total communications sector, which itself represents about 3.1% of GDP. Except for this fixed 5% per year quality adjustment made for voice switches since 1996 and a very modest adjustment for cell phone minutes, the government hasn't been measuring performance or quality improvements for any other parts of the communications products and services sector.

For two reasons this has resulted in a severe undermeasurement of quality-based contributions from communications products and services to real GDP output and productivity growth. First, many of the fastest growing telecom services are brand new and are therefore undercounted when the government estimates product weightings in its survey results. The BLS freely admits that this is the case, especially for cellular phone service in the Consumer Price Index (CPI). Most consumers who have bought a cell phone service knows exactly how much faster, better, and cheaper his or her handset and service are compared to the old ones. But the weighting for cell phone service for the CPI was last estimated in 1995–1997 when cell phones were in their infancy.

It should also not come as a surprise that as a relatively new phenomenon, there is no home yet for the Internet in GDP except for Internet service providers such as AOL buried four levels down in GDP accounts. In the government's defense, for the Internet there are very large measurement issues regarding what should be measured, where it should be measured—and how to gauge the size as well as the price and performance improvement of this rapidly evolving new communications service. But they should be addressed. What is the annual increase in value of Internet access to the "road warrior" business traveler who is relying increasingly on checking his or her e-mails and retrieving more complex documents or even digital imaging? Certainly not zero incremental value as is measured today.

The second and by far more important reason the government is not reporting quality improvement in the communications industry is that except for voice-based switches and extra minutes for cell phone service, it is not yet performing quality or performance improvement by hedonic or other statistical methods for the vast majority of communications hardware or services. You can't report what you haven't measured, despite your best intentions.

Even if you had up-to-date (annual) weightings, rather than weightings estimated every 5 years, it still would be difficult to estimate the annual contribution to deflation and to productivity from the rapid advances being made in telecommunications without creating price–performance indices for each of a burgeoning number of new products and services. Routers, handheld wireless data devices and services, Internet access, content, and services are all generating double-digit rates of performance improvement every year, but none of these gains is being captured and reported. Advances in optical technology have been doubling data transmission rates every 9 to 12 months.

Analyst after analyst at the BLS expresses a desire to do more work on measuring quality improvement in communications as well as other industries, but they all cite a lack of funding and staffing resources. Nonetheless, serious efforts are already under way to measure quality improvement in telecom equipment. If the results are anything like what was seen in the computer industry, they should have very favorable implications for the economy and for investors.

Historically, the government has measured the communications sector to be inflationary in some years and deflationary in other years. However, if proper adjustments are made to reflect estimated quality improvements in telephone, cable, radio, wireless, Internet, and other communications equipment and services, the communications sector will be found to be hugely deflationary at a rate estimated at 15% per year as will be shown in the next chapter. Communications will be a growing contributor of Digital Deflation and productivity to the New Economy.

Why does this matter? If the government continues to under-measure the ongoing quality improvements being made to software products and to communications equipment and services, the result would be continued overstatement of reported inflation and understatement of reported productivity growth. The Fed would run the economy at a slower growth rate than it could if it had been given better data. There would be less wealth created, investors would realize lower returns, and people would lose jobs unnecessarily. One might argue that this was the case in 2000–2002.

## THE HUGE HEALTHCARE QUALITY MISMEASURE

Healthcare is a different matter. It's not just about the economy. It's about the quality of life, and even life itself. One of the greatest travesties to result from the lack of accurate data on quality improvement in products and services is the dramatic overstatement of reported inflation in healthcare costs, which arguably has led to questionable fiscal policy toward healthcare practices and a degradation in the quality of care.

Because the government has not been making any adjustments for continuously improving healthcare quality in diagnostics, instruments, pharmaceuticals, surgical procedures, and even diet and preventive medicine, the entire healthcare industry has been measured and reported to be only highly inflationary. The result has been undue pressure placed on healthcare providers and the pharmaceutical and medical instruments companies and, in too many cases, the underdelivery of proper care.

Unfortunately, it is easier to get people upset over reports of "soaring healthcare costs" and to even make a political career out of it than it is to make the effort to measure the improving quality of care and convert that into proper adjustments that may more than offset healthcare cost inflation. Healthcare is one area where the quality of economic statistics is extremely important to society and to the welfare of the average person. Make no mistake, incomplete and inaccurate economic data have resulted in an unnecessary deterioration in the quality of healthcare service in the United States as healthcare service providers have had to sacrifice the delivery of some quality to limit expenditures and reduce "reported" price inflation.

In the decade of the 1990s, the government estimated medical care services to be inflationary at an average rate of 4.3% per annum, with no adjustments for quality. However, an informal survey of a variety of medical care professionals yielded an estimated rate of improvement in the quality of medical care of about 10% per year over the last several years, despite the political pressure brought on the industry. Even if, for modeling purposes, a more conservative 6% rate of quality improvement is assumed for medical care services and 7% per year is assumed for pharmaceuticals and medical instruments, *healthcare expenditures would have been deflationary, adjusted for quality improvement.*

Further study may well result in an upward revision in both of these quality improvement estimates, particularly when consideration is given to rising success rates for surgery and medical treatment, faster patient recovery times, increases in life expectancy and the whole issue of pain, suffering, and the quality of life. In addition, over the next 10 to 20 years, pharmaceuticals and medical care services are likely to both take quantum leaps in quality as scientists leverage the continuing advances in biotechnology and the mother lode of new data from the Human Genome Project.

There is no question that medical care services are contributing significant amounts of Digital Deflation to the economy—and it is even likely that healthcare is delivering deflation net of the 4.3% nominal price increases that the government has been measuring for this important sector. Healthcare is squarely in the New Economy, and the mismeasure of healthcare quality improvement has huge implications for an aging society that will no doubt require more medical care in the years to come.

It would be a grave mistake if we allow ourselves—and our politicians—to remain burdened by bad data. This will only lead to misconceptions about the true costs and quality of healthcare. For senior citizens and aging Baby Boomers, the prognosis would not be encouraging. The likely outcome would be the delivery of a lower quality of care that would fall significantly below the potential of the healthcare industry. In future years, it will become increasingly critical that we properly measure the improvement in healthcare quality so that the industry can attract the capital to continue to develop and deliver faster, better, and safer care.

## THE SERVICE SECTOR IS GROSSLY UNDERMEASURED

One of the biggest reasons for the decline in *measured* productivity growth from 1965 to 1995 was the absence of any measurement of quality or performance improvement in the diverse and rapidly expanding service sector of the economy. For decades, economists have wondered why the service sector has not been able to produce the productivity gains reported by the manufacturing sector. In fact, limp reported productivity gains in the rapidly growing service sector have often been blamed for the decline in overall productivity growth in the 1970s, 1980s, and early 1990s.

The irony is that productivity gains *are* being generated by many areas in the service sector in the form of higher quality and value to the consumer per dollar. It's just that the faster, better, more convenient service sector improvement hasn't been measured.

Medical care services is only one of many subcomponents of the enormous service sector not counted for gains in quality. If you ask just about any service provider, they will gladly cite the many ways that they have become more productive, more efficient, and better able to deliver *higher quality, more convenient service* to the customer through the use of computers, cell phones, wireless e-mail devices, and the Internet. ATMs, Internet banking and shopping online have all introduced a new level of convenience, saving time, energy, and in many cases money for the consumer.

Economists don't deny that the quality of service from retailers, banks, brokers, insurance companies, lawyers, accountants, educators, and financial analysts have all been boosted by advances in technology. Again, it's just that nobody can agree on how to count the annual improvement in the value and quality of these services.

The trick for properly counting quality is that for services—even more than for products—the focus should be placed on estimating the improvement in the *level of service* or *value to the consumer*. This contrasts with the more traditional value measures which are based on the increase in the *dollar cost of the service for the provider*. Old Economy models only look at prices paid and provider costs. New Economy models will need to look at the increase in benefits to the consumer of a product or the user of a service, beginning with the initial shopping experience and extending through the consumption and use of the product or service.

Many of these services enhanced by digital technologies are creating completely new buying habits. For example, for the many people whose families live in different parts of the country, it can be far more convenient, satisfying, and practical to shop over the Internet for a Mother's Day flower arrangement. You can examine many more options at any time of the day. During the holiday shopping season, what is the value of being able to shop online and not fight the shopping mall traffic? This increase in convenience for the consumer is not measured *anywhere* in the government's statistics.

Admittedly, measuring services for annual quality improvement will not be easy. Service quality measurement is complicated by the fact that many consumers figure out new utilitarian uses for a new service that add considerable value to the consumer well after purchase but are not captured in the price of the service. This is particularly true for wireless devices, as increasingly mobile and untethered consumers, for example, may want to use the global position finder on their cell phones to find the nearest Starbucks or to show their spouse that "we're not really lost."

Comparing service quality improvement between different service industries will be difficult as each different service will have unique Key Performance Attributes. Even within each service, these attributes also vary in relative importance from one customer to the next. Some consumers will add creative new uses for their cell phones, and some won't care.

There will be many examples of degradation in service, such as longer lines at airport security or having to fly two legs through a hub to get to one destination. The strength of the economy no doubt will also affect the quality of some services—as seen in the 1990s when labor shortages led to diseconomies of scale. The government's statistical agencies will have to make enormous changes in how they count the quantity and quality of services shopped for, purchased, and consumed in a rapidly changing New Economy. It will not be easy.

## THE SERVICE SECTOR SUPPLY CHAIN

The strongest form of the Theory of Digital Deflation would stipulate that all parts of the supply chain involved in delivering and servicing products with performance-oriented digital components are themselves delivering Digital Deflation in direct proportion to the performance improvement of the digital end product.

This would include the salespeople, wholesalers, distributors, retail sales clerks, help desk personnel, computer, networking, and telecommunications maintenance people, as well as computer software and hardware consultants. They are all involved in the delivery and upgrading of existing digital products to the new faster, better, and cheaper models. The value-added cost of their service, therefore, should be accorded the same deflationary adjustment as the digital equipment itself.

An example might help. If an independent computer software consultant is installing a new software revision that is 50% better (enhanced security, faster backup, Web access, and new functions) than the 3-year old legacy software at a customer site, isn't his or her service 50% more valuable to the customer? In contrast, what if the installer was on the payroll of the original computer software vendor? His or her salary would then be bundled in the cost of the installed product, and the value of the installation service would be counted in the Digital Deflation generated by the hardware and software. What's the difference?

Now, as is often the case, what if the independent consultant is charging the customer 10% more to install and debug the software than he would have charged for the old version 3 years earlier? The customer getting 50% better software is now coming out ahead by 40% in additional real value, net of the 10% price inflation.

How should the economists count it? Compared to 3 years ago, this consultant would be delivering 50% greater value and Digital Deflation, less 10% adjustment for his price increase, for a net increase of 40% in real value and productivity contributed to the economy.

Today, however, the government would measure this software consultant as *only adding inflation to the economy* by charging 10% more over a 3-year period even though the services performed are on a piece of software that is 50% more valuable. The government would also see no improvement in productivity, and in fact would measure the opposite. It would see the consultant's 10% higher price as inflationary, and therefore would record a 10% reduction in real GDP output and a 10% reduction in productivity growth over 3 years. This mismeasurement by the government is one of the biggest reasons why the service sector as a whole has been reported by the government to generate very little in productivity gains over the last several decades.

Digital Deflation in the service sector supply chain is probably going to be one of the more debated claims made by the Theory of Digital Deflation. Valid points can be made on both sides. Many people will just not be able to accept that a retail assistant selling digital cameras or handheld organizers is adding 20% to 30% more value and 20% to 30% more productivity to the economy each year just because the products he or she is selling are improving in performance by 20% to 30% per year. However, the validity of the supply chain thesis can be made more clear by distilling the issue down to asking a couple of questions:

1. If you look at the consumer's Total Cost of Ownership of the digital product, how much more is the consumer getting in real

value per dollar for the product shopped for, purchased, and used this year versus the model bought 1 year earlier? If the digital camera has 30% better resolution, 30% longer battery life, and outputs directly to a TV, isn't the camera that much more valuable to the consumer? Isn't the retail assistant explaining the new features just a small but important part of the total price paid for the product that is being lifted in value by the rapidly advancing digital technology drivers—the semiconductors, software, and displays?

2. What is the Total Cost of Delivery of the rapidly improving product or service to the customer? Why should we arbitrarily draw a line that excludes the sales assistant, the installer, or the maintenance person for one product and not another? Aren't they all part of the supply chain delivering the improving digitally driven product or service to the customer? Do you treat differently personal computers sold through retail channels versus those that are sold direct over the Internet? Should we exclude the cost of Dell Computer's online sales and support people in the supply chain if we exclude the cost of the retailer helping to sell an HP-Compaq PC at Staples?

If you're going to try to estimate the benefits of Digital Deflation for specific products and services to the economy in terms of increments to real GDP and to productivity, its seems that you should make the calculation complete and measure all the benefits to the final point of consumption. That may be a person shopping for, buying, and using a digital camera, or it may be a major corporation purchasing a maintenance contract for an enterprise-wide network. To exclude any of the necessary services in the supply chain—whether it is the camera retailer, the software installer, or the maintenance person—would be arbitrary and inaccurate.

## SOLVING THE MYSTERY OF RISING CAPITAL SPENDING AND DECLINING PRODUCTIVITY

This chapter has focused largely on the undercounting of the recurring and rapidly improving quality in digitally driven products and services, the resulting overstatement of inflation, and the underappreciated lift in *quality*-based productivity gains to create a New Economy.

Many economists have also claimed that the government must be undercounting the more traditional *quantity*-based productivity gains (more units produced per hour) from high technology's contribution to real output—mainly because this form of productivity growth has not kept up with capital spending trends. This disconnect of rising capital spending and declining productivity growth was alluded to in prior chapters. The reality is that the government probably has been counting traditional productivity gains fairly accurately. Units are fairly easy to count.

A problem arises, however, because the government is including in corporate capital spending the cost of capital investments made to improve product performance and quality improvement, but it is not measuring much of the benefit or boost to real output and productivity growth resulting from these quality-enhancing investments.

Classical economics would stress that economists should look for traditional quantity-based productivity gains by tracking the growth in high-technology capital investments and examining how they help leverage worker output in terms of units produced per hour. This traditional thinking has been quite evident in Fed statements, including Chairman Greenspan's February 13, 2001 speech to the Senate Committee on Banking, Housing, and Urban Affairs: "The synergies of key technologies markedly elevated prospective rates of return on high-tech investments, led to a surge in business capital spending, and significantly increased the underlying growth rate of productivity."

It is a little surprising that the Fed has persisted in using the standard model relating productivity gains to capital spending despite the fact that for the 30 years until the late 1990s, reported productivity gains had been *declining* at the same time that business capital spending had been soaring. This was particularly evident in the 1970s and 1980s. But again, you can't blame the Fed if it didn't have the data or the models to fully evaluate and understand the magnitude and extent of quality improvement in the digitally deflating New Economy.

What really happened is that over the years, as digital technologies became faster, better, and cheaper, more companies in more industries found it attractive to grow market share and profits by allocating more of their capital budgets to improve the price performance and *quality* of their products and services. Many companies have also found for competitive reasons that they had no choice but to make these investments to improve product performance or lose market share. This meant, however, that at the margin they had less of their capital budget to allocate for more traditional investments to increase the *units* of output produced per hour on the production line (quantity-based productivity growth).

As the mix of the R&D and capital budgets shifted more toward improving product performance and quality versus quantity, *it is only natural that the growth in traditionally measured productivity slowed down.* The government wasn't measuring most of the quality-based gains in real output and productivity, which explains how reported aggregate productivity growth slowed in the 1970s, 1980s, and early 1990s at the same time that total capital spending had been accelerating.

As it turned out, the government was counting the capital expenditures dedicated to increasing both the quantitative and qualitative gains in real output, but it was counting only one productivity gain—that of the traditional quantitative units of output produced per person-hour worked. When the government begins to count more of the recurring and rapidly improving quality of products and services across the economy beyond just computers, it will have a more complete picture. It will be counting more accurately both the capital expenditures and the productivity gains for quantitative and qualitative increases in real output.

The next chapter will show how in 2001, the undercounted quality improvement in products and services amounted to an estimated 2.1% of additional real output and productivity growth not being included in government reports. This would imply that the government has been counting only about *half* of the total productivity growth being generated in the U.S. economy. It should now be clear why for almost three decades reported productivity growth had been declining while capital spending was rising. For an economist, it was like paying to see a really great movie and hearing the sound but only seeing half the screen. You know there is an exciting story there somewhere.

## THE "PRODUCTIVITY REVOLUTION" IS UNDER WAY

We have discussed how the absence of data showing the quality improvement from the application of digital technologies in products and services across the economy has effectively reduced reported total productivity growth rates below where they should have been for over 30 years. Ironically, the resulting downtrend in *reported* productivity growth in the midst of rising capital spending has created another interesting dynamic.

For three long decades, the government's productivity reports punished any economist who dared to predict a rise in productivity growth. That's a career for most. Many times burned, economists are still understandably very shy to talk about any kind of a secular rise in productivity growth. Many refuse to accept the late 1990s' rise in productivity growth as anything more than a bubble. (To its credit, the Greenspan Fed is one of the few exceptions.)

What all of this means, of course, is that like Pavlov's dog that has been overconditioned, economists have not noticed that a productivity revolution is already well under way. When the government goes back and restates prior years for uncounted quality improvement in a whole host of digitally driven products and services—as it did for computers made for final sale—we will see that actual productivity growth has been in a secular uptrend for many years. Depending on how much of the quality improvement the government is able to measure—as well as how quickly they count it—we will see as much as a 2% per year upward revision to recent productivity growth rates— no small adjustment.

Due to three decades of under-reported productivity gains, economists are not only conservative on the level of expectations for future productivity growth, but also reluctant to predict any uptrend or upward slope in productivity growth commensurate with rising IT capital spending trends in the future. This is evident in the official forecasts of the Congressional Budget Office showing *totally flat* productivity growth of 2.5% per year over the next 10 years.[2]

Yet over the next one to two decades, as IT capital spending recovers and resumes its five-decade pattern of rising as a percentage of GDP, there should be an upward bias in the more traditional quantity-based productivity gains. The growth in quantity-based productivity should rise over the long term, not remain flat.

What is also exciting to contemplate is that as the government begins to count more of the *quality*-based productivity gains (rising real value per unit) in the future, this will provide a second upward boost to total productivity growth rates. Recall that this rising quality-based productivity growth will be accompanied by increasing Digital Deflation, which should put inflation in a long-term secular downtrend. This downward trend in inflation, coupled with strong productivity growth, will allow for significantly more accommodative monetary policy and faster *nominal* economic growth.

In the end, economists will then have little choice but to raise their sights for more traditional quantity-based productivity growth in the future. Combined with government efforts now under way to count more of the Digital Deflation and quality-based productivity gains, it will become increasingly obvious that *we have already started a powerful productivity revolution*. We've only just started to count it.

## DISAGGREGATION INTO THE NEW ECONOMY AND THE OLD ECONOMY

It is one thing to understand what is driving the New Economy and why Digital Deflation will continue to create more real value and productivity growth over the next 10 to 20 years. It is another thing to be able to model the New Economy and carry out policies that allow it to reach its full potential. Because the New Economy and the Old Economy are so different, they are very likely to react very differently to changing government policies. It would be helpful to establish models to "disaggregate" the economy into two separate pieces. Policy changes can then be modeled for each sector, Old and New. The results then can be "reaggregated" to determine the net effect of a fiscal or monetary policy change on the overall economy.

As the capital markets seek to adjust to the new realities of the Digital Revolution, it would be helpful for the public to have new theories and new models that will define and explain what's driving the New Economy. New models will be needed to better understand the new and improved quality-adjusted data that most assuredly will be forthcoming from the government over the next few years. Only then can there be properly informed and open debate over the optimum path of growth for the U.S. economy. Only then can policymakers, corporate managers, and investors make intelligent decisions in an economy that will be transforming rapidly and breaking a lot of old economic models and theories along the way.

## NOTES

1. "Digital Economy 2000," Department of Commerce, June 2000.
2. "The Budget and Economic Outlook: Fiscal Years 2001–2011," Congressional Budget Office, August 2001.

# 7
## CHAPTER

# New Models for the New Economy

I skate to where the puck is going, not where it has been.
*Wayne Gretsky*

*Unique new models help measure the effects of demographics, productivity, Digital Deflation and the wealth effect on the economy. They reveal why inflation has been in a secular downtrend, and more recently, why reported productivity growth has strengthened in the United States. Models will show why actual productivity gains have been significantly higher and actual inflation lower than what has been reported. These models will prove to be invaluable tools for predicting the economy, inflation, interest rates, corporate profits, and the stock market in a world of increasing Digital Deflation.*

## BETTER MODELS, BETTER FORECASTING

This chapter presents several new models and methods for measuring the New Economy and predicting our economic future, both short term and long term. These models cover fundamental new forces that are combining to drive the New Economy and the Old. They all contributed importantly to the development of new theories needed to help solve the mystery of the New Economy:

  I. Models used to develop and confirm the Demographic Theory of Economics
  II. Models to help find the missing growth in labor productivity
  III. Models used to detect and prove the Theory of Digital Deflation
  IV. Models to understand wealth creation and the wealth effect

The models were developed in various stages over the course of several years, and only recently was it realized how they fit together like pieces of a puzzle to explain what many refer to as the New Economy. They have been brought together in this book to provide investors, managers, and policymakers with a better understanding of the New Economy and with the tools to have greater success at forecasting the economy and stock market in these murky and uncertain times.

This is necessarily a long chapter. As indicated above, the models and methods offered in this chapter fall naturally into four distinct categories. But they remain part of a bigger picture, and it therefore seemed artificial to break them up into several smaller chapters. Graphs are used to help illustrate the most important points.

Taken as a group, the models are internally consistent and mutually reinforcing. For example, several models strongly suggest or confirm the government's overstatement of inflation and undermeasurement of productivity gains in the 1990s and earlier. It is also interesting to note that the predictions of several models improved in accuracy if the historical reported data for inflation were reduced by 1 or 2 percentage points. This was done experimentally to test for the government's undermeasurement of Digital Deflation. Similarly, correlations for productivity also improved if historical productivity data were adjusted upward by a couple of percentage points to reflect the undermeasurement of quality improvement that should have been counted as equivalent increases in real GDP. These results provided encouragement and additional support to the belief that the government's data needed to be more accurate.

# I. DEMOGRAPHIC MODELS

## A DEMOGRAPHIC FOUNDATION FOR THE NEW ECONOMY

The Demographic Theory of Economics as discussed in Chapter 2 identifies the subtle but powerful relationships that exist between long-term changes in the labor force and various indicators of the health of the economy. It was established that favorable demographics in the 1980s and 1990s created an environment for low inflation and the need for labor productivity gains if the economy was going to grow at all. However, since most economists do not fully appreciate these demographic forces even at this date, they are likely to confuse the favorable disinflationary effects of benign labor force growth with the favorable effects of other new forces contributing to the New Economy.

Exhibit 7-1 shows what many economists have been missing. These graphs reflect the same 1983 demographic model that was used to predict the 1982–1999 stock market boom as described in Chapter 2. However, in this 2001 version of the demographic model, the data have been updated through the year 2000, adjusted to substitute the more widely used S&P 500 for the S&P 400 returns and revised to reflect the Bureau of Labor Statistics' minor revision in the age range of the youngest segment of the labor force.

Interestingly, the addition of the last 18 years of data—which included some very unusual economic times and the broadening of the labor force data to include 16- and 17-year-olds—did not alter materially the strong correlations between changing demographics and the economy discovered 18 years ago. It is quite encouraging that the strong correlations in the original demographic research have been fully confirmed by the last 18 years of data. More importantly, the demographic relationships proved to be symmetrical. They not only held up during the acceleration of growth in the youngest segment of the labor force in the late 1960s through the 1970s, but they held up equally well during the slowdown in labor force growth in the 1980s and 1990s, lending further support to the validity of the Demographic Theory and its models.

## THE DEMOGRAPHIC–INFLATION MODEL

The strongest relationship found in the group of demographic models was between the Consumer Price Index (CPI) and growth in the youngest segment of the workforce lagged by 5 years. The correlation, or R statistic, was an unusually high 0.93 between these two variables. The coefficient of determination, or R-squared statistic, was 0.87. This means that the level of inflation as measured by the CPI over 5-year periods can be 87% explained (or was 87% determined) by the rate of change in the youngest segment of the workforce 5 years earlier. Higher labor force growth produced higher inflation, and lower labor force growth led to lower inflation in the immediately following 5 years. This was confirmed by over 50 years of data and can be seen easily by comparing the bottom two graphs in Exhibit 7-1.

The 0.87 coefficient of determination between two seemingly unrelated variables (labor force growth and inflation) is highly significant

EXHIBIT 7-1

How Changes in the Labor Force Affect Inflation, Productivity, and Real Returns on Common Stocks

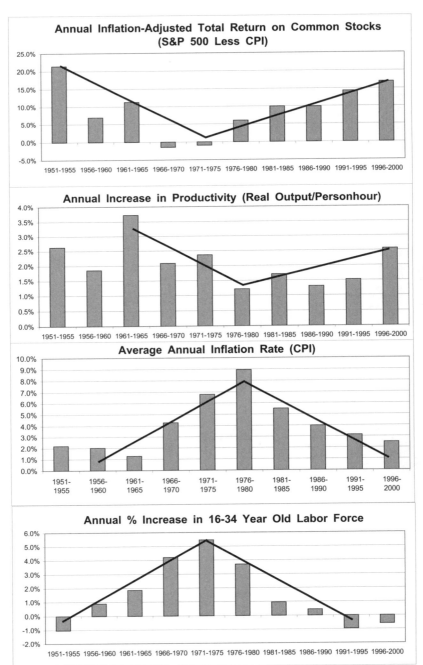

Sources: Department of Commerce; Bureau of Labor Statistics; Tanaka Capital Management, Inc.

and strongly suggests that the primary cause of the massive and crippling surge in inflation from the late 1960s to the early 1980s was the surge in the Baby Boomers and Working Women entering the workforce. Likewise, the dramatic decline in inflation from the early 1980s through the 1990s was primarily caused by the reduction in the growth of the workforce since the Baby Boomers and Working Women had already entered the labor markets in the 1970s. With close to zero growth in the youngest segment of the workforce, there would be a great need for productivity gains if the economy was to grow at all.

The implications of a strong cause and effect between labor force growth and inflation are enormous and innumerable. Perhaps the most important is that while many economists, including some at the Fed, continue to fear even today that inflation will return to the double-digit levels of the 1970s and early 1980s, the reality is just the opposite. The underlying demographic forces remain so favorable that given the proper environment for fostering capital spending, and sufficient new ideas and new technologies for boosting productivity, *it would be extraordinarily difficult to return to very high inflation anytime soon.*

For the Fed's critics, yes, the strong implication is that ever since the early 1980s, the Fed at the margin has been inadvertently too tight, waiting in that time period for the return of inflation that would not come back. Moreover, this result does not incorporate the further inflation-dampening effects of uncounted Digital Deflation. These effects will be revealed by Digital Deflation models which will be presented later in this chapter.

Admittedly, the very high 0.87 coefficient of determination between inflation and the single variable of labor force growth is partly explained by the use of 5-year averages which serve to smooth any existing relationships. However, these 5-year periods were selected in the original 1983 demographic studies because of the long-term nature of demographic change and the short-term volatility of common stock returns. Five-year averages remain appropriate today. The fundamental economic rationale for the high 0.87 coefficient of determination (0.93 correlation) is that the relative balance of supply and demand for capital and labor, the two most basic elements of a market-based economy, are the most dominant determinants for setting price levels and the rate of change in price levels (inflation) over long periods of time.

From a policy point of view, what is exciting is that this strong labor force-inflation bond means that almost *regardless of who was president, who was Fed chairman, and whether they made the right or wrong policy decisions over the short term, the course of inflation over the long term (5-year periods) seems to have been more heavily influenced by changing demographics than anything else.*

This does not mean that the economy and inflation in particular can't be heavily influenced in the short term by changes in fiscal and monetary policy, or by wars or oil cartels for that matter. It does mean that labor force dynamics are more dominant over the long run. This in turn suggests that policymakers, economists, and business planners need to better understand the powerful effects that changes in the labor force have on the economy before they formulate and carry out major changes in policies or strategies even over the short term. Major decisions should not be made with a blind spot for demographics.

As an aside, there are some who believe that policymakers and central bankers should minimize their "micromanagement" of the economy. For example, some feel that the Federal Reserve magnifies economic cycles by moving short-term interest rates up and down well after market forces have already started. The very strong fundamental relationship between demographics and inflation should be encouraging to those who are fiscal or monetary policy minimalists.

## THE DEMOGRAPHIC–STOCK MARKET MODEL

The Demographic Theory of Economics doesn't stop with inflation. It turns out that labor force growth has had an equally enormous impact on capital asset pricing, and more specifically on common stock returns. This is only logical since an economy and its capital and labor markets are constantly adjusting—seeking a balance between the changing costs of labor versus the changing costs of capital, debt, or equity. Of course, consideration must also be given to the expected returns on labor (factoring in productivity gains and unit labor costs) and returns on capital.

When first conceived in 1982, the Demographic Theory of Economics was an unproven hypothesis that was based on logic and an extension of well-established views that capital and labor are to some degree substitutable or interchangeable. The thought was that surpluses or shortages in one would affect demand and pricing for the other. That seems to have been the case as born out by the demographic model generated in 1983 and revalidated in 2001 showing a strong relationship between labor force growth and capital asset (stock market) pricing. In later chapters, it will be seen how common stock (equity) financing will likely take on an increasingly important role in providing much needed capital to feed the expanding New Economy in an increasingly scarce labor environment.

The top graph in Exhibit 7-1 shows a strong inverse correlation between real returns on common stocks (S&P 500 Index less the CPI) versus changes in the youngest segment of the workforce shown in the bottom graph. The R-squared coefficient of determination is a very significant 0.82 (–0.90 correlation), suggesting that changes in the youngest segment of the workforce would explain 82% of the average real return over 5-year periods during the last 50 years. It is important to realize that a real return is expressed as the net of the nominal return on common stocks minus the CPI inflation rate, so that the correlation with inflation again comes into play. However, this particular relationship measures the real return on stocks for the exact same 5-year periods as the labor force changes, without the 5-year lag that yielded the unusually high labor force–CPI correlation. More important, from a practical real-world standpoint, investors want to know what kinds of returns they can expect on common stocks *net of inflation*.

The demographic–stock market model and the accompanying graphs would strongly suggest that the double-digit real returns on common stocks over the last two decades were based very much upon favorable labor market conditions and were fundamentally justified. Investors can rest assured that these strong returns were not a statistical fluke or an act of irrational exuberance that must be "given back" by investors. In fact, they were built upon a solid foundation of low inflation that can continue well into the future given the outlook for continued moderate labor force growth.

This second demographic model, which correlates real returns on common stocks versus labor force growth, should provide a powerful and invaluable model to investors, particularly those seeking a long-term view for asset allocation, retirement planning, and pension fund actuarial assumptions. Again, there are many other variables that come into play, particularly for periods of time shorter than 5 years. Other variables will be examined later in this chapter.

## THE DEMOGRAPHIC–PRODUCTIVITY MODEL

From the three original demographic models studied 20 years ago, the one big disappointment was that the labor force–productivity model predicting a rise in productivity for the 1980s and 1990s did not pan out until the late 1990s. This is despite the fact that of the three major economic indicators studied—inflation, productivity, and real common stock returns—one would have expected labor productivity growth to have had the highest correlation with changes in labor force growth. Instead, the coefficient of determination between reported productivity gains and changes in the labor force was virtually zero for the same 5-year periods to 2000, and only improved to 0.12 with a –0.35 correlation if labor force growth was lagged by 5 years.

One would think that if the labor force grew, productivity would suffer, and that if labor force growth slowed, productivity would have to rise if the economy were to grow at all. This labor force–productivity disconnect is what suggested to this writer that maybe the productivity data were wrong—or that something else wasn't being measured properly.

## DEMOGRAPHIC–PRODUCTIVITY MODEL ADJUSTED FOR UNMEASURED DIGITAL DEFLATION

For the 1991–2000 decade, if the average productivity gains were retroactively increased by 2.0% per year to adjust for uncounted Digital Deflation, the labor force–productivity relationship improved dramatically. The coefficient of determination between productivity and labor force growth lagged 5 years improved to an R-squared of 0.31 versus 0.12 without the adjustment, with the correlation improving to an impressive –0.56 from –0.35 for the 1952–2000 period.

The 2.0% upward adjustment to productivity is the amount by which it is estimated that the government has undermeasured Digital Deflation, including deflation from nondigital quality improvements in the 1990s. When more detailed analysis is performed, previously reported productivity gains may have to be adjusted upward by more than 2.0% per year over the course of the 1990s. As the government makes appropriate adjustments for unmeasured quality improvement for the 1990s, it will undoubtedly restate inflation downward and productivity upward in the 1980s and the 1970s as well.

Restatements will be smaller farther back in time as the quality-generating IT such as computers and non-IT industries such as healthcare were smaller proportions of GDP in the earlier decades. Nevertheless, making all these upward revisions to productivity is likely to improve the demographic-productivity correlations even further, perhaps to the point that economists could conclude that labor force growth and productivity gains are indeed inversely related as common sense would suggest. In addition, it would provide additional evidence to help identify the missing productivity that economists have been seeking for years.

## DEMOGRAPHIC–GDP MODELS

In the 2001 updating of the demographic models, a more extensive analysis was performed on the relationship between labor force growth and other economic variables. Exhibit 7-2 presents graphs for these other demographic models. Over the last 50 years, using the same 5-year periods, the rate of growth in nominal GDP showed a very strong 0.87 R-squared coefficient of determination and a 0.93 correlation with growth in the youngest segment of the labor force lagged 5 years. It would appear, however, that this was more a result of the very strong correlation between inflation and growth in the youngest segment of the workforce. Inflation, of course, is incorporated in nominal GDP but not in real GDP. Indeed, the relationship between real GDP growth rates and changes in the youngest segment of the workforce demonstrated a meager 0.02 R-squared coefficient of determination (0.15 correlation) showing little long-term relationship between real GDP and growth in the labor force.

## THE STOCK MARKET AND REAL GDP

It is interesting to note that real returns on common stocks showed a very strong 0.82 coefficient of determination (–0.90 correlation) with labor force growth, but growth in real GDP showed only a 0.20 coefficient of determination (0.45 correlation) with real returns on stocks. (See the bottom two graphs in Exhibit 7-2.) The analysis indicates that over the long term, common stock returns are driven only modestly by growth in real GDP and are far more sensitive to the balance of labor and capital and the related rate of inflation. This is consistent with earlier demographic models which showed that labor force growth, inflation, real returns on common stocks, and to some degree, productivity, are very closely correlated, rendering other macroeconomic independent variables less significant than is generally believed.

Demographics Drive the Stock Market More Than Growth in Real GDP or
Corporate Profits

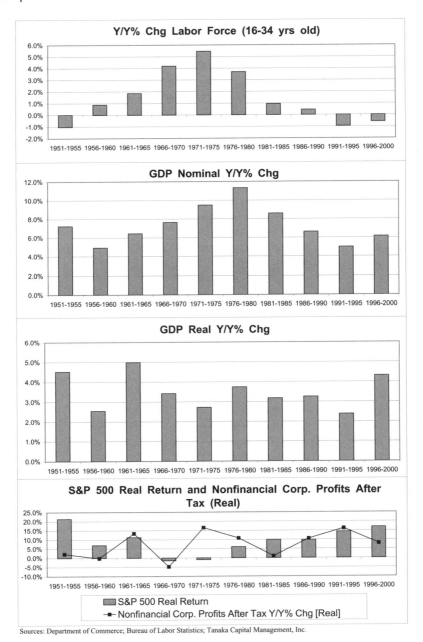

Sources: Department of Commerce; Bureau of Labor Statistics; Tanaka Capital Management, Inc.

## THE STOCK MARKET AND CORPORATE PROFITS

What about corporate profits? Surprisingly, changes in nominal and real corporate profits also seemed to have very little correlation with either changes in the youngest segment in the workforce (coefficients of determination were insignificant at only 0.01 and 0.007, respectively) or with real returns on common stocks (coefficients of determination were virtually zero for both over the 5-year periods). For 50 one-year periods, correlations were no better. It appears that over the long term, real returns on common stocks in the aggregate are not driven significantly by rates of growth in corporate profits, as surprising as this seems. It appears that aggregate common stock returns are driven more by changes in the rate of inflation than by changes in the rate of growth in corporate profits.

At first blush, the poor correlation between changes in nominal or real corporate profits and real returns on common stocks would seem to be counterintuitive. Stock market returns are widely thought to be driven by expectations for growth in corporate profits. However, the absence of good correlations for corporate profit growth only indicates the existence of more important determinants of common stock returns. These will be discussed in the next two chapters.

## "POTENTIAL PRODUCTIVITY"

If there is one message from the Demographic Theory of Economics, it is that there appears to be an ideal economic equilibrium rate of low growth in the youngest segment of the labor force which creates the need for productivity gains to generate economic growth. These productivity gains can support rising wages with little inflation pressure or could be converted into higher profit margins—or a combination of both.

With the balance of labor and capital shifted more in the direction of increasing capital input, the opportunities are greater for the corporate sector to make the kinds of capital investments that will lead to higher labor productivity growth—with the very important benefit being a direct reduction in inflation. In other words, it appears that based on the last 50 years of data there is an ideal stable demographic equilibrium state of close to zero growth in the youngest segment of the labor force which would create a certain potential for greater productivity gains, lower inflation, and higher real returns on common stocks.

That "potential productivity" is very much like the concept of potential GDP. At the micro level, it would reflect the potential for individual companies to substitute capital for labor and create enough productivity growth to generate a positive return on investment and improve overall profitability. *Potential productivity* is really a series of millions of opportunities when multiplied across the economy, and each would depend upon a wide variety of investment considerations. They would include consumer demand, capacity utilization, innovation and product development, new technologies and processes, the cost and availability of capital, the profit potential, and a tax structure that encourages rather than discourages investing.

At the macro level, if potential productivity is optimized, the result would be greater GDP growth with low inflation, declining unemployment, rising corporate profitability, and above-average real returns on common stocks—much like what we saw in the 1990s. The primary drivers would be benign growth in the youngest segment of the labor force and rising growth in productivity. With favorable demographics and an environment that maximizes potential productivity, everything else follows.

# II. PRODUCTIVITY MODELS

Traditionally, there are two approaches that economists have taken over the years to triangulate on growth in productivity: one from the capital spending or input side, and one from the corporate profits or output side. The theory is that if corporations invest more heavily in capital equipment, they should produce a return on that investment and generate higher productivity gains via higher output and higher revenue per fixed unit of labor cost. Similarly, if corporations are able to boost productivity gains, corporate profit margins should rise as revenues grow faster than labor costs. Unfortunately, at least in the statistics reported by the government, the productivity results have been decidedly mixed.

## THE CAPITAL SPENDING–PRODUCTIVITY MODEL REVISITED

As seen in Exhibit 7-3, only in the 1950s and early 1960s did an increase in capital spending as a percent of GDP result in an increase in

**E X H I B I T   7-3**

Nominal Capital Spending vs. Productivity Gains

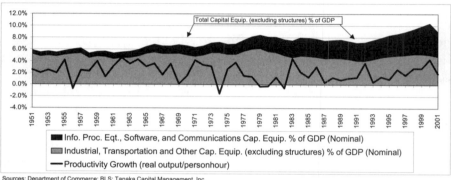

Sources: Department of Commerce; BLS; Tanaka Capital Management, Inc.

measured productivity growth. Then for 30 years from 1964 to 1994, the graph shows quite clearly that reported productivity growth declined at the same time that total capital spending rose dramatically as a percentage of GDP. As alluded to in the previous chapter, this was not supposed to happen. The negative correlation implies that higher capital spending as a portion of GDP would result in lower growth in productivity.

What's worse, the much-anticipated information technology revolution that was supposed to be producing enormous productivity gains seemed to have had little effect. As can be seen, the portion of capital spending or business fixed investment devoted to Information Processing (IP) Equipment and Software had been growing dramatically as a percent of GDP since the 1970s. In fact, IP spending provided virtually all of the rather remarkable growth in total equipment capital spending as a percentage of GDP throughout the 1970s, 1980s, and 1990s. IP capital expenditures grew from about 1.6% of GDP in 1970 to 5.3% of GDP by 2000, while capital spending for non-IP equipment remained fixed at around 4% to 5% of GDP for 50 years.

As can be seen, despite the surge in total capital spending and the much acclaimed boom in IP capital spending, reported productivity did not show any lift until the late 1990s. Reported productivity gains finally did start to rise significantly in the late 1990s just as IP capital spending accelerated and grew to become a dramatically higher percent of GDP. From 1994 to 1999, productivity gains grew from 1.3% to 2.3%, and IP capital expenditures grew from 3.3% to 4.7% of GDP.

As discussed in the last chapter, this late 1990s relinking of reported productivity gains with rising capital spending and surging capital spending for computers in particular was the first sign that the government was beginning to measure what was going on in the New Economy. The inclusion of quality-adjusted data for just one category, computers made for final sale, provided a significant boost to measured productivity growth in the late 1990s and helped explain why productivity growth started moving in the same direction as capital spending after diverging in opposite directions for three decades.

At the same time, the inclusion of better data for computer quality improvement gives hope that other quality adjustments can be identified and made to reveal how additional large amounts of quality-based productivity gains were undercounted during the prior 30 years, contributing to the breakdown of the normal capital spending and productivity relationship. There is no doubt that when the government begins to count more of the quality-based productivity gains in GDP accounts, the upward restatement of productivity will help bring about a more normal relationship showing a strengthening in productivity in line with a rise in capital spending.

## HOW LONG HAS THE GOVERNMENT UNDERMEASURED PRODUCTIVITY?

Exhibit 7-4 shows the same capital spending and productivity indicators as Exhibit 7-3, but expressed in real dollars and as 3-year moving

### E X H I B I T   7-4

Real Capital Expenditures vs. Productivity Gains (3-Year Moving Averages)

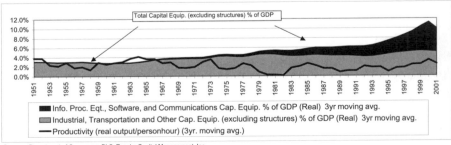

Sources: Department of Commerce; BLS; Tanaka Capital Management, Inc.

averages to smooth volatility and improve visualization. Although the use of real capital spending data divided by real GDP data is not entirely statistically correct given the government's conversion to chain-weighted price data, it serves the purpose of showing how sharply the government's reported productivity growth and capital spending trends diverged and became unhinged, possibly as early as 1964.

By looking at the industries with the largest potential for under-measuring quality, you can see how the government undermeasured productivity as far back as several decades—at least to the 1960s. Information technology was a very small part of the economy back then, and there is not a lot of data on the sector going back that far. However, even in the 1960s, several non-IT industries were generating significant improvement in performance and quality, driven by digital and other technology breakthroughs.

Healthcare and communications services presented significant opportunities for the government to undermeasure quality, overstate inflation and undermeasure productivity even back in the 1960s when they represented 2.5% and 2.2% of GDP, respectively. For example, if these two categories were delivering 5% quality gains per year in the 1960s, they would have been generating about 0.23% lower inflation and 0.23% higher productivity gains than the government measured.

More recently, the government reported that Information Processing equipment and Software represented 5.3% of GDP in 2000, up significantly from only 1.0% of GDP in the 1960s. This shows how the opportunity for the government to undermeasure performance improvement in information technology has risen fairly dramatically over the last 30 to 40 years. As mentioned earlier, an excellent study, "Digital Economy 2000"[1] by David Henry and others at the Department of Commerce, estimates that information technology actually represented an even larger 8.3% of GDP in 2000 when intermediate goods producers of IT products and services were considered. With a rising base of quality-improving IT and non-IT categories in GDP accounts, this suggests an even greater opportunity for the government to undermeasure productivity in the future.

## PRODUCTIVITY AND PROFIT MARGIN MODELS

Perhaps the only traditional productivity models to hold up reasonably well over the last 50 years are those that correlate reported productivity gains with various measures of corporate profitability. As can be seen in Exhibit 7-5, there has been an excellent fit between

**E X H I B I T  7-5**

## Productivity Growth vs. Profit Margins

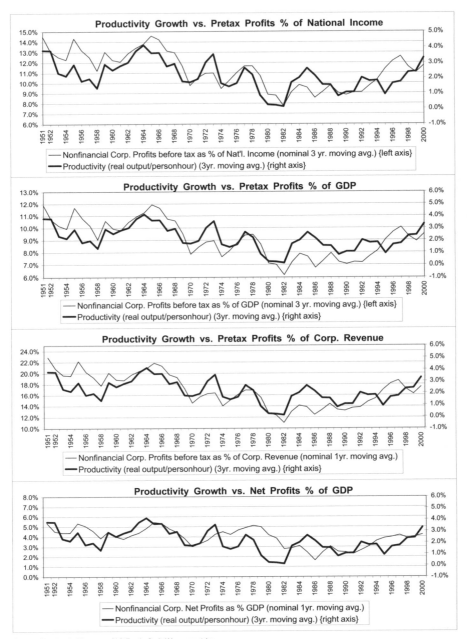

Sources: Department of Commerce; BLS; Tanaka Capital Management, Inc.

gains in productivity expressed as a 3-year moving average and pre-tax corporate profits, whether they are expressed as a percent of nominal GDP, national income, or corporate revenues. Net profit margins (after tax) correlate less with productivity gains, as changes in tax rates appear to interfere with the correlation between productivity growth and profit margins.

The productivity and profit margin models have worked surprisingly well over the last 50 years, through periods of rising and falling inflation and economic expansion and contraction. Over the years, in fact, changes in productivity gains have provided a fairly accurate short-term indication of corporate profit margins as well as of returns on common stocks. The linkage, of course, is that productivity growth drives corporate profit margins, which helps boost returns on common stocks. These relationships were reviewed in a study on "Productivity and Profitability" which I distributed right at the beginning of the 1980s and 1990s once-a-generation superbull market, in February 1983:

(1) Corporate pretax margins when expressed as a percent of GNP or sales are the lowest in 35 years. There is a potential for improved profitability simply from a recovery in profit margins to more "normal" levels.

(2) There are numerous explanations for the decline in profitability, but the strongest reason is the *insidious decline in productivity* gains (output/manhour) in the U.S. from an average of 2.6%/year in the 1948–1965 period to only 1.3%/year in the 1966–1982 period.

(3) The historic linkage between corporate pretax margins and gains in productivity became startlingly apparent when we looked at changes in pretax margins versus productivity: In the last 35 years, pretax profit margins of the S&P 400 increased in all 12 of the 12 years in which productivity rose by over 3%. Margins rose in only 2 of the other 23 years.[2]

## THE 120% RULE OF THUMB

The strongest historical correlation between productivity growth and the various measures of pretax profits shown in Exhibit 7-5 is the one relating pretax profits as a percent of GDP to productivity growth. The coefficient of determination was a fairly strong 0.57, and the correlation was 0.75 for the last 50 years. As can be seen in Exhibit 7-5, it appears that profit margins are leveraged to rise more than productivity gains and decline more than productivity gains. For those who would like a rule of thumb: Pretax profits as a percent of GDP = 6.5% + 120% times productivity growth.

This model provides a handy tool for being able to predict approximately a 1.2% uptick in corporate pretax profit margins for every 1.0% increase in productivity growth across the economy. The 120% rule of thumb for productivity and corporate profits will provide an important link in Chapter 9 on the New Economy stock market for projecting stock market returns over the next two decades.

## THE OVER 3.0% PRODUCTIVITY GROWTH RULE

The 1983 "Productivity and Profitability" study included an analysis of the annual changes in productivity and profits, and this analysis has also been updated through the year 2000 and presented in Exhibit 7-6. The graphs reveal two important points:

1. Profit margin percentages rose from the prior year in 13 of the 16 years that productivity was reported to rise by over 3.0% (middle graph). However, profit margin percentages rose in 6 other years in the 1990s when productivity was reported to rise by less than 3.0%. The Over 3.0% Productivity Rule worked almost perfectly in the 1950–1992 period but seemed to break down after 1992. This provides further evidence that the government was undermeasuring productivity gains in the 1990s, because rising corporate profit margins implies that productivity should have increased by over 3.0% in each of those 6 years.
2. Nominal common stock total returns in the 1950–2000 period were positive in 10 of the 13 years where there was both an increase in productivity of over 3.0% and an increase in pretax profit margins versus the prior year (top graph). However, there were 9 additional years from 1984 to 2000 when profit margins increased and common stock total returns were positive but productivity gains were reported to be less than 3.0%. This evidence also suggests the underreporting of productivity gains, this time in the 1984–2000 period.

## THE NEW ECONOMY PRODUCTIVITY–PROFIT ENIGMA

How is it that over the last 30 years the demographic-productivity and the capital spending–productivity models were completely thrown off

## EXHIBIT 7-6

The Over 3.0% Productivity Rule*

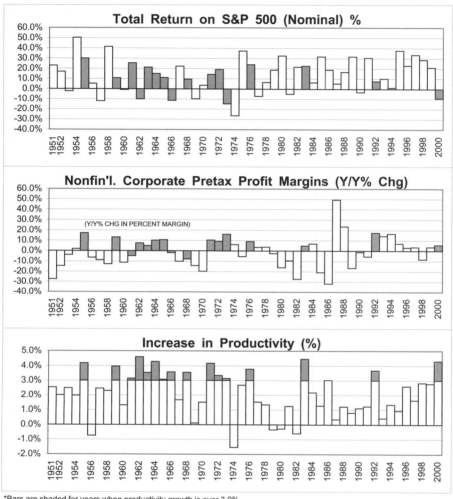

*Bars are shaded for years when productivity growth is over 3.0%.
Sources: BLS; Tanaka Capital Management, Inc.

by the undermeasurement and underreporting of productivity gains, while the productivity–profit margin models held up reasonably well? The answer appears to be that the quality improvement–based real gains in output that have not been counted by the government also have not tended to be priced by New Economy Companies to produce higher margins at the gross profit margin level.

It seems that New Economy Companies tend to price their products and services based on nominal dollars of profit versus nominal dollars of costs without regard to the higher real value of the products and services being delivered with each new design cycle. In essence, this means that companies in the New Economy are passing virtually all of the quality improvements on to the consumer, making little or no incremental profit on the faster and better-performing newest model.

After many years of receiving the fruits of Digital Deflation, the consumer expects no less. He or she has been conditioned to expect 30% or 40% better performing PCs, cell phones, etc., every year for free, period. There is no going back, and most markets are so competitive that many of the companies delivering digital products and services are content to move rapidly down the price curve as long as they don't fall behind the competition. If they can make an acceptable profit return on nominal dollar sales and their R&D investment, they don't seem to think about making a gross profit on the incremental quality or value added with new each design cycle.

On a macroeconomic basis, what this seems to imply is that corporate percentage profit margins should not necessarily rise in direct proportion to the rise in *quality*-based productivity gains, only to the increase in the more traditional nominal dollars of *quantity*-based productivity gains. Can this be true?

## ARE QUALITY GAINS EMPTY CALORIES?

You might ask why companies spending good hard cash to develop new technologies and better-performing products would not price their wares to capture at least some profit return on their product performance enhancements. Certainly, they all try and only those with a truly proprietary position can operate for any length of time with unusually high gross margins. Microsoft, Intel, and Cisco come to mind as rare examples of companies that have been able to leverage proprietary technologies and remain at the leading edge of product design cycles to generate high gross margins and strong sales growth for years.

However, the technology landscape is littered with companies that attempted to charge above-industry average prices to achieve higher margins for a proprietary product advantage. They can end up losing market share and sales growth. Apple Computer is a company with great technologies and a loyal following. However, it has priced its products with gross margins well above the "Wintel" (Windows-Intel) platform of personal computer companies, such as IBM, Gateway, and Dell, who standardized on a more open platform. Apple chose to price to capture a profit on its value-added improvements rather than to pass it all on to its customers. One can only guess what market share Apple might have commanded if it had passed all of its innovative advances on to the consumer without charging a premium for its superior performance.

As innovative companies have found over the years, passing on most if not all of the newest product or service performance improvements to the consumer at the same price is what will drive unit sales growth and gain market share. With greater market share, of course, comes all the benefits of economies of scale on purchasing, production, and marketing. These economies result in lower unit costs which—if even partly passed on to the consumer—drive further gains in market share and expand the market. For the New Economy Company, this pattern creates a "virtuous circle" of rapidly rising sales volume, increasing economies of scale, declining per unit operating costs, and rising operating profit margins—one of many virtuous circles rewarding the enablers and beneficiaries of the Digital Revolution.

Every product has a unique *price elasticity of demand*. This elasticity reflects how much demand might rise if the price on a product is reduced or how much demand might decline if a price is increased. That can be tested fairly easily. However, it is far trickier to estimate how many more units might be sold if say 30% more value is offered on a newly designed model for the same price. Given the very large magnitude of annual performance improvement offered by most digitally driven products, every company involved in the New Economy should know the price elasticity of demand for each of its major products. It is surprising, but very few really do.

Dell Computer, well known for its "Dell Direct" sales and fulfillment model, also understands quite clearly the importance of knowing its product price elasticity curves. It is not widely appreciated, but because Dell had already developed and perfected its product "price elasticity algorithms" over the years, it was able to respond faster than its competitors when demand slowed in 2000 and 2001. By performing product tests in a few markets, they noticed that there was not the predicted "pop" in demand when prices took the normal "step-down parallel pricing"* moves. Dell's response was to test the market with

---

*I use "step-down parallel pricing" to describe the downward stair-step price curve that each digitally deflating product follows with each periodic price cut, making room at the top for the enhanced next-generation version to start a new price curve.

even lower prices until they were again able to stimulate demand even in a weak economy. At a modest sacrifice in gross margins, this allowed the company to meet its corporate objective of continuing to gain market share and gain further economies of scale.

In the end, pricing to pass on to the consumer all of the quality or performance improvement gains of each new design cycle is not producing "empty calories" for the New Economy Company. Pricing to offer faster, better, and cheaper products and services is what stimulates and drives rapid growth in unit demand from new customers as well as from faster cycles of replacement demand from existing customers. It is what has driven industry sales in PCs and cell phones to new heights, defying the forecasts of the industry naysayers who warned even 5 and 10 years ago that the PC and cell phone markets would become saturated and decline.

This is not to say that demand for PCs and cell phones will "grow to the sky." But pricing to pass on quality improvements to the customer is what is accelerating digital product replacement cycles, continuously providing the Digital Revolution with fresh legs to run a lot longer than most realize. It is, in fact, an integral part of the process that is delivering wave upon wave of performance enhancements to the consumer, helping the New Economy to grow faster than the Old. Along the way these New Economy Companies are creating more Digital Deflation for the whole economy.

The New Economy Companies that pass on most of their digitally generated performance and quality improvements to the consumer may not increase their gross profit margin as a percent of sales. However, they certainly will stimulate faster growth in unit demand for their products and therefore produce faster growth in nominal dollars of profits. It is this faster growth in nominal dollars of profits which contributed to higher returns in the stock market for many New Economy Companies in the 1990s. By not pricing to make an extra gross profit on the quality improvements from technology enhancements, this appears to be one of those rare instances when a company doesn't earn higher gross margins, but really does make it up on volume.

By leveraging economies of scale, New Economy Companies can actually expand their operating pretax profit margins and net profit margins even though they are passing on their quality improvement to the consumer. They can benefit from enormous economies of scale by spreading their relatively fixed research, selling, and other corporate expenses over faster growing sales volumes. In the 1990s, the Intel business model was to focus on stabilizing gross profit margins in the "50% plus range," passing on virtually all of the 50% a year or more improvement in microprocessor performance to the consumer. Despite holding gross profit margins flat, Intel was able to expand operating profit margins by 54% (from 29.3% to 45.2%) and net income margins by 90% (16.6% to 31.6%) from 1990 to 2000. It was by no means empty calories for Intel.

The fact that Intel and other New Economy Companies could pass on all their quality improvement to the consumer without price increases—and still increase their percentage pretax profit margins—confirms that quality-based gains in output and productivity *can* lead to higher profit margins. This observation is important for the overall Digital Deflation thesis. It is not just productivity gains from capital spending to increase the *quantity of output per hour* that produces higher profit margins for companies. In addition, it is quite evident that productivity gains from capital spending to increase *product quality* can also produce higher profit margins. In reality, companies have to make an attractive return on capital expenditures dedicated to improve product quality as well as to increase units of output per hour or the companies won't make the investments.

## THE FED'S PRODUCTIVITY AND CAPITAL DECOMPOSITION MODEL

Many of the 220 economists at the Federal Reserve have devoted considerable time and energy to understanding how information technology has contributed to the important rebound in reported productivity in the late 1990s. The almost doubling in reported productivity from the first half of the decade to the second had been cited repeatedly by Fed Chairman Greenspan during 1999–2001 in endeavoring to explain why the 1990s' economic boom had been setting records for length and strength without inflation. The tacit message was that the Fed would let the economy continue to boom as long as it was comfortable that some part of the elevated productivity gains might be structural, long lasting, and sufficiently large enough to offset any cyclical inflationary pressures.

It is notable, however, that in the 1990s, despite a record-long expansion, there was in fact no significant appearance of inflationary pressures on general price levels. This was true despite the fact that reported inflation numbers were overstated by not counting the effects of Digital Deflation. This was true despite the significant round of monetary loosening instituted in 1998–1999 to bring the economy out of the Asia crisis and provide liquidity in advance of any Y2K lockdown. This was true even despite sharp price spikes in oil and gas in 2000–2001.

In early 2001, after a record 9 years of economic expansion, the Fed still saw no signs of a pickup in reported inflation except for energy. On January 3, 2001, in a move to reduce interest rates on federal funds by one-half percent, Alan Greenspan said that "inflation pressures remain contained" and that "to date there is little evidence to suggest that longer-term advances in technology and associated gains in productivity are abating."

Some unknown forces were holding down inflation and at the same time driving productivity gains to new heights—and it was becoming even more important to determine the causes. A number of studies focused on the obvious candidate, information technology. An important analysis was performed by Federal Reserve economists Daniel Sichel and Stephen Oliner and published from February through May 2000. It was titled "The Resurgence of Growth in the Late 1990's: Is Information Technology the Story?"

In this landmark study, the Fed economists used what's called a *neoclassical growth-accounting model* to decompose the measured and reported productivity numbers by source of contribution. By estimating how much capital was employed by the computer hardware, software, and communications industries to manufacture their goods as well as how much capital was employed by "users" of information technology equipment to produce other goods, the Fed economists determined that "the *use* of information technology and the *production* of computers accounted for about two-thirds of the 1 percentage point step-up in productivity growth between the first and second halves of the decade."[3]

The Fed study was very helpful in validating the thesis that information technology was indeed providing a significant boost—in fact the largest boost—to reported productivity gains in the United States in the late 1990s. This was refreshing. After three decades of declining productivity gains, it had become quite common to see studies showing how computers were *not* adding to gains in labor productivity—because they were difficult to learn or not very user friendly. So it was reassuring to see a new model from a very credible source directly associating the rise in productivity in the late 1990s to the growth of information technology capital assets.

Exhibit 7-7 shows how much the Fed economists estimated that information technology industries contributed to growth in real GDP output (top graph) and to total labor productivity growth (middle graph) in each year since 1974. These graphs reflect only how much the *use* of IT equipment contributed to the output and productivity growth of other products. They do not reflect how much output and productivity may have been increased during the *production* of IT equipment, which is increasing in real value each year from quality improvement that is not being counted. (The bottom graph in Exhibit 7-7 is discussed in the next section.)

From the graphs it is quite easy to see that (1) the contribution from IT capital spending to output and productivity growth has been rising significantly over the years (directly proportionate to the size of the capital stock invested in IT) and (2) the contribution of IT has provided a steadying influence on the volatility of both growth in real GDP and growth in productivity. When published in early 2000, these data had to be reassuring to the Federal Reserve Board of Governors as they reviewed the tight monetary policy program they had initiated beginning in July of 1999 to slow down the economy.

## NEW MODELS FOR PREDICTING INFORMATION TECHNOLOGY'S CONTRIBUTION TO GDP AND PRODUCTIVITY

The data from the Fed's Sichel and Oliner productivity decomposition model provided a fresh opportunity to develop new predictive models for the future. Based on the Fed's new data, two new models were developed at Tanaka Capital Management (2000).[4] They are regression models that take the Sichel and Oliner estimates for IT's contribution to real GDP output and productivity and correlate those two streams of data with the ratio of the component of GDP called *fixed investment in Information Processing Equipment and Software* to total GDP for each year since 1974. This Information Processing Equipment and Software category includes computers and peripherals, software, and communications equipment, and will be referred to as *IT capital spending*.

In these new regression models, the R-squared coefficients of determination were very high at 0.90 for IT's contribution to real output

## E X H I B I T   7-7

Information Technology's Contribution to GDP and Productivity

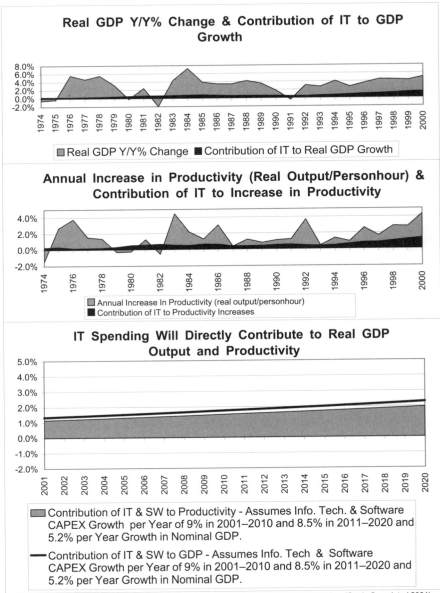

Sources: Federal Reserve Board; Bureau of Labor Statistics; Tanaka Capital Management, Inc. (Study Completed 2001)

and 0.83 for IT's contribution to (reported) productivity. The correlations or R statistics were 0.95 and 0.91 for real output and productivity, respectively. These correlations are very high but would seem to pass the "smell test" as higher IT capital spending as a percent of GDP should logically contribute directly to higher GDP output and greater productivity gains.

Employing Tanaka Capital's IT Capital Spending–IT Contribution to Output and IT Contribution to Productivity regression models and making assumptions for growth in IT capital spending and nominal GDP over the next several years, projections can be made for how much more IT capital spending will contribute to both real output and productivity. Using historically conservative assumptions for future growth in nominal IT capital spending and nominal GDP, the predicted results are very encouraging.

Assuming a straight-line growth rate of 9% per year for IT capital spending and a growth rate of 5.2% per year for nominal GDP growth from 2000 to 2010, IT capital spending alone is projected by 2010 to contribute 1.9% per year to real output GDP growth and 1.6% per year to growth in productivity. This compares to estimates of IT capital spending contributions to real GDP and productivity growth of 1.4% and 1.3%, respectively in 2000. The 9% future growth assumption for IT spending should be fairly conservative given that IT spending grew at an average rate of 11.6% per year in the 1980s and 9.7% per year in the 1990s. Nominal GDP averaged 7.9% per year growth in the 1980s and 5.4% per year in the 1990s.

From 2010 to 2020, assuming growth in IT capital spending of 8.5% per year and nominal GDP growth of 5.2% per year, IT capital spending is projected to contribute 2.8% to real GDP growth and 2.3% to productivity gains by the year 2020. The projections for the next two decades are shown on the bottom graph in Exhibit 7-7.

These projections involve compounding many years out into the future, so much can go wrong to throw them off course. However, the direction and the magnitude of the potential contribution to economic growth and, more important, to inflation-reducing productivity gains have enormously positive implications for society. It must be pointed out that as positive as these projections are, they reflect only historical relationships based on measured and reported output and productivity as well as on what the Fed economists estimated to be the benefits from the *use* of IT capital spending equipment and software to produce quantity-based output and productivity gains. Again, these projections reflect only future *quantity*-based gains in output and productivity from IT capital spending. They reflect little contribution to real GDP and productivity growth from the uncounted *quality* improvements from rapid advancements in digital technologies. Nevertheless, they go a long way toward explaining the very strong growth in real GDP and in productivity in the second half of the 1990s and the year 2000.

It is very important to note that the analysis by the Fed economists' models as well as Tanaka Capital's IT Capital Spending–Productivity model dissected only what had been *reported* as productivity by the Bureau of Labor Statistics (BLS). In their study the Fed economists referred to the BLS numbers as "actual" productivity. Again, the economists at the Fed took a classical approach to estimating how much capital was used in the production or use of IT to boost reported productivity. They did not challenge or question the accuracy of the BLS productivity or inflation data.

The Theory of Digital Deflation goes further as shown in the models discussed in the next section. They reveal that there are large amounts of undermeasured real productivity gains that have been left out of the BLS calculation of productivity due to the undercounting of product quality improvement in a wide variety of large and rapidly growing industries.

# III. DIGITAL DEFLATION MODELS

The Theory of Digital Deflation was developed by observing and marveling at how new digital products are introduced and how each new design dramatically renders the old products obsolete. In analyzing the process, it was realized that the cycles had been repeating themselves for years at fairly consistent rates. In researching the underlying technology or "digital drivers" it was evident that the product design cycles will continue for 10 to 20 years into the future, at rates of performance improvement very similar to the past.

Like clockwork, these very high 15% to 40% per year rates of performance improvement will be driven by advances in technology that are as constant as Moore's Law calling for a doubling of the number of transistors on a silicon chip every 18–24 months. Recurring advances will continue to be made in a variety of other key digital technologies—in software, magnetic storage, displays, and optical transmission. Over the years, new technologies and new digital drivers will surely emerge. Except for computers and to a small degree for software and switches, these rapid 15% to 40% gains in product performance just do not show up in government reports.

## ESTIMATING THE UNDERMEASUREMENT OF DIGITAL DEFLATION

The Digital Deflation models discussed below are first attempts to estimate the total undermeasured contribution of digital technologies, which if reported properly, would result in the boosting of real output and productivity and the reduction of inflation across the whole economy. They are approximations. My hope and expectation is that they will be improved upon through more detailed surveys and analyses.

To obtain the best estimates of undermeasured quality and performance improvement by industry, data on industry size and deflators were obtained from GDP by industry accounts, formerly called *Gross Product Originating* or *Gross Domestic Income.* GDP by industry measures income or value added by each major industry including those at the intermediate goods level and therefore provides a more complete and accurate presentation of the value of output by individual industries than standard GDP accounts. The commonly quoted standard GDP accounts only measure the output of industries that have final product sales to the consumer, business, or government, and therefore do not report the output of semiconductors and other "intermediate goods" generating large amounts of uncounted Digital Deflation.

As mentioned briefly in Chapter 3, early in the process of researching Digital Deflation it became obvious that a study performed by the Department of Commerce (DOC) for a completely different purpose would become very helpful for estimating quality improvement. This particular study was requested by the Clinton administration because it wanted to understand how the Internet was affecting the economy and also to identify all parts of the economy contributing to the Internet. The result was a special effort made by economists at the DOC to come up with a more complete breakdown and identification of technology industries than could be determined before from standard GDP accounts. The first edition, "The Emerging Digital Economy," was published by the DOC in 1998 and was followed by annual updates, including "Digital Economy 2000." This series is among the best studies produced by the U.S. Government and is highly recommended reading.

The initial DOC study estimated the total size of information technology industries at 8.3% of GDP for 1998, a number that was significantly larger than the 5% one could obtain for IT from standard GDP accounts because it used GDP by industry data. Remember, GDP by industry includes computers and semiconductors that are components and therefore do not show up in standard GDP accounts because they are not final sales. Although what most people took away from this study was the widely publicized estimate that information technology represents over 8% of the U.S. economy. Buried deep inside the study were some new data that were even more important.

What was most astonishing was that the report estimated that "In 1996 and 1997, declining prices in IT industries lowered inflation by 1 full percentage point."[5] It is ironic that this statement carried enormously favorable implications for future inflation and indirectly for productivity, yet it has garnered very little press or attention from economists. It was even more significant considering that information technology is likely to keep growing faster than the rest of the economy. Of course, what the statement meant was that *if* the government had measured quality improvement for the computers and semiconductors sold as components rather than just computers and semiconductors made for final sale, then inflation *would* have been significantly lower than what was reported.

In the "Digital Economy 2000" report published 2 years later, the DOC revised their estimates for IT's reduction in overall U.S. inflation to 0.5% per year on average for the years 1995 to 1998. However, this was still a large deflationary force for offsetting inflation in the rest of the economy, and the study only estimated the deflationary benefits from computer and semiconductor quality improvement.

As discussed in Chapter 3, this series of DOC studies on information technology provided an important clue for solving the mystery of the New Economy. The studies confirmed the existence of significant deflation being generated by digital technologies that was not being reported in the GDP Deflator, the CPI, the Producer Price Index (PPI), or any other inflation gauges. The reason was that these studies for the first time estimated how much price deflation was being generated by *all* computers and semiconductors—whether they were listed in final sales or were ending up as components lost in the reporting of larger final goods and services.

## THE GDP DEFLATOR–DIGITAL DEFLATION MODEL

There are several avenues by which the government is currently un-dermeasuring Digital Deflation, and thereby overstating inflation and understating productivity growth. They can be grouped into three major categories:

1. Computers, semiconductors, and other digital *technology compo-nents* currently measured for quality improvement but *not counted as final sales* or in other ways underweighted in GDP accounts
2. *IT industries not currently measured for quality* or performance im-provement including software, communications hardware and services, and IT services
3. *Non-IT industries* not yet measured for quality improvement such as healthcare, autos, and military procurement, as well as parts of the service sector that leverage constantly improving digital technologies in their design and delivery and services

To construct a model of unmeasured Digital Deflation, estimates were made for the amount of uncounted annual quality improvement being generated by all of the IT industries as well as the major non-IT industries likely to be delivering the most continuous improvement in product and service quality. The annual rates of quality improvement were multiplied by the relative weighting of each product or service as a percent of GDP by Industry. The results are presented in Exhibit 7-8. This model focuses on 1998, the latest year for which the most complete data are available from the DOC's "Digital Economy 2000" study showing the relative size of each IT industry.

Adding up the weighted contribution from each major product or service component, the total estimated unmeasured Digital Defla-tion for 1998 totaled 1.96%. In other words, when the government starts to count quality improvement for each of the industries pre-sented in Exhibit 7-3 in a manner similar to how they are already counting quality and performance improvement for computers, it will find that *inflation for the overall economy was approximately 1.9% lower* than what they reported for 1998. Accordingly, by reducing the GDP Deflator by 1.9%, *real GDP growth and productivity gains would also have to be adjusted upward by about 1.9%* more than the government reported for 1998.

The implications of a 1.9% downward adjustment in the overall inflation rate and a 1.9% upward adjustment in the rates of growth in

## E X H I B I T   7-8

### The GDP Deflator–Digital Deflation Model (1998)

| IT INDUSTRIES | QUALITY ADJUSTED IN GDP DEFLATOR | QUALITY ADJUSTMENT ALREADY IN GDP DEFLATOR (A) | ESTIMATED ANNUAL QUALITY IMPROVEMENT (B) | EQUIVALENT UNMEASURED DIGITAL DEFLATION (FOR GDP DEFLATOR) (B) |
|---|---|---|---|---|
| **Hardware** | | | | |
| Computer and Eqt. | Yes | -0.25% | 34% | -0.19% |
| Semiconductors | Yes | NM | 40 | -0.26 |
| Instruments | No | 0.00 | 20 | -0.06 |
| **Software** | No (C) | -0.02% (C) | 15% | -0.13% |
| **Computer Services** | No | 0.00 | 15 | -0.16 |
| **Communications** | | | | |
| Services (incl. Internet) | No | 0.00 | 2-15 | -0.30 |
| Optical (Longhaul/ Metro) | No | 0.00 | 50/20 | -0.03 |
| Other Commu. Equip. | No (D) | NM (D) | 15 | -0.06 |
| **Total IT** | | -0.27% | | -1.19% |
| **NON-IT** | | | | |
| **INDUSTRIES (SELECTED)** | | | | |
| Healthcare Services | No | 0.00% | 6.0% | -0.33% |
| Depository Instit. | No | 0.00 | 4.0 | -0.13 |
| Pharmaceuticals | No | 0.00 | 7.0 | -0.08 |
| Motor Vehicles (E) | No | 0.00 | 2.5 | -0.06 |
| Aerospace | No | 0.00 | 3.0 | -0.05 |
| Medical Instrum. | No | 0.00 | 7.0 | -0.04 |
| Secur. Brokers | No | 0.00 | 3.0 | -0.04 |
| Defense Procurement | No | 0.00 | 8.0 | -0.02 |
| Household Appl. | No | 0.00 | 3.0 | -0.01 |
| Photographic Equip. | No | 0.00 | 4.0 | -0.01 |
| **Total Non-IT** | | 0.00% | | -0.77% |
| **TOTAL IT AND NON-IT** | | -0.27% | | -1.96% |
| **DIGITAL DEFLATION INDEX FOR 1998** | | | -2.23% | |

( A ) Calculated from Department of Commerce, Bureau of Economic Analysis data (1998 is latest data available for Information Tech breakdown)
( B ) Tanaka Capital Management Inc. estimates
( C ) Bureau of Labor Statistics (BLS) adjusts only prepackaged software by fixed 3.1%/year for quality
( D ) BLS adjusts only voice switches by fixed 5%/ year for quality
( E ) BLS adjusts autos for only the higher cost of the value-added components.

real GDP and productivity are significant. They will be discussed in the remaining chapters of this book.

The GDP Deflator–Digital Deflation model in Exhibit 7-8 shows estimates of how much Digital Deflation has been measured and not measured by the government as of 1998. The two columns on the left show for a variety of IT and non-IT industries whether the government has been measuring quality improvement, and by how much the government is already adjusting the GDP Deflator for quality improvement in computers and for a portion of software. The government was already capturing quality improvement or Digital Deflation in the GDP Deflator for a very significant 0.25% for computers sold as finished goods and a very small 0.02% for prepackaged software. The annual rate of quality improvement was estimated for each IT and non-IT sector shown, and the equivalent estimate of unmeasured Digital Deflation is presented in the column on the far right weighted for its effect on the GDP Deflator.

## COMPUTER AND SEMICONDUCTOR DIGITAL DEFLATION "LOST" AS INTERMEDIATE GOODS

In information technology "hardware" industries, the government is currently only estimating quality or performance improvement for *computers* and *semiconductors*, in the range of 30% to 35% and about 34% per year, respectively. However, much of the benefit to the economy in lowering inflation and boosting productivity is lost in the process of calculating GDP accounts. GDP is intended to measure final goods and services sold in the United States, and the numbers are generally regarded as quite accurate. However, GDP is not intended to measure products and services that are components or parts absorbed into a final product or service sold. If computers and semiconductors are only components of a final sale item, they are called *intermediate goods* and are included in GDP only to the extent they are a cost of producing the final item sold.

Computers installed in commercial and military aircraft or in autos are only counted as a cost item, even if they act as a "digital multiplier" to disproportionately lift the performance of the entire final product. Since GDP Deflators are only applied to final goods sold, as a cost component these intermediate goods computers cannot be quality-adjusted. The GDP Deflators, which the government has so painstakingly developed to track quality improvement for computers and semiconductors, are not being applied to close to 40% of computer value shipped, and they are not being applied to most semiconductors. When the Bureau of Economic Analysis (BEA) multiplies the quality-adjusted deflator index times nominal GDP to convert to real GDP, they are not applying it to computers and semiconductors that are only intermediate components. It is estimated that the counting of unmeasured Digital Deflation from computers sold as intermediate goods would have reduced overall inflation in the United States by 0.19% in 1998. This would have been an additional 0.19% beyond the 0.25% already being counted by the government for computer quality improvement that contributed so importantly to the lower reported inflation and higher reported productivity of the late 1990s.

It is worthwhile to focus on semiconductors because they generate such rapid improvement in performance and are so grossly undercounted. Since very few consumers and businesses buy semiconductors as a final product—generally only as add-on memory—it turns out that the only GDP category that directly captures the improvement in semiconductor performance is in net exports of chips shipped out of the United States. But typically, chip imports are approximately equal to chip exports so net exports of semiconductors are virtually nil. The result is that the huge 41–56% per year gains in semiconductor performance from Moore's Law doubling the number of transistors every 18–24 months is lost as a mere component in the sea of calculations of GDP accounts.

It should be pointed out that indirectly, semiconductor improvement does get picked up to the extent that chips contribute to the performance improvement in computers that are made for final sale. In fact, as computer components, semiconductors are so critical to boosting the performance of computers that they act as "digital performance multipliers," creating far more value in boosting computer performance than the mere cost of the chips themselves. In PCs microprocessor chips enjoy proprietary pricing partly because they drive the improvement in performance of the entire PC, although they represent only one-third the manufacturing costs. In this case, semiconductors act as important digital drivers helping to improve computer performance with each new design cycle.

It is important to realize, however, for the vast numbers of chips used to drive the performance of cars and trucks, military and commercial aircraft, medical instruments, machine tools, power generation equipment, and consumer electronics, these semiconductors are only included as computer component costs. Since these and other non-IT final products and services are not measured for performance or quality improvement, the government can't measure either the direct annual improvement in semiconductor performance or any of the performance lift from semiconductors acting as digital performance multipliers in these large non-IT categories of GDP. This means that the great work being done by the BLS to hedonically measure the annual performance and quality improvement in the semiconductor industry is being diluted as it is not being applied directly to any final products in GDP accounts except through computers made for final sale. The counting of unmeasured Digital Deflation from semiconductors in 1998 would have reduced overall inflation in the United States by an estimated 0.26%, or about as much as the Digital Deflation already being measured from computers made for final sale.

## IT INDUSTRIES NOT YET MEASURED FOR QUALITY IMPROVEMENT, INCLUDING COMPUTER SERVICES, SOFTWARE, AND COMMUNICATIONS

Since computers represent virtually the only final product category of IT that is currently measured for quality gains, that leaves three very large categories of IT that are largely not quality adjusted—computer services, software, and communications. Given the rather high rates of quality improvement for these categories, the potential for under-measurement of performance gains and Digital Deflation is quite large. Significant improvements continue to be made in software and communications equipment, and these are very large and rapidly growing GDP categories. In 2000 they made up 2.3% and 1.9% of GDP, respectively, much larger than the 1.1% for computers made for final sale.

As discussed in the previous chapter, *computer services* should be accorded the same rates of quality improvement as the computer hardware and software being installed or maintained if they are integral to the performance of those products. For example, computer integrated system design and computer processing and data design are integral to the installation and operation of computers and networks. If the computer hardware is being improved by 34% per year, on average so should the performance or value of the computer services performed. For this model, however, computer services were estimated conservatively to improve the quality of services by only 15% per year. On a weighted basis, a 15% per year improvement in computer services would have contributed an estimated 0.16% of additional Digital Deflation to the economy in 1998 had they been measured more properly for quality improvement in these services. It will not be known whether this estimate is in fact too conservative until more research is performed on computer services—and in fact all services that deliver digitally enhanced or generated products.

Despite the existence of such a wide variety of *software* and a wide range of annual performance improvement which varies with the type of software, it appears that there is an overall pattern or law in software whereby the average software package during the course of its product life is improved in "features and functions" by about 15% per year. This estimate was based on a survey of a wide variety of software providers from the largest publicly traded software company to small independents. The range of annual performance improvement, however, was found to be quite wide depending upon the type of software, with the most rapid improvement exhibited by the newest types of software serving the youngest and most dynamic end markets. These included internet security and Web-based database reporting and analytical software tools, which have supported annual improvement in performance or features and functions on the order of 50% to 100% per year.

Interestingly, even the most mature software companies, regardless of age, size, specialty, or whether operating system or application software, could point to annual maintenance-based improvement or "tweaks" of about 10% per year. In addition, there are quantum leaps in performance with each major new revision or "rev"—usually every 2 to 3 years. For example, Scott Cook, Chairman of Intuit, the maker of Quicken and TurboTax, estimates small increases in more mature financial programs, but a tripling of the value to the user of its new tax package that allows Internet downloading of financial data from banks and brokerage firms. The current Microsoft Windows operating system may offer 10 to 20 times better functionality than Windows 1.0, and the latest Office might be 20% to 40% better than the prior version of Office. Software performance is certainly subjective, and admittedly, from user to user "your mileage may vary."

Making estimates of software performance gains from a survey of informed software executives and IT officers may be criticized, but it is a first step in the right direction. The government's current practice is to make very small estimates of quality gains only for one category, prepackaged software, leaving the vast majority of software quality gains uncounted. Making very rough estimates of the quality improvement and Digital Deflation generated by the software industry is considerably more desirable than knowing with 100% certainty that large amounts of software quality improvement are not being measured.

In the future, performance benchmarks should be tailored for each particular type of software, and more formal user-based consumer surveys should be conducted to more accurately estimate quality improvement from the point of view of the ultimate user. Simplifying assumptions will have to be made about how much of a software package's capabilities are utilized by the average consumer from product generation to generation. Different users will use different features. The average mainframe software user will utilize about half of the typical mainframe package, but different users will use different halves. The Key Performance Attributes for software are more difficult to identify and quantify than for computers but not impossible.

There is no doubt that software is creating more quality-based productivity gains and Digital Deflation with each new revision or software product design cycle. The government has been quietly assuming a modest 3.1% fixed annual quality improvement for prepackaged software only. This converts to about 0.02% of Digital Deflation for the overall economy. In sharp contrast, assuming a 15% annual rate of quality improvement for the average software product, software is contributing an additional 0.13% per year of uncounted good deflation in the overall economy.

The communications sector is also estimated to be generating significant amounts of quality improvement annually. As can be seen in Exhibit 7-8, the Digital Deflation model reflects approximately 0.39% of uncounted Digital Deflation from communications in 1998. Much of this estimated contribution was from *communications services*, which represented 82% of the communications sector and 2.5% of the economy. Communications services will have to be adjusted for large amounts of currently uncounted Digital Deflation due to the advent of many brand-new services that are underweighted in the government statistics as well as for very rapid rates of annual quality improvement in some of these services. My estimates for the rate of improvement in performance of communications services varied from 5% for television broadcasting and cable services to 15% for telephone and telegraph communications. The latter may seem high but is bolstered to adjust for rapid rates of annual gains in performance of wireless services and Internet access, content and data transmission services, as well as for rapid growth in new Internet and wireless services.

Even though the government is working on measuring more aspects of the growth in Internet service and content providers, data are currently quite sparse. Fortunately, Statistics Canada, the Canadian counterpart of the DOC and the BLS, has been very active in estimating quality improvement and therefore Digital Deflation in a number of areas including the Internet. One study, "Trends in Internet Access Prices," estimated that the quality-adjusted price index for Internet access declines at about 14% per year in Canada.[6]

How and where in GDP accounts does one value the Internet and the ever-improving content on company and public service Web sites? Surely there is a value for the consumer to be able to shop for a baseball bat by going to sportsauthority.com or to shop for a fax-copier-printer at staples.com for basic shopping information and consumer ratings with a click of a mouse button. For a consumer, even if a purchase is ultimately made at an actual bricks-and-mortar store, how should the government account for the total shopping experience? This "clicks and bricks" shopping pattern is rapidly entering the mainstream of consumer purchasing activity in the American economy. Yet nowhere is the information value of Internet content recognized in GDP accounts—only the provider's cost of building and updating the Web site are recognized. Of course, with no associated value measured, the government would measure these Web site costs as purely inflationary.

The same logic would apply to public service Web sites. How do you measure the value to the consumer of government Web sites offering unprecedented services, such as the renewal of drivers' licenses online, or the posting of school cancellations, or revised T-ball game schedules? There is currently no attempt to associate the true real value to the consumer of these services with the taxes paid by the consumer for these government services, so these Internet services are also only counted as inflationary.

The communications services sector probably most understates the true weightings of rapidly growing and rapidly improving new products and services. This is particularly evident from the perspective of real value and total cost of ownership for the consumer. Much like automobiles in the 1920s and 1930s, people are constantly creating new uses for the Internet—and for their wireless devices. This subset of the service sector may well be one of the most difficult for the government agencies to estimate in terms of both the rates of quality improvement and the size of the industries. How do you count brand-new services that are proliferating new uses faster than you can measure?

*Communications hardware* represents only about 0.5% of the economy but is contributing a disproportionately large amount of Digital Deflation due to the rapid advances being made in electronics and the 100% annual gains being generated in the optical transmission of voice, video, and data. The infrastructure is being built out to carry several orders of magnitude more information at lower costs than the old copper wire landlines and the old cellular networks. While expenditures for fiber optic transmission equipment totaled only about $8.6 billion or 0.1% of GDP in the United States in 1998, the bandwidth for long-haul fiber optic transmission has been doubling every 9 to 12 months, creating 100% improvement in performance per year.

This model assumes only a 50% annual improvement in long-haul optical transmission going forward. When combined with about a 20% improvement in the metro markets, optical technologies are contributing about 0.03% Digital Deflation to the overall economy. Other communications equipment is estimated to contribute about 0.06% Digital Deflation per year to the overall economy based on a conservative 15% per year improvement in various nonoptical communications equipment. A recent Brookings Institute study, "Prices for Local Area Network Equipment" found that when hedonic regressions and matched model analyses were performed on LAN equipment, the quality-adjusted price declines were about 14% per year for routers from 1995 to 1999, 22% per year for switches from 1996 to 2000, 18.3% per year for LAN cards, and 19% per year for hubs.[7] This study clearly supports the existence of large amounts of uncounted Digital Deflation in communications equipment, since the government only counts a very small fixed amount of quality improvement for voice switches that is too small to be meaningful in the GDP Deflator.

## NON-IT INDUSTRIES NOT YET MEASURED FOR QUALITY IMPROVEMENT, INCLUDING HEALTHCARE, FINANCIAL SERVICES, AUTOS, AEROSPACE, AND THE MILITARY

Analysts and economists within the BLS and BEA freely admit that they are not capturing quality improvement in many industries that are not in the information technology sector but that are heavily influenced by advancing digital technologies. The industries most often cited are healthcare products and healthcare services and the service sector in general. Healthcare is by far the most important non-IT area of undermeasured quality improvement, rivaling computers, software, and communications in the generation of Digital Deflation. In reality, semiconductors, software, magnetic storage, digital displays, and other digital drivers are becoming so pervasive throughout the economy that the quality or performance of products or services in almost every industry is benefiting from leveraging these advancing digital technologies.

The few industries most likely to have the largest uncounted quality improvements were selected for this analysis and the Digital Deflation model presented in Exhibit 7-8. However, they only represent about 18% of the economy, no doubt leaving out of the analysis many other non-IT industries that are generating undermeasured quality gains and uncounted Digital Deflation.

As with the IT industries, estimates of annual quality improvement were made by identifying Key Performance Attributes and from informal surveys or analyses of each industry. Surveys and analyses were performed from the point of view of the consumer and were therefore more utilitarian in approach than the typically cost-based approach taken by the government's statistical agencies. A cost-based approach is not able to capture any of the digital performance multiplier or lift that a utilitarian approach at least has a chance to measure. The consumer knows best, and in this Information Age consumers are likely to have a fairly accurate understanding of how much more quality and value they are getting in the latest IT or non-IT services. It is envisioned that over time, the BLS will measure quality improvement in many non-IT products and services that are receiving performance boosts from digital components. These performance boosts will be worth multiples of the often very low incremental cost of the semiconductor or other digital components.

*Healthcare services* are estimated to be contributing the largest amount of uncounted Digital Deflation to the overall economy from the non-IT industries at about 0.33% per year. The rate of unmeasured quality improvement in medical services was estimated to be about 6.0% per year, which implies a doubling of the quality of healthcare services every 12 years. Consideration was given to input from doctors as well as the outright reduction in mortality from diseases. Much work needs to be done in the various areas of medical services, and new models with new indices and Key Performance Attributes will have to be identified and measured. For example, disease indices can be created to measure how treatment alters outcomes, success rates, recovery times, and quality of life.

A CAT scan in 1975 might have taken five minutes, said Dr. Robert Longnecker, a nephrologist affiliated with Stamford Hospital in Stamford, CT. Now, the procedure takes 20 to 30 seconds. The cost is actually cheaper, too, around $400 compared to $800 to $1,000 a quarter of a century ago. The increased speed of the newer CAT scanners means that a machine that costs a million dollars can now do 50 to 100 procedures a day compared to 15 procedures a day 20 to 25 years ago. The increased productivity also provides greater quality treatment for patients. Hospitals now use CAT scanners to diagnose appendicitis, avoiding exploratory surgery. "They're using CAT scanners to stage lymphomas and cancers whereas before they used to open people up and see if they had lymph nodes along the aorta that were full of tumor cells," said Longnecker. "It's the kind of thing that's hard to measure, but these are major advances. People lament the cost of technology but they forget that recovering from that surgery to stage a lymphoma took weeks." Clearly, we need to measure these quality improvements.

Admittedly, healthcare services are very subjective and will prove to be very difficult to measure for quality improvement. Indeed, it may not be easy to arrive at consensus for Key Performance Attributes for healthcare quality. As described by Carol Ben-Maimon, President of Barr Research, Inc., "The problem is that unlike the consumer buying Tide detergent, there are three different parties involved in healthcare: the person receiving the care, the payer or the insurance company, and the doctor or healthcare provider—and the three don't communicate." Analysts at the BLS readily agree that healthcare is the most difficult area to measure for quality. No doubt, there are some aspects of healthcare that are not improving, but the larger service categories are delivering improving quality. In any case, the public would probably be fairly unanimous in its belief that healthcare is the most important non-IT industry for the government to start measuring properly for quality and performance improvement.

This brings up an interesting theoretical question. How much can we improve the quality of care simply by improving the quality of our healthcare data? Dr. Marc Grodman, Chairman of Bio-Reference Labs, has been very active in the area of quality measures. He estimates that "the quality of healthcare has gone up by 5% to 10% per year over the last 10 years." More importantly, he feels that in the future "It should go up at twice that rate if we have better data." Given the aging population in the United States and overseas, there will be even greater demands placed on healthcare services—and an even greater need to get the numbers right on quality improvement in healthcare.

*Pharmaceuticals* have played a very important role in improving healthcare and in reducing mortality. For example, mortality rates for rheumatic fever and rheumatic heart disease declined by 5.5% per year from 1965 to 1996 with the aid of antibiotics. Death rates from ulcers of the stomach and duodenum dropped by 4.0% per year for the same period with the help of H2 blockers and proton pump inhibitors.[8] The chairman of one pharmaceutical company estimates that drugs are three to four times more effective than 15 years ago. This would equate to a 7.6% to 9.7% per year improvement in drug performance. He cites three important reasons that the unmeasured increases in performance of drugs have been huge: (1) Drugs are more effective with greater success rates, (2) drugs have much lower side effects, and (3) people can take their doses when they should, not at awkward times and not by injections, improving patient compliance and producing better outcomes.

Again there is the issue of how you measure quality. Eugene Melnyk, Chairman of Biovail, a specialty pharmaceutical company, feels that "what's most unmeasured is the benefit of applying technology to pharmaceuticals and turning them into products dosed on a once-a-day basis." How do you measure the value of better patient compliance because they only have to take their pills once daily? He points out that "as the population gets older, we will have patients taking more drugs in multiple doses, more often, and it's impossible to expect that every dose, every day will be taken by everyone properly." He cites studies which show that up to 30% of the people on chronic medications don't take their medications properly, especially in the cardiovascular area. He estimates that once-a-day dosing may have doubled or tripled the value of the average medication in the last 10 years.

With consideration given to measurement issues, this Digital Deflation model estimates that the quality improvement from pharmaceuticals is averaging about 7% per year, which implies a doubling in drug performance every 10 years.

*Military* use of information technology to improve effectiveness and accuracy has been extensive. It was very difficult to obtain performance or quality improvement data on the effectiveness of the U.S. military mainly for security reasons. It is obvious, however, that the U.S. Department of Defense has been leveraging the Digital Revolution to improve the performance of weapons and personnel to improve strike capability and reduce casualties. As the Afghanistan conflict appeared to be winding down in December of 2001, Forrest Sawyer did an interesting story for MSNBC called "America's Hi-Tech War." He interviewed a Special Forces staff sergeant who showed him how much information technology has improved over the last few years. Among the items demonstrated were the precision munitions guided system for laser-marking of military targets from up to 10 kilometers, global positioning ostensibly for search and rescue as well as the reduction of losses from "friendly fire," and ruggedized laptops for satellite-linked data communication using digital cameras for live battle scenes.

Make no mistake, the U.S. Armed Forces have been making great strides in benefiting from ongoing advances in technology, many of which the public may not see—until they are put to use. How much has information technology (IT) lifted military performance? Perhaps it was summed up best by the staff sergeant. He was asked, "How much more effective is a soldier than 10 years ago?" Without hesitation, he responded, "He's 100% better, sir!"

If the military has not tried to quantify its performance lift from digital technologies, it should. Whether it is reported to the public is another matter. However, it would be helpful for economists, policymakers, military personnel, and ultimately the voting public to know that the billions of dollars being spent on defense procurement and training is resulting in a tangible lift in performance—as well as a reduction in losses—for our military personnel and for civilians. It would also materially reduce the amount of inflation attributed to government spending and the overall economy.

The Digital Deflation model reflects an estimated 8% per year of annual improvement in the quality or performance for defense procurement. This in fact may be low considering the importance of the lives saved during the Gulf War in the early 1990s and the Afghanistan conflict in 2002. As unbelievable as it sounds, except for higher component costs, current economic data measures zero quality improvement for the category of defense procurement. This category includes stealth aircraft, laser-guided "smart" bombs, infra-red detection, and night vision. As with healthcare, the Defense Department is currently only measured as very inflationary.

Many other non-IT industries are also generating significant amounts of uncounted quality improvement and hence Digital Deflation. Some of the more obvious currently unmeasured contributors to lower inflation and higher productivity in the U.S. economy are listed in Exhibit 7-8. There are clearly other industries omitted from the model that are generating lesser amounts of quality improvement. These omissions serve to make the Digital Deflation thesis even stronger.

The few select non-IT industries included in this model created an estimated 0.77% of uncounted Digital Deflation for the overall economy in 1998. When combined with the 1.19% of uncounted Digital Deflation from IT industries, they produced a total estimated uncounted Digital Deflation of about 1.96% in the U.S. economy in 1998. When the estimated 1.96% of uncounted Digital Deflation is combined with the 0.27% of Digital Deflation that was counted by the government, the Digital Revolution contributed a total of about 2.23% of lower inflation and 2.23% of higher real output and productivity growth to the U.S. economy in 1998. These numbers will only get larger as IT continues to grow faster than the rest of the economy.

## THE QUALITY IMPROVEMENT QUOTIENT

A Quality Improvement Quotient or Quality IQ™ can be calculated for each product or service, and for each division within a company to track growing or shrinking product performance advantages (or disadvantages) versus the competition. Managements should know how their product or service quality improvement is changing over time or from one product design cycle to the next. How else can they measure the return on investment for R&D and capital spending for the rising quality or value of new products relative to returns on spending for increasing the units of output produced per hour? Increasingly, managements will want metrics for gauging whether they are using advancing technologies to be faster, better, and cheaper than the competition.

Exhibit 7-9 presents the Digital Deflation product performance curve with several of the IT and non-IT industries shown for their relative rates of performance improvement and their time to double their performance or quality. All company managements should

Digital Deflation Product Performance Curve

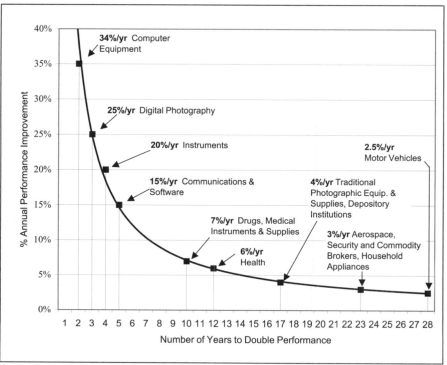

Source: Tanaka Capital Management, Inc.

know where they are on this curve and whether they are sliding down the slippery slope or moving up in performance.

## THE CPI–DIGITAL DEFLATION MODEL

The GDP Deflator–Digital Deflation model described above estimates the undercounted Digital Deflation based on an analysis of both IT and non-IT industries. Economists pay particular attention to the GDP Deflator because it gives a more complete picture of inflation across the whole economy. However, the public and the press understandably focus mostly on the Consumer Price Index as the CPI is intended to reflect how much more the consumer has to pay each year for the same goods and services.

Exhibit 7-10 presents a CPI–Digital Deflation model based on an analysis of the consumer products and services estimated to be generating the most quality improvement and Digital Deflation. As shown, the unmeasured Digital Deflation for the CPI was estimated at 0.98% for the year 2000. In other words, the CPI was overstated by about 0.98%.

It should be pointed out that this 0.98% of unmeasured quality improvement and Digital Deflation estimated in the CPI model is only half of the 2.09% of unmeasured quality improvement and Digital Deflation estimated in the GDP Deflator model for 2000. Why such a big difference? The CPI applies to only the two-thirds of the economy that is represented by consumer spending, so there is a very different mix of products and services in the consumer's market basket. There is a considerably higher proportion of digitally deflating New Economy content in the entire economy (GDP) than in personal consumption expenditures. In essence, proportionately more high-tech equipment and IT services are bought by the corporate sector and the government sector than is spent by individuals on PCs.

Although the CPI appears to require only half the adjustment needed than the GDP Deflator, a 1% overstatement of the CPI is still quite significant. When the government's statistical agencies begin to capture more fully the deflationary effects of quality improvement in consumer goods and services, it will have to make significant reductions in reported inflation for the CPI. Specifically, the CPI for 2000 should be restated closer to 2.4% versus the published CPI report of 3.4%. The core CPI (excluding food and energy) for 2000 should be restated downward from the published rate of 2.4% to closer to 1.4%. Particularly at these low levels of inflation, these are not small changes.

In this first CPI–Digital Deflation model the industries selected for analysis represent only 16.4% of the CPI by weightings. It is important to realize that for most of the categories of the CPI, the BLS does count the increase in quality of products but only to reflect the incremental cost of the addition of a new component or feature to the old product—not for any improvement in quality beyond the cost of the new component. As in the case of the GDP Deflator model, there is little in the way of quality adjustments to deflators for anything but computers and a handful of small consumer electronics goods such as camcorders. Similarly, the product areas with the greatest uncounted Digital Deflation include medical professional services (doctors), hospital services, medical care commodities (drugs), personal computers, cellular service, and new vehicles.

**E X H I B I T   7-10**

## The CPI–Digital Deflation Model for Year 2000

| BLS Industry | Quality Adjustment | Weighting Adjustment | Adjustment To CPI** |
|---|---|---|---|
| Info. Process ex Telephone | | | |
|   Personal Computers | -35.00% | 0.328% | -0.124% |
|   Computer Software | -15.00% | 0.046% | -0.010% |
|   Computer Info. Processing | -30.00% | 0.000% | -0.006% |
|   Other Info. Processing | -30.00% | 0.000% | -0.008% |
| Medical Professional Services | -6.00% | 0.000% | -0.173% |
| Cellular Service | -30.00% | 0.459% | -0.146% |
| New Vehicles | -2.50% | 0.000% | -0.117% |
| Medical Care Commodities | -7.00% | 0.000% | -0.088% |
| Hospital and Related Service | -6.00% | 0.000% | -0.082% |
| Tuition College/HS/Elementary | -5.00% | 0.000% | -0.076% |
| Used Car and Truck | -2.50% | 0.000% | -0.047% |
| Toys | -10.00% | 0.000% | -0.035% |
| Rent & Lease Car and Truck | -2.50% | 0.000% | -0.023% |
| Sporting Goods | -4.00% | 0.000% | -0.018% |
| Financial Services | -4.00% | 0.000% | -0.013% |
| Appliances | -3.00% | 0.000% | -0.010% |
| Photography | -4.00% | 0.000% | -0.010% |
| | | = | -0.985% |
| BLS Reported CPI in 2000 | | | 3.40% |
| Total Adjustment to CPI for Digital Deflation | | | -0.985% |
| CPI Adjusted for Digital Deflation | | = | 2.41% |
| Core CPI (Excluding Food & Energy) | | | 2.40% |
| Total Adjustment to Core CPI | | | -0.985% |
| Core CPI Adjusted for Digital Deflation | | = | 1.41% |

** CPI adjustment reflects quality adjustment times category weightings.

NOTE:  Category weightings not shown.

Source: Tanaka Capital Management, Inc.

Unlike the GDP Deflator–Digital Deflation model, the CPI–Digital Deflation model reflects very significant adjustments to the *weightings* for certain categories, notably cellular service, personal computers and computer software. This is because the BLS is still using the initial weightings for computers and software first calculated in 1982–1984 and weightings for cell phones calculated in 1993–1995. This makes the weightings significantly understated for these relatively fast-growing categories. In addition, due to a quirk in the method of calculation of the CPI, any product category that experiences a reduction in its price index has a directly proportionate reduction in its weighting. For example, since the BLS estimated that personal computers had a quality-adjusted decline in price of 23.2% in 2000, the weighting for PCs actually declined by 23.2% in 2000. The CPI–Digital Deflation model makes appropriate adjustments to recalibrate the weightings for these fast-growing categories.

The estimated annual rates of uncounted quality improvement for CPI product categories reflect the same rates of uncounted improvement in the GDP Deflator model. Again, they are based on informal surveys of consumers and reflect estimates of increases in value as perceived by the consumer as opposed to the cost-based approach currently used by the government.

How does this new CPI–Digital Deflation model compare with the results of the Boskin study of the CPI? The answer is that they are not that different. The February 2000 "Update of the Boskin Commission's Estimate of Bias" estimated a 0.60% overstatement of the CPI attributed to not properly measuring "new products/quality change." This represented virtually no change from what was first pointed out in the initial Boskin report in 1996.

The CPI–Digital Deflation model estimates a higher 0.98% upward bias or overstatement of the CPI due to undercounted quality improvement and underweightings of new and rapidly growing digital products and services. This difference is a result of a different approach taken in the Digital Deflation model than that taken by the four economists on the Boskin panel. The Digital Deflation model reflects changes in real value as perceived by consumers, and the Boskin Commission took the more traditional cost-based approach. Both approaches, however, make strong cases for the BLS to start measuring in earnest the unmeasured quality improvement in consumer products and services.

The Boskin panel's charter was to focus only on the CPI, so it did not address the larger issue of the overstatement of reported inflation for the overall economy. It would be interesting to see what a Boskin Commission analysis of the GDP Deflator would uncover as the overstatement due to new products and quality improvement.

At this point, it should be clear that there are significant amounts of uncounted quality improvement that are not reflected in the government's economic data and that this is resulting in a significant overstatement or upward bias in our inflation data. The two Digital Deflation models represent a first attempt at estimating this uncounted increase in real value being generated by our economy. Because they take a different approach by focusing on the basic underlying digital drivers and estimating the recurring increases in real value to the consumer, it is anticipated that there will be critics. Yet, our government statisticians are already using similar techniques to successfully measure quality improvement for computers made for final sale, so the approach is not unproven and not even revolutionary.

What may be a bit more revolutionary is the idea that it is not just computers that are improving in value with every design cycle, but that there are recurring cycles of improvement in *many* products and services across the entire economy that benefit from rapidly improving digital technologies. The Digital Deflation models merely aggregate these quality improvement benefits to arrive at an estimate of the total magnitude of the mismeasure. The result is a new perspective that shows us that perhaps our data are so fundamentally incomplete that we may be making important policy mistakes.

The conversion of rapid and recurring quality improvement into the economic gift of Digital Deflation can only be associated with a larger, systemic phenomenon like the Digital Revolution. As far out as we can project for this Digital Revolution, these Digital Deflation models can provide a means for translating faster, better, and cheaper products and services into what economists can measure as increasing real value and wealth creation in the future.

# IV. WEALTH MODELS

## HOUSEHOLD TANGIBLE AND NET FINANCIAL ASSETS

One of the great marvels of American households is that over the years, they have been able to adjust or maintain their allocation of net worth according to the outlook for inflation. In times of high or rising inflation you would expect households to hold more tangible assets as an inflation hedge. In times of low or declining inflation they should hold more in financial assets to benefit from declining interest rates and higher stock price–earnings (P/E) ratios. Except for the 1980s, they did so masterfully. The fact that households were able to increase real net worth at all during the highly inflationary 1970s reflected the tendency for households to do the right thing for the times. In the face of soaring inflation, at the margin they accumulated real estate and other tangible assets, which acted as a natural hedge against inflation. In the 1970s, financial assets tended to lose value during a highly inflationary environment, and households were not major net buyers of common stocks or mutual funds.

Individuals will make the right choices if they have the right information, and this applies most assuredly in matters of money and net worth. In the 1950s, 1960s, and 1970s, households allocated their net worth appropriately relative to the outlook for inflation. Only in the 1980s did households err by holding a disproportionately high percent of net worth in tangible assets fearing a return of hyperinflation.

The household allocation of net worth between tangible assets and financial assets relative to inflation was revealed in a study which I published in 1983. It showed that there was in fact a very high correlation (0.84) between the CPI and the percent of net worth that households held in either tangible assets or in net financial assets (financial assets such as stocks, bonds, and money market funds minus liabilities such as mortgages and auto loans).[9] That study predicted that household ownership of financial assets minus liabilities would surge in the 1980s along with a forecasted decline in inflation. This net worth allocation thesis was consistent with the Demographic Theory's prediction of a secular decline in inflation and a once-a-generation bull market in stocks, both of which did in fact begin in 1982.

No doubt, some of the correlation between tangible and net financial assets as a percent of net worth versus inflation was related to the direct effect of inflation on the valuation and pricing of tangible and financial assets. Nevertheless, for decades households allocated their net worth as they saw fit given the outlook for inflation. This all changed in the 1980s and early 1990s.

Although inflation did peak in 1982 and came down rather precipitously during the late 1980s, fearing a return of sky-high inflation,

### EXHIBIT 7-11

Tangible and Net Financial Assets as a Percentage of Net Worth vs. CPI Model

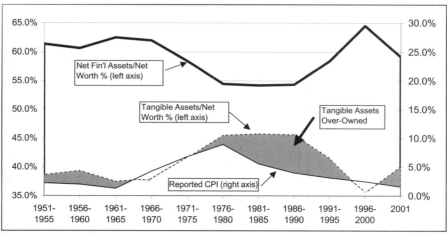

Sources: Department of Commerce; Tanaka Capital Management, Inc.

households stubbornly persisted in allocating more to tangible assets than the Tangible–Net Financial Asset Model predicted. This can be seen in Exhibit 7-11. The overholding of tangible assets lasted until the mid-1990s, when households finally began to accept that inflation might not return to double-digit levels. In other words, purely from the perspective of the average household's tendency to own tangible versus net financial assets, the stock market was primed for appreciation entering the 1990s. This was because American households entered the 1990s still so pessimistic about inflation from their 1970s and early 1980s experience that they overowned tangible assets and underowned net financial assets even before going into another decade of declining inflation in the 1990s.

During the 1990s, however, households readjusted their asset allocations, buying more financial assets and reducing liabilities as a percent of net worth. Coupled with the significant appreciation in the stock and bond markets, American households invested more in common stocks and very quickly brought their net financial asset allocations up to where they should have been relative to reported inflation of 2.5% on average for the CPI in the late 1990s. This can be seen on the right side of Exhibit 7-11, where the 5-year average of net financial assets moved up to about 65% of net worth. This was right in line with the 1983 Tangible–Net Financial Asset model, which implied households should hold net financial assets equal to 65.3% of net worth—consistent with the CPI at a 5-year average of 2.5% in the 1996–2000 time period. (The 1983 model was utilized to exclude distortions from the consistently excessive inflation expectations in the 1980s and early 1990s.)

It is interesting that even near the peak of the stock market at the end of 1999, household allocations to net financial assets as a percent of net worth rose to only 67.2% (individual years are shown in the table in Appendix B—Household Tangible, Financial and Equity-like Assets and Net Worth). This was only modestly above the 65.6% level suggested by the 1983 Tangible–Net Financial Asset model relative to the CPI reported for that year of 2.2%. This meant that based on the fairly low inflation rate of 2.2% in 1999, households had only overowned net financial assets by 1.6% of net worth. Said another way, households only overheld stocks, bonds, and other financial assets by 1.6%, even after the bull market of the 1990s.

What about adjusting for uncounted Digital Deflation? If the CPI is adjusted downward for the approximately 0.94% of uncounted Digital Deflation in 1999, the adjusted CPI would have been 1.2%. The model would imply that households *should* have owned 66.5% in net financial assets as a percent of net worth. But even at the peak of the 1990s' stock market boom, American households still only held 67.2% in net financial assets (net of their liabilities), or just 0.7% more than they should have held relative to this more accurate portrayal of inflation.

At the end of 2001, following two years of stock market declines and rising home prices, American households held only 59.2% of their net worth in net financial assets, with tangible assets rising to 40.1% of net worth from 32.8% at the end of 1999. With inflation weighing in at only 1.6% for 2001, this implied that households were *under*holding net financial assets by a whopping 7.0% versus the 66.2% they should have held to be consistent with the reported CPI of only 1.6%. Adjusting the CPI to exclude the 13% decline in energy prices by using the core CPI of 2.7%, but also adjusting the CPI for an estimated 1.0% of uncounted Digital Deflation would produce an adjusted core CPI of 1.7% for 2001. With this more accurate CPI of 1.7%, the 1983 Tangible and Net Financial Asset model suggests that households should have held about 66.1% of net worth rather than the 59.2% they actually held in net financial assets. This would imply that entering 2002, American households underowned financial assets by more than $2.7 trillion relative to inflation both reported and as adjusted for uncounted Digital Deflation.

Because the Digital Revolution and Digital Deflation are imposing such dramatic change on the economy, like many of the other old models, it may be that the old historical relationship between the CPI and how households allocate their wealth to tangible and net financial assets will not hold up. It may be one of many models that worked well in the Old Economy but may lose its predictive ability and needs to be revised for a rapidly growing New Economy.

Nevertheless, over the next 20 years, households will likely hold an increasingly higher percent of net worth in common stocks and other net financial assets. This will be a natural result of an aging population choosing to own more liquid financial assets, as well as a continued decline in inflation. Low inflation will cause households to shift asset preferences from tangible to net financial assets—much as we saw in the late 1980s and 1990s.

In addition, as will be shown in the next two chapters, common stocks should generate superior returns as Digital Deflation's dual benefits of strong real earnings growth and declining inflation become even greater in a rapidly growing New Economy.

## THE WEALTH EFFECT

In a July 1999 study, "How Important Is the Stock Market Effect on Consumption?" economists at the Federal Reserve Bank of New York concluded: "It appears that we have a way to go before we can make inferences about movements in consumption based on movements in the stock market." In September 2000, a prominent Wall Street economist reported from a survey that "88% of all Americans and 90% of investing Americans say that changes in the stock market over the past year have had no effect on their spending levels."[10] In early 2001, economists at another leading Wall Street brokerage firm estimated that the rise in household net worth contributed more than 1% to the growth in GDP per year from 1995 to 2000, while the savings rate declined. Interestingly, to a large degree they were all correct.

## THE CONSUMER WEALTH EFFECT

As with anything behavioral, the "wealth effect" is not the same for all people, and it is not the same for all seasons. Exhibit 7-12 shows in the

**E X H I B I T  7-12**

Investor-Consumer Wealth Effect

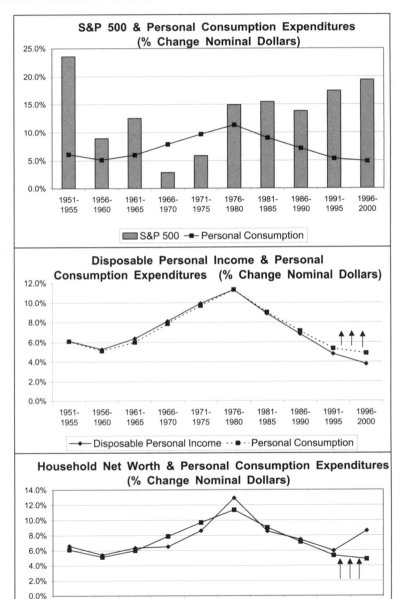

top graph how over the last 50 years there appeared to have been no
clear relationship between average returns on common stocks and increases in consumer spending. However, a deeper analysis of the data
over long time periods reveals that at certain times, the increase or decrease in the stock market had stronger or weaker effects on consumer
spending. The middle graph shows how American consumers increased their spending in lockstep with the growth in disposable personal income for over 40 years—until the 1990s when spending grew
faster than incomes.

The bottom graph provides a fairly clear explanation. It shows
how consumer spending also grew at rates very similar to the growth
in household net worth—again until the 1990s. This was when the
New Economy took hold, producing more real growth while at the
same time generating more productivity and Digital Deflation to offset inflation in the Old Economy. This was when the stock market
started its extended meteoric rise, boosting net worth for *Investor-Consumers*—those consumers with common stock portfolios or mutual
funds—increasing their propensity to consume and accelerating overall spending to grow faster than disposable income. Although not
every Investor-Consumer boosted his or her spending due to the rise
in stock prices, and although some obviously increased their spending more than others, the net effect was for the rising stock market to
boost overall spending beyond historical relationships with income
growth.

Exhibit 7-13 presents two additional methods for modeling the
wealth effect on consumer spending. The left two columns show how
consumer spending (personal consumption expenditures) averaged a
fairly steady 89.1% of disposable personal income from 1950 to 1995,
but then jumped to 93.6% of income in the 1996–2000 period. Similarly, consumer spending averaged a fairly steady 18.5% of net worth
from 1950 to 1995, but then *declined* to 15.8% in the 1996–2000 period.
It is obvious that the late 1990s' surge in stock portfolios and net
worth elevated consumer spending to levels that exceeded the historical norm versus levels of disposable personal income.

Likewise, it is quite apparent that consumer spending grew significantly slower than the rate of growth in net worth, as Investor-
Consumers did not convert all of their market winnings into higher
spending. In other words, American Investor-Consumers are apparently more conservative and less irrational than many seem to believe. If they benefit from increases in the stock market and rising net

## Consumer Capital Gains Wealth Effect

| | Consumer Spending | | Capital Gains Wealth Effect | | | |
|---|---|---|---|---|---|---|
| | % of Disposable Personal Income | % of Household Net Worth | S-T & L-T Realized Capital Gains ($ Mil.) (a) | Average Effective Cap Gains Tax Rate | Realized Gains as % of Disposable Personal Income | Disposable Personal Income ($ Bil.) |
| 1950 | 91.5% | 18.5% | N/A | N/A | N/A | 211 |
| 1951 | 90.2% | 18.2% | N/A | N/A | N/A | 231 |
| 1952 | 90.2% | 18.4% | N/A | N/A | N/A | 244 |
| 1953 | 90.2% | 19.0% | N/A | N/A | N/A | 259 |
| 1954 | 90.9% | 18.2% | 7,157 | 14.1% | 2.7% | 265 |
| 1955 | 91.4% | 18.0% | 9,881 | 14.8% | 3.5% | 283 |
| 1956 | 89.8% | 17.7% | 9,683 | 14.5% | 3.2% | 303 |
| 1957 | 89.7% | 18.3% | 8,110 | 13.7% | 2.5% | 320 |
| 1958 | 89.7% | 17.3% | 9,440 | 13.9% | 2.9% | 331 |
| 1959 | 90.6% | 17.7% | 13,137 | 14.6% | 3.7% | 351 |
| 1960 | 90.7% | 17.8% | 11,747 | 14.4% | 3.2% | 366 |
| 1961 | 89.6% | 16.9% | 16,001 | 15.5% | 4.2% | 382 |
| 1962 | 89.7% | 17.5% | 13,451 | 14.5% | 3.3% | 406 |
| 1963 | 90.0% | 17.5% | 14,579 | 14.7% | 3.4% | 426 |
| 1964 | 88.9% | 17.5% | 17,431 | 14.2% | 3.8% | 463 |
| 1965 | 89.1% | 17.5% | 21,484 | 14.0% | 4.3% | 499 |
| 1966 | 89.4% | 18.5% | 21,348 | 13.6% | 4.0% | 539 |
| 1967 | 88.3% | 17.5% | 27,535 | 14.9% | 4.8% | 576 |
| 1968 | 89.2% | 17.1% | 35,607 | 16.7% | 5.7% | 626 |
| 1969 | 89.7% | 18.3% | 31,439 | 16.8% | 4.7% | 675 |
| 1970 | 88.1% | 18.7% | 20,848 | 15.2% | 2.8% | 737 |
| 1971 | 87.6% | 18.3% | 28,341 | 15.3% | 3.5% | 802 |
| 1972 | 88.7% | 17.6% | 35,869 | 15.9% | 4.1% | 869 |
| 1973 | 87.1% | 18.7% | 35,757 | 15.0% | 3.7% | 979 |
| 1974 | 87.0% | 20.4% | 30,217 | 14.1% | 2.8% | 1,072 |
| 1975 | 87.2% | 19.8% | 30,903 | 14.7% | 2.6% | 1,181 |
| 1976 | 88.5% | 19.6% | 39,492 | 16.8% | 3.0% | 1,300 |
| 1977 | 89.0% | 20.0% | 45,338 | 18.2% | 3.2% | 1,436 |
| 1978 | 88.6% | 19.8% | 50,526 | 18.0% | 3.1% | 1,615 |
| 1979 | 88.3% | 19.2% | 73,443 | 16.0% | 4.1% | 1,808 |
| 1980 | 87.3% | 18.5% | 74,132 | 16.8% | 3.7% | 2,020 |
| 1981 | 86.5% | 18.9% | 80,938 | 15.9% | 3.6% | 2,248 |
| 1982 | 86.4% | 18.8% | 90,153 | 14.3% | 3.7% | 2,407 |
| 1983 | 88.4% | 19.1% | 122,773 | 15.2% | 4.7% | 2,586 |
| 1984 | 86.5% | 19.5% | 140,500 | 15.3% | 4.9% | 2,888 |
| 1985 | 87.9% | 18.9% | 171,985 | 15.4% | 5.6% | 3,087 |
| 1986 | 88.7% | 18.3% | 327,725 | 16.1% | 10.0% | 3,263 |
| 1987 | 89.8% | 18.5% | 148,449 | 22.7% | 4.3% | 3,459 |
| 1988 | 89.5% | 18.3% | 162,592 | 23.9% | 4.3% | 3,752 |
| 1989 | 89.6% | 17.8% | 154,040 | 22.9% | 3.8% | 4,016 |
| 1990 | 89.2% | 18.7% | 123,783 | 22.5% | 2.9% | 4,294 |
| 1991 | 88.7% | 18.1% | 111,592 | 22.3% | 2.5% | 4,475 |
| 1992 | 88.5% | 18.5% | 126,692 | 22.9% | 2.7% | 4,755 |
| 1993 | 90.3% | 18.6% | 152,259 | 23.7% | 3.1% | 4,935 |
| 1994 | 91.3% | 19.2% | 152,727 | 23.7% | 3.0% | 5,165 |
| 1995 | 91.6% | 18.2% | 180,130 | 24.6% | 3.3% | 5,423 |
| 1996 | 92.2% | 17.5% | 260,696 | 25.5% | 4.6% | 5,678 |
| 1997 | 92.3% | 16.4% | 364,829 | 21.7% | 6.1% | 5,983 |
| 1998 | 93.0% | 15.8% | 455,223 | 19.6% | 7.2% | 6,286 |
| 1999 | 94.2% | 14.9% | 555,000 (E) | N/A | 8.4% (E) | 6,640 |
| 2000 | 96.7% | 15.3% | 652,000 (E) | N/A | 10.0% (E) | 6,511 |

(E) = Estimated

Sources: (a) Department of the Treasury; Federal Reserve; Tanaka Capital Management, Inc.

worth even over a several-year period, they are likely to spend only a bit more on consumer purchases and to salt away most of their gains. In fact, a study by economists at the Federal Reserve estimated that during the 1992–2000 stock market boom, Americans tended to spend only $3.25 to $5.00 for every $100 increase in net worth, depending on their level of income and education.[11]

## THE REALIZED CAPITAL GAINS WEALTH EFFECT

While the classical approach to measuring the wealth effect is to analyze changes in spending versus income and net worth, some Investor-Consumers may not think in those terms. Many people will only spend what they feel they earned, so an analysis was performed on actual realized capital gains. The data are presented in the right three columns in Exhibit 7-13. Not surprisingly, it was found that consumer spending rose significantly as a percent of disposable personal income in the mid 1980s and late 1990s, exactly when realized capital gains soared as a percent of disposable personal income.

In addition, as might be expected, consumer spending as a percent of disposable personal income *declined* in the early 1970s during exactly the same period when realized capital gains declined. This clearly demonstrates the existence of a *reverse wealth effect* where investor-consumers reduce their rate of spending as a percentage of disposable income as their common stock portfolios decline or fail to meet expectations and as they realize lower capital gains.

It is fairly clear that in periods of rising or falling stock prices there will be an increase or decrease in realized capital gains. Historically, in the United States, realized capital gains have reached as high as 10.0% of disposable personal income in 1986 and again in 2000, and as low as 2.6% of disposable income in 1975. These kinds of swings would naturally act as a stimulant or depressant on consumer spending. It also appears that the wealth effect is cumulative and that several years of a rising stock market and rising net worth will tend to provide a greater lift to consumer spending than if the stock market rose for just 1 or 2 years. There is clearly opportunity for much more work to be done in modeling and understanding the consumer wealth effect.

## THE CORPORATE WEALTH EFFECT

While there has been much discussion and debate about the existence of a wealth effect for consumers, surprisingly, there has been little if anything mentioned about the existence of a "corporate wealth effect." Rising or falling stock prices also affect corporate spending. Higher stock prices are critical for providing equity capital to finance future capacity expansion and to fund new ventures. Equity capital is the lifeblood of the New Economy.

Fast-growing companies will need to raise capital if their capital requirements are growing faster than their ability to generate cash flow internally. This kind of risk or growth-based capital is not always available in the debt markets or from banks. Growth capital often has to come from common stock investors via initial public offerings and secondary offerings. Falling stock prices and restricted access to equity capital will result in a slowing in the rate of capacity expansion and new product development. It would also lead to a slowing in IT capital spending and the creation of less Digital Deflation and productivity, as seen in 2001–2002.

The top graph in Exhibit 7-14 shows corporate sector capital spending on information technology and total capital spending as a percent of corporate cash flow. After leveling off at about 30% and 70% of cash flow, respectively, in the 1980s and early 1990s, IT capital expenditures and total capital expenditures took off in the late 1990s. The bottom graph shows how the stock market rose at a much faster rate than capital spending, providing the opportunity for most corporations in the late 1990s to raise equity capital, improve their balance sheets, and make the necessary capital expenditures to make their systems Y2K compliant.

In a manner very analogous to the consumer who spends a part of his or her increase in net worth, companies in the late 1990s were able to improve their balance sheets to supplement their growth in cash flow. The result was a rise in capital spending above and beyond their growth in cash flow. Much of the capital spending surge, of course, was for new computers and software in advance of Y2K. But it was clear that there was a "corporate wealth effect" that was an important contributor to capital spending trends in the 1990s. The reverse corporate wealth effect goes a long way toward explaining the sudden drop in corporate capital spending in 2000 to 2002, in sync with the stock market decline.

## EXHIBIT 7-14

Stock Market Fuels Corporate Capital Spending

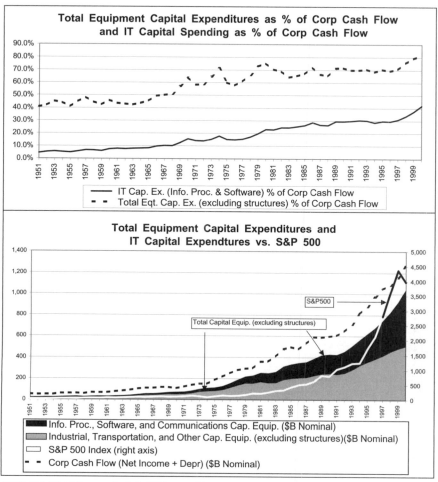

Sources: Department of Commerce; Tanaka Capital Management, Inc.

Just as with consumers, corporations also generate realized capital gains, and the swings from year to year can be very significant. Exhibit 7-15 shows that in 1997, the latest year that the data are available, corporate net capital gains swelled to a very large 19.2% of corporate cash flow, up from an average of 11.4% the prior 20 years. The table shows how beginning in 1980, for the first time ever, IT capital expenditures jumped up to exceed 20% of corporate cash flow at exactly the

EXHIBIT 7-15

## Corporate Capital Gains Wealth Effect

| | Corp Cash Flow (Net Income + Depr) ($B Nominal) | IT Cap. Ex. (Info. Proc. & Software) % of Corp Cash Flow | Total Eqt. Cap. Ex. (excluding structures) % of Corp Cash Flow | Corporate Net Capital Gains ($ Bil.) | Corporate Net Cap. Gains as % of Cash Flow |
|---|---|---|---|---|---|
| 1950 | 43 | 4.3% | 41.5% | 1.0 | 2.3% |
| 1951 | 49 | 4.4% | 40.7% | 1.1 | 2.3% |
| 1952 | 47 | 5.2% | 42.0% | 1.1 | 2.3% |
| 1953 | 48 | 5.6% | 45.1% | 0.8 | 1.7% |
| 1954 | 47 | 5.2% | 44.0% | 1.8 | 3.8% |
| 1955 | 58 | 4.8% | 41.0% | 1.7 | 2.9% |
| 1956 | 59 | 5.7% | 44.9% | 1.7 | 2.9% |
| 1957 | 60 | 6.7% | 47.9% | 1.6 | 2.7% |
| 1958 | 56 | 6.5% | 44.5% | 2.8 | 5.0% |
| 1959 | 67 | 6.0% | 42.5% | 1.8 | 2.7% |
| 1960 | 65 | 7.4% | 45.7% | 2.6 | 4.0% |
| 1961 | 67 | 7.8% | 43.6% | 4.0 | 6.0% |
| 1962 | 75 | 7.6% | 43.0% | 3.4 | 4.5% |
| 1963 | 82 | 7.9% | 42.5% | 3.6 | 4.4% |
| 1964 | 90 | 8.1% | 43.7% | 3.9 | 4.3% |
| 1965 | 102 | 8.3% | 45.5% | 5.2 | 5.1% |
| 1966 | 110 | 9.7% | 49.3% | 5.4 | 4.9% |
| 1967 | 110 | 10.2% | 50.0% | 7.5 | 6.8% |
| 1968 | 118 | 10.1% | 50.7% | 8.9 | 7.5% |
| 1969 | 117 | 12.5% | 57.0% | 7.8 | 6.6% |
| 1970 | 108 | 15.5% | 63.7% | 5.2 | 4.8% |
| 1971 | 123 | 14.1% | 58.1% | 7.4 | 6.0% |
| 1972 | 140 | 13.9% | 58.5% | 10.1 | 7.2% |
| 1973 | 152 | 15.2% | 64.7% | 9.5 | 6.3% |
| 1974 | 151 | 17.7% | 71.4% | 7.7 | 5.1% |
| 1975 | 188 | 15.1% | 59.9% | 8.9 | 4.7% |
| 1976 | 219 | 14.8% | 57.8% | 10.6 | 4.8% |
| 1977 | 252 | 15.3% | 61.1% | 14.0 | 5.5% |
| 1978 | 283 | 17.1% | 66.1% | 16.7 | 5.9% |
| 1979 | 297 | 19.7% | 73.0% | 21.0 | 7.1% |
| 1980 | 302 | 23.0% | 75.2% | 27.1 | 9.0% |
| 1981 | 360 | 22.9% | 70.4% | 28.8 | 8.0% |
| 1982 | 363 | 24.5% | 68.9% | 29.1 | 8.0% |
| 1983 | 411 | 24.5% | 64.3% | 42.0 | 10.2% |
| 1984 | 480 | 25.3% | 65.5% | 46.7 | 9.7% |
| 1985 | 498 | 26.3% | 67.2% | 75.2 | 15.1% |
| 1986 | 481 | 28.6% | 72.1% | 124.0 | 25.8% |
| 1987 | 532 | 26.7% | 66.7% | 82.9 | 15.6% |
| 1988 | 591 | 26.4% | 65.5% | 80.1 | 13.6% |
| 1989 | 587 | 29.5% | 71.6% | 82.9 | 14.1% |
| 1990 | 597 | 29.5% | 71.7% | 62.8 | 10.5% |
| 1991 | 608 | 29.8% | 70.0% | 62.2 | 10.2% |
| 1992 | 648 | 30.5% | 70.0% | 70.9 | 10.9% |
| 1993 | 712 | 30.2% | 70.7% | 90.8 | 12.8% |
| 1994 | 817 | 28.6% | 68.7% | 71.0 | 8.7% |
| 1995 | 880 | 29.8% | 70.5% | 115.5 | 13.1% |
| 1996 | 972 | 29.6% | 69.4% | 132.9 | 13.7% |
| 1997 | 1,049 | 31.0% | 70.9% | 201.1 | 19.2% |
| 1998 | 1,087 | 33.8% | 75.8% | N/A | N/A |
| 1999 | 1,158 | 37.4% | 79.2% | N/A | N/A |
| 2000 | 1,270 | 41.9% | 81.6% | N/A | N/A |

Sources: Department of Commerce; Bureau of Economic Analysis; Tanaka Capital Management, Inc.

same time that corporate net capital gains surged for the first time ever to 9% of cash flow. Clearly, more work can be done on the analysis of the sources of realized capital gains and the wealth effect for the corporate sector.

Given the rising importance of equity capital for IT capital spending and new product development in both the New Economy and the Old Economy, policymakers, investors, and corporate managements should have a better understanding of the corporate wealth effect and its effect on the overall economy.

It should be abundantly clear that there is a wealth effect—and a reverse wealth effect, both for consumers and for the corporate sector. Consumers will alter their spending habits up or down, based on increases or decreases in the stock market and net worth. So will corporate top managements as they make their capital spending plans. It is also evident that the wealth effect is getting a boost from a unique New Economy that is leveraging Digital Deflation and rising productivity gains to generate growth in economic activity, higher corporate profitability, lower inflation, and rising asset values. At the same time, in a rising stock market, the wealth effect also contributes to the economy by providing the mechanism by which consumers and corporations can convert enriched balance sheets into above-average spending—which itself provides for future growth.

This wealth effect can be a "virtuous circle," one of many resulting from the Digital Revolution. However, it raises at least as many questions as it answers, particularly in regard to how to manage monetary and fiscal policy. No doubt, there are other new forces on the economy relating to the Digital Revolution and its effect on the New Economy; but demographics, productivity growth, Digital Deflation, and the wealth effect are four of the more important phenomena to understand. All four are already significantly altering how the economy can be managed, and all four will determine who will benefit the most in the upcoming new era of prosperity.

## NOTES

1. "Digital Economy 2000," David Henry, et al., Department of Commerce, June 2000.

2. "Productivity and Profitability," Graham Y. Tanaka, February 1983.

3. "The Resurgence of Growth in the Late 1990's: Is Information Technology the Story?" Stephen D. Oliner and Daniel E. Sichel, Federal Reserve Board, February, March and May 2000.

4. "Contribution of IT and Software Capital Spending to Output and Productivity," Graham Y. Tanaka, Tanaka Capital Management, Inc., 2000.

5. "The Emerging Digital Economy," David Henry, et al., Department of Commerce, 1998.

6. "Trends in Internet Access Prices," Marc Prud'homme and Kam Yu, Statistics Canada, February 2001.

7. "Prices for Local Area Network Equipment," Mark Doms and Christopher Forman, Brookings Institute, February 23, 2001.

8. "The Pharmaceutical Industry Profile 2000," Pharmaceutical Research and Manufacturers of America (PhRMA), 2000.

9. "Disinflation, Consumer Spending, and a Healthy Surge in Financial Assets," Graham Y. Tanaka, May 1983.

10. "More Affluent Than Ever: The American Age of Affluence Continues," Edward Kerschner, Paine Weber, September 8, 2000.

11. "Disentangling the Wealth Effect: A Cohort Analysis of Household Saving In the 1990's," Dean M. Maki and Michael Palumbo, Federal Reserve, April 2001.

# 8

**C H A P T E R**

# The Wealth in Our Future

I've been rich and I've been poor. Rich is better.
*Sophie Tucker, actress (1884–1966)*

*Over the next 10 to 20 years, Digital Deflation will deliver the dual benefits of near-zero inflation and strong real economic growth simultaneously. For investors, corporate managers, and the public at large, the potential is there for the greatest creation of wealth in the history of mankind.*

## THE 2020 VISION

By helping to produce more real growth in the economy while at the same time reducing inflation to near zero, the Digital Revolution and Digital Deflation offer the prospect of creating enormous wealth in the United States over the next two decades. This scenario can be achieved as New Economy Companies utilize new technologies to continuously improve product and service quality, delivering more value to the consumer and the corporate buyer. As more of this increase in quality or value is counted by the government and converted into the equivalent of price reductions, the result will be a decline in reported inflation, an equal rise in reported real output and productivity, and an important opportunity for monetary and fiscal policies to pursue faster economic growth.

In concert with strong real growth and low inflation, interest rates will decline and common stock valuations will rise in the United States, creating the potential for individuals and corporations to produce and accumulate more wealth than in any other 20-year period in

American economic history. With more Americans owning common stocks directly or through retirement plans and other equity-like assets, household net worth will grow and balance sheets will get more liquid just as the Baby Boomers will be starting to look to those savings for retirement. Society as a whole will benefit as real wages rise, unemployment reaches record lows, and crime rates move into a secular decline.

In the corporate sector, smart managers will fortify balance sheets by taking advantage of higher stock valuations and lower interest rates. In the public sector, governments at the federal, state, and local levels should return to the mode of generating budget surpluses and reducing tax rates as both income and real estate–based tax revenues rise and social expenditures decline as a percent of gross domestic product (GDP). There will be a window of opportunity to fund the looming Social Security requirements of the Baby Boom generation, arguably the greatest fiscal, social, and political challenge facing America in the next 20 to 30 years.

All of the above trends will act collectively to create the potential for an enormous increase in wealth in both real dollars and in percentage terms. Over the next two decades, the Digital Revolution will go global, creating more wealth for countries encouraging corporate investment in information technology to drive quality improvement, productivity gains, low inflation, and increasing wealth for investors in a growing New Economy worldwide.

Early in the book it was explained how the recurring creative forces of rapidly advancing digital technologies have contributed to improving the quality and performance of products and services across the U.S. economy and how these cycles are likely to continue well into the future. To help solve the mystery of the New Economy and help define and measure it, old economic models were tweaked and new models were presented. This chapter will utilize these models to predict how the Digital Deflation phenomenon can translate into powerful economic forces of declining inflation and rising productivity to create wealth in the next 20 years.

Rising valuations on common stocks and other equity-like assets will boost the wealth of individuals and at the same time help to strengthen the balance sheets of America's corporate sector. Through a growing consumer wealth effect, rising stock prices will in turn enhance the ability of American Investor-Consumers to buy more New Economy products and services—and Old Economy products as well.

In an almost Zen-like balance matching the growth in supply with the growth in demand, the declining cost of capital and the corporate wealth effect will provide corporate America with the necessary capital to fund the development and production of future generations of faster, better, cheaper products and services to match the consumer's growing appetite.

It should come as no surprise that the two most important economic variables that will determine how much wealth will be created over the next two decades will be the rate of inflation and the rate of growth in productivity. It will be seen that due to Digital Deflation's unique mechanism of action, both will improve with productivity growth going to new highs and the rate of inflation to new lows.

## A WIDE RANGE OF POSSIBLE OUTCOMES

The range of possible scenarios for real economic growth and wealth creation over the next several years is surprisingly wide, which is both exciting and daunting at the same time. Not surprisingly, the analysis shows that the 1990s' boom left the U.S. economy and stock markets in a potentially precarious position. By exiting the decade with historically very low inflation, very low interest rates, record high price–earnings (P/E) ratios and record high household percentage holdings in common stock, the 1990s' economy created a very hard act to follow in terms of wealth creation. More importantly, if all of the above indicators merely return to historical average levels during the next 10 years, it would mean a turn toward mediocre returns for investors and very little generation of new real wealth.

Over the next decade, for the stock market to produce anywhere near the 1980s' or 1990s' rates of return and wealth creation, P/E ratios will have to expand to significantly higher levels than the 22 to 24 times earnings at the end of the last decade. This means that inflation will have to move significantly lower than the already low 1.2% to 2.3% range on the GDP Deflator in recent years. Similarly, interest rates will have to move significantly lower than the 4% to 5% area on 10-year Treasuries. It would be a tough act to perform indeed. Unless inflation can move significantly lower, the potential for the Digital Revolution to repeat the 1990s' creation of wealth will be just a dream.

Ironically, the good news is that because the government has not yet started to measure quality improvement in so many products and services across the economy, there remains tremendous potential to count more Digital Deflation and to make significant downward adjustments for reported inflation in the current decade. These downward adjustments can range from 2 percentage points currently on the GDP Deflator to almost 3% by 2010 and almost 4% by 2020. There is a lot of work for the government to do as it is only measuring approximately 0.30% per year of quality-based Digital Deflation today.

Before we explore just how much wealth can be generated by the Digital Revolution and the growing New Economy, it would be important to first examine for the next two decades: (1) how much value will be created annually from quality improvement in the New Economy, (2) how to measure and link value and wealth creation in the New Economy, (3) the favorable demographic foundation for the New Economy, (4) how Digital Deflation will create wealth, and (5) how to properly adjust the GDP Deflator and the CPI for Digital Deflation.

## VALUE CREATED FROM DIGITALLY DRIVEN QUALITY IMPROVEMENT

One of the basic economic underpinnings of the Theory of Digital Deflation is that digital technologies are creating more value in the output of goods and services than the government is measuring and that this value creation is generating wealth in the process. The debate can be never-ending over how much wealth can be created or how much wealth should be created for a particular action or in a particular period of time. However, few people will begrudge the person or the company that is able to make a fortune by coming up with the "Next Big Thing" that everyone wants to buy. Few people will begrudge the thousands of millionaires created among the employees and investors in Microsoft for the delivery of value-added software to computer users with every new design cycle.

It's a simple combination of psychology and incentive-based economics. If you deliver something of perceived value to someone, you should be rewarded by some measurable increase in wealth. The problems come up when value is delivered and little or no wealth is generated as a reward, or if wealth is created with little or no delivery of perceived value to the consumer. These latter two cases are inherently unstable, which brings us to the burning issue of whether the massive wealth creation in the 1990s was justified and therefore will or will not be "given back" over the next few years.

Based on the economic statistics reported by the government, some economists and investment strategists have become a little queasy about record-high stock market valuations and justifiably so. However, if the economic reports are adjusted to reflect the true value of goods and services being delivered to the buyers of ever-improving PCS, cell phones, digital cameras, pharmaceuticals, and other goods and services, stock market valuations and the resulting wealth creation don't look so irrational. In fact, common stock and bond valuations look quite cheap if the inflation and productivity numbers are adjusted properly for uncounted Digital Deflation. With these adjustments, throughout most of the 1990s, stock market valuations for the Dow Jones and the S&P 500 averages were justified.

The Internet Bubble at the end of the decade, however, was a different matter. In the 1999–2001 period, dot-com and telecom companies were valued at ridiculous P/E ratios, and many of these companies could not even show the prospect of profitability anytime soon. In many cases, wealth was created with the delivery of little or no real value to the consumer—it was an inherently unstable situation.

In the process of generating wealth, value has to be created somewhere nearby. The Theory of Digital Deflation provides a fairly simple and convenient methodology for estimating the amount of value being created each year from product performance and quality-based improvement produced annually by the Digital Revolution. The numbers are large but not surprising. The economic value can be determined by adding up the price-adjusted improvement in performance and quality of both products and services across the economy due to digital technologies.

For example, it was shown in Chapter 7 that in 1998, the U.S. Government was already measuring and counting 0.27% of GDP per year in quality improvement and Digital Deflation due mostly to performance improvement in computers made for final sale and to a very modest degree in packaged software. Recall from the Digital Deflation model that the estimated *uncounted* Digital Deflation was an *additional* 1.96% of GDP in 1998—mostly from quality and performance improvement in semiconductors, software, computer services, communications services, pharmaceuticals, healthcare services, and financial services. For an $8.8 trillion economy, these percentages amounted to $24 billion of counted and $172 billion of uncounted real economic value being created from digitally driven quality improvement in 1998 alone. In other words, the government actually counted and reported $24 billion of value produced from quality improvement but did not count and report an estimated $172 billion of value produced in 1998.

The counted and uncounted quality improvement combined for a total of $196 billion of value, or about 2.23% of GDP, being generated by the Digital Revolution—just from improving product quality and performance. This amount of quality-based value is truly staggering but provides an important explanation as to why the United States has continued to seemingly defy gravity and grow so rapidly despite already being the world's largest economy. As a counterpoint to the Old Economy, the $196 billion of value created solely from digitally driven counted and uncounted quality improvement almost equaled the $219 billion value of vehicle shipments by the auto industry in the same year.

The above example was for 1998, the most recent year for which reasonably accurate industry data is available for estimating counted and uncounted Digital Deflation. Each year these numbers get even larger as New Economy industries offer ever faster, better, cheaper products and services and take a larger piece of the economic pie. Over each of the last five decades, IT industries grew at rates that were 44% to 100% faster than the overall economy. These above-average growth trends are expected to continue as consumers and corporate buyers perceive greater value and take advantage of the continuous improvement in product quality per dollar spent on digitally driven products.

By 2001, digital technologies created an estimated 0.30% of quality improvement or Digital Deflation counted by the government and 2.16% of quality improvement uncounted by the government. They combined to generate a total of $255 billion of value equal to 2.46% of GDP being created from digitally driven quality improvement in a $10.4 trillion economy. For 2002 and beyond, the numbers become even larger and the impact greater as IT and industries driven by digital technologies grow faster than the Old Economy. In 2002, there will have been approximately 0.31% of counted quality improvement and 2.23% of uncounted quality improvement from digital technology advances, producing a combined 2.54% of GDP or $275 billion of added value in an economy of about $10.9 trillion.

## TWO MORE DECADES OF VALUE CREATION

Over the next 20 years, with the power of compounding of faster growth products and services driven by advancing digital technologies, the value to be created by improving quality and performance will become even more impressive. By 2010, further gains in product and service quality will generate at least 0.40% per year of counted quality improvement and about 2.89% per year of uncounted quality improvement. The former number will be higher and the latter number lower to the extent that the government captures more quality and performance improvement for more industries.

It is fully expected that over the next several years, the Bureau of Labor Statistics and the Department of Commerce will be measuring many more industries, products, and services for quality and performance improvement than just computers and the portion of software and voice switches that they measure today. So while the split between counted and uncounted quality improvement will no doubt start to shift toward more quality being counted, the total amount of quality-based value being created by the Digital Revolution will be perceived by consumers and will continue to grow annually. By 2010, a total of about $540 billion of greater real value will be created per year by technology-driven quality improvement in products and services, equal to about 3.3% of a $16.3 trillion economy.

Projecting out another 10 years, by the year 2020, ever-advancing digital technologies will create $1.2 trillion of real value per year in the form of quality and performance improvement. This will represent 4.4% of a $27 trillion economy. It is important to recall that the economic accounting for that $1.2 trillion of quality and performance improvement delivered to the consumer "for free" in 2020 will be reflected as a $1.2 trillion reduction in prices. It is, of course, this large reduction in prices across the economy that creates Digital Deflation equal to *minus* 4.4% on the overall GDP Deflator—when properly counted by the government's statisticians.

This counting of good deflation means that by 2020 the Old Economy could generate and contribute 4.4% of inflation toward the aggregate GDP Deflator, and the overall economy will still end up with zero inflation. The implications, of course, are staggering. Government fiscal and monetary policy will have to be looked at in a new light. It certainly underscores the importance of properly counting quality improvement and the need to disaggregate the economy into the digitally deflating New Economy and the traditionally inflating Old Economy to truly understand the economy of the next two decades.

## VALUE TO WEALTH: THE NEW ECONOMY'S VIRTUOUS CIRCLE

Recall that the consumer does not perceive that he or she is charged for this extra value from quality improvement, so the higher quality appears to be delivered to the consumer for free. However, it must be remembered that it does cost New Economy Companies real dollars to develop and deliver higher-value new generation products, particularly if they are charging only the same or lower prices than they did for the older generation products. They must have the opportunity to earn an attractive profit or return on their investment, or they will not have the incentive to make the investment to develop the new technologies and products.

This is, of course, the mechanism by which the advancing Digital Revolution becomes a self-renewing and regenerative process—a virtuous circle. Higher value products are created for consumers for which New Economy Companies are rewarded with above-average revenue growth, higher incremental profitability, higher stock valuations, and access to lower-cost capital. Recall that incremental profit margins are higher on the next digital widget sold, a direct result of the economies of scale benefits of spreading fixed costs over more units produced. These higher incremental profits are reinvested into the development, production, and delivery of the next generation of higher-value products, generating wealth at the same time for the company's investors via rising stock prices.

Of the increase in stock market wealth, a small but increasingly important part is used by the Investor-Consumer to increase spending to rates above historical levels of disposable income, in the process creating more demand for New and Old Economy products and services (the wealth effect). But as shown in Chapter 7, the vast majority of the increase in wealth is left in the stock market, which will help to finance the growth in supply of both quantity- and quality-based output of New and Old Economy products and services.

This is the process by which increasing *value creation* from quality improvement is translated into stock market–driven *wealth creation* in the New Economy. Investors would not be inclined to continue to allocate a large portion of their net worth to common stocks unless they believe their stocks will go up. They are rewarded if their holdings in common stocks appreciate, which generally results from earnings growth, but can be even more sensitive to changing P/E ratios for the overall stock market. It was the dramatic rise in the market P/E ratio that contributed most to the outsized gains in the 1990s. It is this *rise in P/E ratios* that provides the key linkage in converting value creation to wealth creation in the New Economy.

Importantly, improving product quality and increasing Digital Deflation will exert more downward pressure on inflation every year. Lower inflation brings on lower interest rates and higher P/E ratios. Higher P/E ratios create new wealth, and that incremental new wealth will finance the next generation of technology advances, product improvement, value creation, and wealth creation. This again, through the wealth effect, will create more demand.

It is important to understand this direct linkage between New Economy value creation and New Economy wealth creation, because this is a large part of what ultimately justified and legitimized much of the expansion in P/E ratios that created so much wealth during the decade of the 1990s. Put differently, without an understanding of why productivity gains have been surprisingly high and how they have helped to reduce reported inflation, one should be wondering why P/Es have been so high and might be heading lower. On the other hand, with a new understanding of how improving product quality and Digital Deflation are reducing inflation, one can better understand not only current interest rates and P/E ratios but the potential that exists for even higher productivity, lower inflation, lower interest rates, and higher P/E ratios over the next two decades.

In essence, this key linkage between quality-based value creation from digital technology advances and stock market–based wealth creation says a lot about whether common stock investors are irrationally exuberant or whether shares are rationally priced. If the New Economy productivity gains of the late 1990s recede back to the 1% to 1.5% range of the previous 20 years, P/E ratios are probably too high. If productivity gains can remain at the 2.5% level or higher, then common stock P/Es are rationally valued. The "value-to-wealth" virtuous circle of the New Economy is critical to the outlook for common stock investors and for the potential for further wealth creation.

In trying to understand how much wealth the New Economy will create in this ongoing virtuous circle of the future, defining wealth is a good place to start.

## MEASURING WEALTH

Arguably, the best single measure of wealth in an economy is household net worth, and such data are readily available and reported annually in the Federal Reserve's "Flow of Funds" report. It is a measure of household assets, including housing, common stocks, bonds, money market funds, and pension reserves, less total debt, including mortgages, credit card debt, and auto loans. Since individuals own virtually all privately held companies and most corporate equities directly or as pension beneficiaries, household net worth also effectively includes the vast majority of corporate net worth. Here, the Fed's household balance sheet data are reasonably accurate except for the understatement in the reporting of the value of "Non-Corporate Business" or privately held companies, as well as the understated value of bond holdings.

There has been much publicity over how household net worth in the United States declined in the year 2000 for the first time in over 50 years. Exhibit 8-1 shows how growth in net worth accelerated in the late 1990s with the rising stock market but came back down to the long-term growth curve with the fall in the stock market in 2000 and 2001. It is remarkable for any economy to have enjoyed 50 consecutive years of growth in any single measure of wealth. It is even more amazing given the size of the U.S. economy. What is more important to the individual household, however, is the pace of growth in *real* household net worth or the purchasing power of that net worth after adjusting for the wealth-punishing effects of inflation. The bottom graph in Exhibit 8-1 shows how real net worth in fact declined several times over the last 50 years, most notably in the 1970s when demographic-induced inflation took its heavy toll on purchasing power and net worth. Notwithstanding all the negative press, in real terms the decline in net worth in 2000–2001 was not all that unusual.

In reality, despite occasional declines both in nominal and real terms, household net worth in the United States has demonstrated an amazing ability to grow fairly consistently over the decades as shown in Exhibit 8-2. Of the last five decades, the 1990s generated the largest absolute increase in wealth with an astounding $22 trillion rise in nominal net worth for American households versus only an $11.8 trillion increase in net worth in the 1980s. Household net worth *totaled* just $22.7 trillion in 1992, so in absolute dollar terms, the $22 trillion increase in net worth was something to behold. Americans by and

## E X H I B I T   8-1

Net Worth vs. the Stock Market

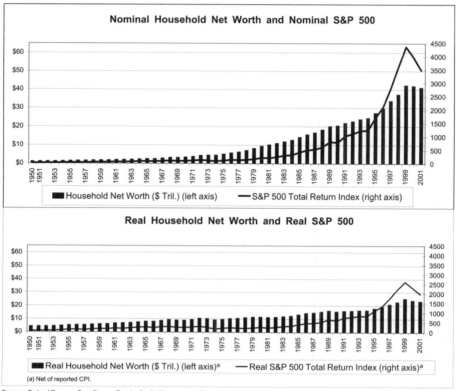

Sources: Federal Reserve; Bear Stearns; Tanaka Capital Management, Inc.

large felt wealthier than when they began the decade, and they were. This most recent decade, of course, benefited from a surging stock market and the compounding of large numbers.

All five decades showed large percentage gains in nominal net worth. It is interesting, however, that when adjusted for reported inflation, the 1990s' gain of 56.3% in *real* net worth appears to have been only as strong as the 1950s' gain of 54.8% and not much greater than the real gains of the 1960s and the 1980s. In other words, using the government's Consumer Price Index (CPI) to adjust for inflation, the 1990s' gain in real wealth seemed little different from prior decades. Despite these lackluster reported statistics, the average consumer knew better, and so did the average investor.

EXHIBIT 8-2

Five Decades of Wealth Creation

| | Nominal Net Worth | | | Real Net Worth |
| --- | --- | --- | --- | --- |
| | End of Period Net Worth (Tril.) | $ Increase In Net Worth (Tril.) | % Change in Nominal Net Worth | % Increase in Real Net Worth (a) |
| 1950s | $1.8 | $0.8 | 86.5% | 54.8% |
| 1960s | $3.3 | $1.5 | 84.1% | 46.5% |
| 1970s | $8.3 | $5.0 | 152.0% | 27.4% |
| 1980s | $20.2 | $11.8 | 143.0% | 42.4% |
| 1990s | $42.3 | $22.2 | 109.9% | 56.3% |
| | | | | |
| 2000 | $42.0 | –$0.4 | -1.0% | -5.6% |
| 2001 | $41.1 | –$0.9 | -2.1% | -2.4% |
| (a) Net of reported CPI | | | | |

Sources: Federal Reserve, Tanaka Capital Management, Inc.

## ADJUSTING WEALTH FOR DIGITAL DEFLATION

We should not be surprised that when an appropriate downward adjustment is made to inflation for uncounted quality improvement and Digital Deflation, the gain in real household net worth in the 1990s was actually much larger than 56.3%. Recall that by adjusting for Digital Deflation, the CPI was estimated to have been overstated by about 1.0% in 2000 and by slightly less in the late 1990s from the undercounting of quality improvement. Assuming that uncounted quality improvement in the CPI averaged 0.8% per year in the 1990s, an adjustment downward in CPI of 0.8% per year would have made the cumulative gain in real household net worth closer to 69.6% during the decade of the 1990s rather than the 56.3% real gain using the reported CPI data. This adjusted 69.6% growth in real net worth is probably a lot closer to what the average American felt happened to his or her wealth and purchasing power in the 1990s as the dollar was able to buy higher-quality products and services.

In other words, while the economic data as reported show that the gain in nominal and real net worth in the decade of the 1990s only approximated the rates of gain in wealth in the 1950s, 1960s, and 1980s, the public knows that the real gains in the 1990s were significantly larger. In fact, the 1990s *only* showed significantly better growth in wealth if appropriate adjustments are made for uncounted quality improvement and Digital Deflation. This is a real-world validation of the Theory of Digital Deflation as it shows by inference the existence of more real growth and wealth than the government has been measuring. That unmeasured real growth and wealth was, of course, related to uncounted quality improvement.

The impact of just a 0.8% downward adjustment to inflation demonstrates how significant a small annual correction to government inflation statistics can mean for the wealth of a nation when compounded over several years. Importantly, for investors attempting to discern the future value of their investments, the effects of significantly lower inflation and interest rates as they approach zero are even more dramatic, because the relationships between P/E ratios and interest rates and inflation are nonlinear and exponential. A small 1 percentage point correction in fact will become quite large, especially as inflation and interest rates move to new lows. As reported inflation declines from 3% to 2%, the 1 percent reduction will have a much bigger impact (−33%) than when inflation dropped from 5% to 4% (−20%). And as inflation drops from 2% to 1%, the 1 percent change will be an even more dramatic 50% decline.

Over the next several years, the federal government's statistical agencies will begin to count more completely the quality improvement in consumer and corporate purchases, so the reported rise in real net worth will be greater. Further, the 1.0% downward adjustment to the CPI for uncounted Digital Deflation in 2000 will grow and become an even larger 1.8% reduction in the CPI by 2020 as Digital products and services grow to become a larger share of the consumer economy.

## A STRONG DEMOGRAPHIC FOUNDATION FOR GENERATING WEALTH

It is clear that inflation, or more specifically the absence of inflation, is a critical ingredient for the generation of substantial national wealth. Earlier, it was shown how the greatest single long-term determinant of inflation in the United States over the last 50 years was the rate of growth in the labor force. Recall that the correlation was 0.93 between growth in the youngest segment of the labor force and the CPI. The really good news is that during the next two decades, the pivotal youngest segment of the labor force is projected to grow at a benign rate of only 0.1% per year, which is virtually no growth at all. Barring a major change in immigration rates, these demographic labor force projections can be made with fairly good accuracy based on excellent data showing how many children are 1, 2, 3 . . . 18 years old.

By utilizing the demographic–inflation model described in Chapter 7, projections can be made with a fairly high degree of confidence that based on very little growth in the youngest segment of the workforce, inflation as measured by the CPI will average about 2.6% per year over the next 20 years to 2020. This compares quite favorably with an average reported inflation rate of 5.5% and 3.0% for the CPI respectively in the 1980s and the prosperous 1990s, and it doesn't yet factor in most of the benefits of uncounted Digital Deflation. Thanks to the favorable demographics of low labor force growth, there will continue to be low inflationary pressures from the relative balance of labor and capital on the producing or supply side of the economy.

Given a scenario of low inflation and lower interest rates over the next two decades, it would follow that common stocks should also generate attractive returns. Utilizing the demographic–stock market model and given modest growth in the labor force, projections can also be made with a high degree of confidence (a correlation of 0.89 over the last 50 years) that real returns on common stocks should average about 13.4% per year over the next 20 years, net of inflation. These returns would be less than the real returns of 16.0% per year enjoyed in the heady 1990–1999 period, which benefited from pre-Y2K spending and the Dot-com Bubble, as well as declining inflation. But real returns of 13.4% per year would be extremely high, especially when compounded on top of the massive amounts of real wealth already created in the stock market in the 1980s and 1990s.

Exhibit 8-3 presents the projections for inflation, productivity, and real returns on stocks over the next four 5-year periods based on the Demographic Theory of Economics. Inflation, productivity, and real returns on stocks are projected to average 2.6%, 2.3% and 13.4% per year, respectively. Even if the stock market excesses of the late 1990s borrowed some of the projected returns from the 2000s, it is very clear that favorable demographics would suggest the potential for prosperous times ahead. Unlike the inflation-accelerating demographics of the 1970s and early 1980s, but very much like the 1990s, benign growth in the labor force in the United States over the next 20 years will create a strong foundation of demographically low inflation and the need for productivity gains for the economy to grow at all.

How Changes in the Labor Force Will Affect Inflation, Productivity, and Real
Returns on Common Stocks

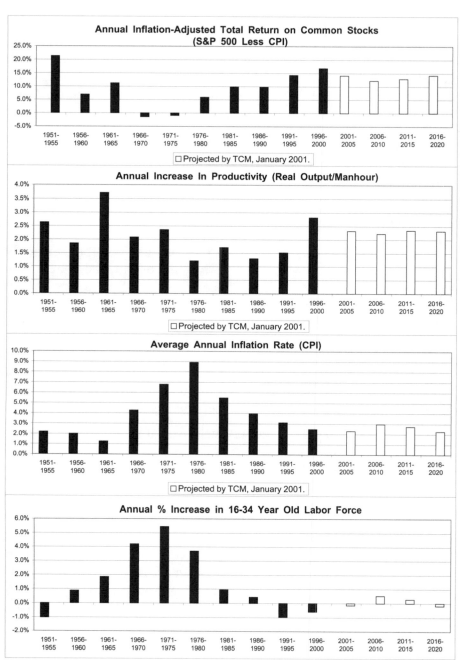

Sources: Department of Commerce; Tanaka Capital Management, Inc.

In the bleakest of terms, with very little growth in the workforce there will be close to zero real growth in the economy unless labor productivity rises. Fortunately, the almost total dependence of the economy of the future upon gains in labor productivity for growth will coincide with a proliferation of new digital technologies that will generate growing amounts of performance and quality improvement, and hence, more Digital Deflation. Over the next two decades, it will be these growing amounts of quality-based Digital Deflation that will lead to a dramatic surge in real economic growth and rising productivity. Growing Digital Deflation will be the key enabler for the economy to achieve much of the fairly sanguine potential suggested by the demographic models for inflation and productivity.

## THE DIGITAL DEFLATION WEALTH MULTIPLIERS

With all the value being delivered to the consumer by the constantly improving product quality and performance enhancements, how much wealth will be created for those who contribute to the Digital Revolution? The answer is that there is the potential for record amounts of wealth to be generated for investors, employees, and managers in the New Economy as it grows and delivers ever more value to the consumer.

From a macroeconomic perspective, there are really two simple but very powerful benefits that continuously improving digital technologies will contribute to the creation of wealth:

1. *Lower inflation* as the government counts and converts more quality improvement into lower price deflators for the overall economy. This will translate into lower interest rates and higher P/E ratios for the stock market.
2. *Rising productivity* as the government counts more of the real value of digitally driven products. Strong labor productivity growth has generally resulted in above-average real revenue growth, incremental operating leverage, and rising profit margins for companies helping to deliver more value to consumers through higher-performing, higher-quality products and services. Employees delivering higher productivity should earn higher real wages and salaries.

What this means is that as the government begins to count more of the quality improvement from advancing technologies, reported inflation will be adjusted downward significantly, and real output and productivity growth will be adjusted upward significantly. The result is that more wealth will be created from the dual benefits of rising P/E ratios on stocks due to declining inflation—and rising profit margins due to increasing productivity growth. However, while it is declining inflation that will have by far the greater incremental boost to wealth creation through lower interest rates and higher P/E ratios, it is the unusual combination of both strong growth and declining inflation that places the New Economy head and shoulders above other periods of wealth creation. The decade of the 1990s was just the beginning.

Through the eons of economic history, it has been very unusual for both rapid growth and low inflation to occur at the same time. In fact, if you were to poll people as to what would happen to the economy and the stock market if they were to become convinced that inflation will decline by a full 2 percentage points, the vast majority would still say that the economy will be going into a recession or worse. This view is common despite all the evidence to the contrary from the 1990s' experience during which the economy racked up 9 years of record expansion and yet inflation declined. These were the first hints of what the naturally deflating New Economy can contribute to the U.S. economy for decades to come.

Over the next two decades, by significantly reducing inflation on a sustainable and secular basis, constantly improving digital technologies and growing Digital Deflation can dramatically increase the value of *all assets* by driving interest rates down to record lows, boosting P/E ratios on common stocks to record highs, and even raising cash flow multiples on income-producing tangible assets. Indeed, as Digital Deflation acts to lower inflation over the next 10 to 20 years, it will act to create value as a significant "wealth multiplier," creating more wealth by boosting all valuation metrics and the value of already existing assets.

Essentially, with inflation and interest rates going to record lows and cash liquidity to very high levels, investors will be willing to pay more for assets and for a future stream of earnings, dividends, and interest income. Interest yields on cash instruments will look very unattractive, encouraging investors to shift more assets at the margin into longer-maturity fixed income securities and into common stocks.

## THE KEY TO WEALTH IS LOW INFLATION

It is apparent that the key to the *preservation of wealth* is sustained low inflation, and the key to the *creation of new wealth* is declining inflation.

The problem with rising inflation is that it erodes not only the value of goods being produced a particular year but also the value of the vastly larger pool of already existing assets. This was why the 1970s and early 1980s felt so painful. Hyperinflation not only hurt the real value of goods being produced, it eviscerated the real value of already existing assets and therefore net worth. On the other hand, with inflation in a secular decline in a New Economy world of increasing Digital Deflation, in aggregate there will be less erosion in the value of goods produced and assets owned. Lower and/or nonexistent inflation ahead also means that the ownership of a right to a future stream of cash flows or dividends (future assets) will not be eroded significantly with the passage of time.

Over the next several years, as the government counts more quality improvement, inflation expectations can decline by more than 2.0% on the overall GDP Deflator and by more than 1.0% on the CPI. Investors will reduce the rate by which they discount future interest payments or dividends back to the present, significantly increasing how much an investor will pay to own the right to that same stream of future interest payments or dividends. Even if the future stream of interest payments and dividends doesn't change, as soon as investors start to believe that inflation will be declining, that future stream of interest and dividends immediately becomes more valuable to them.

As inflation expectations start to decline, interest rates will decline, moving bond markets higher and elevating common stock P/E ratios. This is why the stock and bond markets whip around so much right around the announcement of inflation news or on comments by Fed officials on inflation. With inflation declining to lower levels, not only will owners of stocks and bonds become more wealthy, corporations will be able to raise funds more cheaply to fund product development and capital-spending programs for future growth, and governments will be able to borrow at cheaper rates.

## A "NEAR-ZERO EXPERIENCE"

Over the next 20 years, the deflationary benefits of the Digital Revolution will only get larger. As the recurring cycles of improving digital technologies result in ever faster, better, cheaper products and services, they collectively will offer the prospect of generating enough Digital Deflation to produce close to zero inflation in the aggregate economy. As unbelievable as it sounds, zero inflation is not only feasible but, for the overall or aggregate economy, it is already here. If corrected for 2.1% of uncounted quality improvement in products and services and for Digital Deflation, actual inflation for the overall economy as measured by the GDP Deflator was running at around 0% by the end of 2000. In 2001, inflation as measured by the GDP Deflator nudged up to around 2.3%. Making the adjustment for the estimated 2.2% of uncounted Digital Deflation in 2001 would result in an adjusted GDP Deflator of 0.1%, again close to 0%.

Similarly, if adjustments are made for uncounted quality improvement in the consumer sector of the economy via the Consumer Price Index, the CPI would be about 1.0% lower than the approximately 2.8% level reported in the late 1990s and early 2000s, or around 1.8%. With zero inflation in the overall economy (GDP Deflator) and 1.8% inflation for the consumer sector (CPI), the two principal indicators of inflation adjusted for quality average out to 0.9%, or near-zero inflation.

At the micro level, many businesspeople have been saying for years that "There is no inflation in the economy!" They often lament that they have no pricing flexibility. This is perhaps more true than they realize as the Digital Revolution is creating increasing Digital Deflation in the New Economy. Old Economy Companies are feeling the heat, and it will only get worse. It will become more and more difficult for Old Economy companies to compete for the consumer's wallet as they raise prices to cover their traditional cost increases while New Economy companies offer increasingly more real value to the consumer at lower prices.

## PICTURING ZERO INFLATION WILL BE DIFFICULT FOR MANY

The U.S. economy has not enjoyed zero inflation at any other time in recent history, so you can only imagine what it would be like if your dollars, your income, savings, and investments did not become eroded over time. Yes, prices will rise in many parts of the Old Economy, but inflation in the Old Economy will be offset by improving product quality and Digital Deflation in the New Economy, with the net or total result being close to zero inflation.

As exciting or unbelievable as it may seem for many to consider a near-zero inflation scenario today, the future looks even brighter. As information technology grows to become a larger part of the U.S. economy and as quality improvement becomes better measured during the next 20 years, the reported GDP Deflator could drop well below zero, and the CPI to less than 1.0%. The implications for interest rates, P/E ratios, and wealth creation are quite significant, and the implications for monetary and fiscal policymakers are profound—if the government counts Digital Deflation properly.

At this point it is worth repeating from prior chapters that Digital Deflation is good deflation and positive for the economy. Recall that Digital Deflation is created as economists convert increasing quality in upgraded digitally driven products sold at the same price into the economic equivalent of lower-price deflators for those new products. It is in no way to be associated with the negative cyclical deflation associated with severe recessions and the price-cutting that many fear could turn into a downward spiral of wage reductions. In an era of increasing Digital Deflation, the exact opposite is true as increasing quality-based productivity gains result in real wage increases. Increasing Digital Deflation also should not be confused with the economy-wide deflation related to a reduction in the money supply as was experienced in the early 1930s when the Fed inadvertently reduced the money supply by 25%.

## THE GDP DEFLATOR ADJUSTED FOR DIGITAL DEFLATION

Exhibit 8-4 presents the GDP Deflator adjusted for Digital Deflation as reflected in the Digital Deflation model for the years 1998 through 2010, plus the year 2020. These estimates differ significantly from the Congressional Budget Office (CBO) projections, which have the GDP Deflator leveling out at 1.9% per year from 2004 to 2010. The graph begins with the year 1998 when very good industry data are available for estimating uncounted quality improvement from advancing digital technologies as explained in Chapter 7. In 1998, the GDP Deflator was reported at a very low 1.10%. If the estimated uncounted Digital Deflation of 1.96% for 1998 is subtracted from 1.10%, the resulting GDP Deflator adjusted for Digital Deflation would place the Deflator at closer to *minus 0.86%* for 1998.

From 1999 to 2010, the growth in uncounted Digital Deflation is assumed to approximate the rate by which the growth in capital spending for Information Processing Equipment and Software exceeds the growth in nominal GDP. Over the next 10 years, IT capital spending is estimated to grow by 9.0% per year, and nominal GDP to grow by 5.2% per year, yielding a rising contribution of uncounted Digital Deflation

## E X H I B I T   8-4

### GDP Deflator vs. GDP Deflator Adjusted for Digital Deflation

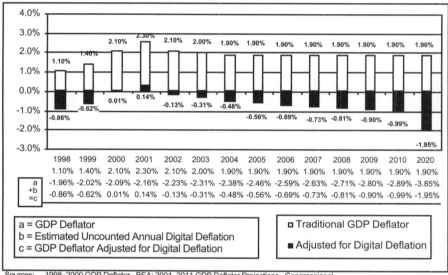

| | 1998 | 1999 | 2000 | 2001 | 2002 | 2003 | 2004 | 2005 | 2006 | 2007 | 2008 | 2009 | 2010 | 2020 |
|---|---|---|---|---|---|---|---|---|---|---|---|---|---|---|
| a | 1.10% | 1.40% | 2.10% | 2.30% | 2.10% | 2.00% | 1.90% | 1.90% | 1.90% | 1.90% | 1.90% | 1.90% | 1.90% | 1.90% |
| +b | -1.96% | -2.02% | -2.09% | -2.16% | -2.23% | -2.31% | -2.38% | -2.46% | -2.59% | -2.63% | -2.71% | -2.80% | -2.89% | -3.85% |
| =c | -0.86% | -0.62% | 0.01% | 0.14% | -0.13% | -0.31% | -0.48% | -0.56% | -0.69% | -0.73% | -0.81% | -0.90% | -0.99% | -1.95% |

a = GDP Deflator
b = Estimated Uncounted Annual Digital Deflation
c = GDP Deflator Adjusted for Digital Deflation

□ Traditional GDP Deflator

■ Adjusted for Digital Deflation

Sources:   1998–2000 GDP Deflator - BEA; 2001–2011 GDP Deflator Projections - Congressional
Budget Office; 1998–2020 GDP Deflator Adjusted for Digital Deflation - Tanaka Capital
Management, Inc.

as a percent of GDP with each year into the future. Projected growth rates for nominal GDP are borrowed from the Congressional Budget Office (CBO), and the projected growth in IT capital spending is estimated at a fairly conservative 9.0% per year compared with average annual growth in IT capital spending for the 1950s, 1960s, 1970s, 1980s, and 1990s of 9.5%, 13.8%, 14.9%, 11.4%, and 9.6% per year, respectively.

As IT continues to rise as a percent of GDP, it is estimated that the GDP Deflator should be adjusted downward for currently uncounted quality improvement by minus 2.09% in 2000, by minus 2.89% in 2010 and by minus 3.85% by 2020. As a rough rule of thumb, the GDP Deflator should be reduced by about 2% in 2000 and a little less than 3% and 4% in 2010 and 2020 to adjust for uncounted gains in quality improvement.

It should be pointed out that there will be expansion of reported Digital Deflation in the few areas where the government is already counting quality improvement. Assuming that computers and prepackaged software grow at the same rate as information technology over the next two decades and that the rates of quality improvement are maintained at the same pace, reported Digital Deflation from computers and prepackaged software will grow from 0.27% in 1998 as mentioned in the last chapter to about 0.31% in 2002, 0.43% in 2010, and 0.61% in 2020. Even if the government does not count quality improvement for any other products or services, there will be a downward bias for inflation and an upward bias for productivity over the next two decades as the New Economy grows faster than the Old.

Back to adjusting the GDP Deflator for uncounted Digital Deflation, it can be seen in Exhibit 8-4 that except for 2000 and 2001, the GDP Deflator–Digital Deflation Model shows how the U.S. economy is already in a deflationary mode. Furthermore, as the New Economy continues to grow faster than the Old Economy and as the government begins to count quality improvement for more products and services, aggregate deflation as indicated for the GDP Deflator will get larger and larger with each passing year.

Obviously, as our government counts more of the currently uncounted quality improvement, the appearance of a negative GDP Deflator will open the door for the Federal Reserve to stimulate the Old Economy to produce enough inflation to offset the rising Digital Deflation in the New Economy. All of this presumes that the Fed chooses to keep aggregate inflation at zero on the GDP Deflator. It is indeed ironic that after spending decades trying to keep inflation down, the Fed may have to learn new tricks to try to keep inflation up in the Old Economy! In the end it is envisioned that the Fed would elect to run the economy with a modestly negative GDP Deflator and a modestly positive CPI. There will be more on this subject in Chapter 10.

## THE CPI ADJUSTED FOR DIGITAL DEFLATION

Exhibit 8-5 shows how the CBO has projected the CPI to level out at 2.5% per year from 2004 extending out to the year 2010. It is interesting that the CBO does not use demographics as a major input in its complex models, but it arrives at roughly the same level for the CPI as the 2.6% predicted by the demographic model for the next 10 years. The CBO also does not yet adjust its forecasts for uncounted quality improvement and Digital Deflation. However, as the U.S. statistical agencies add more and more products and services to their list of quality-adjusted industries, the CBO, and the Federal Reserve for that matter, will have more accurate data to make more accurate projections.

## EXHIBIT 8-5

Reported CPI vs. CPI Adjusted for Digital Deflation

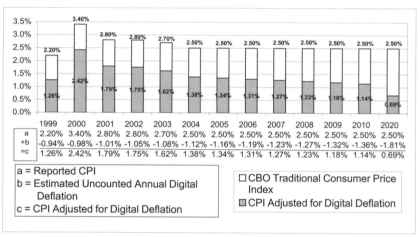

| | 1999 | 2000 | 2001 | 2002 | 2003 | 2004 | 2005 | 2006 | 2007 | 2008 | 2009 | 2010 | 2020 |
|---|---|---|---|---|---|---|---|---|---|---|---|---|---|
| a | 2.20% | 3.40% | 2.80% | 2.80% | 2.70% | 2.50% | 2.50% | 2.50% | 2.50% | 2.50% | 2.50% | 2.50% | 2.50% |
| +b | -0.94% | -0.98% | -1.01% | -1.05% | -1.08% | -1.12% | -1.16% | -1.19% | -1.23% | -1.27% | -1.32% | -1.36% | -1.81% |
| =c | 1.26% | 2.42% | 1.79% | 1.75% | 1.62% | 1.38% | 1.34% | 1.31% | 1.27% | 1.23% | 1.18% | 1.14% | 0.69% |

a = Reported CPI
b = Estimated Uncounted Annual Digital Deflation
c = CPI Adjusted for Digital Deflation

☐ CBO Traditional Consumer Price Index
■ CPI Adjusted for Digital Deflation

Sources: 1999–2000 CPI - Bureau of Labor Statistics; 2001–2010 CPI Projections - Congressional Budget Office;
Office; 1999–2020 CPI Adjusted for Digital Deflation - Tanaka Capital Management, Inc.

Similar to the GDP Deflator–Digital Deflation model, the CPI–Digital Deflation Model can be used to project the uncounted Digital Deflation for the CPI out well into the future. Assuming the same growth in consumer-based information technology goods and services relative to overall consumer spending, the adjustment for un-counted Digital Deflation for the aggregate CPI is projected to expand from a minus 0.98% in 2000 to a minus 1.36% in 2010 and a minus 1.81% by 2020. If properly adjusted for Digital Deflation, the CPI should drop from 3.40% to 2.42% in 2000, from a projected 2.50% to 1.14% in 2010, and from an estimated 2.50% to 0.69% by 2020. This fa-vorable downward trend contrasts with the CBO's baseline projection of a flat 2.5% per year for each of the next 10 years. Properly counted over the next 20 years, the CPI will remain modestly inflationary while the GDP Deflator will reflect net deflation.

## WHY THE CPI AND GDP DEFLATOR WILL DIVERGE

It is important to recall that Digital Deflation has a greater effect on re-ducing inflation in the overall economy than in the roughly two-thirds of the economy that is made up of consumer spending. Again, this is because corporate capital spending has considerably higher digital content than the market basket of goods and services that the consumer buys in a given year. Accordingly, the GDP Deflator is estimated currently to have undermeasured Digital Deflation by roughly 2.0% per year, and the CPI by only 1.0% per year.

For those who have wondered why the GDP Deflator has been creeping downward versus the CPI in recent years, one big reason is that the government is already counting quality improvement at about 0.30% per year for computers in the GDP Deflator that virtually doesn't show up in the CPI. Another reason is that steadily rising quantity-based productivity gains from rising IT capital spending helps the GDP Deflator more than the CPI.

Therefore, when quality improvement is properly counted, it is apparent that the consumer stands to benefit annually from only 1.0% lower inflation on the CPI and thus has only 1.0% greater purchasing power when adjusted for Digital Deflation. In contrast, the overall economy will be shown to benefit from more than 2.0% lower inflation and therefore 2.0% higher real growth and productivity, as reflected in the GDP Deflator adjusted for Digital Deflation. The 2% lower inflation for the overall economy will benefit investors. Furthermore, unless the digital content in the CPI's market basket of goods and services grows faster than IT capital spending, the differences between Digital Deflation for the GDP Deflator and the Digital Deflation for the CPI will widen from a 1.11% spread in 2000 to about 2.04% by 2020.

## WHICH IS THE RIGHT INFLATION RATE?

As it is clear that the GDP Deflator and the CPI will diverge further over time, which inflation index should people use? That depends on what you're buying. Investors in financial assets are presumably more interested in how future inflation will affect interest rates and the long-term value of their dollar-denominated assets across the economy rather than a change in the value of a more narrow market basket that a consumer would purchase in the next year. Hence, bond and common stock valuations are likely to be more sensitive to changes in the GDP Deflator than the CPI. Accordingly this analysis utilizes the GDP Deflator for predicting interest rates and for determining common stock P/E ratios.

Most investors, however, are also Investor-Consumers who are interested in the purchasing power of their investments. So this analysis utilizes the CPI for more conservatively determining the real return on common stocks as being equal to the nominal total return on the stock market less the CPI. Real net worth for the average household is also calculated to be equal to nominal net worth less the CPI.

In the end, the key to generating real wealth over the next two decades will depend less upon which inflation rate is appropriate for which purpose and more upon how much more quality improvement the government will measure—or not measure. There should be no doubt that growing amounts of Digital Deflation will help in the wealth creation process. The critical question remains as to how much Digital Deflation will be counted. Future rates of reported inflation and productivity growth will depend increasingly upon the accuracy or inaccuracy of the government's data.

## FOUR SCENARIOS FOR THE WEALTH IN OUR FUTURE

Chapter 9 presents a scenario which assumes that by the end of each of the next two decades, the U.S. Government will count only 50% or half of the remaining uncounted quality improvement and Digital Deflation estimated to be generated by advancing digital technologies. Outcomes are also presented for a second but highly unlikely scenario in which the government will measure no additional quality improvement beyond that which it is already measuring in computers and the small amount of performance improvement in software and switches. A third scenario shows the equally unlikely "ideal case," in which the government counts 100% of the estimated uncounted annual quality improvement and Digital Deflation, and the fourth case, in which 75% of the uncounted quality improvement and Digital Deflation is measured.

The 75% scenario can be viewed as approximating what some well-run companies in the private sector refer to as a *stretch goal*, which is theoretically achievable but only with committed management and strong execution by the government. The 50% case should be attainable but will require a more concerted effort by the government to count quality improvement across the economy.

By examining the four cases, it will be seen how incredibly sensitive stock market returns and real wealth creation will be to the long-term reported rates of inflation and productivity growth. It will become more obvious why economists and policymakers spend so much time and effort trying to understand inflation and productivity.

More important, the analysis will show that because each percentage point increase in Digital Deflation translates into a direct one-for-one 1% reduction in inflation and a direct one-for-one 1% increase in productivity, stock market returns and real wealth creation will be highly sensitive to the amount of quality improvement the government will measure.

In the four cases, it will be seen that for the government's counting of 100%, 75%, 50%, and 0% of the currently uncounted Digital Deflation, the expected nominal returns on common stocks over the 2000–2009 decade will vary from approximately 16.6% per year to 13.7%, 11.3%, and 7.7% per year, respectively. Real returns on stocks will vary even more, from 15.2% per year to 11.8%, 9.2%, and 5.9% per year, respectively, in the four cases, due to the greater importance of inflation in calculating real returns.

The growth in nominal net worth in the United States will range from +$61 trillion to +$44 trillion, +$34 trillion, and +$21 trillion over the 2000–2009 decade, depending upon whether the government counts 100%, 75%, 50%, or 0% of the currently uncounted quality improvement and Digital Deflation. These are enormous differences in the projected wealth of the nation and obviously have significant social and political implications.

The rate of growth in real net worth per household will range from +110% to +71%, +46%, and +15% for each of the four scenarios over the course of the decade. As described at the outset of this chapter, the projected rate of growth in real net worth is what really counts as it reflects what American households will accumulate in terms of real purchasing power. A 46% gain in real net worth in the decade is a real possibility if the government is able to count half of the remaining uncounted quality improvement being generated in the economy. It would compare quite favorably with the 42% real gain in the 1980s and the 56% real gain in the 1990s.

On the other hand, it is likely that there will be only about a 15% gain in real net worth in the decade if the government counts no further quality improvement than it is currently counting for computers and for nominal amounts in software and switches. This 15% gain would compare poorly even with the 27% real gain in net worth in the awful decade of the 1970s.

These above indicators of wealth creation reflect quite a wide range of possible outcomes and underscore how critically important it will be for the government to count the performance and quality improvement being generated by digitally driven products and services. This improvement is being created every year and will only grow larger over the next two decades.

## FAIR VALUE P/Es AND WEALTH

Following the recession of 2001 and the stock market declines of 2000, 2001, and 2002, many investors have wondered quite justifiably whether the 1990s' boom was just a fluke. The answer, as it turns out, will depend most critically upon what direction the fair value P/E ratio on common stocks will take from current levels. The fair value P/E, or the market multiple relative to inflation and interest rates, will depend importantly on what the government will report as the "true" inflation rate, which in turn will depend upon the level of measured Digital Deflation. Of course, it will also depend on what investors believe will be the long-term inflation rate. Depending upon expectations for what this inflation rate will be over the long term, the range of possible fair value P/Es over the next two decades can be extremely wide.

This chapter describes qualitatively why there is an enormous potential for wealth to be created over the next two decades as a direct result of the Digital Revolution and the New Economy. The next chapter will provide investors with a quantitative means for determining fair value P/E ratios in a world of growing Digital Deflation and, therefore, just how fast or slow household wealth can grow to the year 2020.

# 9
## CHAPTER

# The New Economy Stock Market

Without standards no rational method of value measurement is possible.

*Benjamin Graham, et al., Security Analysis, 1962*

*If measured properly, Digital Deflation will accelerate earnings growth and boost price–earnings (P/E) ratios to new highs. This will convert otherwise mediocre returns on the stock market over the next two decades into average to above-average returns, creating record amounts of wealth that could rival even the prosperous 1980s and 1990s.*

## THE IMPORTANCE OF EQUITIES

In the last chapter it was shown how the rising stock market of the 1990s contributed to an enormous growth in wealth that was made even more meaningful in real terms by a significant decline in the rate of inflation. Common stocks and other equity-like assets surged from a four-decade average of 46% of household net worth at the beginning of the 1990s to 64.8% of net worth by the end of the decade in 1999 and 58.5% of net worth by the end of 2001. This high starting point for the new decade virtually assures that financial assets in general, and common stocks in particular, are likely to be significant determinants of the rate of growth in household net worth for the next several years.

With higher household weightings in common stocks and other equity-like assets, wealth creation in the United States will be even more sensitive to the swings in inflation and the stock market, up or down. Consumer spending is also likely to be affected more by a larger wealth effect—and reverse wealth effect—as common stock holdings are now larger relative to net worth and consumer spending levels. Accordingly, it is even more important that investors, policymakers and economists understand how increasing Digital Deflation will reduce inflation and interest rates, boost real output and productivity growth, and enhance the real market value of common stocks and other equity-like assets.

Although bond holdings will benefit from declining inflation and bond yields, common stocks should continue to be the financial asset that will benefit most from the ongoing Digital Revolution and the rapidly growing New Economy. This is because Digital Deflation will deliver the dual benefits that will boost common stock returns—declining inflation, which should boost fair value price–earnings ratios, and rising productivity, which should boost profit margins and earnings growth rates. With these factors in mind, a New Economy stock market model has been developed and custom-tailored to focus on these two most significant benefits of Digital Deflation: (1) declining inflation and (2) rising productivity growth.

## A NEW ECONOMY STOCK MARKET MODEL

Below is a fairly unique stock market model as it has been designed to be driven by two variables not often seen in stock market models— the average annual percentage change in corporate profits *as a percent of GDP* and the average annual *percentage change in P/E ratios*. These two variables were isolated for this model because the percentage change in pretax corporate profits as a percent of gross domestic product (GDP) can be very sensitive to changes in productivity growth as shown in Chapter 7, and changes in the level of P/E ratios are primarily driven by changes in the outlook for inflation as will be shown below.

To highlight the truly long-term nature of changing demographics and the growth in Digital Deflation, this stock market model focuses on decades of average annual change. In drawing on models introduced previously, this New Economy Stock Market model translates the benefits of favorable demographics, growing Digital Deflation, lower than expected inflation, and rising productivity gains into real returns on common stocks.

The first three lines of Exhibit 9-1 simply dissect the average annual growth rates in pretax corporate profits over the last five decades into the contribution from the average annual rise in nominal GDP and the contribution from the average annual change in pretax profit margins as a percent of GDP. This grouping will allow the direct translation of rising productivity gains from increasing Digital Deflation into rising pretax profits as a percent of GDP and then into rising earnings per share for a market index, in this case the S&P 500.

Lines 3 and 4 show that for some decades in the past, average annual growth rates in earnings for the S&P 500 varied somewhat from the rates of annual growth in overall corporate pretax profits due to changes in effective corporate tax rates and write-offs. However, growth rates for pretax and after-tax profits have tracked fairly closely over the five decades overall, so a simplifying assumption will be made. Projections will assume little change in effective corporate tax rates and hence that lines 3 and 4 will be fairly similar for the two decades ahead. (Incidentally, this is where alterations in corporate tax rates by Congress directly help or hurt stock market returns and wealth creation for all investors.)

It is important to note that in the 1950s, 1960s, 1970s, and 1980s, pretax profits *declined* as a percent of GDP. This is not surprising since this was during an extended period when growth in productivity was on a steady decline. Similarly, we should not be surprised that pretax profits as a percent of GDP surged by 2.3% per year in the 1990s when measured productivity growth finally started to move upwards and out of its extended slump. Rising growth in productivity was a major reason that stock market investors profited so handsomely in the 1990s, as it enabled corporate pretax profits to grow by a vigorous 7.8% per year. This is how in the 1990s corporate profit growth rates exceeded the rate of growth in the overall economy (GDP)—ending four long decades of declining corporate profit margins.

Will productivity gains significantly move the needle again on profits as a percent of GDP during the next two decades? The answer is critical, because growth in productivity will be a major determinant of whether profits will grow faster or slower than nominal GDP in the decades of the 2000s and 2010s.

There was a second reason that common stocks performed so well in the 1990s. Price–earnings ratios expanded dramatically in concert with the decline in inflation and interest rates. Line 5 in the New Economy stock market model shows how *P/E ratios on the S&P 500 ex-*

## E X H I B I T   9-1

A New Economy Stock Market Model

|  | Decades of Annual Averages | | | | |
|---|---|---|---|---|---|
|  | 1950s | 1960s | 1970s | 1980s | 1990s |
| [1] -- Nominal GDP Growth multiplied by: | 6.6% | 6.9% | 10.0% | 7.9% | 5.4% |
| [2] -- Imputed % Rise in Pretax Profits as a % of GDP [a] equals: | -0.1% | -1.0% | -0.9% | -1.7% | 2.3% |
| [3] -- Change in Pretax Profits | 6.5% | 5.8% | 9.0% | 6.1% | 7.8% |
| [4] -- Change in S&P 500 EPS [b] multiplied by: | 4.8% | 5.7% | 9.1% | 8.1% | 6.7% |
| [5] -- Change in P/E Ratios [S&P 500] equals: | 9.6% | -0.4% | -5.4% | 4.7% | 8.8% |
| [6] -- Annual Capital Appreciation plus: | 14.9% | 5.3% | 3.2% | 13.2% | 16.1% |
| [7] -- Dividend Return [S&P 500] [c] equals: | 4.4% | 2.0% | 4.3% | 5.0% | 2.9% |
| [8] -- Nominal Total Return [S&P 500] less: | 19.3% | 7.3% | 7.5% | 18.2% | 19.0% |
| [9] -- CPI equals: | 2.1% | 2.3% | 7.1% | 5.6% | 3.0% |
| [10] -- Real Total Return | 17.2% | 5.0% | 0.4% | 12.6% | 16.0% |

Notes:
[a]  May differ slightly from reported due to rounding.
[b]  Uses operating net income (excluding non-recurring items) for S&P 500
from 1980-2000 and reported EPS from 1950-1979
[c]  Compound dividend return on beginning of year index.

Sources: Federal Reserve; Bureau of Labor Statistics; Tanaka Capital Management, Inc.

*panded by a staggering 8.8% per year in the 1990s,* which was almost one-half of the extraordinary 19.0% average annual return on common stocks experienced in the decade. One could legitimately question whether these rates of return can ever be seen again—or at least any-time soon. It's also fair to ask whether these returns were so strong that they will have to be reversed in the years ahead.

The answers, as you'll recall from previous chapters, will depend very much on the direction of inflation which will largely determine P/E ratios over the next several years.

A further examination of line 5 reveals the volatility of the average annual percentage change in P/E ratios over the decades. For common stock investors, one could say that "it's all about P/Es" because the strongest decades of nominal and real returns on stocks were the 1950s, 1980s, and 1990s—when P/E ratios expanded by 9.6%, 4.7%, and 8.8% *per year*, respectively. The worst decade for investors was the 1970s when P/E ratios declined by 5.4% per year and real returns on common stocks averaged a paltry 0.4% per year. Given the importance of P/Es, the next section of this chapter will provide a convenient path for translating predicted declines in inflation from growing Digital Deflation into lower interest rates and rising P/E ratios.

Lines 7 and 8 show how dividend yields have also been an important part of nominal common stock returns over the last 50 years. However, after the dramatic rise in stock market valuations in the 1990s, careful investors should be aware that going into the new decade, dividend yields are starting out very low, with a yield of only 1.1% on the S&P 500. This will make it even more difficult for common stocks to generate attractive total returns (capital appreciation plus dividend yields) anywhere near the 18.2% and 19.0% per year returns of the 1980s and the 1990s. Dividend yields averaged 5.0% and 2.9% per year, respectively, in the 1980s and 1990s.

There is another reason that dividend yields are low. As thoughtful policymakers are becoming increasingly aware, fiscal policy is stacked decidedly against the payment of dividends. This is because dividends are still taxed twice before they reach investors—even after the 2003 tax law changes. This has discouraged company managements from raising dividends in line with earnings growth and has instead encouraged share buyback programs—adding to financial leverage, stock market volatility, and risk.

What about real returns? After adjusting for inflation using the reported Consumer Price Index (CPI), as shown in lines 9 and 10, real total returns on common stocks in the 1990s were actually *lower* than real returns in the 1950s. This may be surprising to many readers. In this light, the stock market boom of the 1990s was not as unusual as many believe—or fear.

Nonetheless, the rising stock market, particularly in the late 1990s, left the market in a precarious position—at least in terms of historical valuations. Given the already record high P/E ratios and very low dividend yields on common stocks going out of the 1990s and into the decade of the 2000s, investors will be fortunate to have any chance of enjoying double-digit returns in real or even in nominal terms over the next several years.

In fact, the *only* way investors will be able to enjoy double-digit real or nominal returns on common stocks over the next decade or two is if P/E ratios rise significantly. This will only happen if (1) reported inflation takes another significant decline from already low levels or (2) *real* bond interest rates (10-year Treasury yield minus the rate of inflation) decline from the high levels of the last 20 years—or if both happen. This is where Digital Deflation comes into the picture.

As discussed earlier, with benign labor force growth and a significant increase in productivity growth, reported inflation has the potential to experience a major decline—without a recession. Fortunately, there is an excellent chance that this will come about as the government properly counts more of the quality improvement and Digital Deflation that are already being generated by the Digital Revolution. With another quantum level drop in inflation expectations over the next several years, P/E ratios can move up to new highs. This is how investors will most fully notice and realize the wealth-generating benefits of the Digital Revolution.

As alluded to above, the second major opportunity for P/E ratios to make a sustainable move upward from already historically high levels is if the bond markets demand a lower real interest rate on long-term bonds. The reason is that bond yields directly affect stock values, and currently most economists and most investors are expecting that the real interest rate on long Treasury bonds may remain at historically high levels—and they may not. For example, the Congressional Budget Office is forecasting that the real interest rate on 10-year Treasury bonds will average about 3.9% over the next 10 years.

To be conservative, this New Economy stock market model also assumes a 3.9% real rate in predicting the market P/E ratio at the end of each of the next two decades—even though this may be too high. The 3.9% real rate assumption is a very large 0.9% greater than the 2.99% average of the last 46 years. If the real bond rate declines toward the long-term average, the nominal 10-year bond yield can move lower relative to reported inflation, paving the way to a rise in stock market P/E ratios.

The next few pages will show more explicitly how lower inflation from increasing Digital Deflation can lead to higher P/E ratios over the next two decades, as well as how growing Digital Deflation can increase productivity and contribute to a rise in corporate profit margins as a percent of GDP.

## INFLATION, INTEREST RATES, AND FAIR VALUE P/Es

Over the years, many stock market P/E valuation models have been devised and optimized for predicting P/E ratios under various economic or market conditions. Fortunately, two of the most consistent and accurate valuation models over longer periods of time are also simple and easy to understand. The first is the model that relates the P/E ratio of the stock market with the rate of inflation, and the second is a model that relates P/E ratios with interest rates on long-term Treasury bonds. The latter is often referred to as the *Fed model* as it has been used by the Federal Reserve to gauge whether the stock market is over- or undervalued—at least relative to bonds.

Both models are easy to understand because the inverse of the P/E ratio is itself a yield called the *earnings yield*, or earnings divided by price (E/P). The inverse of a 50 P/E is 1 divided by 50, or a 2% earnings yield. The earnings yield reflects how much profit return is earned for the shareholder relative to the price of a stock, and this earnings yield can quite easily be compared to another yield, such as the interest yield on bonds, as well as the rate of inflation in the overall economy.

In setting out to develop a stock market model for an era of rising Digital Deflation, the challenge on the one hand was to capture the major benefits to the stock market of Digital Deflation, but on the other hand not fall victim to the inherent shortcomings of the existing models. As with all models, the P/E ratio versus inflation and the P/E ratio versus interest rate models have their weaknesses. It turns out that for these particular P/E models to work efficiently, they have to assume that the rate of long-term earnings growth and the riskiness of common stock returns remain constant over time—that they are not affected by whatever is causing inflation or interest rates to move up or down.

This is a problem. Most economists and investors would accept a simplifying assumption that all things influencing the risk of equity returns such as the risk of economic cycles, political upheaval, wars, oil shortages, and other kinds of event risk, will average out over the next several years to be similar to the last several years. But, the Achilles' heel of these models has always been that historically, the cyclical forces acting to reduce inflation also act cyclically to reduce earnings growth. In other words, if inflation is going down, that's great for stocks and P/E ratios should rise, but not if earnings growth is also slowing down due to a weak economy that brought on the low inflation.

This is where the combination of the long-term, once-a-generation benefits of favorable demographics, as well as the unique dual benefits of Digital Deflation become so powerful. Low labor force growth has created a multiyear foundation of low inflation and the need for productivity growth if the economy is to grow at all. At the same time, constantly improving quality and performance in digitally driven products and services will create both lower inflation and the equally important increase in real economic growth *simultaneously*. This is the New Economy phenomenon that was first seen in the late 1990s, and it will continue for as long as the New Economy continues to grow faster than the Old.

The Digital Revolution can deliver the quantity- and quality-based productivity gains and real output growth that are absolutely required for the economy to enjoy any significant growth in an environment of low labor force growth. Yet, at the same time, when quality improvement is properly counted, Digital Deflation will also create a long-lasting and growing downward pressure on reported inflation. Since this reduction in inflation from Digital Deflation is not a result of a cyclically weakening economy, but is actually accompanied by a *strengthening* economy, these P/E ratio models relating stock market valuations directly to inflation and interest rates make them ideal for our analysis. They can be used to translate the beneficial effects of the New Economy and Digital Deflation into projections of future common stock returns and wealth creation.

Arguably, it is possible that faster earnings growth rates from rising productivity growth will act to raise P/E ratios even higher than the current New Economy stock market model would suggest. This is an opportunity for further analysis.

Over the years, P/E ratios have tended to move inversely with both inflation and interest rates, as seen in Exhibit 9-2. If inflation (in this case the GDP Deflator) goes down, P/E ratios tend to rise. If in-

P/E Ratios Move Inversely with Inflation and Interest Rates

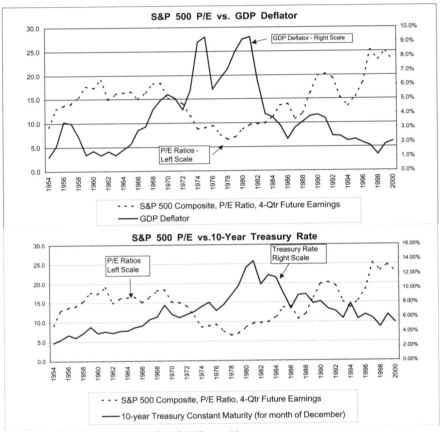

Sources: Standard & Poor's; Department of Commerce; Tanaka Capital Management, Inc.

terest rates (in this case, 10-year Treasury bond yields) go down, P/E ratios also tend to rise.

Using the S&P 500 Index and the 12-month forward earnings per share on the S&P 500, the correlations are a fairly strong –0.72 on the P/E ratio versus inflation model, and an even stronger –0.84 on the P/E ratio versus interest rate model. These strong correlations reflect the constant arbitrage between the stock market and the bond market and their common sensitivity to inflation. Their strong relationship, in fact, enables the adoption of the term *fair value P/E* in these models to refer to stock market P/E valuations that are priced fairly and consistently versus the level of interest rates on 10-year Treasury bonds and the P/E versus 10-year Treasury model.

Exhibit 9-3 presents the same data for each of the two models in scatter diagram format. It is fairly clear that there are strong patterns, particularly for the P/E versus interest rate model at the bottom. Both relationships are exponential, meaning that the P/E ratio curves move sharply upward as the GDP Deflator and the 10-year Treasury yields approach zero. The models cease to function when either inflation or interest rates drop below zero. In fact, both models produce unreasonably high P/E ratios when either inflation or 10-year Treasury rates drop to near zero.

Although both P/E ratio models are useful, they don't always agree. For the purpose of the prediction of P/E ratios in a world of increasing Digital Deflation—with near zero aggregate inflation and very low interest rates—it was felt it would be most practical to use the 10-year Treasury model. This is not only because it has demonstrated a tighter correlation with P/Es historically, but because interest rates have a lot more room to decline from the 4.00%–5.00% level before they approach zero. Inflation is already near zero.

With the recent level of interest rates on 10-year Treasury bonds in the 4.0%–5.0% area, the P/E ratio versus 10-year Treasury model would suggest a fair value theoretical P/E ratio on the S&P 500 of 27 to 21 times next 12-month forward earnings. (Again, *fair value* is defined for this model as the P/E ratio consistent with the P/E ratio versus 10-year Treasury bond model.) However, by making appropriate downward adjustments on the GDP Deflator for all 2.2% of the currently uncounted Digital Deflation, the 10-year Treasury yield would be closer to 2.0% to 3.0% than 4.0% to 5.0%, and the P/E ratio adjusted for Digital Deflation would be closer to 40 to 60 times forward earnings.

This P/E ratio range of 40 to 60 times earnings is highly theoretical at this point. It presumes that the government is counting 100% of the estimated 2.2% of annual quality improvement and Digital Deflation that it is currently not measuring—and that investors accept this quality-based reduction in inflation. It also assumes a steady growth economy free of external threats, and it assumes that the capital markets fully discount an extended period of near zero inflation or modest deflation. The real usefulness of this exercise is to show where price–earnings ratios would be if the government were fully counting quality improvement actually being generated in the economy today.

**E X H I B I T   9-3**

P/E Ratio Scatter Diagrams

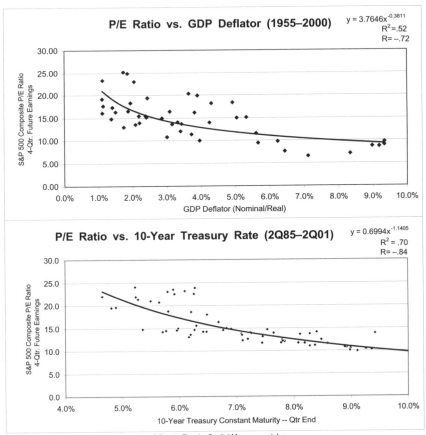

Sources: Department of Commerce; Standard & Poor's; Tanaka Capital Management, Inc.

## P/E RATIO FORECASTS FOR THE NEXT TWO DECADES

As indicated in the last chapter, in making estimates for the next two decades of the effect of Digital Deflation on inflation and P/E ratios, *this analysis assumes that the government will count only 50% of the currently uncounted Digital Deflation* projected out to the end of each of the next two decades. The ends of the decades are 2009 and 2019, just as 1999 marked the end of the 1990s. For additional conservatism, this analysis begins with baseline Congressional Budget Office (CBO) projections of 5.80% on 10-year Treasuries and 1.90% on the GDP Deflator for the next 10 years, implying a 3.90% real 10-year Treasury bond yield (10-year bond yield minus the GDP Deflator).[1] To reiterate, the 3.90% real rate assumption on the 10-year T-bond may prove to be overly conservative since it is 90 basis points or 0.90% above the 2.99% average of the last 47 years that 10-year T-bonds have traded.

Adjusting the above conservative baseline assumptions to reflect that the government by 2009 and 2019 will be counting 50% of the currently uncounted Digital Deflation, the P/E ratio on the S&P 500 is projected to be about **26.5** times earnings by 2009 and **32.3** times earnings by 2019, as summarized in Exhibit 9-4. Note that this analysis assumes that **1.40%** of counted Digital Deflation by 2009 and **1.87%** by 2019 will reduce bond yields by the same amounts down to levels of 4.13% by 2009 and 3.47% by 2019. For common stock investors, this model projects that P/E ratio expansion will add 1.21% per year to common stock returns in the decade ending 2009 and 2.01% per year in the decade ending in 2019. This is off a relatively high base of 23.5 times earnings in 1999. For those who wish to examine various scenarios for the P/E ratio versus 10-year Treasury yields, Appendix A contains a handy conversion table.

## HIGHER PRODUCTIVITY AND PROFIT MARGINS IN THE NEXT TWO DECADES

As shown in Exhibit 9-1, the most stable contributor to nominal returns on stocks over the last five decades has been the growth in nominal corporate earnings, averaging 7.0% per year. In the 1990s, nominal corporate pretax profits grew by 7.8% per year, of which an unusually large 2.3% per year was from the average annual rise in corporate profit margins as a percent of GDP.

As surprising as it sounds, the next two decades are also likely to benefit from a rise in corporate profit margins as a percent of GDP as corporate profitability will benefit directly from accelerating growth in labor productivity. The two main sources of rising productivity will be: (1) quantity-based productivity gains from IT capital spending rising as a percent of GDP and (2) quality-based productivity gains from the continuous improvement in the quality and performance of digitally driven products and services.

## E X H I B I T   9-4

P/E Ratio Expansion in the New Economy

|  | End of Decade | | |
|---|---|---|---|
|  | **1999** **(Actual)** | **2009** | **2019** |
| GDP Deflator (w/CBO Estimates) [a] | 1.40% | 1.90% | 1.90% |
| - Deflation from Rising IT as % GDP | 0.00% | -0.27% | -0.46% |
| - Counting 50% of Uncounted Digital Deflation | 0.00% | -1.40% | -1.87% |
| GDP Deflator Adj. For Digital Deflation | N/A | 0.23% | -0.43% |
|  |  |  |  |
| Real 10-year Treasury Bond Yield | 4.88% | 3.90% | 3.90% |
|  |  |  |  |
| 10-year Treasury Bond Yield w/ CBO Estimates [a] | 6.28% | 5.80% | 5.80% |
| - Deflation from Rising IT as % GDP | 0.00% | -0.27% | -0.46% |
| - Counting 50% of Uncounted Digital Deflation | 0.00% | **-1.40%** | **-1.87%** |
| 10-year Treasury Bond Yield Adj. for Digital Deflation | N/A | 4.13% | 3.47% |
|  |  |  |  |
| S&P 500 P/E (Next 4 Qtrs. EPS) |  |  |  |
| (A) - GDP Deflator Model P/E Projection[b] | 23.5 | 38.1 | 125.9 |
| (B) - 10-year Treasury Bond Model P/E Projection | **23.5** | **26.5** | **32.3** |
| % Increase in P/E Ratios/Year in Decade (CAGR) |  |  |  |
| Using 10-yr Treasury Bond Model [b] | 8.8% | 1.21% | 2.01% |

[a] Congressional Budget Office projections out to 2011 are assumed to extend to 2020.
[b] GDP Deflator models for market P/E's become non-functional with negative inflation rates, so a "near zero" 0.01% rate was assumed.

Sources: Department of Commerce; Congressional Budget Office; Tanaka Capital Management, Inc.

Corporate profit growth has the potential to surprise economists and investors on the upside. Why? Expectations are low, and rising productivity gains are likely to power corporate profit margins to record highs. Rising profit margins would help boost annual earnings growth rates to approximately 8.9% and 6.5% per year, respectively, for each of the next two decades. That would be very fast growth indeed because low inflation will hold down nominal growth in the next two decades. Also, it would be difficult for corporate profits to grow much faster than

GDP over the long term. There is obviously a Malthusian limit to profit expansion, as profits can only grow to be but so large as a percent of GDP.

Nevertheless, as can be seen in the New Economy Stock Market model in Exhibit 9-1, over the last five decades, nominal corporate pretax profits have grown at decade average annual rates of 5.8% to 9.0% per year, largely during periods of *low* productivity growth—so projected growth of 8.9% and 6.5% per year for the next two decades appear reasonable and within historical bounds.

Exhibit 9-5 shows how the projected pretax corporate profit growth rates of 8.9% and 6.5% per year are derived for each of the next two decades. The estimates start with the CBO's baseline long-term expectation that nominal GDP will grow by 5.2% per year through 2011, and it is assumed that the 5.2% rate of growth will continue to 2020. The CBO's long-term estimates are used for the GDP Deflator, real GDP and productivity, and adjustments are then made to account for Digital Deflation over the next two decades. It is important to note that IT capital spending is estimated to continue to grow at a faster rate than nominal GDP based on the corporate need for enhanced productivity and the ongoing advances to be made in digital technologies.

The estimates for uncounted Digital Deflation from quality improvement are derived from the Digital Deflation–GDP Deflator model described in Chapter 7, reflecting faster rates of growth in IT and the New Economy relative to overall GDP growth. It should be understood that the federal government for political or other reasons may decide not to count even these conservative amounts of quality and performance improvement. Hence, the full 2.4% per year of estimated real growth and Digital Deflation for the 2000–2009 decade and the 3.3% per year estimated for the 2010–2019 decade may not be reported even though they will be delivered to consumers.

A key assumption for this profit margin analysis, however, is that even if the government is not counting the full amount of quality-based productivity gains during the next 20 years, consumers will perceive that the products and services are of higher value each year and will buy more at the margin. Over the next two decades, just as in the 1990s, New Economy Companies will not be selling "empty calories." They will be creating and offering more value for the dollar to their customers and will grow faster than Old Economy Companies, which by and large will only be offering the same quality products at higher prices.

**E X H I B I T   9-5**

Rising Productivity and Profitability (75% Conversion of Rising IT to Productivity)

| | Average Annual Increase Per Year | | | | | | |
| | | | | | | 2000-2009 | 2010-2019 |
| | 1950s | 1960s | 1970s | 1980s | 1990s | 2009 | 2019 |
|---|---|---|---|---|---|---|---|
| IT Equipment & Software Capital Spending (Nominal) | 9.5% | 13.8% | 14.9% | 11.4% | 9.6% | 9.0% | 8.5% |
| Nominal GDP (w/CBO Estimates) | 6.6% | 6.9% | 10.0% | 7.9% | 5.4% | 5.2% | 5.2% |
| % Incr.IT Capital Spending/% Incr. Nominal GDP | 0.7% | 1.2% | 1.8% | 2.9% | 3.6% | 6.0% | 8.9% |
| Non-Farm Productivity Gain (CBO Estimate) | 2.8% | 2.9% | 2.0% | 1.4% | 1.9% | 2.5% | 2.5% |
| Quantity-based Productivity Gain from Rising IT Cap. Spending (a) | - | - | - | - | - | 0.4% | 1.1% |
| Quality-based Productivity Gain from Digital Deflation | - | - | - | - | - | 2.8% | 3.7% |
| Fully Counted Productivity Gains (a) | - | - | - | - | - | 5.7% | 7.3% |
| % Conversion of Quality-based Prod. Gains to Profit Margins | - | - | - | - | - | 75.0% | 75.0% |
| Adjusted Prod. Gains Converting Directly to Higher Profit Margins | - | - | - | - | - | 5.0% | 6.4% |
| Pretax Profit as % GDP at End Of Decade (b) | 10.6% | 9.5% | 8.7% | 7.2% | 8.9% | 12.5% | 14.2% |
| Increase in Pretax Corp. Profits as % of GDP/yr. (c) | -0.1% | -1.1% | -0.9% | -1.9% | 2.1% | 3.5% | 1.3% |
| % Growth in Pretax Profits/yr. (CAGR) | 6.5% | 5.8% | 9.0% | 6.1% | 7.8% | **8.9%** | **6.5%** |

(a) Productivity growth in last year of 2000-2009 and 2010-2019 decades.
(b) Pretax Corp. Profits with IVA and CCA as % GDP equals 6.5% + 1.198x(Productivity Growth Rate).
(c) Projections assume annual percentage increases in Corp. Profits as a % GDP solely due to rising Productivity Growth Rates. May differ slightly from Imputed % Rise in Pretax Profits as a % of GDP.

Source: Tanaka Capital Management, Inc. Estimates

The productivity and profit margin model described in Chapter 7 was used to adjust productivity gains from Digital Deflation and to translate the adjusted growth in productivity into increases in pretax corporate profits as a percent of GDP. Recall that the correlation was a reasonably strong 0.75, and the rule of thumb for the model is that for every 1.0 percentage point increase in productivity growth, pretax profits as a percent of GDP have historically risen by 1.2 percentage points.

For the purpose of this model, however, to be conservative, it is assumed that a rise in productivity due to rising real output growth from Digital Deflation will result in only three-quarters of the historical rise in pretax profits as a percent of GDP. In other words, for every 1.0 percentage point rise in productivity growth, profit margins will be assumed to rise by only 0.9 percentage point (rather than by the 1.2% rule of thumb).

This conservative assumption is made because the Digital Deflation thesis is so new that there are very little data relating quality-based real growth in GDP and productivity to rising corporate profit margins. However, there is little doubt that the delivery of faster and better products at cheaper prices will stimulate more unit demand and higher dollars of revenues for digitally improving products. When revenues grow faster than operating expenses, the result will be higher operating profit margins and higher pretax profit margins—both as a percentage of revenues and as a percentage of GDP.

In Chapter 12, it will be seen how during the 1990s, New Economy Companies delivering increasing quality-based value to the customer and Digital Deflation to the economy produced significantly faster sales and profit growth than Old Economy Companies that tended to generate or pass on Old Economy inflation. If the history of the 1990s is any indication, it could be that the assumption of only a three-quarters' conversion of *quality*-based productivity gains to pretax profit margins will prove to be too conservative. Much more analysis is needed to develop an accurate estimate of just how much of the traditional pretax profit lift will be generated in the future from *quality*-based productivity gains versus the historical correlation with *quantity*-based productivity gains of the past.

In estimating the total boost to productivity—and therefore to pretax corporate profit margins—from the Digital Revolution, a second but smaller upward adjustment was made to the CBO's long-term flat line forecast of 2.5% productivity gains. This was done to reflect in projections the increasing amount of *quantity*-based productivity growth generated from rising IT capital spending as a percent of GDP. Like the CBO, most forecasters simply assume a constant or flat rate of productivity gains into the future, without recognizing and providing for the upward trajectory for IT spending as it grows to become a larger percentage of the economy. The IT capital spending and productivity model introduced in Chapter 7 shows an unmistakable positive relationship between rising IT capital expenditures as a percentage of GDP and rising productivity growth, with a very strong 0.91 historical correlation.

Rising IT capital spending as a percent of GDP should contribute an incremental 0.4% per year to productivity growth by 2009 and an additional 0.7% per year by 2019. Using the 120% rule of thumb for the full 1.2% profit margin gain per 1.0% rise in quantity-based productivity growth, this would translate into about a 0.5% increase in corporate pretax profit margins as a percentage of GDP by 2009 and an additional 0.8% of higher pretax margins by 2019 solely as a result of rising IT capital expenditures as a percentage of GDP.

As shown in Exhibit 9-5, the addition of *quantity-based productivity gains* from rising IT capital expenditures plus *quality-based productivity gains* from Digital Deflation to the CBO's baseline projection of 2.5% productivity growth over the next decade produces total theoretical productivity gains of 5.7% by 2009 and 7.3% by 2019.

Making the conservative assumption that only three-quarters or 75% of the quality-based productivity gains will be converted directly into higher profit margins, Exhibit 9-5 shows how that the adjusted increase in productivity gains that will convert into higher margins will be about 5.0% and 6.4% for 2009 and 2019, respectively.

The model suggests that pretax corporate profits should still rise to about 12.5% of GDP by 2009 and 14.2% of GDP by 2019, which would be record highs for the last 50 years. By way of reference, pretax profits ranged from 9.1% to 12.0% of GDP in the prosperous 1950s and 1960s. They then declined in the late 1960s and 1970s just when the demographics turned negative and it became easier to substitute excess labor for capital.

The rationale for record high margins is that the demographic scarcity of labor will call for greater capital inputs in the economy so that gains in labor productivity will result in more goods and services being produced with little incremental labor input. The higher margins are consistent with the higher return on sales needed for the increase in capital input (relative to labor input) required per dollar of sales. Nonetheless, this is new ground with little data correlating quality-based productivity gains to increases in profit margins. So, this productivity-profit margin model is likely to be less accurate than the interest rate–P/E ratio model.

In terms of their contribution to average annual profit growth, rising pretax corporate profit margins as a percentage of GDP should enhance corporate earnings growth by about 3.5% per year in the decade of the 2000s and by 1.3% per year in the decade of the 2010s. Multiplying these increments times the projected growth in nominal GDP of 5.2% per year produces projected growth rates in pretax corporate profits of **8.9%** per year in the 2000–2009 decade and 6.5% per year in the 2010–2019 decade, as seen at the bottom of Exhibit 9-5.

It is worthwhile to recognize that the maximum productivity gains of 5.7% per year and 7.3% per year by 2009 and 2019, respectively, are theoretical and would seem incomprehensible to most investors and economists at this time. That is to be expected with any new economic phenomenon. Remember that they were used only in the productivity–profit margin model, and the model only assumed three-quarters of the historical productivity-to-profit lift.

It is highly unlikely that these theoretical productivity gains will ever be fully counted, because it would require that the government statisticians count 100% of the currently uncounted Digital Deflation. But it is very important for the public and policymakers to know how high the theoretical limit or "potential productivity" could reach in less than two decades if the government fully counted real quality improvement. It will be our monetary and fiscal policymakers that will largely determine how close we get to that potential.

In 1983, the demographic models yielded predictions of 3.0% inflation for the next 10 years, a level that was hard for people to believe in the early 1980s when inflation on the CPI was running 6% and had recently been as high as 13.5%. But inflation indeed declined to 3.0%, and it trended even lower in the 1990s during the longest and strongest economic expansion in modern U.S. history. In a similar manner, over the *next* two decades, the projected benefits of Digital Deflation will be built on a favorable demographic foundation of modest labor force growth to provide the potential for labor productivity gains to reach record high levels—even if only half the annual gains in quality improvement are measured by the government.

These are the kinds of large order anomalies, of course, that create major investment opportunities. The Digital Revolution and Digital Deflation can add one or two more decades of very positive returns to the demographic-based once-a-generation super bull market that began back in 1982.

## NEW ECONOMY STOCK MARKET PROJECTIONS

Exhibit 9-6 presents the New Economy stock market model with projections for nominal and real returns on stocks for each of the next two decades. Profit growth rates and changes in P/E ratios are taken from the above two models for pretax profit margins and P/E ratios.

For each of the next two decades, earnings growth rates of 8.9% and 6.5% per year are combined with annual increases in P/E ratios of 1.2% and 2.0% per year and with very modest dividend yields of 1.1% and 0.8% per year to produce nominal total returns on common stocks of 11.3% and 9.5% per year. The more important *real* total return on common stocks (nominal return minus the CPI) will average about 9.2% per year and 7.7% per year over each of the next two decades. These returns will fall very short of the exceedingly high real common stock returns of the 1950s, 1980s, and 1990s, but will be significantly better than the mediocre returns of the 1960s and the nonexistent returns of the 1970s.

The prudent investor would be wise to be very cautious about expected returns over the next decade after the highly unusual stock market gains of the last 20 years. At a minimum, the demographic, productivity, Digital Deflation, and New Economy stock market models provide some confirmation and comfort that nominal common stock returns could approximate the often quoted long-term average returns of 10% to 11% experienced in the U.S. equity markets since the 1920s. Again, this model would require that the government count about 50% of the currently uncounted quality improvement and Digital Deflation being created today.

On the upside, two less likely but possible scenarios are presented later in this chapter in which stock market returns could be materially higher than the average returns projected in the model above. On the downside, one scenario is presented in which stock market returns could be significantly lower than projected in the case of 50% counted Digital Deflation.

Immediately below is a discussion of how record amounts of wealth can be created by the New Economy—even if there are only average returns on stocks over the 2000–2009 and 2010–2019 decades, as suggested in the model assuming 50% counted Digital Deflation.

## TWO MORE DECADES OF WEALTH CREATION

As noted previously, the next two decades could be very much like the late 1980s and 1990s in that inflation will fall well short of

## EXHIBIT 9-6

New Economy Stock Market Projections—Case C (Profit Margins Assume 75% Conversion of Rising IT to Productivity Growth, and P/E Expansion Assumes 50% Counted Digital Deflation)

| | Decades of Annual Averages | | | | | Projections | |
| | 1950s | 1960s | 1970s | 1980s | 1990s | 2000-2009[E] | 2010-2019[E] |
|---|---|---|---|---|---|---|---|
| [1] -- Nominal GDP Growth multiplied by*: | 6.6% | 6.9% | 10.0% | 7.9% | 5.4% | 5.2% | 5.2% |
| [2] -- Imputed % Rise in Pretax Profits as a % of GDP (a) equals: | -0.1% | -1.0% | -0.9% | -1.7% | 2.3% | 3.5% | 1.3% |
| [3] -- Change in Pretax Profits | 6.5% | 5.8% | 9.0% | 6.1% | 7.8% | 8.9% | 6.5% |
| [4] -- Change in S&P 500 EPS (b) multiplied by*: | 4.8% | 5.7% | 9.1% | 8.1% | 6.7% | 8.9% | 6.5% |
| [5] -- Change in P/E Ratios [S&P 500] equals: | 9.6% | -0.4% | -5.4% | 4.7% | 8.8% | 1.2% | 2.0% |
| [6] -- Annual Capital Appreciation plus: | 14.9% | 5.3% | 3.2% | 13.2% | 16.1% | 10.2% | 8.7% |
| [7] -- Dividend Return [S&P 500] (c) equals: | 4.4% | 2.0% | 4.3% | 5.0% | 2.9% | 1.1% | 0.8% |
| [8] -- Nominal Total Return [S&P 500] less: | 19.3% | 7.3% | 7.5% | 18.2% | 19.0% | 11.3% | 9.5% |
| [9] -- CPI equals: | 2.1% | 2.3% | 7.1% | 5.6% | 3.0% | 2.1% | 1.7% |
| [10] -- Real Total Return | 17.2% | 5.0% | 0.4% | 12.6% | 16.0% | 9.2% | 7.7% |

* The multiplier is 1 plus the change.

Notes:
(a) May differ slightly from reported due to rounding.
(b) Uses operating net income (excluding non-recurring items) for S&P 500 from 1980-2000 and reported EPS from 1950-1979.
(c) Compound dividend return on beginning of year index.
Sources: Federal Reserve; BLS; Tanaka Capital Management, Inc.

people's expectations, and the economy will get stronger as it ages. Returns on both labor and capital will increase as growth in IT spending and rising labor productivity combine to boost corporate profitability.

Much like the late 1990s, rising corporate profit margins will provide the opportunity, particularly in a scarce labor environment, for more investors to earn attractive returns in exchange for providing much needed capital. Real wages will increase at the same time that profit margins improve, both enabled of by the rise in measured productivity.

This bodes well for more wealth creation in the United States. In the 1990s, things were so good that even after the Post '90s sell-off, U.S. stock markets still stood at levels that were several times higher than they were at the beginning of the 1990s. Likewise, over the next two decades, U.S. capital markets will rise to price levels that will be at multiples of existing levels.

In many ways, though, the next two decades will be very different from the 1990s. As more Digital Deflation is counted by the government, inflation and interest rates will move to record lows, dramatically altering the way Investor-Consumers spend, save, and invest. Society as a whole is likely to change. Productivity gains will reach higher levels than the late 1990s, pushing corporate profit margins as a percentage of GDP to levels not seen since the 1950s. Politicians may be tempted to tax these profits, but they would be well advised not to "kill the golden goose"—the investment in the ongoing Digital Revolution that will create rising productivity gains and near-zero inflation.

Although common stocks will not likely generate anything like the 19.0% per year nominal returns experienced in the 1990s, the next two decades will produce nominal returns close to the 10%-plus average of the last 75 years. Real rates of return on common stocks will also fall short of the 16.0% per year real returns of the 1990s, but will benefit over the next 20 years from an even lower level of inflation than we enjoyed in the 1990s.

Perhaps it will come as a surprise, but despite lower common stock returns than in the 1990s, real household net worth will grow at almost the same annual rate over the next two decades as it did in the 1990s. This is because common stock and other equity-like assets will start each decade as much larger percentages of household net worth than the 1990s, and common stocks will continue to be the fastest appreciating asset class. In addition, aggregate inflation will be lower in the overall economy, and in an interesting twist, Digital Deflation will surprise economists in another very unlikely asset class—housing.

Housing and other tangible assets, long thought of as inflation hedges that go up in price as inflation rises, will actually benefit from declining inflation in the aggregate economy—or, more specifically, from expanding deflation in the New Economy. This is because growing Digital Deflation in the New Economy will allow the Federal Reserve to accommodate more traditional inflation in the Old Economy without it being seen as raising the aggregate inflation rate. In essence, there can be more home price appreciation in the Old Economy because it will be offset by price reductions in the New Economy.

In addition, rising productivity and declining inflation from Digital Deflation will result in lower interest rates and lower monthly payments on mortgages and other consumer loans (e.g., zero interest rate auto loans). In effect, this will enable buyers to pay higher prices for tangible assets. A significant decline in interest rates is one of the important reasons why housing and auto demand remained much stronger than economists and analysts expected during the 2000–2002 economic slowdown. This is only a taste of things to come.

## A NEW ECONOMY WEALTH MODEL

Exhibit 9-7 shows how household net worth is likely to grow during each of the next two decades due to the projected growth in tangible and equity-like financial assets. In the case of the government counting 50% of uncounted Digital Deflation, net worth should rise by more than $33 trillion in the current 2000–2009 decade and by more than $60 trillion in the next decade, both considerably greater than the $21.9 trillion increase in net worth in the 1990s.

These would be record gains in wealth for any economy and would be staggering for those outside the United States to contemplate. It should be noted, however, that in percentage terms, the projected increase in nominal net worth will look less impressive, with gains of only 80% for each of the two decades versus 109% gain in nominal household net worth during the 1990s. But thanks to two consecutive decades in the 1980s and 1990s of rapid gains in net worth, U.S. households will only need to be compounding modest percentage growth rates on top of the already high base to generate large dollar gains in net worth.

Of course, what is important is what households can buy with their net worth. After adjusting for inflation, the outlook appears a lot brighter for American households. Real net worth is projected to increase by 46% in the 2000–2009 decade and by 52% in the 2010–2019 decade—rather impressive when compared with the 42% gain in real net worth in the 1980s and even the phenomenal 56% real gain in the 1990s. In real terms, if the government counts half of the Digital Deflation to be produced over the next two decades, Americans can look forward to the same kinds of gains in real net worth as the very prosperous 1980s and 1990s. The odds of any four decades of large gains in real wealth occurring consecutively are very low, but it can be a reality with a force as powerful as Digital Deflation expanding rapidly with the Digital Revolution.

**E X H I B I T   9-7**

A New Economy Wealth Model

| | 1950s | 1960s | 1970s | 1980s | 1990s | 2000s | 2010s |
|---|---|---|---|---|---|---|---|
| Incr. in Equity-Like Assets | | | | | | | |
| $ Trillions | $0.4 | $0.8 | $2.1 | $5.7 | $17.9 | $29.5 | $56.4 |
| % Increase | 105.6% | 90.9% | 128.7% | 153.5% | 190.7% | 108.3% | 99.3% |
| Incr. in Net Financial Assets | | | | | | | |
| $ Trillions | $0.5 | $0.9 | $2.4 | $6.6 | $17.2 | $29.5 | $56.4 |
| % Increase | 76.8% | 82.0% | 120.1% | 149.9% | 155.5% | 104.6% | 97.6% |
| Incr. in Tangible Assets | | | | | | | |
| $ Trillions | $0.4 | $0.6 | $2.6 | $5.2 | $4.7 | $4.2 | $4.4 |
| % Increase | 107.6% | 85.5% | 201.4% | 133.8% | 51.3% | 30.5% | 24.3% |
| Incr. in Nominal Net Worth | | | | | | | |
| $ Trillions | $0.8 | $1.5 | $5.0 | $11.8 | $21.9 | $33.7 | $60.7 |
| | | | | | | | |
| Nominal Net Worth | | | | | | | |
| End of Period  - $ Tril. | $1.8 | $3.3 | $8.3 | $20.2 | $42.0 | $75.8 | $136.5 |
| % Increase Per Decade | 86.5% | 83.0% | 152.0% | 142.0% | 109.0% | 80.3% | 80.2% |
| % Increase Per Annum | 6.4% | 6.2% | 9.7% | 9.2% | 7.7% | 6.1% | 6.1% |
| | | | | | | | |
| Inflation (CPI) | | | | | | | |
| % Increase Per Decade | 23% | 26% | 99% | 71% | 34% | 23% | 19% |
| % Increase Per Annum | 2.1% | 2.3% | 7.1% | 5.5% | 3.0% | 2.1% | 1.7% |
| | | | | | | | |
| Real Net Worth ([a]) | | | | | | | |
| % Increase Per Decade | 52% | 45% | 27% | 42% | 56% | 46% | 52% |
| % Increase Per Annum | 4.3% | 3.8% | 2.4% | 3.6% | 4.5% | 3.9% | 4.3% |
| | | | | | | | |
| ([a])    Net of reported CPI | | | | | | | |

Sources: Federal Reserve; Tanaka Capital Management, Inc.

Exhibit 9-7 shows that the vast majority of the projected gain in net worth is expected to come from increases in net financial assets (financial assets minus loans) which in turn are expected to come entirely from the appreciation and incremental purchases by households of common stocks and other equity-like assets of more than $29 trillion in the first decade and more than $56 trillion in the second decade. Household equity-like assets include directly owned common stocks, mutual funds, pension fund reserves, ownership of noncorporate businesses (partnerships, etc.), and bank trust accounts. Estimates for annual appreciation in each of these categories are shown in the Appendix C table, Decades of Growth in Equity-like Assets.

## GROWTH IN EQUITY-LIKE ASSETS

Over the next 20 years, the investing public will be faced with unattractively low interest rates in the 0% to 2% range on money market funds and other money market instruments due to record low inflation and rising liquidity from a buildup in financial assets. With an increasing need to save more for their retirement, American investors will have little alternative but to invest incrementally more of their household net worth in directly-held common stocks and other equity-like assets such as mutual funds and pension reserves. Bond yields are also expected to decline by about 2% to 3%, consistent with the 2% to 3% drop in inflation from Digital Deflation and the growing New Economy. With declining interest yields on bonds, directly owned common stocks and equity-like assets will offer at least the prospect of growth even though they are also likely to offer record-low dividend yields, as well as greater volatility.

Despite only modest 7.7% to 9.2% real returns projected to be generated per year on common stocks over the next 20 years, households will nevertheless benefit from compound growth in the value of their holdings of common stocks, and this will build upon an unusually high beginning base of 64.8% of net worth invested in equity-like assets at the beginning of the new decade. To understand the significance of this allocation to equity-like assets, one need only consider that the proportion of net worth held by households in equity-like assets at the beginning of each of the last five decades was only 44.4% to 48.9%. These trends can be viewed in the Appendix B table, Household Tangibles, Financial, and Equity-like Assets and Net Worth.

Thanks to the 18-year super bull market (1982–2000) and the rise in popularity of mutual funds, IRAs, and 401(k)s, more people own more stock than ever before. These investors—and other new investors who will most certainly enter the equity markets over the next several years—will be the main beneficiaries of a new era of prosperity that will result from the further expansion of the Digital Revolution and the benefits of growing Digital Deflation.

No doubt, it will be difficult at first for households and investors to accept near-zero inflation—as well as near-zero money market interest rates and 2% to 4% Treasury bond yields over the next two decades. It happened in the 1950s. Yet, in the late 1980s and early 1990s it took investors more than 8 years to accept that just maybe inflation wasn't heading back up to double digits again. Accepting near-zero inflation will be no easier. Over time, however, more people will realize that inflation and interest rates are headed to new lows and that with declining yields in bonds and cash, common stocks will continue to generate the most attractive returns.

## HOW DIGITAL DEFLATION HELPS HOMEOWNERS BUILD WEALTH

At this point, it seems appropriate to address the other major asset class that has been historically a steady source of increasing household net worth—tangible assets. Exhibit 9-7 shows how tangible assets have also grown fairly dramatically over the decades. In fact, before the New Economy broke economic molds in the 1990s, American households allocated a very large 45% of their net worth to tangible assets, including housing and consumer durable goods (see Appendix B).

In 2001, a record high 67.7% of Americans, or 72.3 million families, owned homes. From a wealth-building perspective, home ownership has been the right thing to do. During the 1990s, household real estate declined from 32.2% of net worth to 27.1% but rose in dollar terms from $6.6 trillion to $11.1 trillion. Interestingly, this $4.5 trillion increase in the value of real estate holdings over the decade was almost as much as the $5.2 trillion surge in the value of *directly* owned common stocks (excluding mutual funds and other equity-like assets).

What is ironic is that home prices in the 1990s consistently appreciated at a rate greater than that of reported inflation. This occurred during a 10-year period of declining inflation! Although most people generally view housing as an excellent hedge against the ravages of inflation, the reality is that home prices have tended to appreciate more than reported inflation—both in times of high inflation and in times of low inflation. This can be seen in Exhibit 9-8.

Although it may not be immediately obvious, homeowners benefit rather nicely from Digital Deflation. In fact, to the extent that Digital Deflation reduces inflation in general, price levels for the overall economy, owners of all assets—tangible or financial—are better off. For each 1 percentage point that Digital Deflation reduces overall inflation and improves the value of the dollar, there is a 1 percentage point increase in the relative real value of *all assets* that are nominally priced in dollars, including real estate.

For example, in 2000, the median sales price of a single-family home rose by 4.5%, exceeding the 3.4% rise in the reported CPI by

**EXHIBIT 9-8**

How Home Ownership Builds Wealth

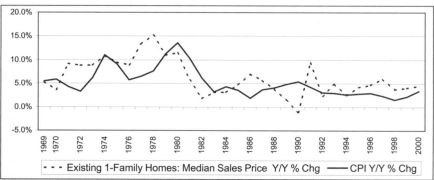

Sources: Department of Commerce; Tanaka Capital Management, Inc.

1.1%. One could conclude that to the extent that the mix of median home sales prices are representative of home values, in the year 2000 homeowners enjoyed a 1.1% increase in the real value of their homes. Correcting for the 1.0% overstatement in the CPI due to the under-counting of Digital Deflation, the CPI was really up only 2.4%, making the real home appreciation 2.1% rather than 1.1%.

Thanks to Digital Deflation, more of the rise in nominal home prices is converted to an increase in real value and real wealth for the homeowner. Why? Digital Deflation creates value across the economy by holding down overall or aggregate inflation while at the same time, individual Old Economy assets are rising in price. As digitally driven products continue to get faster, better, and cheaper, the consumer can afford to buy other goods and services of all kinds, including housing.

Said another way, because you can pay less for a computer or a cell phone service than you did a year ago, you can use the money saved to buy more shelter, food, clothing, or other products, whether in the Old or New Economies. By improving the purchasing power of the dollar, Digital Deflation acts as a wealth multiplier for all assets, even housing.

## DIGITAL DEFLATION HELPS TANGIBLE ASSETS BY DRIVING INTEREST RATES LOWER

There is another indirect, but very powerful way that Digital Deflation acts as a wealth multiplier. By reducing inflation, Digital Deflation will be at work helping to drive down mortgage and other interest rates.

In 2001, many economists marveled at how the American Investor-Consumer could continue to spend at fairly high levels despite a surge in job cuts, a major drop in the stock market, and the first decline in nominal net worth in more than 50 years. A major reason was the record levels of mortgage refinancings. Lower interest rates allowed Americans to pull cash out of the rising equity values in their homes. They could monetize their home price appreciation by taking out larger mortgages at lower interest rates and still make the same monthly payments. All of this was done, of course, without the Fed having to print more money. This important new source of liquidity was enabled by declining inflation and declining interest rates.

This is just one example of how Digital Deflation will help American Investor-Consumers build wealth and increase their purchasing power for Old Economy tangible assets over the next 10 to 20 years. This is the process by which tangible asset appreciation based on a secular decline in inflation and interest rates can produce its own wealth effect. It is every bit as important as that of an appreciating stock market.*

As homeowners continue to benefit from real house price appreciation in excess of general price inflation, it's worth remembering that a larger and larger part of the perceived increase in real wealth from rising home prices will, in reality, be created by the inflation-reducing and interest rate–reducing forces of improving product quality and Digital Deflation in the New Economy. For a New Economy wealth model in an era of growing Digital Deflation, appreciating tangible assets will add to the wealth-building process. Housing will not subtract from wealth creation—as might be the case if we were in an era of cyclical or monetary deflation instead of Digital Deflation. Monetary deflation will be addressed in Chapter 10.

## THE ENORMOUS UPSIDE POTENTIAL FOR WEALTH CREATION IN THE UNITED STATES

Over the next two decades, the 2000s and the 2010s, the U.S. economy has the potential to create enormous amounts of wealth. But the range

---

* A caveat should be added. Real estate is a very local market, and housing in individual regions and cities can become over- or underpriced relative to nationwide valuations.

of possible outcomes for wealth creation can vary dramatically. All other factors being equal, wealth creation will depend on three factors: (1) the proportion of the quality improvement and Digital Deflation that will be counted by the government, (2) whether fiscal and monetary policies will be carried out to nurture the New Economy or to inadvertently restrict it, and (3) how high a real interest rate the capital markets will require on Treasury bonds.

The case examined in this chapter assumes that the government will count about 50% of the currently uncounted quality improvement by the end of the decade. This would require that the government measure 1.4% of the 2.8% of currently uncounted Digital Deflation estimated to be created by 2009 and 1.9% of the 3.7% of currently uncounted Digital Deflation estimated to be created by 2019. This will require a concerted effort by the Department of Commerce and the Bureau of Labor Statistics to count digitally driven quality improvement across a number of industries. As pointed out in prior chapters, they have the methodologies, and they know how to use them.

The summary wealth creation table in Exhibit 9-9 shows four different scenarios, in which the government counts 100%, 75%, 50%, or 0% of the Digital Deflation to be generated by the end of each of the next two decades (beyond that which is already being counted for computers made for final sale and the small amounts for software and switches). It can be seen that the range of possible expected nominal and real returns on common stocks and the amounts of nominal and real wealth creation are quite wide. This chapter has been examining Case C, which assumes that the government will count about 50% of the uncounted quality improvement by the end of the decade.

However, depending upon whether the government counts 100%, 75%, 50%, or 0% of the Digital Deflation to be generated, nominal stock market returns will vary from about 16.6% to 13.7%, 11.3%, and 7.7% per year in the current decade. Similarly, increases in real net worth will vary from 110% to 71%, 46% and 15% in the decade. This is an enormously wide spread that depends entirely on how much Digital Deflation the government counts. The ranges of potential outcomes are equally dramatic for the four cases in the 2010–2019 decade.

## ON THE UPSIDE

To focus on one example on the upside, it is clear that if the government counts a full 75% of currently uncounted Digital Deflation as in

# E X H I B I T  9-9

## Summary Table of Four Cases for Wealth Creation in the United States

| | 1ST DECADE (2000-2009) | | | | 2ND DECADE (2010-2019) | | | |
|---|---|---|---|---|---|---|---|---|
| | CASE (A) | CASE (B) | CASE (C) | CASE (D) | CASE (A) | CASE (B) | CASE (C) | CASE (D) |
| % Digital Deflation Counted by end of decade | 100% | 75% | 50% | 0% | 100% | 75% | 50% | 0% |
| % Conversion of Productivity to Profits As % GDP | 75% | 75% | 75% | 75% | 75% | 75% | 75% | 75% |
| **DIGITAL DEFLATION & PRODUCTIVITY MODELS:** | | | | | | | | |
| Additional Digital Deflation Counted by the End of the Decade (a) | 2.8% | 2.1% | 1.4% | 0.0% | 3.7% | 2.8% | 1.9% | 0.0% |
| CBO's Productivity Growth Projections | 2.5% | 2.5% | 2.5% | 2.5% | 2.5% | 2.5% | 2.5% | 2.5% |
| Quality-Based Productivity Gains fr. Digital Deflation (a) | 2.8% | 2.1% | 1.4% | 0.0% | 3.7% | 2.8% | 1.9% | 0.0% |
| Quantity-Based Productivity Gains fr. Rising IT Cap. Ex.(a) | 0.4% | 0.4% | 0.4% | 0.4% | 1.1% | 1.1% | 1.1% | 1.1% |
| Total Counted Productivity Adjusted for Rising IT & Digital Deflation (a) | 5.7% | 5.0% | 4.3% | 2.9% | 7.3% | 6.4% | 5.5% | 3.6% |
| **STOCK MARKET MODEL:** | | | | | | | | |
| % Chg. in S&P 500 EPS per year | 8.9% | 8.9% | 8.9% | 8.9% | 6.5% | 6.5% | 6.5% | 6.5% |
| GDP Deflator Adj. For Rising IT and Digital Deflation (a) | -1.17% | -0.47% | 0.23% | 1.63% | -2.30% | -1.37% | -0.43% | 1.44% |
| 10-year Treasury Bond Yield Adj. for Rising IT & Digital Deflation (a) | 2.73% | 3.43% | 4.13% | 5.53% | 1.60% | 2.54% | 3.47% | 5.34% |
| P/E Ratio in Last Year of Decade | 42.5 | 32.8 | 26.5 | 19.0 | 78.1 | 46.2 | 32.3 | 19.8 |
| % Chg. in P/E Ratio/Yr. (CAGR) using 10-Yr. Treas. Model | 6.10% | 3.37% | 1.21% | -2.11% | 6.28% | 3.51% | 2.01% | 0.40% |
| Nominal Return on Comm. Stocks (S&P 500) CAGR | 16.6% | 13.7% | 11.3% | 7.7% | 14.0% | 11.1% | 9.5% | 7.8% |
| Real Return on Comm. Stocks (CAGR) | 15.1% | 11.8% | 9.2% | 5.0% | 13.1% | 9.7% | 7.7% | 5.3% |
| **WEALTH MODEL:** | | | | | | | | |
| Incr. In Nominal Net Worth per Decade ($Tril.) | $61 | $44 | $34 | $21 | $165 | $91 | $61 | $36 |
| % Incr. In Nominal Net Worth per Decade | 144% | 105% | 80% | 50% | 161% | 105% | 80% | 57% |
| % Incr. In Inflation (CPI) per Decade | 16% | 20% | 23% | 30% | 10% | 14% | 19% | 28% |
| % Incr. In Real Net Worth per Decade | 110% | 71% | 46% | 15% | 137% | 80% | 52% | 23% |

(a) Rate in last year of decade.

Source: Tanaka Capital Management, Inc.

Case B, projected fair value P/E ratios for 2009 will rise to 32.8 times earnings from 26.5 in Case C. Nominal stock market annual returns also will jump significantly from 11.3% to 13.7% per year in the decade. Even more dramatically, the increase in nominal net worth in the decade would rise from $34 trillion in the 50% scenario to $44 trillion in the 75% scenario. Obviously, the addition of $10 trillion of incremental wealth creation would be nontrivial.

No doubt, greater Digital Deflation, lower inflation, lower interest rates, and higher P/E ratios would allow many wealthy people to become wealthier. But more importantly, it would provide the opportunity for a much greater number of low- and middle-income Americans to save, invest, and have a chance to accumulate their own real net worth. Broadening the base of wealth in the United States will strengthen the economy. Giving more people not just hope, but a real stake in the system, will make the economy more durable—and society more stable—over time.

## ON THE DOWNSIDE

If the government counts no more quality improvement and Digital Deflation beyond that which it is currently measuring, fair value P/E ratios will decline toward 19 times earnings and nominal stock market returns will drop from a projected 11.3% per year in the 50% counted Digital Deflation scenario to only 7.7% per year in the 0% scenario. If the government counts no further quality improvement, the increase in nominal net worth in the decade will be reduced from a $34 trillion gain in the 50% scenario to only a $21 trillion gain. That $13 trillion difference in net worth over the decade will average out to about $45,000 per man, woman, and child in the United States.

While disproportionately hurting those owning more common stocks and other equity-like assets, the pain and suffering from the downside scenario of 0% counted Digital Deflation will be felt at all levels of income and household net worth. The 0% scenario will mean not just lower common stock returns, but also lower real growth, lower productivity gains, higher inflation, higher interest rates, higher unemployment, and higher federal, state, and local budget deficits.

## MOST LIKELY SCENARIO

It is encouraging to note that the 1990s turned out to be a very prosperous decade even though the government had only begun to count modest amounts of Digital Deflation—approximately 0.3% per year by the end of the 1990s. In the upcoming two decades, the statistical agencies will likely be counting more quality improvement than they did in the 1990s, as they appear to be on track to add new products and services every year. This analysis assumes that with additional public awareness and motivation, the government will count about 50% of the currently uncounted quality improvement and Digital Deflation that will be created by the end of the next two decades.

It is hoped that this book and further research by the Bureau of Labor Statistics, the Department of Commerce, and others in the area of quality improvement and Digital Deflation will help to accelerate this all-important measurement effort. It is also hoped that our fiscal and monetary authorities will be encouraged to better understand, accommodate, and even welcome a growing New Economy that won't act at all like the Old. Whether our policymakers completely or only partly perceive the opportunity, it would be useful and even exciting to see what potential the future holds in a world of increasing Digital Deflation.

## THE SURPRISING IMPORTANCE OF THE REAL BOND RATE

Over the next two decades, real U.S. Treasury bond rates present a second major potential upside for stock market returns and wealth creation—after the potential from counting a higher percent of currently uncounted Digital Deflation. The real Treasury bond rate has frustrated investment strategists, economists, and investors for decades. It is supposed to measure the long-term borrowing cost for the U.S. Government net of inflation. Since Treasuries are backed by the full faith and credit of the U.S. Government, U.S. Treasury bonds are generally referred to as *risk-free*. So, for the capital markets, Treasuries serve as a key benchmark rate for determining the relative value of riskier bonds as well as for stock market P/E valuations. Yet real Treasury bond rates have fluctuated wildly over the years.

The real rate on 10-year Treasury bonds (10-year Treasury yield minus the GDP Deflator) has ranged from 1.7% to 3.0% in the 1960s, from a negative 1.5% to a positive 2.1% in the 1970s, from 3.6% to 7.8% in the 1980s, and from 3.3% to 5.7% in the 1990s. Over the last 46 years since the 10-year bond has been trading, the real 10-year Treasury bond rate has averaged 2.99%, but the CBO is projecting a 3.90% rate for the next 10 years. For consistency and to be conservative, this analysis uses the CBO's 3.90% real 10-year bond rate in making projections for the next two decades in Exhibit 9-9 (page 246).

A case can be made, however, that real 10-year Treasury bond rates will continue the last 18 years' downward trend and move lower—perhaps closer to the 2.99% historical long-term average during the next several years. The reasoning is that U.S. Treasury bonds are not really "risk free" after all, and that the actual risks for holders of U.S. bonds will be declining consistent with the long-term downward trend in inflation.

Real rates for any type of bond appear to be quite sensitive to the level and volatility of inflation and interest rates. In that vein, during the last few decades, real bond yields have been penalized by the memories of high and volatile inflation and interest rates in the 1970s and 1980s. But with the prospect for another one or two decades of declining and less volatile inflation—due in part to steadily increasing Digital Deflation—there may be additional opportunity for real bond rates to shrink, perhaps to *below* the 2.99% average of the last 46 years.

On the other hand, Treasury bond rates represent the price that the U.S. Government has to pay to borrow and should logically be sensitive to the risk of large government budget deficits. There continues to be a very real fear that ballooning budget deficits will lead to a flooding of the market with the sale of more government bonds. Exhibit 9-10 shows how the real rate on 10-year Treasuries surged in the early 1980s when the Reagan Revolution took hold with tax cuts and defense spending increases that *temporarily* produced rising budget deficits and large auctions of new long-term Treasury bonds. Real rates then declined in the late 1980s as the lower tax rates kicked in to produce faster economic growth, which contributed to smaller deficits and eventually budget surpluses in the 1990s.

Looking beyond the recession-induced budget deficits of the early 2000s, a resurging U.S. economy should again place the U.S. Government into a surplus mode, leading to a net reduction in the supply of government bonds during most of the rest of the current decade. The result should be a reduction in the bond risk premiums associated with the lower risk of massive bond sales by the government. This should act to reduce real Treasury bond rates over the next several years.

**E X H I B I T   9-10**

Nominal and Real 10-Year Treasury Yields

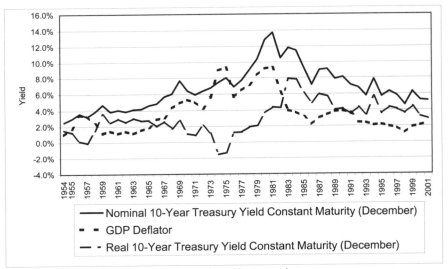

Sources: Federal Reserve; Dept. of Commerce; Tanaka Capital Management, Inc.

It should be pointed out that real 10-year Treasury bond yields could drop into the 2% to 3% range as seen in the 1960s. As of this writing it is difficult to assess the long-term reduction in real Treasury bond yields that would result from the level of perceived geopolitical risk and the effect of investors fleeing to the safety of U.S. Government bonds.

What was startling to discover was the sensitivity of the New Economy Stock Market model to the real rate on 10-year Treasury bonds. If a lower real bond rate of 3.00% is plugged into the model—instead of the 3.90% rate that the CBO projects—then P/E ratios, the return on common stocks, and the increase in household net worth *all rise dramatically for both decades.*

Take Case C (Exhibit 9-9), which assumes that the government counts 50% of the uncounted Digital Deflation. If the real rate on Treasuries declines to 3.00% versus 3.90%, the projected fair value P/E ratio by the end of the first decade (2009) rises to 35.1 times earnings versus 26.5 times earnings, and nominal returns on stocks jump to a compound average growth rate of about 14.4% per year in the first decade versus an 11.3% return under the 3.90% real rate scenario. The increase in nominal household net worth would jump from $34 trillion to $48 trillion, the percentage gain would rise from 79% to 114% and the increase in real net worth would jump up from 45% to 79%.

The full range of scenarios for stock market returns and wealth creation, assuming a reduction in the real 10-year Treasury rate from 3.90% to 3.00%, is shown in the Appendix D revised version of the Summary Table of Four Cases for Wealth Creation in the United States (Exhibit 9-9). The table shows the same four cases of the government counting 100%, 75%, 50%, and 0% uncounted Digital Deflation, but with predictably higher projected P/E ratios, stock market returns, and rates of growth in net worth for each case under the 3.00% real bond rate assumption versus the 3.90% real bond rate scenario.

The results suggest a very large potential upside to P/E ratios that will vary with great sensitivity depending upon how large a real rate bond investors will demand in a world of declining and more stable inflation and interest rates. In fact, the more Digital Deflation the government is able to measure, the greater will be the sensitivity and upside potential of P/E ratios to shrinking real Treasury bond rates. This is because higher Digital Deflation and lower real bond rates will compound upon each other.

With a 3.00% real Treasury bond rate assumption, for the four cases of the government counting 100%, 75%, 50%, and 0% of the uncounted Digital Deflation, the projected fair value P/E ratio rises to 67.1, 46.3, 35.1, and 23.3 times earnings by 2009. Nominal returns on stocks would rise to 22.0%, 17.6%, 14.4%, and 9.9% per year for each of the four cases in the first decade. The decade increase in nominal net worth would jump by 242%, 159%, 114%, and 67%, and the decade increase in real net worth would rise by 193%, 117%, 74%, and 29% for each of the four cases. The upper ranges of these common stock returns and gains in net worth are astronomical. While theoretically feasible, they would be very dangerous to build into expectations. However, this analysis does serve to underscore the importance of the real 10-year Treasury bond rate as a reflection of capital market inflation expectations, fair value P/E ratios, and investor upside, particularly in a world of increasing Digital Deflation.

It would certainly help to have some confidence that the real bond rate will have greater stability over the next several years since it provides such an important link between inflation in the economy and stock market fair value P/E valuations. Unfortunately, the real bond rate is one of the more difficult interest rates to predict, so there may be little relief on this issue. Based on the preceding analysis, however, there is no doubt that real bond rates should become the focus of more research and scrutiny by economists and investors.

## STOCKS, WEALTH, AND THE NEW ECONOMY

The purpose of this chapter is to use the Digital Deflation and productivity models from Chapters 7 and 8 to help investors, economists, and policymakers understand how growing Digital Deflation over the next two decades will translate rising productivity into rising profit margins, and also transform declining inflation into declining interest rates and rising P/E ratios on common stocks. As shown, depending on how much annual quality improvement the government is able to measure beyond the 0.30% being counted today, the potential total return on common stocks and the concomitant rise in wealth over the next two decades can be enormous—or merely mediocre.

Economics is not an exact science, and no set of estimates and projections can be expected to be completely accurate. Nevertheless, the models introduced in this chapter, together with those preceding them, are intended to help bring the science of economics and the challenge of investing closer to the reality of a rapidly changing and often perplexing economy.

As seen in the New Economy Stock Market model, the targeted outcomes for returns on common stocks and wealth creation for American households for the next two decades will vary widely depending upon how much quality improvement the government will be able to measure, as well as the future real rate on long-term Treasury bonds. Of course, there will be other determining factors, some of which we do not yet know.

As with the Demographic Theory of Economics described earlier, the Theory of Digital Deflation will take years to evolve and become fully validated by real world experience. Hence, the uncertainties as to timing of forecasts based on this long-term theory should be considered in addition to the normal vagaries and unpredictability of the stock market when viewing long-term stock market predictions.

With the above caveats, projections are provided below for where the broader stock market indices could theoretically go over the remainder of the current decade and the next decade if the government is able to *count 50% of the currently uncounted quality improve-*

*ment* and Digital Deflation and if real 10-year Treasury bond yields average 3.90%. The Dow Jones Industrial Average is assumed to approximate the projected nominal return on the S&P 500 excluding dividends:

- The S&P 500 can rise from 1469 at the beginning of the current decade (12/31/99) to 3880 by the end of the current decade (12/31/09), and to 8930 at the end of the following decade (12/31/19).
- The Dow Jones Industrial Average can rise from 11,497 at the beginning of the current decade (12/31/99) to 30,360 by the end of the current decade (12/31/09), and to 69,900 at the end of the following decade (12/31/09).

As developed in the New Economy Stock Market model (Exhibit 9-6), the projections shown above reflect capital appreciation of 10.2% per year and 8.7% per year in the decades of the 2000s and 2010s, respectively, compared to the average of 10.5% per year over the last five decades. It should be noted that because of the inadvertently tight monetary policy—and geopolitical and recession-related stock market downturns in 2000, 2001, and 2002—the S&P 500 and Dow Jones Average are deeper in the hole and will have to climb out and appreciate at much higher rates over the remaining years in the current decade to reach the projected endpoint for the end of the decade in 2009. Given the negative events and tensions worldwide during the early years of the decade, it may take a few additional years to reach those endpoints.

Nevertheless, these are lofty expectations for the next two decades. Meeting them will require that the government is able to count 50% of the currently uncounted Digital Deflation or about 1.4% of the 2.8% Digital Deflation estimated to be created by the year 2009 and 1.9% of the 3.7% Digital Deflation estimated to be created by 2019.

What would happen in a most conservative, base case scenario? Should the government *count no further quality improvement* and Digital Deflation by the end of the next two decades, inflation on the GDP Deflator might approximate 1.6% and 1.4% by 2009 and 2019, respectively, rather than the 0.2% and minus 0.4% estimated in the 50% scenario. Accordingly, 10-year Treasury bonds might yield about 5.5% and 5.3%; P/E ratios might approximate 19.0 and 19.8 times earnings for 2009 and 2019; and nominal capital appreciation might average only 6.6% per year in the 1999–2009 decade and only 7.0% per year in the 2009–2019 decade. The S&P 500 and the Dow Jones Industrials would then be projected to end the next two decades at approximately only two-thirds of the levels that would be achieved if the government were to count half the currently uncounted Digital Deflation:

- The S&P 500 can rise from 1469 at the beginning of the current decade (12/31/99) to 2780 by the end of the current decade (12/31/09), and to 5460 by the end of the next decade (12/31/19).
- The Dow Jones Industrial Average can rise from 11,497 at the beginning of the current decade (12/31/99) to 21,780 by the end of the current decade (12/31/09), and to 42,840 by the end of the following decade (12/31/19).

Importantly, these projections assume greater geopolitical stability worldwide. They also require that monetary and fiscal policies will be carried out with a fundamental understanding of the large and growing positive forces driving productivity and good deflation as a result of the ongoing Digital Revolution. As can be seen in the two cases above, the opportunity for healthy gains in the stock market and enormous amounts of wealth creation will hinge largely on how much more quality improvement can be measured by the government and whether policymakers will accommodate and encourage the expansion of the New Economy—or inadvertently inhibit its further development.

Given favorable labor force demographics and the likelihood that the government will continue to add new categories for measuring quality improvement, reported inflation should be declining over the next several years. This suggests that prospectively, U.S. common stocks are the cheapest they have been since the early 1980s.

## NOTE

1. "The Budget and Economic Outlook: An Update," Congressional Budget Office, August 2001.

# 10

## CHAPTER

# Monetary Policy: New "Speed Limits" for the Fed

In the information economy, it remains up to us to organize and use that information in ways to improve the quality of decision making.
*Alan Greenspan, August 31, 2001*

*As the Federal Reserve Board adjusts monetary policy for a rapidly changing New Economy, it will want to understand how Digital Deflation reduces inflation, increases productivity, and raises potential GDP growth rates. Without heating up the economy, unemployment rates can go lower, wage rate gains can go higher, and other speed limits will have to be recalibrated as Digital Deflation in the New Economy offsets traditional inflation in the Old Economy. By dutifully focusing on inflation numbers that happen to be flawed and outmoded, the Fed has inadvertently been too tight, causing unnecessary economic hardship and societal pain and suffering both in the United States and abroad. Will the Fed avoid the mistakes of the 1920s and 1930s? Or will the Fed slow the Digital Revolution, much as the Fed and the Great Depression put an end to the Industrial Revolution?*

### THE FED'S CHALLENGE

Given wise policy-making, there should be a very strong economic tailwind over the next two decades, as declining inflation and continued strong economic growth should generate wealth and prosperity in many respects reminiscent of the 1990s. It should be made very clear, however, that if the government does not continue to make major strides in counting quality improvement in products and services

255

across the economy, there is a very real danger that monetary and fiscal policies will be conducted in a manner that will inhibit or totally abort the wealth-building process. As we proceed further into the new millennium, it will be critical for economists, government policymakers, corporate managers, investors, and the public at large to understand the policy implications of the New Economy so that the aggregate economy can reach its fullest potential.

The greatest danger is that a persistent undercounting of Digital Deflation and a continued overstating of reported inflation will lead to overly tight monetary policy. If the Federal Reserve thinks that inflation is higher than it really is, it will inadvertently maintain interest rates higher than they should be. Or it may believe that it is providing economic stimulus when it is not—as was likely in the early 2000s. The Fed may even try to move price earnings ratios lower than they should be if it believes the stock market is exhibiting "irrational exuberance" based on the application of its stock market models to a level of reported inflation and therefore interest rates that are overstated.

The result of an inadvertently tight Fed would be a reduction in the availability of capital and the choking off of the innovation, risk-taking, and entrepreneurial efforts that are so vital for the continued advancement of the Digital Revolution. Fewer jobs would be created, real wages would rise more slowly, and more demands would be placed on government safety nets for the unemployed. A well-engineered monetary policy response to bad data can sink the economy—or certainly make it very difficult to embark on a course of one or two more decades of wealth creation.

## A TALE OF TWO ECONOMIES

Nobody ever said that managing the nation's monetary policy was easy, and new challenges have been introduced with the arrival of the New Economy. Previous chapters talked about the need to disaggregate the overall economy into the Old Economy and a New Economy that doesn't act at all like the Old. New economic models were offered to help predict where the New Economy, the aggregate economy, and the capital markets are likely to be going in the future.

When you analyze how the Old and New Economies react to changes in monetary policy, you'll find that the greatest difference relates to the pace of the economy and inflation. In general, faster growth in the New Economy sector will create more Digital Deflation. Faster growth in the Old Economy sector will create more traditional inflation.

If the Federal Reserve restricts monetary policy too severely for too long, it will reduce demand for technology-based capital goods and other naturally deflating products and services. In a manner that is counterintuitive to Old Economy thinking, by raising interest rates and slowing demand for technology goods and services, the Fed will inadvertently reduce the creation of Digital Deflation from the New Economy and thereby *increase* aggregate inflation for the whole economy. If the New Economy slows down faster than the Old Economy, it is entirely possible that the aggregate economy will lose more *deflation* from the New Economy than the amount of *inflation* that is lost from a slowing Old Economy.

This is what happened in 2000–2002 as the Fed inadvertently layered a tight monetary policy regimen on top of a New Economy that was already reeling from the post-Y2K IT capital-spending downturn and the Dot-com Bust. In this particular case, restrictive Fed monetary policy was reflected in the fairly high real interest rates of close to 4.0% and by the downward sloping yield curve (short-term rates higher than long-term rates) maintained from the spring of 2000 to the spring of 2001.

The result was a recession in the overall economy, and in the New Economy, a severe recession that contributed to a reverse *corporate* wealth effect, lower productivity gains, and less generation of Digital Deflation. At the same time, the slower-growing but more stable Old Economy continued to grow in real terms and continued to inflate. The Old Economy defied most economists' predictions by the strength in demand for housing and autos as lower mortgage interest rates boosted home values, household net worth, and the consumer wealth effect. In the 2000–2001 period, the Fed unknowingly reduced New Economy deflation but didn't reduce core inflation from the Old Economy as housing prices soared.

With the benefit of hindsight, much of the New Economy slowdown in 2000–2002 was unavoidable given the tremendous temporary pop in demand from Y2K spending and the Dot-com Bubble. However, some analysts have pointed out that the Fed's well-intentioned but overly aggressive creation of money in 1999 in advance of Y2K and its reflexive overtightening of monetary policy in 2000–2001 inadvertently magnified the swings in the economy both up and down. Ironically, the Fed's focus on making sure plenty of money was available for a possible lockdown of computers due to the anticipated millennium software bug contributed to a rising and an irrationally exuberant stock market in 1999, particularly for stocks related to the Internet. The Federal Reserve Board then felt compelled to restrict the availability of money in 2000–2001, leading to the recession of 2001, a severe contraction in the New Economy, and a sharp correction in the stock market. The real tragedy was that these things didn't need to happen with such severity.

With much of the economy's incremental growth occurring in pre-Y2K spending for computers and software as well as for the build-out of the Internet infrastructure, an enormous amount of Digital Deflation was being created—producing actual deflation in the aggregate economy. Recall that the GDP Deflator adjusted for Digital Deflation is estimated to have been –0.86% in 1998 and –0.22% in 1999. Because the government was not counting much of the "good" Digital Deflation being generated, all that the Fed saw in its headlights was a booming economy, a soaring stock market, and possible inflation, so it jammed on the monetary brakes. Again, without accurate data for measuring real quality improvement in the New Economy, it was hard for the Fed to know what was really happening in the Old and New Economies.

The Federal Reserve's overly stimulative and then overly restrictive policy moves in 1999 and in 2000 to 2001 are reflected in both the Fed's interest rate actions, as well as in reported changes in liquidity. The Fed began a program of lowering the targeted federal funds rate from 5½% in September 1998 to 4¾% by November 1998 and held "funds" at that level until June 1999, creating considerable liquidity in advance of Y2K. The Fed then initiated a program of hiking the federal funds target rate from 4¾% in June 1999 to the 6½% level by May 2000, maintaining that level until January 2001. Since inflation on the broad GDP Deflator was running at only 2.4% during 2000, the Fed had imposed a very high real interest rate of 4.1% on the economy.

Many economists, business leaders, and policymakers criticized the Fed for maintaining high nominal (6.5%) and real (4.1%) interest rates for as long as it did (from May 2000 to January 2001), particularly considering that employment and other statistics demonstrated weakness as early as mid-2000. In reality, real interest rates were even higher, at closer to 6% if appropriate adjustments were made to reduce the inflation rate for uncounted Digital Deflation of 2%. A real rate regimen of 6% is an enormous depressant on *any* economy. It goes a long way toward explaining how the Fed and the vast majority of other economists could be so surprised by the recession in 2001.

The Fed's over- and undercreation of liquidity is corroborated on the demand (for liquidity) side by dramatic swings in the St. Louis Fed's data for the adjusted monetary base, sometimes called *high-powered money*, as shown in Exhibit 10-1.

In defense of the Fed, it is not easy for it to optimize the management of two separate and distinct economies, because it can only administer one monetary policy to both. Because the concept of Digital Deflation is so new, it is underanalyzed and it will take time for the Federal Reserve and others to find the new delicate balance of optimal growth in the Old and New Economies. It will also take time for the government to count more fully the beneficial effects of Digital Deflation, lowering reported inflation, and raising reported productivity gains to more accurate levels.

**E X H I B I T   10-1**

Percent Change in Adjusted Monetary Base (Rolling 12-Month Percentage Change)

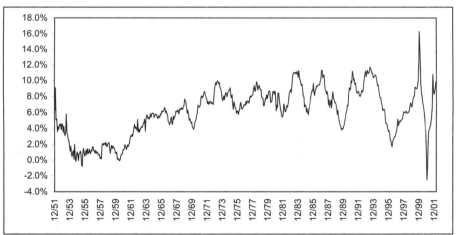

Sources: Federal Reserve Bank of St. Louis; Tanaka Capital Management, Inc.

## AVOIDING A REPEAT OF THE 1920s AND 1930s

At the outset, the initial expectation for this book was that the Digital Revolution would be shown to be clearly superior to the Industrial Revolution due to the recurring nature of technology's advances. However, in the end it became quite clear that the two revolutions are not all that different. While the recurring nature of the quality improvement from digital technologies does indeed act to extend the Digital Revolution for decades, both revolutions share in common a couple of extremely important characteristics. They both have benefited from periods of major innovation and dramatic improvement in the quality of products and services. More significantly, both revolutions also have suffered from the undercounting of their respective enormous gains in quality improvement and the underappreciation of the beneficial effects on the economies of their day.

Why? In both periods, the government was not able to measure and record the real economic value of entirely new categories of products and services being sold. In both periods, moreover, the governments lacked measures of quality improvement to indicate the real productivity gains and good deflation being generated by these new inventions.

The Industrial Revolution and the Digital Revolution both generated enormous amounts of economic growth, and both dramatically improved the quality of life. Indeed, the rapid adoption of the Internet has often been compared to the widespread distribution of electricity, and the personal computer has become as ubiquitous as the automobile. Consumers in both eras could easily see the value of these new products and services.

What is of great interest, however, is how the Industrial Revolution *ended*, and what its demise might imply for the current Digital Revolution. Most people think that the Industrial Revolution ended with the onset of the Great Depression, which was triggered by the Smoot-Hawley Trade Act and the Stock Market Crash of 1929. The reality was that the Depression was very much the product of a monumental mistake in monetary policy. Without even the benefit of having accurate data for GDP accounts or monetary aggregates, in December 1928 the Federal Reserve began to shrink the money supply by what would become a total cumulative reduction of 25.1% over a 4½-year period that finally ended by June 1933. That was a large enough dose of monetary "restraint" for a long enough period to choke off any healthy economy, cripple the strongest of stock markets, stifle innovation, and put an end to decades of growth and wealth creation from the Industrial Revolution.

Although the Fed back in the 1920s had only a very small fraction of the economic data that the modern-day Fed has today, it did see an economy that was booming and a red-hot stock market in the 1920s. This might sound eerily familiar. Was the Federal Reserve of the late 1920s and early 1930s intent on protecting the American economy from the kind of hyperinflation that had ruined the Weimar Republic in Germany? Would it have acted any differently if it had known that if adjusted for quality improvement, inflation was running 1 or 2% lower than the –1.7% (deflation) reported for the Consumer Price Index (CPI) in 1928 or the 0.0% inflation reported for the CPI in 1929? Surprisingly, the answer is "No." According to a senior Fed official, the reality was that the Fed of the 1920s and 1930s did not look at inflation, and it did not look at the money supply. This might seem unbelievable today, but the view back then was that deflationary periods were the inevitable response to speculative excesses. It was a Victorian view that people equated with moral rectitude—a stock market boom had to be followed by a bust. Some people hold these beliefs today.

In the 1920s and 1930s, what the Fed did look at was member bank borrowings and nominal interest rates. Since they were both low in that era, the Fed believed that it was accommodative, and it was doing its job. After all, the Federal Reserve Act of 1913 stipulated that the Fed should provide an elastic currency and meet the needs of trade. To the Fed back then, that meant that if the economy weakened, it should provide less liquidity, and if the economy strengthened, it should provide more liquidity. The Fed's original charter made the Fed "procyclical," and it was only much later that the Fed took on the role of providing an anticyclical stabilizing force for the economy. In essence, the Fed today knows that it can be much smarter about smoothing rather than magnifying economic cycles.

Can the Industrial Revolution tell us much about how we can better manage or accommodate the Digital Revolution? There are certainly parallels between the two. Yes, both the 1920s and the 1990s benefited from vibrant economies and rising stock markets, but both decades at the same time *also enjoyed low and declining inflation and interest rates.* This can be seen in Exhibit 10-2 where the data for the two decades are presented with the years 1929 and 2000 superimposed. Focusing on the top graph, by mentally making a 2% downward ad-

# EXHIBIT 10-2

Monetary Policy in the 1990s vs. the 1920s and 1930s

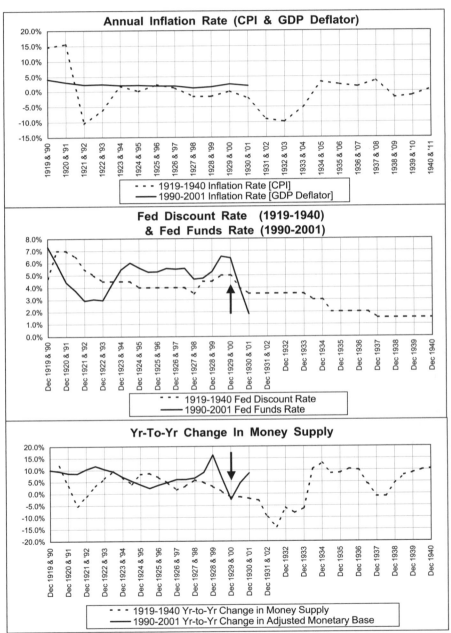

Source: Federal Reserve; Bureau of Labor Statistics; Tanaka Capital Management, Inc.

justment to the GDP Deflator for the 1990s for uncounted Digital Deflation, it can be seen that the inflation rate in the most recent decade would be close to zero for the broadly defined inflation index. Interestingly, inflation in the 1920s also averaged close to zero for the CPI, the broadest inflation index for that era.

The middle graph in Exhibit 10-2 superimposes the Federal funds rate of the 1990s over the then-equally important Fed-controlled discount rate of the 1920s and 1930s. Again, the graphed lines are centered on 1929 and 2000 because these were the years of peak interest rates from the two Feds, both of which were tighter and more restrictive than they realized. Ironically, they show the Fed in the 1990s to be nominally tighter with higher interest rates than the Fed of the 1920s.

The bottom graph is less instructive as money supply growth had lost some of its significance in the 1980s and 1990s. However, it does show the inadvertent, but severe and prolonged, tightening with a cumulative 25% reduction in the money supply by the Fed in the late 1920s and early 1930s—and the severe tightening with negative high-powered money growth by the current-day Fed in the year 2000.

In another parallel, it is interesting that in the 1920s, labor productivity growth is known to have surged in the United States, similar to the rise in productivity growth in the United States in the late 1990s. While U.S. government data on labor productivity does not exist prior to 1948, a study written for the Organization for Economic Cooperation and Development (OECD) by economist Angus Maddison has estimated that labor productivity gains in the United States averaged 2.4% per year in the 1913–1929 period, up from 1.9% per year in the 1870–1913 period.[1] A Goldman Sachs study published in August 2000 estimated that total factor productivity (gains in output from higher labor productivity growth, higher output from capital assets, and other factors) in the United States accelerated to 2.7% per year in the 1920–1929 decade, up from –0.6% per year in the 1913–1920 period.[2] It seems then that the decades of the 1990s and the 1920s both shared in common rising growth in labor productivity as well as strong economies, rising stock markets, and low and declining inflation and interest rates.

In hindsight, it was clearly wrong for the Fed of the late 1920s and early 1930s to shrink the money supply when reported inflation was running at zero or slightly below zero. In reality, the economy of the 1920s and 1930s was a lot more deflationary than the reported inflation numbers suggested because the statistics reflected absolutely no quality improvement in the plethora of new products and services being offered to the American consumer. Unlike today, the government was not counting *any* of the higher real value of the fruits of the Industrial Revolution. This means that the Federal Reserve's monetary policy error, the reduction in the supply of money, was magnified by the fact that the economy was actually in a highly deflationary mode if appropriate adjustments were made for quality improvement. In other words, the economy of the 1920s was already in a mode of good deflation *before* the Fed reduced the money supply, ushering in years of ruinous monetary-based "cyclical deflation."

Looked at from the point of view of providing adequate liquidity or dollars to satisfy the needs of a growing economy, just because the consumer was able to buy more value per dollar in the 1920s and 1930s didn't mean that the Fed should shrink the supply of dollars in the hands of the public. It was just the opposite. More consumers worked to be able to buy more units of the higher-value fruits of the Industrial Revolution, so more dollars should have been printed, not less.

The visibly vibrant economy of the Roaring Twenties was being driven by innovation that produced the 1920s equivalent of today's Digital Deflation. Like the 1990s' version, this "Industrialization Deflation" was not a cyclically based deflation resulting from a recession but rather from new product innovation, economies of scale, rising efficiencies, and faster, better, cheaper autos, home appliances, and other new products of that era. It was a result of higher-quality goods and services being delivered per dollar, and this phenomenon should have been counted as lower inflation and higher real output and productivity gains. (It was 60 to 70 years later, in the late 1980s, before the government eventually did start to make its first quality adjustments—for computers.)

In the late 1920s and early 1930s, instead of printing more money to "accommodate" the higher real value of goods and services being transacted, the Fed inadvertently shrank the money supply, and the rest was history. The Stock Market Crash of 1929, the banking collapse, the ruinous rise in the unemployment rate to 25% of the labor force, and the soup lines were all part of the Great Depression that slowed down innovation and brought the Industrial Revolution to an early demise.

## LEARNING FROM THE 1920s AND 1930s

It is by no means being suggested that the U.S. economy of today is heading for anything close to a depression or the end of the Digital Revolution. However, it is instructive to view the current economy in the context of the 1920s and 1930s. Virtually every economist today would agree that the economic data of the 1920s and 1930s were woefully inadequate for measuring the economy during that era. Monetary policies and disciplines were also underdeveloped, and when combined with bad data, the results were catastrophic.

Today, we would like to believe that the Federal Reserve is armed with much better data. However, significant improvements need to be made to present-day economic statistics regarding the timely addition of new products and services, and the recurring and rapidly improving quality of products and services driven by the Digital Revolution. Advances will continue to be made for years out into the future in silicon, software, magnetic storage, optics, and a whole host of other rapidly improving digital technologies—as well as in healthcare and other products and services benefiting from the *use* of new and improving technologies.

If the current-day Fed continues to have to struggle with Old Economy numbers that do not reflect the truly enhanced value of goods and services being sold in today's New Economy, it will be in danger of committing mistakes similar to those in the 1920s and 1930s. The mistakes would be the same, differing only in degree. In the 1930s, very poor economic data, as well as a lack of understanding of the influence of liquidity and money on the economy, contributed to monetary policy blunders that plunged the United States into the Great Depression and brought an end to the Industrial Revolution in the United States and worldwide.

Early in the 2000–2010 decade, economic data that do not properly convert the dramatic double-digit gains in the value of technology-driven products and services into good deflation have already led the Federal Reserve down a monetary policy path that is more restrictive than it perceives. The result has been unfulfilled growth in the economy, fewer jobs, the destruction of wealth, and a deceleration of the Digital Revolution. If these restrictive policies continue to be pursued, they will lead to a slowing in the pace of innovation, lower rates of performance and quality improvement in digitally driven products and services, and less creation of Digital Deflation in the years ahead. The Digital Revolution may not die, but it will fall far short of its potential.

## COUNTING QUALITY IMPROVEMENT WILL MAKE THE FED'S JOB EASIER

There is much hope for the future, however, as the Bureau of Labor Statistics and the Department of Commerce appear quite committed to the task of adjusting more products and services for quality improvement. In addition, it is quite fortunate that the current Fed chairman is very focused on the importance of productivity growth and has a keen interest in technology's role. Alan Greenspan has often provided variations of the speech he delivered in June 2000 when he said, "Most of the gains in the level and the growth rate of productivity in the United States since 1995 appear to have been structural, largely driven by irreversible advances in technology and its application—irreversible in the sense that knowledge once gained is almost never lost."

The Federal Reserve is already aware that the economic data are not complete, and it is reported that some Fed Board members employ their own "fudge factor" in adjusting the numbers downward for inflation and upward for productivity. Nevertheless, it is also clear from various speeches that the Federal Reserve Board of Governors is populated with anti-inflation hawks that seem intent on fighting inflation even though reported inflation remains at historical lows. It is hoped that these Fed Board members become more appreciative of the existence of Digital Deflation and can take a more balanced approach to monetary policy. This was an important reason for writing this book.

At least until the reported data are corrected for quality improvement, it may be more appropriate for the Fed to lean toward what might *appear* to be a more accommodative or even stimulative posture relative to what would be called for by more traditional monetary "speed limits." At a minimum, the ever-vigilant Fed might at least question whether in a world of increasing Digital Deflation it will continue to be appropriate to maintain its historical bias toward erring on the side of restraint.

Lower inflation and higher productivity from the New Economy should give the Fed enormously greater flexibility in conducting monetary policy in the future. When corrections are made to count more of the quality and performance improvements being made to digitally driven products and services, the Fed could let the aggregate economy run faster and still result in actual inflation that is approximately in the same 1.0% to 3.0% range that has been reported in recent years. On the other hand, if the Fed made no adjustments to monetary policy following a correction for quality improvement, nominal GDP growth wouldn't change, but reported inflation would be 2.0% lower, and reported real GDP growth 2.0% higher. This would produce an economy tantalizingly close to Chairman Greenspan's wistful but prescient comment some years back that the U.S. economy could achieve a state of zero inflation.

Given the conservative nature of the Federal Reserve Board, it is more likely that initially the Fed will operate somewhere in between, accommodating slightly faster nominal GDP growth and making mental adjustments that inflation is lower than what is being reported. It is hoped that no Fed governor will labor under the belief that our inflation data are accurate.

The Fed, as usual, will do its best to keep the debate from being politicized, but hopefully there will be healthy debate. What is optimal? Is it zero inflation with slower GDP growth than the New Economy–enhanced higher potential GDP "glide path" would permit? Zero inflation would result in considerably lower interest rates and higher P/E ratios on stocks. However, fewer people at the margin would be employed than if the Fed allowed the economy to expand at a faster rate. Having to decide between zero inflation, modest growth, and what appears to be full employment under the Old Economy metrics versus the alternative of faster growth, super full employment, and modest inflation is a difficult decision that many foreign central bankers would like to have to make.

Whatever path the Fed chooses over the next few years as more changes are made to the government's data to count more fully the benefits of Digital Deflation, interest rates should go down because reported inflation will go down. However, this adjustment process may take years if history is any guide. It took the capital markets over 18 years to adjust to the decline in inflation from the demographically induced double digits of the late 1970s and early 1980s to the end of the 1990s. Many still are fearful that inflation will come roaring back as evidenced by persistently high real interest rates. It may take years for the lower inflation numbers from a more complete counting of Digital Deflation to be accepted by the public.

It may take years for the public to understand and accept the inflation-lowering, productivity-enhancing effects of the New Economy. During those years, as the bond and stock markets "climb their walls of worry," long-term interest rates should move begrudgingly but inexorably lower, and common stock P/E ratios should move higher. Just as it seems almost comical today that computers weren't measured to show any performance improvement before 1985, in 10 years it will seem just as strange that software, communications, healthcare, and other products and services aren't being measured for quality improvement today.

## NEW SPEED LIMITS FOR THE FED

In the late 1970s, a prominent economist at a major Wall Street brokerage firm visited bank trust departments and talked about an economy that was growing so fast that it was careening out of control, bouncing off trees as the Fed tried desperately to stay on the road. While the story elicited laughter, the economic reality was fairly grim in that era of high inflation and "profitless prosperity."

Fortunately, economic conditions today are quite a bit more favorable. If the 1990s taught us anything about monetary policy, it was that the old economic speed limits are no longer valid. We saw an economy that could grow at vigorous rates and drive unemployment to surprisingly low levels during a record 10-year expansion, and yet inflation continued to move downward to the 1% to 3% range. Interest rates dropped to the low single digits, yet the dollar strengthened as foreign investors wanted a piece of the New Economy. Most importantly, in the second half of the 1990s, reported productivity gains moved up out of the 1% to 1.5% range to the 2.5% area, giving the Fed more room to let the economy grow faster without igniting inflation.

As the government begins to count more quality improvement in products and services and the benefits of Digital Deflation become more visible, the Federal Reserve is likely to feel more comfortable raising the speed limits for economic growth. In fact, in a vibrant, but low-inflation economy with increasing Digital Deflation, it is quite possible that some of the traditional economic speed limits should be eliminated—at least until the new safe driving speeds are better understood in a Digitally Deflating New Economy.

**The GDP Growth Rate Speed Limit.** The 1990s' experience showed this limit to be virtually ineffective. The growth rates of real and nominal GDP completely delinked from the rate of inflation and often moved in opposite directions. Yet despite the experience of the 1990s, the stock and bond markets continue to fear strong economic expansion, plunging frequently on reports of above-average GDP growth. The capital markets need not fear vigorous economic growth if it is accompanied by strong productivity gains and Digital Deflation to offset inflation in the Old Economy. If economists insist on monitoring a real GDP growth speed limit, at a minimum, they should consider revising the limit upward, by at least 1% to 2%.

**The Unemployment Rate Speed Limit.** The NAIRU, or Non-Accelerating Inflation Rate of Unemployment, is supposed to be the lowest level that the jobless rate can go without pushing up inflation. Several years ago, 6% was accepted as the limit. After the 1990s' experience, the median estimate was revised down to about 4.5%, according to a September 2000 survey of economists by the National Association for Business Economics (NABE). But only 37% of those economists surveyed thought NAIRU was still a useful concept. Another 40% said it was of "very limited use" and 17% said it was "useless." So much for the Phillips Curve theory, which postulates that the unemployment rate and inflation are inversely related. Perhaps the NAIRU is not so useless, but merely set at too high a level of unemployment for a growing New Economy. As inflation rates are revised lower due to adjustments for quality improvement, economists may wish to revise downward their views on the unemployment rate speed limit, probably closer to 3.0% to 3.5% currently and possibly lower in the next decade.

**The Inflation Speed Limit.** The modern Fed's long-run goals have been to achieve "price stability and sustainable economic growth." Some economists feel that to achieve price stability, it is best to adjust monetary policy by keying directly off of reports of inflation. Bob McTeer, highly regarded president of the Dallas Federal Reserve Bank and information technology enthusiast, wrote that "the way to minimize inflation risk is to focus directly on inflation indicators, regardless of the strength of the real economy and employment."[3] Nonetheless, it is well known that inflation reports tell us where inflation has been, not where it is going. The challenge is that while inflation is viewed in the rear view mirror, changes in monetary policy take 6 to 9 months to have an effect on the economy down the road. In addition, many economists, including some at the Fed as noted earlier, do not accept the inflation reports to be entirely accurate. The Digital Deflation thesis suggests that inflation is overstated by about 2%

on the GDP Deflator and about 1% on the CPI, and that these over-statements will rise as digitally deflating products and services grow to take a larger share of the economy.

Will the inflation target devotees at the Fed be willing to mentally alter monetary policy speed limits to reflect Digital Deflation or will they insist on waiting years for the Department of Commerce and Bureau of Labor Statistics to more accurately measure performance and quality improvement in the New Economy? As the government begins to measure more quality improvement across the economy, there will be more frequent monthly reports of negative inflation, particularly for the GDP Deflator. Economists, investors, and policymakers will want to know how much of this condition of net deflation in the aggregate inflation rate is caused by Old Economy, recession-based deflation as experienced by Japan in the 1990s and how much is a result of New Economy, technology-based Digital Deflation.

**Money Supply Speed Limits.** Monetary aggregates have not been utilized to guide monetary policy for years as companies and consumers have become more efficient in their use of cash. In 1993, Alan Greenspan stated that "the historical relationships between money and income, and between money and the price level have largely broken down, depriving the aggregates of much of their usefulness as guides to policy." Nonetheless, many economists still refer to the growth in the various money supply aggregates to get a feel for the creation of liquidity and demand for money. A few economists are tracking the St. Louis Fed's adjusted monetary base (bank reserves and currency) shown earlier in Exhibit 10-1 as a monetary speed limit; however, more research needs to be done on this measure.

**Interest Rate Speed Limits.** Since the late 1980s, the Fed has been guiding monetary policy to focus on interest rate targets for the nominal federal funds rate, the rate charged on overnight borrowings at the Fed from one bank to another. For example, on May 7, 2002, the Federal Open Market Committee (FOMC) announced that it "decided today to keep its target for the federal funds rate unchanged at 1¾ percent." This rate target is set with the Fed's best guess at creating just the right amount of liquidity to maintain price stability and sustainable economic growth. It is also used to help communicate to the markets the Fed's intentions. In reality, more information would be communicated if the Fed announced its targets for real interest rates. Exhibit 10-3 shows how the real Fed funds rate declined in the 1970s

## EXHIBIT 10-3

### Nominal and Real Fed Funds Rates

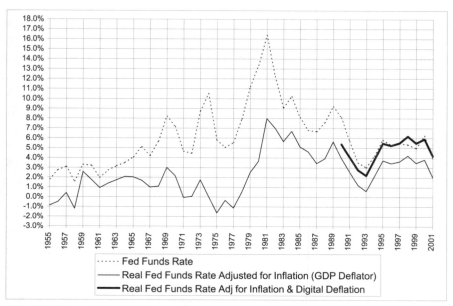

Sources: Federal Reserve; Tanaka Capital Management, Inc.

as the Fed was accommodative to meet the Politics of Need at that time to create jobs for the burgeoning Baby Boomers.

The Fed raised real rates in the 1980s to bring down inflation expectations, became more accommodative in the early 1990s—and then unfortunately raised real rates again to the 4.0% area on real Fed funds in the late 1990s. Furthermore, when adjustments are made to the real Fed funds rate for estimated uncounted Digital Deflation for each of the years in the decade of the 1990s, it can be seen that the Fed was much tighter than it realized—as tight as the 1980s. The real Fed funds rate adjusted for 2% per year of uncounted Digital Deflation is shown by the heavy line to have been kept at a very high 5.0% to 6.0% range in the late 1990s and throughout the year 2000. In hindsight, this speed limit clearly shows the Fed to have been inadvertently highly restrictive from 1995 through 2000 and even into 2001, particularly with the economy already weakening. If the Fed wishes to focus on real interest rates, of course, it should insist on more reliable data on inflation. Chairman Greenspan has spoken at least once about the need for better inflation data.

**The Oil Price Speed Limit.** Since the first OPEC oil embargo in 1973, every spike in oil prices has been followed by a recession as the Fed has reacted to rising oil prices with great concern that they would trigger a new round of soaring inflation as they appeared to do in the 1970s. As discussed in prior chapters, the surge in inflation in the 1970s and early 1980s was caused primarily by record numbers of Baby Boomers and Working Women piling into the workforce. While the sharp rise in oil prices did act as a tax on the consumer from 1973 to 1981, oil prices alone did not cause a spiral in inflation. In fact, personal consumption expenditures for energy (gasoline, fuel oil, electricity, and gas) after rising from 3.9% of GDP in 1972 to a peak of 5.7% of GDP in 1980, had fallen steadily to a low of 2.9% of GDP in the first quarter of 2002 (Exhibit 10-4).

This cost of energy to the consumer is significantly lower than the 4.0% and 4.3% average of the 1950s and 1960s—before the "oil crisis." The effect of oil prices on inflation was exaggerated by the experience of the 1970s. Cartel-manipulated oil prices should not be used as a major indicator of the direction of inflation or of the pace of the economy, nor should they be used as a speed limit for monetary policy. Chairman Greenspan's statement on April 17, 2002 was not inconsistent with this view: "When simulated over periods with observed oil price spikes, these models do not show oil prices consistently having been a decisive factor in depressing economic activity." With a

**E X H I B I T   10-4**

Declining Personal Consumption Expenditures for Energy as a Percentage of GDP

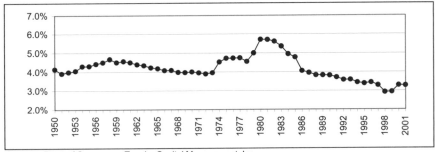

Sources: Dept. of Commerce; Tanaka Capital Management, Inc.

faster-growing New Economy, this Old Economy commodity is likely to continue to decline as a percentage of GDP and should not be considered a major speed limit for monetary policy.

**The Fed's Newest Speed Limit, the Wealth Effect.** Until the late 1990s, there was very little evidence of a wealth effect to suggest that the stock market materially influenced consumer spending or inflation. However, as seen in the late 1990s, a combination of rapid real economic growth and declining inflation can combine to create enormous wealth and rising net worth for the average American household as well as improve corporate balance sheets. This increase in wealth can have a significant effect on spending in both the consumer and corporate sectors. With a more accurate counting of quality improvement and Digital Deflation over the next several years, inflation and interest rates should move lower, stimulating the economy even further. Great care must be taken to understand that growth is not necessarily inflationary, especially if it is based on rising Digital Deflation and quality-based productivity gains. The increase in liquidity from the appreciation of financial or tangible assets creates the potential for greater consumer and corporate spending in a manner quite different from the printing of more money by the Federal Reserve. The increase in equity in the hands of the public is likely to be far less inflationary than the printing of the equivalent amount of money by the Fed because it is associated with the delivery of higher-value goods and services in the economy. Much more research needs to be done on the wealth effect, and much can be learned about whether the creation of wealth from the appreciation of tangible assets such as housing is any more inflationary than the appreciation of financial assets such as stocks.

## RUNNING OUT OF ROOM AT THE FED

What happens to monetary policy if interest rates approach zero? Will the Fed lose control of the economy?

Voting members of the Federal Reserve Open Market Committee (FOMC), economists, and investors should not be surprised that in a world of increasing Digital Deflation, changes in aggregate price levels are likely to turn deflationary at times, and on occasion *interest rates may approach zero*. As discussed earlier, this would be a natural result of increasing traditional productivity gains and a "secular" rise in

Digital Deflation, together with a "cyclically" weak economy, such as in 2001–2002.

The Fed, in fact, has already thought about what it would mean for monetary policy if the federal funds rate approaches 0%, or what it calls the *zero-bound nominal rate*. At 0% interest rates, it is highly likely that the Fed would not be able to conduct normal open market operations to try to stimulate the economy. The January 2002 FOMC minutes stated this concern quite explicitly: "Members discussed staff background analyses of the implications for the conduct of policy if the economy were to deteriorate substantially in a period when nominal short-term interest rates were already at very low levels. Under such conditions, while unconventional policy measures might be available, their efficacy was uncertain, and *it might be impossible to ease monetary policy sufficiently through the usual interest rate process* to achieve system objectives. The members agreed that the potential for such an economic and policy scenario seemed highly remote, but it could not be dismissed altogether."

We may well be closer to zero interest rates than the Fed thinks. Yet, 0% interest rates wouldn't be so bad if they are a result of an increasingly efficient economy producing higher-value goods and services faster, better, cheaper. So while some people are understandably becoming concerned that the Fed will "run out of room" when short-term interest rates reach zero, it will be perhaps less the "end of the world" and more the beginning of a new era.

Yes, at zero federal funds rates, the Fed may effectively lose much of its ability to control liquidity through its *traditional* open market purchases of money. But it can devise other means to control liquidity. Initially, the federal funds rate could drop to zero, and bank lending rates would still be significantly above zero due to the cost of commercial bank operations. More significantly, the Fed can make massive amounts of open market purchases of short-term Treasury notes and even intermediate- or long-term Treasury bonds—and pay for them with newly minted money. Any of these measures would boost liquidity and the money supply, adding slightly different amounts of stimulus to the economy.*

Indeed, one can envision a very new era of monetary policy as we get closer to a world of near-zero inflation and zero interest rates.

---

* This stimulus can be described by the "velocity of money," which is a ratio that simply reflects what percent GDP will rise for each 1% rise in money supply.

Even the Fed's historically clear-cut goal of targeting a specific federal funds rate—or a more theoretical goal of achieving an ideal "equilibrium real interest rate"—becomes quite murky.

There will also be many new structural issues to manage through. For example, just as rising interest rates caused disintermediation in the 1970s with massive fund flows out of savings and loans and into CDs, near-zero interest rates will likely cause "reverse disintermediation," with massive flows out of money market funds and CDs and into bonds, stocks, and other higher risk financial assets.

For the U.S. central bank in the longer term, it should now be evident that as the Bureau of Labor Statistics and the Department of Commerce proceed to count Digital Deflation more accurately, the GDP Deflator will be seen by the public to be negative—and likely to become more negative in the years ahead. The Fed may have no choice but to start to manage monetary policy by means other than by pegging the federal funds rate.

In the shorter term, the Fed could cause serious damage to a highly efficient and productive economy that is producing large amounts of Digital Deflation if it is reluctant to lower interest rates below a certain psychological level (for example, 1.0%) simply because of a fear of running out of room later.

## LESSONS FROM JAPAN'S DEFLATIONARY SLUMP

Most people realize that the Japanese economy is very different from the U.S. economy, as Japan is suffering from structural inefficiencies, cyclical deflation, and a lack of confidence in a dysfunctional banking system so overwhelmed with bad loans that creating liquidity is truly like "pushing on a string." However, the United States is a lot closer to deflation than most people realize, and therefore—in terms of monetary policy—the U.S. economy is a lot closer to the Japanese economy than many people believe.

As reported, the United States has already been flirting with deflation, with deflationary numbers already reported on a quarterly basis for the GDP Deflator in the fourth quarter of 2001 and on numerous occasions for the CPI and the Producer Price Index (PPI). Properly adjusted for quality improvement and Digital Deflation, inflation in recent years has been running on a full-year basis at "near zero" on the GDP Deflator and at only about 1% on the CPI.

The Fed is understandably concerned that the situation might drift into a Japan-like scenario of deflation and near-zero interest rates in which monetary policy stimulus appears ineffective. In a rigorous and eye-opening Federal Reserve study entitled "Preventing Deflation: Lessons from Japan's Experience in the 1990s," 13 economists at the Fed concluded that Japanese policymakers did not anticipate a deflationary slump and that once inflation turned negative and interest rates approached zero, it became difficult for monetary policy to "reactivate" the economy.

The Federal Reserve economists went on to state that "We draw the general lesson from Japan's experience that when inflation and interest rates have fallen close to zero, and the risk of deflation is high, stimulus, both monetary and fiscal, should go beyond the levels conventionally implied by baseline forecasts of future inflation and economic activity."[4] Graphs from this Fed study appear in Exhibit 10-5, showing the sharp decline in the Tokyo stock market (TOPIX) in 1990, the recession beginning in 1993, the appearance of deflation in 1993 and 1994, and the plunge in interest rates to zero in 1995.

It is ironic that this Fed study on Japan was published in June 2002 when the U.S. economic recovery was faltering and just before the Department of Commerce in July 2002 restated the GDP Deflator for the fourth quarter of 2001 downward from a minus 0.1% to a minus 0.5%. It is curious that the study garnered very little press despite the hand-wringing at the time over whether the U.S. economy was slipping into a double-dip downturn. Furthermore, the Federal Reserve itself voted in its next meeting in August to pass on lowering interest rates another notch even though economic indicators had turned sluggish and the bond and money markets had signaled expectations of a rate cut. It was as if the Fed "refused to eat its own cooking." It seemed risky indeed for the Fed to resist taking a preemptive strike at possible deflation after its own Japan study highlighted the risks of waiting too long before taking action at the first signs of deflation.

Exhibit 10-6 (page 279) shows today's stock market peak versus that experienced by Japan in the 1980s and 1990s, as well as the U.S. stock market in the 1920s and 1930s. Given the similarities, one must at least ask the question, "Is there something we can be doing better?"

**E X H I B I T   10-5**

## Japan's Deflationary Slump

### (a) Equity and Land Prices

### (b) Real GDP Growth* and Output Gap**

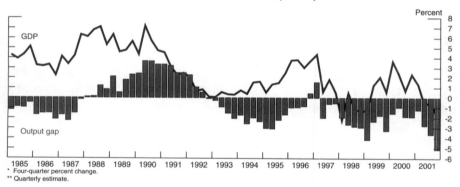

\* Four-quarter percent change.
\*\* Quarterly estimate.

### (c) Inflation* and Unemployment

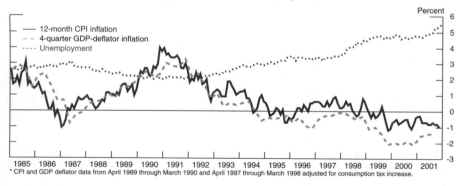

\* CPI and GDP deflator data from April 1989 through March 1990 and April 1997 through March 1998 adjusted for consumption tax increase.

**E X H I B I T   10-5** *(continued)*

### (d) Nominal Policy Rate vs. Real Policy Rate

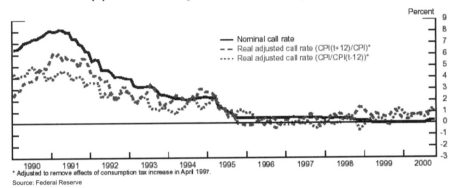

Percent

Legend:
— Nominal call rate
– – Real adjusted call rate (CPI(t+12)/CPI)*
···· Real adjusted call rate (CPI/CPI(t-12))*

* Adjusted to remove effects of consumption tax increase in April 1997.
Source: Federal Reserve

## PRODUCTIVITY GAINS IN A DEFLATIONARY ECONOMY

Productivity gains for 2002 were reported at a very strong 4.8%, the highest since 1950. We should be happy, right? Not if they're the wrong kind of productivity gains that lead to the wrong monetary policy. In the early 2000s, much has been made of productivity gains, but what do they mean for an economy in outright deflation in many sectors, and how can they help a faltering recovery?

The answers to these questions are critical because during much of the Post '90s economic slowdown, the Federal Reserve has been hanging its hat on the hope that strong growth in labor productivity would help rescue the economy from its doldrums. The November 6, 2002, FOMC press release reflected this hope: "The Committee continues to believe that an accommodative stance of monetary policy, coupled with the still *robust underlying growth in productivity,* is providing ongoing support to economic activity."

But what good is strong productivity growth to an economy where companies can't sell more goods, workers can't find jobs, and prices are going down? Perhaps these productivity gains arising out of a deflationary economy are not the salvation that the Fed is hoping for.

As Japan has found out, once in a deflationary trap, it's very difficult to use traditional monetary and fiscal policy means to get out of that trap. One serious result of a deflationary trap is that in the "jobs economy," unemployment rises as companies are forced to cut labor

# EXHIBIT 10-6

Stock Market vs. Prior Peaks
(Current S&P 500 and NASDAQ vs. Dow Jones in 1920s and 1930s and Japan's Nikkei in 1980s and 1990s)

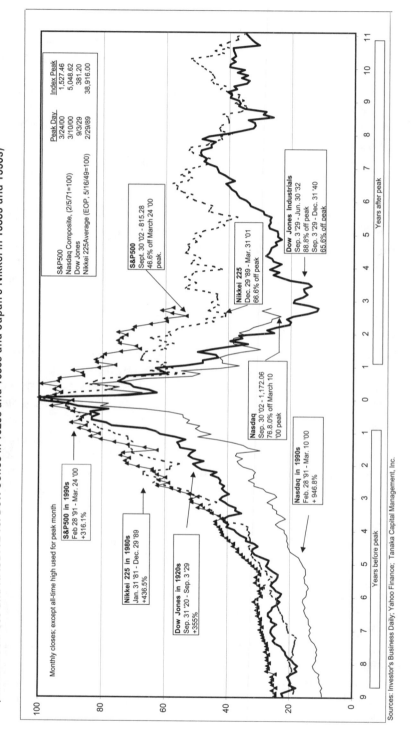

Sources: Investor's Business Daily; Yahoo Finance; Tanaka Capital Management, Inc.

costs to match their end-product price deflation. This is one of the major reasons for the 2.9% average annual productivity gains in the United States during the first 3 years of the new millennium. *The jump in productivity growth very much reflected the successful efforts of the private sector to match end-product price deflation with headcount reductions.* Companies could only cut labor to stay profitable. They had already downsized and reduced their other costs.

We also know that companies in the Post '90s slowdown did not race to make capital expenditures. With depressed sales, they didn't need to increase the output of their existing workforce. Rather, in a world with deflationary price expectations, much of capital spending was limited to rapid payback investments that enabled companies to meet stagnant unit demand and declining end-product prices with a *smaller workforce.*

With soaring energy and home prices in the early 2000s, most economists believed that we were not really in a deflationary economy. The real world suggested differently. GE Chairman Jeff Immelt reported that in 2002, his portfolio of businesses experienced an average price decline of 1.4%. GE's diversified nonfinancial businesses, from aircraft engines and power services to lighting, plastics, medical equipment, appliances, and NBC, were fairly representative of a large part of the economy. Arguably, declining interest rates also represented *interest rate price deflation* in GE's vast financial services operation. What about the consumer sector? In 2002, Wal-Mart passed on to its customers price declines averaging 1.25% across its products, according to CFO Jay Fitzsimmons. This was even better than the 1.0% per year price reductions achieved in the prior 10 years. Wal-Mart would say that much of this was achieved by the use of IT to gain distribution cost advantages, and it plans to continue to generate cost savings for the customer well into the future.

As for the rest of corporate America, we have been hearing for several years now that managers have had "no pricing flexibility." But the appearance of *outright price declines* in companies the size and breadth of GE and Wal-Mart should do more than just raise eyebrows in the debate over whether the United States is already in deflation. And that doesn't even factor into the first 3-year deflation in stock market prices since 1939 to 1941.

During much of the Post '90s slowdown, officials reiterated that the Fed had engineered the fastest interest rate reduction in history. The implication was that this was all it could do—or this was all that was needed—to provide sufficient stimulus to get the economy going again. So why didn't the economy respond? Was it really just "heightened geopolitical risk" that contributed to the "soft spot" in the economy?

The real answer was that the Fed was probably not as "accommodative" as it had thought. This Fed had decades of valuable experience in dealing with inflation, but precious little experience with deflation. It didn't seem to realize that productivity gains resulting from job cutbacks in a deflationary economy can be fundamentally very different from productivity gains in a rapidly growing, inflationary economy.

With interest rates already down to 1.25% on the federal funds rate at the end of 2002, the Fed probably felt it was running out of room. But with outright deflation in the real economy, the Fed was still groping to find the right level of interest rates to get the economy actually growing again.

Few people have ever said the Fed's job was easy.

## THE PAST AND FUTURE FED

No doubt, the U.S. economy benefited in the 1990s from a Federal Reserve that resisted rigid speed limits to pursue a more flexible, eclectic, and common-sense approach to setting monetary policy. Chairman Greenspan should be praised for his focus on productivity and for his Fed's willingness to let the 1990s' New Economy expand at an above-average rate.

However, it may be some time before the public knows why the Fed appeared to reverse its course in the 2000–2002 period from an accommodative, "let the New Economy expand" posture to take on more of an early 1980s' Old Economy approach to fighting inflation. The most likely explanation is that with data that was overstating inflation, it may have appeared, particularly to the anti-inflation hawks on the Fed Board, that the 10-year long economic expansion was getting heated up by the Internet phenomenon and was in danger returning to higher inflation. Without more complete data on just how the New Economy was creating new and different kinds of productivity gains that would take inflation to new lows, and certainly without a specific understanding of the recurring nature of Digital Deflation across the economy, the Fed may have mistaken a dot-com craze and a stock market bubble as indicative of an overheated and inflationary economy.

In general, there is much to be learned about how the New Economy influences the overall economy. Aside from the counting of quality improvement and the creation of Digital Deflation, perhaps the most difficult task ahead is for monetary policy to be adjusted and fine-tuned to reflect the new forces at play. New models will have to be considered, and monetary policy speed limits will need to be revised. The greatest risk to the Digital Revolution and the digitally driven productivity boom would be for the Fed to inadvertently restrict the economy to a growth rate well below its true potential. This would likely create a depressed stock market that would deny equity capital and venture capital to the very creators and enablers of future advances in technology—and economic growth.

It is critical to realize that a lack of understanding and a lack of measurement of the rapidly improving quality of products and services could leave the Digital Revolution unfulfilled in a manner quite analogous to what led to the demise of the Industrial Revolution in the 1920s and 1930s. This perspective puts an even greater onus on the government and the Fed to obtain better data on the New Economy and a better understanding of the workings of Digital Deflation.

## NOTES

1. "Monitoring the World Economy 1820–1992," Angus Maddison, Organisation for Economic Co-operation and Development, 1995.

2. "Is the Internet Better than Electricity?" Martin Brookes and Zaki Wahhaj, Goldman, Sachs, August 2, 2000.

3. "Believe Your Eyes, the New Economy Is Real," Bob McTeer, *Wall Street Journal*, November 18, 1999.

4. "Preventing Deflation: Lessons from Japan's Experience in the 1990s," Ahearne, Gagnon, Haltmaier, Kamin, et al., Board of Governors of the Federal Reserve System, June 2002, www.federalreserve.gov/pubs/ifdp.

# 11

## CHAPTER

# The Politics of Need and Better Data for a Digitally Deflating World

The role of government is not to create wealth. The role of government is to create conditions in which jobs are created, in which people can find work.

*President George W. Bush, January 14, 2002*

*The New Economy presents an unusual opportunity to achieve a super full employment economy and to reduce poverty, as well as to create more wealth and improve the quality of life for the vast majority of Americans. For the New Economy to reach its full potential, the government first needs to allocate more resources to obtain better economic data and measure large amounts of quality improvement being generated from advancing technologies. This is not a luxury, but a necessity. A vibrant economy may be the only viable solution to America's looming Medicare and Social Security needs.*

## WEALTH AND POVERTY IN THE NEW ECONOMY

It is one thing for an economy to generate substantial wealth for the great middle class through real appreciation in financial and tangible assets. It is quite another thing for an economy to create an environment to help people lift themselves out of poverty.

One of the greatest benefits of the New Economy is that digital technologies are generating increasing amounts of Digital Deflation, which allows the Old Economy to run faster and hotter than would be the case if there were no new technologies producing faster, better, cheaper products. With the appropriate fiscal and monetary policies, the result should be full employment—and employment at levels that redefine *full*. Perhaps, *super full employment* would be a more appropriate description. The amount by which economic growth in a super full employment economy exceeds the Old Economy definition of growth at full employment (calculated from the standard noninflationary rate of unemployment) is a function of how much Digital Deflation is created in the New Economy to offset inflation in the Old Economy. The more good deflation created in the New Economy, the more inflation that can be accommodated in the Old Economy, permitting greater traditional employment without a rise in aggregate inflation.

The benefits to society of a super full employment economy are immediate and enormous. In the 1990s, the benefits were obvious to all, regardless of political party. Amidst all the hoopla over the record economic expansion and meteoric rise in the stock market, there was another important story—about how moderate-income individuals and the unemployed benefited from the New Economy.

In the late 1990s, companies hired the marginally employable and used all kinds of creative means to coax, cajole, and entice retired people back into employment, work-at-home, and part-time work. Corporations didn't need government incentives and programs for worker training, though they no doubt helped. A continuation of vigorous economic growth with low inflation for any extended period of time into the next decade would give hope and opportunity to the less advantaged, much as it did in the 1990s.

It is well-documented but worth reviewing the record of the magnificent 1990s from the perspective of the American society as a whole. Real incomes grew dramatically, the number of welfare recipients declined in half, and the poverty rate dropped from over 15% to 11.8% by 1999 (Exhibit 11-1).[1]

What enabled the improvement in these important metrics for society was the combination of favorable demographics, strong economic growth, rising productivity, and declining inflation. The surge in productivity in the late 1990s allowed the Fed to let the economy expand at a faster rate without rekindling inflation. The result was a super full employment economy where companies desperate for labor reached out to the fringes of the labor pool to hire and train many

**E X H I B I T  11-1**

How Society Benefited from the New Economy of the 1990s

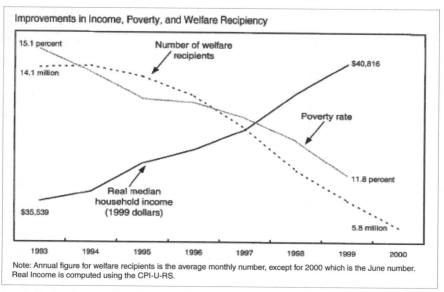

Improvements in Income, Poverty, and Welfare Recipiency

Number of welfare recipients

15.1 percent

14.1 million

$40,816

Poverty rate

Real median household income (1999 dollars)

$35,539

11.8 percent

5.8 million

| 1993 | 1994 | 1995 | 1996 | 1997 | 1998 | 1999 | 2000 |

Note: Annual figure for welfare recipients is the average monthly number, except for 2000 which is the June number. Real Income is computed using the CPI-U-RS.

Source: "Economic Report of the President" January 2001; Department of Commerce (Bureau of the Census) and Department of Health and Human Services.

who would have had difficulty finding jobs in a slower-growth economy. As people moved off the welfare rolls, many became more self-sustaining, with all the psychological benefits of self-achievement. The government found itself with a reduced demand for social services and the need to revise its estimates upward for projected budget surpluses. From a societal point of view, it couldn't get much better. But can it last?

The answer, fortunately, is yes. The great thing about the Digital Revolution is that there is no end in sight. It seems that every time it appears that a technology will run out of steam, a new process, a new technology, or a brand-new innovation appears, to take the product or service to the next level. New technologies will drive quantitative productivity gains to new heights, and constantly improving product quality will drive quality-based productivity gains to higher levels. What it means for society is that gains in productivity should be rising rather than falling over the next couple of decades, as labor force productivity enjoys its own revolution. What it means for the economy is more real and nominal GDP growth and virtually zero aggregate inflation.

With the right fiscal and monetary policies, very much like the 1990s, everyone benefits. The corporate sector gains access to more capital at lower cost. This will be needed to fund the development of future technology advances and product design cycles. For Investor-Consumers it will mean record-low interest rates and higher stock valuations, rewarding those who provide risk capital for these new technologies as well as financing for growth and expansion of both the New and Old Economies. The consumer will be dazzled by an ongoing proliferation of new products and services to improve the quality of life. Federal, state and local governments will collect more revenues, face declining social burdens, and enjoy a greater capacity to provide training and assistance for those who can't make it on their own. For the wage earner, there will be higher real average hourly earnings—much like there were in the 1990s.

## WAGE EARNERS WILL EARN MORE

The key to a better standard of living for hourly wage earners is for them to improve their real hourly earnings, adjusted for inflation. Unfortunately, except for the 1960s, early 1970s, and late 1990s, over the last 35 years, the working man and woman enjoyed little in the way of real wage gains as seen in Exhibit 11-2. The top graph shows how real wage gains suffered immensely from the ravages of inflation. On the other hand, the bottom graph shows how real wage gains benefited directly whenever there was a strong gain in productivity. The reason, of course, is that strong growth in output per person-hour allows companies to raise wages without having to raise product prices or hurt profitability. At the same time, higher productivity reduces overall inflation, which is critical to preserving the purchasing power of the wage earner's hard-earned dollar.

Based on a simple linear relationship that has existed historically between productivity gains and real wages, the future for the hourly wage earner looks quite bright. The outlook for continued favorable demographics, rising IT capital spending, and increasing Digital Deflation would suggest that productivity gains should continue at the high level of the late 1990s and even trend higher. A regression analysis of the last 35 years would suggest that productivity gains would have to average greater than 1.77% per year for real wages to grow.

**E X H I B I T   11-2**

Productivity and Real Wage Gains

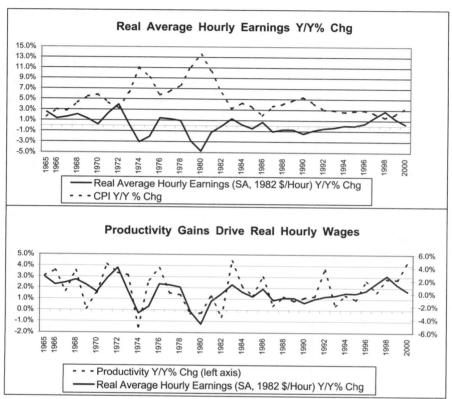

Sources: Bureau of Labor Statistics; Tanaka Capital Management, Inc.

This is because companies have to use some of the benefits of higher labor productivity gains to cover the inflationary cost pressures of all expense categories, not just labor costs.

The good news is that productivity growth is projected by the Congressional Budget Office (CBO) to average 2.5% per year over the next 10 years. This should be a *minimum* expectation. Factoring in the incremental growth in productivity directly from rising IT capital spending as a percentage of GDP, productivity growth should rise at an even faster pace—at about a 2.9% per year by 2010 and by 3.6% per year by 2020, as shown in the IT capital Spending–Productivity model, discussed in Chapter 7. More important, as the government

counts more of the incremental quality improvement and Digital Deflation from the New Economy, total productivity growth can reach
4.3% by 2010 and 5.4% by 2020 (assuming the case of the government
counting 50% of the currently uncounted quality improvement).

Using the historical relationship between productivity gains and
real wage gains, given a productivity growth rate of 4.0%, real hourly
wages should grow at around 4.0% per year. At 5.0% productivity
growth, real wages should grow at about a 5.8% rate. These rates of
growth would be astounding considering that real wages grew by an
average of only 0.2% per year over the last 35 years.

The simple regression between productivity gains and real wage
gains demonstrated a respectable 0.64 historical correlation. However, since there were very few data points where productivity
growth reached levels over 4.0%, the regression model may become
nonlinear and lose some of its predictability at extremely high rates of
productivity growth. Nevertheless, it should be clear that real hourly
wages will be heading much higher, which will be great news for
wage earners. The beneficial real wage aspect of the New Economy is
virgin ground for economists and has exciting implications for the
egalitarian nature of the Digital Revolution. The ultimate challenge
will be to help convert the increases in real wages into savings and investment so that the wage earner can also build wealth in advance of
retirement.

## THE NEW ECONOMY, UNEMPLOYMENT, AND CRIME

It is important to understand that there are incredibly positive implications for American society if the U.S. economy is to enjoy another 10
or 20 years like the 1980s and 1990s. An extended period of above-average economic growth, labor shortages, rising productivity, declining inflation, and increasing wealth will lead to higher real wages and
improving fortunes for those with financial assets. At the same time, it
will change the fabric of American life for the better by providing natural incentives for better education and job training, a decline in crime
rates, better healthcare, and a considerable improvement in the overall quality of life.

Crime rates represent just one example of how an expanding
New Economy can improve the quality of life. Exhibit 11-3 shows
graphically how changes in crime rates in the United States have
tended to mirror changes in the unemployment rate. Simply put,

**E X H I B I T   11-3**

Change in Unemployment Affects the Crime Rate

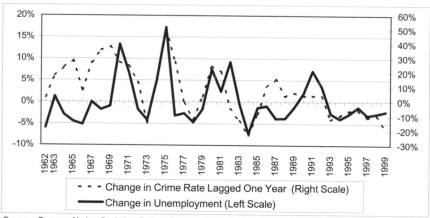

Sources: Bureau of Labor Statistics; Federal Bureau of Investigation; Tanaka Capital Management, Inc.

when unemployment goes down, crime goes down. This relationship has a respectable correlation of 0.48, which can be easily seen in the graph. What is a little surprising is that historically, changes in the crime rate have occurred about 1 year in advance of changes in the unemployment rate. This seems to imply that crime rates rise as jobs get harder to find. This makes sense, since the process begins as the corporate sector shuts down hiring well before it resorts to layoffs. Jobs get scarce before they get eliminated.

The really encouraging news for the American public and for the law enforcement community is that other things being equal, crime rates should decline as the New Economy gets back on its feet. Recall that one of the major benefits of the Digital Revolution is that Digital Deflation from the New Economy offsets inflation in the Old Economy. This allows for a more fully employed economy and a lower unemployment rate before inflation from the Old Economy threatens to significantly exceed good deflation in the New Economy. Exhibit 11-4 shows how crime as a percentage of the American population peaked in 1980 and again in 1991 before beginning to trend down during the more prosperous 1990s.

Many reports have concluded that for a variety of economic, social, and enforcement reasons, the trends in crime have seen their best years and that crime will be headed back up over the next few years.

**E X H I B I T   11-4**

The Crime Rate Started a Major Downtrend in the 1990s

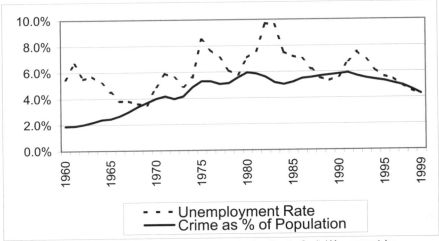

Sources: Bureau of Labor Statistics; Federal Bureau of Investigation; Tanaka Capital Management, Inc.

But, the economic trends would suggest otherwise. Lower unemployment rates spawned by the ongoing expansion of the New Economy and better programs for training and education will likely move crime rates down further. Over the next 10 to 20 years, crime as a percentage of the population is more likely to trend down from 4.0% in 1999 toward the 2.0% level of the 1960s than to return to the 5.9% peak reached in 1991. While one can estimate the economic value of less crime, it is difficult to measure the true value to society of fewer victims and greater peace of mind.

## THE POLITICS OF NEED

As discussed in Chapter 2, the "Politics of Need" in the late 1960s and the 1970s was to create jobs for the Baby Boomers and Working Women entering the workforce at the rate of 3% to 4% per year. That social need was met, but the by-product was an enormous surge in inflation. As the growth in the workforce declined to near zero during the late 1980s and the 1990s, the Politics of Need shifted away from creating jobs to promoting savings, investment, and capital spending—to enable the existing nongrowing workforce to become more productive.

Voters signaled their wishes, and astute elected representatives responded. Congress eliminated the deductibility of consumer interest expense, which had encouraged spending versus saving and investment. Tax rates were reduced on earned income, and importantly, capital gains tax rates were lowered, creating a more favorable environment for what soon would be called the New Economy. Congress did its part by reducing tax rates and contributing to the potential for higher after-tax returns on capital investments and investments in the stock market. With scarce labor conditions, the market mechanism signaled the need for more capital investment and stronger productivity gains. Digital technologies also played an important role, enabling the capital to be put to work more efficiently and, at the same time, providing higher-quality products and brand-new services.

No single politician or even group of legislators should take credit for the Digital Revolution or the New Economy of the 1990s. The truth is that there was a host of contributors including scientists, entrepreneurs, researchers, engineers, product developers, manufacturers, sales reps, investors, and, not the least, consumers.

Fiscal policy, nevertheless, played an important role in the 1990s and can play an enormously important role in the revival and return of the New Economy. Policymakers therefore need to be aware of how digital technologies are providing the critical third fundamental element driving the New Economy, complementing labor and capital. Policies will need to reflect the increasing importance of capital, as it is required to leverage scarce labor and increase productivity if the economy is to grow at all.

On the legislative front, lowering capital gains tax rates and eliminating double taxation of dividends would go a long way toward unlocking capital and providing incentives for investment in new products and new technologies. Both measures will help create new jobs by making it easier for capital to flow out of the Old Economy and into the New Economy—restarting a job engine every bit as powerful as we saw in the 1990s.

Regulating and taxing the Internet would have just the opposite effect. The Internet has become a shared public resource. It is more like the air we breathe than a national highway system that by necessity must be built and maintained by the government. To regulate or tax the Internet would slow down the Digital Revolution—and a reemerging New Economy. The Internet-based supply chain and customer service initiatives on the planning table today will be needed to help deliver the faster, better, cheaper products and services of tomorrow.

Meanwhile, breaking the logjams on wireless spectrum availability, digital music, and video intellectual property rights and local telecommunications access issues are critical next steps for launching the next phase of demand for broadband Internet services. These are not easy issues to resolve. But solving them would help accelerate the resurgence of the New Economy, and further delays would only slow it down.

## BETTER DATA FOR THE NEW ECONOMY

If the New Economy is to return to provide another decade or two of prosperity, it will be absolutely critical that the government make further progress on properly counting the ongoing quality improvement being made in a variety of products and services across the economy. This point cannot be made too strongly.

No amount of legislation to stimulate the economy or to attempt to create jobs would have the same long-term beneficial impact on the economy as the accurate measurement of the real value of output already being delivered in the economy today. What's at stake is another decade or two very much like the 1990s with strong growth in real GDP, productivity, real wages, and real wealth creation. The alternative, as noted, is a decade of unfulfilled growth, moderate productivity gains, little growth in real wages, and mediocre growth in real wealth. With more accurate data, lower reported inflation will allow more accommodative monetary policy and faster economic growth. It's that simple.

What the U.S. Congress needs to do is to provide more funds as soon as possible for the Bureau of Economic Analysis (BEA) at the Department of Commerce (DOC) and the Bureau of Labor Statistics (BLS) at the Department of Labor to more accurately measure quality improvement in technology-driven products and services as well as the more timely addition of brand-new products and services. A handful of economists and analysts at the statistical agencies already have the tools and the desire to measure more products and services for gains in quality, but they are severely short of funding to complete the task.

The National Association for Business Economics (NABE) has been lobbying strongly for several years for greater funding for these statistical agencies. In mid-2000, the NABE said that 7 years of flat funding at the BEA had "resulted in the current hiring freeze and a devastating 7% reduction of staff since 1994. This reduction has occurred during a period of dramatic changes in the economy, which require significant work to update and improve national economic estimates and trade statistics." NABE commented further that data quality "is being seriously compromised" by a lack of sufficient funding.

It's not only the Federal Reserve and other government departments that need accurate, up-to-date economic data on which to base policy decisions. The integrity of these data is also essential to the business community. From the major corporations to the smallest "mom and pop" company, business managers must have the right data to help make vital decisions that will keep the U.S. economy moving and the Digital Revolution thriving. Company managements need to understand the digital content and quality improvement dynamics of their products to compete successfully in an environment of rapidly advancing technologies and product design cycles. The government, meanwhile, needs to know how the private sector is converting these advances into Digital Deflation, and it needs to have the resources to work with each industry to develop the proper guidelines for measurement.

It is encouraging that in a highlighted section called "Better Tools: Improving the Accuracy and Timeliness of Economic Statistics," the January 2002 Economic Report of the President commented that "the quality of existing statistics is far from perfect and could be enhanced with further investment." White House economists then went on to say that "even real GDP, generally thought of as a reliable measure of overall activity in the U.S. economy, is susceptible to considerable revisions . . . the average quarterly revision of real GDP growth over 1978 to 1998 was about 1.4 percentage points in either direction, while the real GDP growth averaged 2.9 percent." The report then finished on an important note striking closer to home:

> Improved quality-adjusted price indexes for high-technology products are also an important area for future research . . . current estimating techniques fail to capture productivity growth in high technology–using service industries. This shortcoming may lead to underestimates of annual productivity growth of 0.2 to 0.4 percentage point or more. As the economy continues to change and grow, the need persists to

create and develop such new measures, to provide decision makers with better tools with which to track the economy as accurately as possible.

The Digital Deflation model would suggest that the overall understatement of productivity is closer to 2.0% per year, and that much of the service sector measurement error is in the uncounted delivery of higher-quality services to the consumer rather than the use of high-tech equipment by the service sector. Yes, the fact that the government wishes to do more research in the area of quality improvement is encouraging. But, it needs to move quickly to catch up—and keep up—with the fast-moving hands on technology's clock.

## THE NEW ECONOMY AND BUDGET SURPLUSES

Federal, state, and local governments were pleasantly surprised by budget surpluses in the late 1990s, as the New Economy produced higher incomes, greater than expected tax revenues, and lower demands on social services. For a brief period, there was even hope that projected budget surpluses could somehow be used to address the looming Social Security and Medicare deficits as the Baby Boomers retire.

The optimism on the budgetary front evaporated quickly in 2001. A tightening of monetary policy, the recession of 2001, and the related fiscal stimulus package passed in 2001 contributed to an extraordinary $4.0 trillion downward revision in the 10-year budget surplus predicted by the Congressional Budget Office (CBO). After predicting a 10-year cumulative $5.6 trillion budget surplus one year earlier, in January 2002, the CBO reduced its 10-year forecast to a mere $1.6 trillion. Forty percent of the reduction was related to a weaker economic outlook. The balance was related to legislation including a major tax reduction program designed to help stimulate an economy.

What happened in the early 2000s was that while monetary policy became inadvertently too tight due to the undercounting of increasing product quality and the overstating of inflation, fiscal policymakers attempted to compensate by becoming more stimulative. This was eminently logical. The White House and Congress could see that the economy was struggling. What they didn't know was that the persistently weak economy was very much a result of a Federal Reserve that was tighter than it realized because it was reacting to overstated inflation numbers. It would have been far more efficient for the Fed to take its foot off the brakes *before* our fiscal policymakers started stepping on the gas. Instead, fiscal policy had to carry the load, resulting in a virtual elimination of the massive planned 10-year budget surplus.

One of the most important benefits of a resurging New Economy would be a return to the creation of large federal budget surpluses. Counting only half of the currently uncounted quality improvement and Digital Deflation in the economy could conceivably add back an estimated $2.6 trillion or two-thirds of the $4.0 trillion of the 10-year budget surplus "lost" in the 2001 budget revision. This estimate is obtained by using the CBO's "rules of thumb" for budget projections and by assuming a 1% adjustment for quality improvement and Digital Deflation resulting in a 1% reduction in overall inflation. Conservatively, it is assumed that a 1% lower inflation rate would allow the Federal Reserve to expand nominal GDP by an extra 1%, producing $2.3 trillion more tax revenues over 10 years. A decline in interest rates of 1%, in line with 1% lower inflation, would contribute an additional $0.3 trillion of surplus, for a total of $2.6 trillion.

Although a 1% reduction in inflation would normally reduce the budget surplus by reducing income tax revenues, it would not do so in this case. This is because the reduction in inflation would come entirely from making downward adjustments to the GDP Deflator for quality improvement, rather than from a 1% reduction in the nominal dollars of GDP. The above example shows how incredibly sensitive the federal budget surplus will be to changes in assumptions for GDP growth, interest rates, and inflation, which again puts enormous pressure on getting the numbers right.

## THE DARK SIDE OF DEMOGRAPHICS

Earlier chapters talked about how the favorable demographics of low growth in the youngest segment of the workforce formed the stable foundation of the New Economy. This positive demographic condition of low growth in the supply of labor will persist over the next two decades, extending the need for growth in the other two basic inputs of economic activity—capital and technology. However, one aspect of the evolving demographics will turn decidedly negative. Over the next 30 years, Baby Boomers will be retiring in record numbers, placing an enormous burden on the government for both medical and re-

## E X H I B I T  11-5

The Approaching Medical and Social Security Challenge

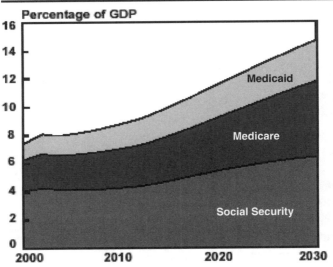

NOTE:   Spending is based on measures from the national income
and product accounts.

Source: Congressional Budget Office.

tirement services. The graph shown in Exhibit 11-5 presents the CBO's projections published in January 2002 estimating that the demand for Social Security, Medicare, and Medicaid will rise from 7.8% of GDP in 2001 to 14.7% of GDP by 2030.

Ironically, the demand that will be placed on our government for more medical and retirement support and services will be further compounded by the increasing quality of medicine and healthcare services. Advances in science and technology will continue to drive mortality rates lower for a variety of diseases, extending the life expectancy of Americans thereby increasing the demand for medical care and Social Security benefits.

While the life expectancy trends shown in Exhibit 11-6 are encouraging, they are likely to be raised further by advances in medical science in general and the human genome in particular. It would be bittersweet if the advances in technology and health sciences extend life expectancy and improve the quality of life but are not counted by the government

## EXHIBIT 11-6

Factors Affecting Demand for Social Security, Medicare, and Medicaid

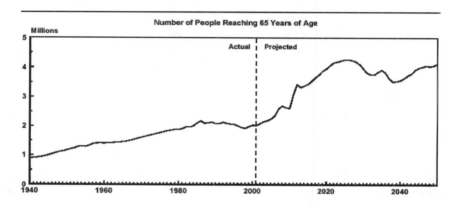

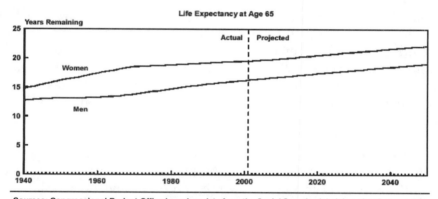

Sources: Congressional Budget Office based on data from the Social Security Administration (intermediate assumptions) and from Social Security Administration, *The 2001 Annual Report of the Board of Trustees of the Federal Old-Age and Survivors Insurance and Disability Insurance Trust Funds* (March 19, 2001), Table V.A4 (intermediate assumptions).

in the measurement of the real value of goods and services. It would be most disappointing if the resulting inaccurate counting of the improving quality of healthcare and other products and services across the economy leads to overly tight monetary policy because the inflation rate would be reported to be higher than it really would be if quality improvement were counted properly. What would be most tragic, however, is if the resulting period of unfulfilled economic expansion and wealth creation resulted in a slowing of the pace of technological advancement and the inability of the government to extend the benefits of medical science and retirement support to more beneficiaries.

This scenario is echoed in the explicit warnings of the CBO in its January 2002 report:

> The pressure to boost spending on health and retirement programs will present the nation with difficult choices. Some combination of reduced spending on other priorities, increased revenues, and diminished outlays for health and retirement programs (below levels projected under current law) will probably be needed to balance the government's finances. Policies that encourage economic growth also could help ease the burden of rising health and retirement spending. If none of those actions is taken, rising budget deficits could ultimately harm the economy.

The goal of the CBO is to provide Congress with economic projections for better decision making in the legislative process, and its warnings are sobering. For our policymakers, it should be quite clear that the Politics of Need in the United States is shifting again. We've already transitioned from a need to create jobs for an expanding labor force in the late 1960s and the 1970s to a need for capital investment and technology advancements to improve the productivity of a stable labor force in the late 1980s and the 1990s. Over the next several years, we will have a new need to provide a strong enough economy to generate sufficient income, investment and wealth creation—and therefore tax revenues—to meet the growing medical and retirement requirements of an aging population.

The looming healthcare and Social Security challenge could be made far more manageable if Digital Deflation is properly counted, permitting the Fed to grow both the Old and New Economies at a faster rate. As our fiscal policymakers search for solutions, it is encouraging to note that they will be better able to confront these budgetary, Medicare, and Social Security issues head on if they only measure more accurately the real gains in output and productivity—and the resulting reduction in inflation—already being generated across the economy today. If we give ourselves the ability to count the quality improvements being created by the Digital Revolution, it will then allow the Federal Reserve to become more accommodative, ushering in a resurgent New Economy, renewed prosperity, and a happier and healthier society.

## NOTE

1. "Economic Report of the President," January 2001.

# 12

CHAPTER

# Wise Investing in the New Economy

If more investors conclude that the giddy days of the 1990's are over
and that the stock market has become a less secure place to put their
money, the virtuous cycle of the 90's could be gone.

*E.S. Browning,* The Wall Street Journal

*Investors will want to know how to participate in the upcoming new era of
prosperity and learn how to identify the "creators and beneficiaries" of Digital Deflation in the next decade. As the New Economy continues to take share
from the Old, it will be helpful to understand which kinds of companies really
did outperform in the 1990s—and why they may or may not repeat that feat.*

## REAL-WORLD INVESTING

A considerable amount of wealth will be created in the New Economy
stock market over the next two decades as the government becomes
more skilled at counting quality improvement, resulting in further declines in inflation, record gains in productivity, and more stimulative
monetary and fiscal policies. But what does it mean for the average
investor, and how can he or she best take advantage of the opportunities that lie ahead? This chapter will provide the reader with some
helpful hints as to which kinds of companies will be the winners and
which the losers over the next one to two decades.

Many of the previously described new theories on demographics, productivity, Digital Deflation and the wealth effect were

grounded on firsthand observations of individual companies that were doing better than others as the New Economy took share from the Old. Accordingly, it should follow that these macroeconomic observations and theories should help the investor figure out at the microeconomic or company level which companies will succeed going forward.

Do these theories work in practice? Do they work in the real world of investing, and will they work in the future? In a quest for validation of the basic Digital Deflation thesis and its usefulness at the individual company level, it became obvious that there was no better way to start than with a representative but manageable group of companies and see how they actually performed in the 1990s.

The Dow Jones Industrials fit the bill, and the 30 Dow companies were divided into two groups—New Economy Companies and Old Economy Companies—based on definitions provided in earlier chapters. In short, companies that were utilizing digital technologies in the decade of the 1990s to deliver more value and more quality to their customers annually, net of price increases, were deemed to be major contributors to the New Economy. The thesis was that if New Economy Companies were delivering more value to their customers per dollar, then at the margin they should be growing their revenues and profit margins faster than Old Economy Companies.

The "creators" of Digital Deflation, those companies creating digital products and services, such as Intel, Microsoft, IBM, and Hewlett-Packard, were the easiest to identify as being in the New Economy camp. Those companies delivering products with high digital content (such as Honeywell and United Technologies), and those using digital technologies to deliver superior products and services (such as GE) or to deliver products at lower prices (such as Wal-Mart and Home Depot) were also placed in the New Economy group. Companies that used advancing technologies to gain market share in the 1990s were major "beneficiaries" of Digital Deflation. Merck and Johnson & Johnson, for example, used digital technologies—as well as advances in combinatorial chemistry and other advances in basic scientific research—to provide drugs with improved efficacy and safety profiles.

The Old Economy group included many companies which, to be entirely fair, have been utilizing digital technologies to improve their products and services. In these cases, it was a tougher call than for others. But if, on a net basis, companies were raising prices for equivalent quality products and services because their more traditional raw material, labor, energy, and other cost pressures exceeded the benefits of digital technologies, they were placed in the Old Economy camp. The toughest decision was to include SBC Communications in the Old Economy camp, but it was determined that this telecom provider on a net basis was not delivering faster and better products and services at lower prices. At the local level, telephone rates were not coming down and broadband deployment has been slow to develop.

The 10-year period from 1990 to 2000 was selected to attempt to minimize the effect of economic cycles, since the beginning and ending years of this period represented final years of two economic expansions. Additionally, it was felt that the period should not end in 1999, the peak year of the pre-Y2K spending surge. Data were then collected for four performance metrics: the percentage change in operating profit margins, compound annual growth in revenues, compound growth in earnings per share, and appreciation in the stock price per annum for each of the companies. Over time, six Old Economy Companies and one New Economy Company had to be excluded from the study due to material mergers, divestitures, or spin-offs during the decade.

## REAL-WORLD RESULTS

The results of the New Economy–Old Economy analysis were viewed with apprehension and excitement, something like that of first-time parents about to view the first ultrasound image of their yet-to-be-born child. What if, in the actual real-world experience of the 1990s, these New Economy Companies performed no better that the Old Economy Companies? This might raise serious questions about the validity of the theory of Digital Deflation.

As it turned out, the data exceeded expectations, as the 11 companies in the New Economy pool outperformed the 12 companies in the Old Economy pool by a factor of about two times, *for each of the four metrics,* in the 1990–2000 decade. The results are presented in Exhibit 12-1.

On average, the New Economy Companies grew their revenues per share by 13.8% per year in the decade, versus a growth rate of only 6.2% per year in revenues per share for the Old Economy Companies. This is fully consistent with the Digital Deflation thesis that companies offering more value to customers every year at the same or lower

# E X H I B I T   12-1

## New Economy vs. Old Economy Company Metrics

| | SALES 1990–2000 CAGR | NET PROFIT % INCREASE IN MARGIN 1990–2000 | E.P.S. 1990–2000 CAGR | STOCK APPRE-CIATION 1990–2000 CAGR | STOCK APPRE-CIATION 2001–2002 |
|---|---|---|---|---|---|
| **OLD ECONOMY:** | | | | | |
| ALCOA | 5.8% | 22.6% | 8.2% | 16.6% | -32.0% |
| AMERICAN EXPRESS (a) | --------- | ------- | ---------- | ---------- | -35.7% |
| BOEING | 3.9% | 2.1% | 4.1% | 11.3% | -50.0% |
| CATERPILLAR | 7.6% | 188.9% | 19.2% | 14.9% | -3.4% |
| CITIGROUP (a) | --------- | ------- | ---------- | ---------- | -31.1% |
| COCA-COLA | 7.9% | 32.6% | 11.2% | 18.0% | -28.1% |
| DISNEY | 12.6% | -46.1% | 6.1% | 13.1% | -43.6% |
| DUPONT (a) | --------- | ------- | ---------- | ---------- | -12.2% |
| EASTMAN KODAK (a) | --------- | ------- | ---------- | ---------- | -11.0% |
| EXXON MOBIL | 3.4% | 74.5% | 9.3% | 12.9% | -19.6% |
| GENERAL MOTORS (a) | --------- | ------- | ---------- | ---------- | -27.6% |
| INT'L PAPER | -0.1% | -37.0% | -4.0% | 4.3% | -14.3% |
| J P MORGAN CHASE (a) | --------- | ------- | ---------- | ---------- | -47.2% |
| MCDONALDS | 9.0% | 14.9% | 10.3% | 16.7% | -52.7% |
| MINNESOTA MINING | 3.6% | 11.0% | 4.6% | 10.9% | 2.3% |
| PHILLIP MORRIS | 7.0% | 53.6% | 11.3% | 9.8% | -7.9% |
| PROCTER & GAMBLE | 5.8% | 73.8% | 11.1% | 6.1% | 9.6% |
| SBC COMMUNICATIONS | 7.6% | 19.8% | 9.4% | 13.1% | -43.2% |
| AVERAGE | 6.2% | 34.2% | 8.4% | 12.3% | -24.9% |
| # OF COMPANIES | 12 | 12 | 12 | 12 | 18 |
| **NEW ECONOMY:** | | | | | |
| AT&T (a) | --------- | ------- | ---------- | ---------- | -63.9% |
| GENERAL ELECTRIC | 4.6% | 100.0% | 12.2% | 31.1% | -49.2% |
| HEWLETT-PACKARD | 14.0% | 30.4% | 16.4% | 23.0% | -45.0% |
| HOME DEPOT | 23.7% | 30.2% | 27.1% | 31.9% | -47.4% |
| HONEYWELL | -0.9% | 148.6% | 12.9% | 21.5% | -49.3% |
| IBM | 5.2% | 5.7% | 5.4% | 11.6% | -8.8% |
| INTEL | 23.5% | 90.4% | 31.4% | 38.0% | -48.2% |
| JOHNSON & JOHNSON | 9.5% | 46.0% | 13.5% | 19.3% | 2.2% |
| MERCK | 18.1% | -27.2% | 14.3% | 7.6% | -39.5% |
| MICROSOFT | 31.5% | 73.7% | 37.6% | 35.4% | 19.2% |
| UNITED TECHNOLOGIES | 2.5% | 94.3% | 9.9% | 20.7% | -21.2% |
| WAL-MART | 19.6% | -17.5% | 17.1% | 21.5% | -4.9% |
| AVERAGE | 13.8% | 52.2% | 18.0% | 23.8% | -29.7% |
| # OF COMPANIES | 11 | 11 | 11 | 11 | 12 |

a   For companies which had significant mergers, acquisitions, sale of assets or spin-offs,
no figures were calculated.  Am. Express - Lehman spinoff 5/94; DuPont - Conoco IPO 10/98;
Eastman Kodak - 1990–1992 includes chemical division; AT&T - 1996 on excludes Lucent,
NCR and AT&T Capital; 2001–2002 stock appreciation adjusted for AT&T Broadband spin-off
and AT&T Wireless dividend.

Fiscal years: Coca-Cola - September 30; Procter and Gamble - June 30; Home Depot -
January 30 following year; Microsoft - June 30.

CAGR = Compound Annual Growth Rate.

Sources: Dow Jones; Value Line; Tanaka Capital Management, Inc.

prices should take market share away from companies offering the same or similar value at higher prices. In addition, in keeping with the thesis that New Economy Companies should earn a higher return for offering more value, higher performance, and higher quality, the pool of New Economy Companies in the Dow also enjoyed a more rapid expansion of profit margins in the decade. On average, they expanded their net profit margins (after-tax profits divided by revenues) by an impressive 52% during the decade versus a 34% improvement in the Old Economy Company net profit margins. This result seems to validate the thesis that New Economy Companies were not giving away their technology-driven product improvement for free ("empty calories"), but in fact were benefiting from higher incremental profit margins on faster incremental sales growth.

For the investor, it's the bottom line that counts. And again, in terms of earnings per share, the New Economy group excelled. The compound annual growth rate in earnings per share averaged 18.0% per year for the New Economy Companies versus an average of only 8.4% per year for the Old Economy Companies. It should be noted that in earnings per share, New Economy Companies performed even better relative to the Old Economy Companies than they did in net profit margin. This is a natural result of companies with improving profitability being able to utilize growing free-cash flow to self-finance their growth, deleverage, accumulate cash, and buy in stock.

Did the superior growth in sales and profits translate into higher returns for shareholders? The answer is that in terms of capital appreciation (excluding dividends), not only did the New Economy Companies significantly outperform the Old Economy Companies, but they did so with great consistency. Common stock prices in the New Economy group appreciated on average by 23.8% per year in the decade, versus only 12.3% per year for the Old Economy group. The difference is even more dramatic in cumulative terms, as the New Economy stocks were up an average of 746% in price during the 10-year period, and the Old Economy stocks were up only 219%.

In the New Economy camp, only Merck significantly underperformed the 12.3% average of the Old Economy pool with a 7.6% price appreciation per year, as it suffered from a succession of major drugs going off patent. All other New Economy Companies delivered strong capital appreciation ranging from 11.6% per year for IBM to a high of 38.0% per year for Intel and 35.4% per year for Microsoft. It is not surprising that Intel and Microsoft earned top honors as they hold leadership positions in silicon and software—two of the fundamental drivers of the Digital Revolution.

In terms of price appreciation, *none* of the Old Economy Companies outperformed the 23.8% per year average of the New Economy Companies. In the Old Economy camp, International Paper produced the lowest capital appreciation at 4.3% per year during the decade, and Coca-Cola generated the highest at 18.0% per year. The 16.6% per year appreciation in the common stock of Alcoa was impressive, demonstrating that management can improve profitability even in a fairly pure Old Economy industry such as aluminum.

Although it was suspected at the outset of the study that there would be a marked (or certainly a statistically significant) improvement in profit performance for companies contributing Digital Deflation to the economy, the consistency of the superior stock price performance for the New Economy Companies was striking. This can best be seen in the "connect the dot" graph in Exhibit 12-2.

In Exhibit 12-2, each of the companies was plotted on the scatter diagram to show its average annual stock price appreciation versus its percentage increase in net profit margins over the decade. Looking at the two groups, it was evident that a few of the Old Economy Companies enjoyed significant increases in net profit margins during the 1990–2000 period. However, across the board, regardless of the percentage increase in net profit margins, the New Economy group consistently delivered dramatically better stock appreciation than the Old Economy Companies.

## DID THE INTERNET BOOM SPIKE THE PUNCH?

In an effort to figure out how stimulative monetary policy, the Y2K spending surge, and the dot-com boom–bust may have artificially spiked the stock prices of New Economy Companies at the end of the 1990s and into the year 2000, the Dow Jones Industrials were examined to see how much more the New Economy stocks declined versus the Old Economy stocks *after* the peak.

The results were rather surprising. Excluding the seven companies with mergers or spinoffs, in 2001 and 2002, the New Economy group actually declined by only 3% more than the Old Economy group. The 11 New Economy stocks declined by an average of 26.6% in the two years, while the 12 Old Economy stocks declined by 23.6%.

**EXHIBIT 12-2**

Stock Performance vs. Profit Margin Growth

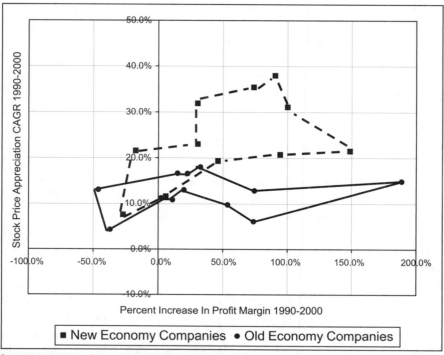

Sources: Value Line; Tanaka Capital Management, Inc.

To see if the exclusion of six Old Economy Companies and one New Economy Company had an effect in the two-year period, the analysis was adjusted to include the stock price performance of these excluded companies. (Only AT&T had a significant corporate event in 2001–2002, and the estimated value of the spinout of AT&T Broadband was included in the price change calculation.) The 12 New Economy stocks gave up an average of 29.7%, and the 18 Old Economy stocks dropped by an average of 24.9% during those 2 years, which is still only a 4.8% difference. Given the much greater advances by the New Economy stocks in the 1990–2000 decade—as well as the greater volatility in high-tech companies—one would have expected that the New Economy stocks would have significantly underperformed the Old Economy stocks on the downside in the following 2 years.

This was certainly quite heartening. High-quality New Economy Companies, delivered faster, better, cheaper products and services throughout the 1990s and during the 2000–2002 Nasdaq collapse—and their stocks performed reasonably well even during the downturn. In fact, three of the New Economy Companies with the highest digital content—Intel, IBM, and Microsoft—were *up* in price in 2001, and Microsoft was up for the 2-year period.

Yes, the headlines for the Dot-com Bubble were dominated by Internet stocks and Internet-related telecom stocks—on both the upside and the downside. However, many of these stocks represented Internet or telecom companies that had little or no sales and earnings and had no fundamental justification for being valued at such high levels.

It bears repeating that *the Internet is not the New Economy*. This book has suggested a different, considerably broader, definition of the New Economy—one that focuses on companies that use digital technologies to offer more value and quality to their customers on a recurring basis. With this broader definition of the New Economy, and considering the analysis in this chapter, it is apparent that the New Economy, and the New Economy Companies, did not die with the end of the 1990s. They took their lumps in the Post '90s era, just like the Old Economy and the Old Economy Companies did. Most importantly, these New Economy Companies are slimmed down and ready to participate in the next decade or two of value and wealth creation.

## INVESTING WISELY IN THE NEW ECONOMY

Perhaps the most important take-away for investors is that common stocks should continue to deliver the best returns over the next two decades. This may be difficult for investors to accept after suffering over 3 years of stock market declines in the Post '90s period. However, this lesson will become more obvious as yields on money market funds decline to paltry levels and bond interest rates move to record lows.

Yes, there is much that can go awry, particularly in the area of monetary or fiscal policy. But with a stable demographic foundation of modest growth in the labor force, with Baby Boomers becoming even greater savers and investors, and with an understanding of the growing Digital Deflation that will take inflation to new lows and productivity gains to new highs, the long-term outlook will be for *even lower interest rates and higher P/E ratios on stocks* than were seen in the 1990s. With better data and a Federal Reserve more aware of the increasing benefits of Digital Deflation, it is more and more probable that the current decade and the next will follow the 1980s and 1990s as the third and fourth consecutive decades of rising prosperity in the United States.

## POINTERS FOR INVESTING IN A RESURGING NEW ECONOMY

Clearly, not every New Economy Company that delivered for its shareholders in the 1990s will excel in the next decade, and not every Old Economy Company that performed poorly or well in the last decade will necessarily repeat its performance in the years ahead. Yet even in an increasingly dynamic world characterized by rapid technology change, shorter product life cycles, and increased competition, there will be certain enduring company characteristics that will determine which companies will be more likely to succeed, and which will be more likely to disappoint.

The following pointers are intended to serve as incremental advice for investors in a rapidly growing New Economy. Some of them are fairly obvious, but they are emphasized here because they will be even more important for investors to remember in the next few years or because, for a variety of reasons, investors seem to forget these ideals in practice as they experience the emotional highs and lows of investing.

- *Take a broad view of the New Economy.* Although many high-technology companies (creators of Digital Deflation) will grow very rapidly and deliver handsome returns for their investors during the next 10 years, the reality is that many more non-tech New Economy Companies will be major beneficiaries of the Digital Revolution, and investing in them will entail a lot less risk for the average investor. The entire healthcare area is one group that immediately comes to mind.
- *Apply the Digital Deflation test.* Are the companies in your portfolio creating or utilizing advancing technologies to deliver more value, quality, and performance to their customers at lower prices than their competition? One only has to look at the experience of Wal-Mart versus Kmart to understand how quickly the

consumer figures out which company is offering a better deal. Managements should know how much quality improvement (Quality Improvement Quotient) they are adding to their product and service offerings yearly.

- *Beware of digital replacing analog.* As digital technologies permeate the economy and find their way into more and more products and services, they often leverage overall product value as they displace old analog products, processes, or services. Producers of traditional silver halide film-based image capture devices and consumables (i.e., traditional 35 mm cameras and film) will find that digital cameras will become increasingly higher performing, feature-laden, cheaper, and easier to use with each technology design cycle.

- *Own technology companies but only if you understand what's driving them.* Over the next several years, a handful of high-tech companies will emerge to become the next Intel or Microsoft, and many more will deliver very high returns. However, for each success story there will be dozens of other promising high-tech corporate aspirants that will fall short and will cost their hopeful shareholders dearly. The reason is simply that high-technology investing is very hard to do right because the underlying technologies are getting more complex, and the product design cycles are getting shorter. This makes it harder for the average investor to keep up.

- *The Internet is a tool.* Try to find companies that are leveraging the Internet to gain an advantage versus their competition. While GE is probably best known for its Six Sigma programs for improving the quality of its products and services, it is light years ahead of much of its competition in terms of using the Internet to reduce costs and provide superior service to its customers.

- *Understand the cycles.* New Economy Companies can be just as cyclical as Old Economy Companies or even more cyclical. A successful new-product upgrade cycle can be even more beneficial to a company than an upturn in end-market demand. The opposite is equally true. This is particularly significant in the computer hardware and storage space, where design cycles are rapid, and performance and quality improvement can jump by 30% to 50% or more per year.

- *Consider the big picture/business plan.* Company managements should be able to articulate in one sentence what they have to do to create shareholder value, and they should have a viable business plan to take them there. Then you need to measure how each company is executing against that plan. Lou Gerstner was praised for his general leadership of IBM, but he especially got IBM to do one thing very well—convert a decades-old mentality and system from selling "big iron" mainframe computers to a total service and software solution for the customer.

- *Identify companies with a sustainable competitive advantage.* Companies are more likely to create superior returns if they have a proprietary technology or process or a highly differentiable product or service that allows them to deliver a better value proposition to their customers than the competition. Intel has been able to sustain its leading position as the PC microprocessor of choice ever since it beat out an equally strong Motorola design for that first IBM PC contract. Once designed in, Intel worked hard to adhere to Moore's Law and stay one step ahead of its competition, delivering greater and greater processor performance and functionality.
- *Find companies with the strongest new product pipeline.* An R&D pipeline full of potentially superior new products will often give an investor a much better indication of the future earnings prospects for a company than the company's current profitability or market share. For 8 straight years in the 1980s, Pfizer went into a slump and couldn't seem to produce a blockbuster drug to buttress its highly profitable but aging product line. So analysts ignored the company's pronouncements that it had the best R&D pipeline ever in the company's history. Two years later, Pfizer began to introduce a stream of new classes of drugs with vastly superior efficacy and safety profiles for several areas of "unmet medical need," pushing the stock to the top of the charts.
- *Stick with quality.* Companies that use the most conservative accounting policies will be dealing from strength. They will tend to be maximizing cash flow, and they will be least likely to hit investors with bad earnings surprises. Enron was not the first, nor will it be the last transgressor. In the high-tech arena, investors in some software companies in the 1990s were severely punished for corporate policies that pushed for aggressive revenue recognition. In contrast, smarter and more confident software company managements will take the more conservative route by opting to delay revenue recognition and to instead build de-

ferred revenues until there is no question that the revenues are completely earned. A perfect example is Business Objects, which operates in the business intelligence (database retrieval, analysis, and reporting) software space, and reports its financials very conservatively.

- *Consider cash on the balance sheet.* Quality also means a strong balance sheet. For New Economy Companies, this means lots of cash on the balance sheet. In a world of rapid technological change where the assets and much of the intellectual property walk in and out the door every day, there is often not much in the way of hard assets to qualify as collateral for bank loans. Bankers know this, and managements know this. Investors should too. In addition, many OEM (original equipment manufacturers) customers and retailers will not design in or commit to distributing or selling a company's products unless it has a rock-solid balance sheet, giving assurance that it will be there to deliver when called upon. For investors during the Nasdaq crash of 2000 to 2002, the amount of cash per share on the balance sheet often put a floor on the stock price that might otherwise have plunged even lower as panicking investors bailed out.

- *Look for increasing market share.* Although companies with the largest market shares tend to benefit from economies of scale, lower cost structures, and higher profit margins, often the better investment can be the strong number-two or number-three player that is gaining market share. Throughout much of the 1990s, ASM Lithography moved up steadily from a position as the number-three supplier of complex photolithography equipment for semiconductor manufacturing to surpass Nikon and Canon and become number one. During that run, ASM Lithography became the top-performing stock in the semiconductor equipment group.

- *Insist on real sales and earnings.* Investors who insisted on investing only in companies reporting real sales and earnings probably missed the dot-com boom—but they also missed the bust. The old adage, "don't buy stories, buy earnings" is even more relevant in the rapidly changing New Economy. It truly made no sense for the average investor to buy shares in companies that were not generating profits, and it made no sense for anybody to invest in companies that could not even present a business plan showing profitability any time soon. At an analyst meeting in

New York, the CFO of eToys could not and would not offer either a time frame or a revenue level at which breakeven profitability could be reached. Don't be fooled by tales of clicks, eyeballs, page views, or even revenue per share. At the end of the day, investors need to know how much profit and how much cash are being generated for shareholders.

- *Look for proven management.* This is a tricky one because it is often violated. The truth is that corporate executives who have proven themselves in the past can make mistakes or get surprised by a competitor with a faster, better, cheaper product in the future. However, there is one management characteristic to watch for that can help keep the average investor out of trouble, particularly in a fast-moving New Economy where so much of the stock's value hinges on future growth rather than last year's earnings. You're more likely to have a successful investment in a company where management underpromises and overdelivers on expectations rather than the other way around. Promotional managements never learned this and are setting up themselves and their investors for a fall. Smart managements learned this early in their corporate careers. In the 1990s, Microsoft was one of the few companies where management had the courage and the confidence in its long-term outlook to make a reference to its stock at one point being temporarily a bit high.
- *Kick the tires.* There is no better way to research a company and its competitive position than to shop the product or service as if you were a customer. If you can't quite understand the product or the underlying technology drivers that are purportedly delivering superior value and performance to the customer, then ask a friend who knows the industry—or seek help.
- *Adopt a valuation discipline.* There is a saying in football and forestry that, "the bigger they are, the harder they fall," and the same can be said for investing. The higher the P/E ratio, the harder it can fall. There are two steps that investors can take to avoid the big fall. One is to concentrate on companies where the P/E on the stock is not much higher than the future growth rate of the company's earnings. This is particularly critical for rapid-growth companies, because even the best New Economy Companies eventually become so large that growth rates much over 20–25% cannot be maintained for long. The second step is to focus on companies where earnings growth is accelerating rather

than slowing down. Admittedly, this is a lot harder for the investor to determine in practice.

- *Don't ignore the Old Economy.* The ongoing Digital Revolution and the growing economic benefits from Digital Deflation are not binary. As in the 1990s, there will be shades of gray, and many Old Economy Companies will benefit from digital technologies and will do quite well for their shareholders even though they will be technically in the Old Economy camp. Remember that the more quality improvement that the government counts from digitally deflating products and services in the New Economy, the more growth and inflation the Federal Reserve will be able to accommodate in the Old Economy. Recall also that through the consumer and corporate wealth effects, the creation of more real wealth for households and corporations will result in higher overall demand for *all* products and services—from both the New and Old Economies. In addition, lower inflation will mean generally lower interest rates, making many Old Economy products—such as housing, autos, and other consumer durables—more affordable. In effect, Digital Deflation will act as a "rising tide that will lift all boats."
- *Recognize that bonds should benefit from lower reported inflation.* As reported inflation numbers are corrected for uncounted quality improvement and increasing Digital Deflation, bond yields should trend downward over the long term. Recall, though, that it took years for the bond market in the 1980s to accept that inflation would not rebound to the levels of the 1970s and early 1980s.

## THE PRELUDE TO A NEW ERA OF PROSPERITY

Following the record 10-year economic expansion and stock market boom in the 1990s, the pre-Y2K spending surge, the Dot-com Bubble, the collapse of the Nasdaq and sharp cutbacks in IT spending, it is only natural that many investors for some time will harbor fears over whether they should own stocks having anything to do with technology—or whether they should even own stocks at all. This is only normal after participating in a fundamentally sound bull market that got carried away on the upside. By the end of the 1990s, virtually *every* investor felt that investing was easy, too easy.

With the full benefit of hindsight, it is now easy to identify when the excesses started—with the well-intentioned overprinting of money by the Federal Reserve in 1999 in advance of what might become a liquidity squeeze due to Y2K lockdown. The resulting overextension of the stock market really got into swing as more companies, individuals, and government entities purchased new computer equipment and software that would be able to recognize the year '00 as 2000 rather than as 1900. This Y2K capital-spending spike became further extended by the extraordinary ease with which new ideas relating to the Internet and the burgeoning technology and telecommunications infrastructure build-outs were attracting equity capital virtually for free from investors via initial public offerings and secondary offerings. Many of these companies were startups, or very young and unproven, and a shocking number were without viable business plans showing profitability or revenue for even 2 years out in the future.

In the end, of course, the Internet Bubble *did* burst, casting a pall on the entire high-technology sector. Since most investors owned at least some technology stocks, for many, the experience naturally raised serious questions about how much faith they should place in common stocks in general. During the next several years, perhaps the biggest mistake that investors can make will be to stay out of equities. They should not confuse the boom at the *end* of the 1990s and the bust that followed with the underlying, fundamentally sound New Economy offering products and services that continually improve in performance and real value. This more broadly defined New Economy powered the *entire* decade of the 1990s, and it will reemerge to fuel the next multiyear economic expansion. The Post '90s stock market downturn has created low investor expectations. But it has also laid the foundation for the next bull market.

The Digital Revolution is not dead. Millions of engineers, scientists, and product designers worldwide are in their labs right now, creating future generations of advanced digital technologies and new product applications. Many more are working diligently to utilize these new technologies to develop faster, better, cheaper wireless devices, consumer electronics, wonderful new drugs and surgical procedures, safer cars, more convenient shopping, and more effective security, networking, and defense solutions. There will be no shortage of ingenuity and no shortage of performance and quality improvement in products and services across the economy.

In sum, there is no question that advancing digital technologies will be converted into ongoing product quality improvement and growing amounts of Digital Deflation to help drive inflation and interest rates to record lows. Most assuredly, both New and Old Economy stocks will move higher. What remains to be seen is how much quality improvement the government will measure, and whether monetary and fiscal policies will respond accordingly to energize or inhibit value and wealth creation in the upcoming new era of prosperity.

# 13

# Digital Democracy: Globalization of the New Economy

*I hear and I forget. I see and I remember. I do and I understand.*
*Confucius (Chinese philosopher) 551–479 B.C.*

*As more major economies beyond the United States begin to properly count Digital Deflation, inflation will trend lower, and real economic growth and productivity will trend higher worldwide. Monetary policy can become more accommodative, elevating potential GDP growth rates and employment to higher levels. The countries that participate most fully will be those that dismantle the artificial support of Old Economy industries and improve productivity by encouraging entrepreneurship and the free flow of capital to New Economy enterprises. First they need to count quality improvement.*

## NEW ECONOMY ENTREPRENEURSHIP

The year was 1972. The scene was the dining room of the baronial Guilford, England, castle of billionaire oil company entrepreneur J. Paul Getty. Mr. Getty was seated at the head of an enormously long table, addressing a handful of American business students. "Come out from under your umbrella," he implored them, "and take a risk." He could have been addressing business students or entrepreneurs anywhere in the world.

315

Getty had already made his fortune exploring the oilfields of North America, and this businessman knew a little about risk-taking. But, he was sincerely anxious that the youth of America, swept up in their involvement in the anti-Vietnam War movement, had forgotten about the importance of entrepreneurship and of going out and taking some risks to be successful in business.

In the ensuing years, of course, the youth of America did fairly well for itself, as Bill Gates, Steve Jobs, Michael Dell, Jerry Yang, Meg Whitman, and legions of other engineers, tinkerers, and entrepreneurs with new ideas and new technologies attracted capital and other bright, motivated, and highly qualified people to deliver faster, better, cheaper new products to the world's consumers. These New Economy entrepreneurs have been delivering increasing real value to consumers at the same or lower prices, and in the process creating Digital Deflation for the U.S. economy and enormous wealth for themselves and their investors.

Of course, this technology-based wealth creation, and the New Economy itself, are not unique to the United States. For practical reasons, prior chapters focused on the expanding New Economy in the United States. But, in fact, *many* countries are demonstrating vigorous growth in the New Economy sectors of their economies—and most of these are reaping the rewards of creating greater value for their consumers.

## DIGITAL DEMOCRACY

Wealth creation from the Digital Revolution is not limited to the United States. Economies that are already benefiting from quantity-based productivity gains as well as from productivity gains from recurring quality improvement in products and services tend to be those countries that: (1) enjoy high or rising digital content in their economies; (2) pursue fiscal policies that encourage entrepreneurship, free market allocation of capital and labor, attractive returns on capital investment, and broad-based common stock ownership; (3) properly count the continuous improvement in the performance and quality of products and services; and (4) enforce laws that protect the value of proprietary technology, intellectual property, and creative digital content.

Depending upon how aggressively foreign policymakers act to remove barriers to the free flow of capital and labor and allow rewards for risk-taking, there is a worldwide potential for one of the greatest periods of wealth creation in the history of mankind. If policymakers in most of the larger economies play their cards right, there will be a true globalization of the New Economy, with lower inflation and more rapid real economic growth spreading to more economies. The result will be an increase in overall efficiency, productivity gains, business activity, and trade on a global scale. The reason is simple: If real and lasting value is created, then so is real and lasting wealth.

The Digital Revolution has already proven to be highly democratic, so in a sense, it knows no borders. Semiconductor plants are popping up in many countries, notably in Ireland and China. Software is being written in India, and a high proportion of printed circuit boards used worldwide are stuffed in Taiwan. Out of necessity and good business practice, most large New Economy Companies have become multinational and multicultural. ASM Lithography, the worldwide leader in photolithography equipment for semiconductor manufacturing, is a Dutch company with an important U.S. subsidiary, a Scottish CEO, lenses supplied from Germany, and customers in the United States, Asia, and Europe.

Yet, just as the level of democracy and free market capitalism varies from country to country, so too does the level of participation in the New Economy. Exhibit 13-1 presents business sector labor productivity data from the Bank for International Settlements (BIS)[1] plotted against data on information and communication technology expenditures as a percentage of GDP from the Organization for Economic Co-operation and Development (OECD).[2] The two sets of data were analyzed to verify whether there was a correlation between the proportion of information technology (IT) in an economy and measured productivity gains in that economy.

The results shown in the scatter diagram indicate quite clearly that those countries with a high proportion of digital content in their economies have tended to also enjoy higher productivity gains. The correlation is not extremely high at 0.57, but the coefficient of determination shows that the level of IT in these economies alone determines on average about one-third of each country's reported productivity growth. Since strong productivity gains tend to lead to lower inflation, higher corporate profit margins and higher real wage gains, countries with high information technology content and strong productivity growth should enjoy greater than average prosperity over the long term.

## EXHIBIT 13-1

Digital Content and Productivity by Country

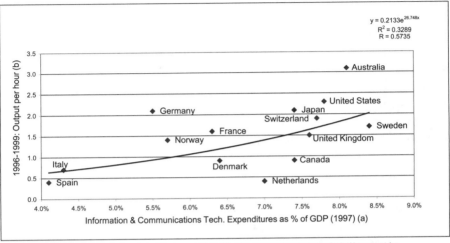

$$y = 0.2133e^{26.748x}$$
$$R^2 = 0.3289$$
$$R = 0.5735$$

Sources: (a) Organisation for Economic Co-Operation and Development; (b) Bank for International Settlements; Tanaka Capital Management, Inc.

As the scatter diagram clearly shows, the United States and Japan are benefiting from high IT content and above-average gains in labor productivity. What is noteworthy is that in the 1996–1999 period, the United States was experiencing strong economic growth while Japan was under depressed economic conditions—and yet both enjoyed high IT content and strong productivity gains. In other words, despite major banking and other structural differences and despite monetary and fiscal policies that were almost diametrically opposed, the two largest economies of the world both benefited directly from high IT content.

At the other end of the spectrum, Spain and Italy suffered in the late 1990s from fairly low IT content in their economies at about 4% of GDP—and fairly low growth in labor productivity, averaging less than 1% per year. Italy is particularly known for restrictive labor laws.

In the late 1990s, Germany, Australia, and the Netherlands were clearly outliers. On the downside, the Netherlands suffered from low productivity gains, which may have also been related to its very rigid labor laws. On the upside, Australia was the only country with productivity growth greater than the United States in the 1996–1999 period, with two-thirds of its 3.1% average productivity growth coming from multifactor productivity, meaning technology, Digital Deflation and other noncapital spending sources. Germany's fairly high 2.1% average productivity growth in the late 1990s was a surprise, considering the relatively low level of IT content in its economy.

Over time, as more countries start measuring quality improvement from advancing digital technologies, and as they all experience faster growth in the New Economy, all countries should see their dots on the productivity–IT content scatter diagram moving upward and to the right. By offering better value at lower prices to consumers and corporate buyers, the IT sector, and the New Economy in general, should grow faster than the Old Economy in each country. The result will be a surprising, almost orchestrated, rise in labor productivity growth worldwide.

## COUNTING DIGITAL DEFLATION AND PRODUCTIVITY PROPERLY

It should not be surprising that the countries with larger and growing IT sectors are generating higher reported productivity growth. In recent years, studies have been published in the United States and other countries showing a correlation between IT spending and traditional quantity-based productivity gains.

What is very interesting, though, is that in a more recent report, the OECD identified five countries that are counting quality improvement for digital products, and four of these five countries have been generating superior productivity growth relative to the amount of IT content in their economies. These countries—Australia, Japan, France, and the United States—all use hedonic deflators to adjust for quality improvement for computers, and they have enjoyed above-average reported gains in productivity.

In the scatter diagram in Exhibit 13-1, it can be seen that these four countries are above the line representing the relationship between productivity gains and IT content for the 14 countries covered in the OECD report. What is happening is that these countries are out ahead of the pack on (1) beginning to properly measure quality improvement and (2) converting rising quality into the equivalent of deflation. In essence, these four countries have been pioneers in beginning to measure some of the Digital Deflation being generated in their respective economies. For these countries this process translates into lower inflation, which opens the door to more rapid GDP growth and higher growth in overall productivity than in the countries that do not measure any of their recurring quality improvement.

Of the five countries reported to be using hedonic deflators for computers, Canada is the only country that has suffered from subpar productivity growth relative to the high amount of measured IT content in its economy. This may relate partly to Canada's counting of quality improvement only for PCs, laptops, and peripherals, but apparently not for mainframes and networked servers. On the other hand, it may point to other inefficiencies in the Canadian labor markets or fiscal and monetary policies, or to its large exposure to commodity-based Old Economy industries, or to some combination of these factors. Productivity gains below 1% have not been helpful to the Canadian dollar exchange rates.

Exhibit 13-2 presents a table from an October 2001 OECD report showing countries that use hedonic or other deflators to try to measure some part of the quality improvement in computers, software, and communications equipment. What is striking is that Germany, Italy, and the United Kingdom do not use hedonics to measure quality improvement in *any* of these three large categories of GDP, raising serious questions about the accuracy of their economic statistics.

## JAPAN AND CHINA CAN CREATE ENORMOUS WEALTH

Over the next two decades, two countries hold the potential to generate substantial wealth from the expanding Digital Revolution: Japan and China. Japan has great potential in part because it is the world's second largest economy, and it is starting from a decade-long, recession-depressed base. Japan has both corporate and household wealth, and a strong middle class. Its economy enjoys high digital content, and it benefits from strong technological innovation. Its labor force is highly educated and can be very productive. But so far Japan seems to have missed an opportunity to build a large class of Investor-Consumers. Most households in Japan did not generally benefit from the surge in stock prices in the prior decades. They instead had much of their vast savings frozen in low rate, interest-bearing postal savings accounts. In addition, the enormously high cost of consumer goods in Japan is legendary.

How could the Japanese economy get into its predicament? The answer is complex. But as many have reported, the Japanese government remains a huge drag on the nation's prosperity. It oversees a

## EXHIBIT 13-2

## Countries Using Hedonics to Measure Digital Deflation

| | Software | IT Equipment | Communication Equipment |
|---|---|---|---|
| Australia | No | Hedonic price index linked to US-BEA computer price index. exchange rate adjusted | No |
| Canada | Adjusted version of US-BEA price index for pre-packaged software (hedonic) and for customized software (partly hedonic) | Hedonic price index for PC's, portable computers and peripheral equipment | No |
| Finland | Weighted Average (50-50) of average earnings index in computer industry and US-BEA hedonic price index for pre-packagaed software | n.a. | n.a. |
| France | No | Hedonic price index for computers; combined measure of hedonic price index for France and the US-BEA computer price index, exchange rate-adjusted | No |
| Germany | No | No | No |
| Italy | No | No | No |
| Japan | No | Hedonic price index for computers | No |
| United Kingdom | No | No | No |
| United States | Hedonic deflator for pre-packaged software; for customized software average of deflators for own-account software (not based on hedonic method) and pre-packaged software | Hedonic deflators for computers and peripheral equipment | Hedonic deflators for telephone switching equipment |

Source: Organization for Economic Cooperation and Development

centrally planned economy, locked in an archaic system of cozy corporate and political "life support" relationships intended to keep the Old Economy barely alive at the expense of the New Economy. Recently, the Japanese government has been showing signs that it may become more responsive to the Politics of Need of its people. But it still has a long way to go in terms of opening up its consumer markets to efficient distribution and lower prices, unlocking its banking infrastructure to the free flow of capital, opening its stock markets to broader ownership by the public, and subjecting corporate management to true accountability for creating shareholder value. All of these conditions are needed for a truly efficient allocation of capital—and for Japan to transform itself from a nation of frustrated savers into a nation of Investor-Consumers.

China is a different story. Over the next few years, China will begin to show signs to the world which direction it will travel, and how it will juggle the interests of a centrally planned, largely agrarian society, juxtaposed with a rapidly advancing New Economy. Is China a crouching tiger preparing to open up its consumer and capital markets to its people and the world? Or is it only a hidden dragon that will remain dormant for another generation? We'll find out soon.

As is true with much of the Developing World, China has the advantage of not having to scrap a lot of old-generation technology infrastructure. For example, it doesn't have to replace old copper wire telecommunication networks. It can go immediately to third generation (3G) wireless technologies for many solutions. China is fast becoming the largest market in the world for cell phones and personal computers; its people are clamoring for consumer goods. With proper policies, China can make giant strides from a bicycle-driven society to a player in the Digital Revolution.

For the rest of the world, as well as for China itself, this rapidly advancing country will not be a zero-sum game if it chooses wisely how it will leverage technology and nurture its New Economy. Both China and the world can benefit immensely from China's low-cost labor and the growing demand from its consumer markets, as well as from what will emerge from its research labs.

This brings up one of the most commonly heard concerns about China. To acquire and develop technology know-how—and to go to the next level—China will have to begin to recognize intellectual property rights. For example, it is estimated that 80% to 90% of software in China is pirated. Indeed, it will have to work very hard to create respect for intellectual property if it wishes to accommodate and encourage free enterprise. And it certainly must move to establish respect and value for ideas well before its inventors develop their own new technologies. The alternative, of course, is that some of the most promising new Chinese-cultivated technologies will be secreted away to other countries that *will* protect the inventors—and their intellectual property—as if they were star tennis or basketball players. The brain drain out of the country could be enormous.

If it's smart, China will also foster the creation of liquid and efficient capital markets. Capital will be needed, along with skilled labor and technology, to accommodate growth in both its New and Old Economies. China will also benefit immensely over the long term if it could work to foster individual stock ownership to help create its own middle class and its own vibrant consumer markets. The potential is there for China to harness its resources, leverage the Digital Revolution, and create significant wealth. China's success would have enormously positive implications for stimulating growth worldwide.

## EUROPE MUST RECOGNIZE DIGITAL DEFLATION TO OPTIMIZE IT

Europe also holds great potential for wealth creation over the next two decades, and it can realize its own New Economy vision. In the 1990s, most of Europe fell behind the United States and Asia, due in part to the distractions of the formation of the European Union (EU). But there was also the decades-long tendency of most of the major European governments to exact a high price for companies moving labor and capital from the Old Economy to the New Economy. By protecting jobs in old and dying industries, and by making it prohibitively expensive for companies to close plants in Europe, protectionist laws have inadvertently acted as huge disincentives for multinational IT companies who have considered coming to its shores.

The exception in Europe has been Ireland, which has leveraged its well-educated workforce and progrowth tax policies to attract some of the largest technology players. Ireland can continue to excel.

Many European countries have great potential to benefit from redirecting fiscal and labor policies to encourage the free flow of capital and labor in the years ahead. To make the right decisions, however, all countries need to generate better economic data. And like the rest of the world, Europe needs to measure quality improvement and

Digital Deflation. Lower reported inflation would show European central bankers that they can grow their economies much faster than they have been—with all the benefits of rising employment and rising stock prices.

At a minimum, if the EU's inflation numbers were overstated, this would help explain the EU's sluggish economy and persistently high unemployment rate of the last several years. The problem is that European central bankers have guided monetary policy to target a specific inflation rate, and its inflation numbers *are* overstated. This combination can be disastrous. For several years now, European monetary policy has been inadvertently too tight. Europe's central bankers are looking at inflation data that simply do not reflect quality improvement.

In Europe, only France and Finland are using hedonic price indices to measure performance and quality improvement in IT spending. Most of the other larger countries are either in discovery or denial on the subject of measuring quality improvement and therefore have been making policy decisions that are counter to taking advantage of the Digital Revolution.

Some European countries have even criticized the United States, claiming that the United States has understated its true inflation and overstated its real output and productivity by adjusting inflation downward to reflect performance improvement in computers. Ironically, the U.S. statistical agencies have had to defend themselves publicly and privately for beginning to measure real quality gains. This international skirmish between the statistical economists even found its way into the January 2001 Economic Report of the President:

> Compared with the United States, a country using a traditional price deflator appears to produce less high-technology output for any given amount of inputs such as workers [productivity] and nontechnology capital. Applying the U.S. deflator [assumedly for computers] to German information technology investment, for example, results in a substantially larger measure of real investment—as much as 170 percent larger—than with the traditional deflator. Over the period since 1991, use of a hedonic price index would have implied that real investment in information technology equipment in Germany increased at a rate of 27.5 percent per year, versus 6 percent using the traditional approach. However, even after correcting for the different statistical methodologies, investment and GDP growth in the United States remain far stronger than in Europe.

Make no mistake. Internationally, the stakes are very high. It is no coincidence that the dollar was so strong in the 1990s against European and other currencies. It is not at all surprising that the U.S. economy had been reporting stronger real growth *and* lower inflation than the EU. Why? The U.S. economy generated—and measured—more productivity and more Digital Deflation than the EU. This allowed the Federal Reserve to grow the economy faster than Europe. If the EU continues to rely on incomplete economic data, it will continue to make suboptimal policy decisions that will lead to the digging of more moats around inflation-generating Old Economy castles—and it will continue to suffer from high levels of unemployment.

If most of the EU continues to deny the existence of quality improvement in its products and services, it will not appreciate the naturally deflating benefits of New Economy industries. The EU will fall further and further behind those countries that optimize and allocate resources to the New Economy. It will have to resort to policies that block greater efficiencies. Some have suggested that the EU decision to block the GE–Honeywell merger ultimately reflected a desire to protect weak industries within the EU. Even worse, if the European public continues to be served bad economic data, it will not be in a position to put pressure on the politicians to make more appropriate policy decisions.

At the margin, the EU consumer will be stuck with higher-priced, lower-quality products, as local manufacturers will feel less pressure to compete with the best that the world has to offer. If EU corporate managements continue to be given bad economic data, they will not make the best business decisions, perpetuating the vicious cycle of protecting dying product lines and outmoded industries.

Perhaps one can only appreciate good economic data when one doesn't have any. The monetary policy of the European Monetary Union is a case in point. Early in 2001, the Federal Reserve in the United States moved rapidly to reduce interest rates when it realized that monetary policy had been too tight. However, its counterpart in Europe didn't move a monetary muscle. The central banks in Europe remained frozen in the headlights of high *reported* inflation and refused to reduce interest rates, fearing a return to the inflation of the 1970s and 1980s. Yes, energy prices had gone up, but high interest rates in Europe alone never did much to force OPEC's hand.

Armed with incomplete economic data, the monetary authorities of the EU succeeded in holding down inflation that was already a lot lower than what was being reported had it been properly adjusted for quality improvement. Unknowingly tight monetary policy unnecessarily costs member states jobs, GDP growth, and the creation of household wealth. In the highly competitive global marketplace, the United States gained market share. American companies were greatly assisted by more accurate economic data from U.S. statistical agencies, generally favorable fiscal policies, and a central bank that has worked hard to understand the new forces stimulating productivity gains and the New Economy.

## COWBOY CAPITALISM AND WEALTH CREATION

When it comes to risk-taking and making the capital investments needed to employ and deploy the newest digital technologies, the United States probably comes closest to an ideal economic model. This probably goes back to its frontier roots.

For the most part, the United States is a society that encourages and rewards entrepreneurship and risk-taking, with all the rewards of building something of value and the promise of creating wealth for themselves and their families. It's woven into the fabric of a nation of immigrants that risked everything to come to the United States to build a better life. The kids in the software labs pulling all-nighters and living on pizza are in many ways analogous to the pioneers and cowboys of the American West in the 1800s. Donna Smith, manager of investor relations of security software developer Rainbow Technologies, describes it this way, "These kids are fearless. They make a mistake. They pick themselves up, learn from their mistakes, and then do it right. These kids are the future of this country."

But a vibrant New Economy takes more than attracting bright and ambitious people. It also requires capital and technology. It places a premium on the attraction of capital as well as labor to the ideas and technologies that offer the greatest risk-adjusted promise for product development and commercial success. By placing a premium on attracting talent that is likely already well compensated—as well as attracting capital from investors who always have other alternatives—the New Economy thrives on free and open labor and capital markets.

While the United States economy has benefited from the relatively frictionless movement of labor as well as capital from the Old Economy to the New Economy, some of this greater efficiency has appeared more recently. In the 1980s, during the rationalization of American industry to become more efficient and more competitive in the global marketplace, the nation endured much pain and suffering.

But it prepared the U.S. economy to be most ready for the ultimate New Economy challenge. The result was a lean and highly efficient economy, able to move quickly to optimize on its scarce labor resource, attract capital to its best use, and utilize rapidly improving technologies, whether in the New or Old economies.

For decades, one of the greatest strengths of the U.S. economy has been its middle class with its great work ethic, its sense of entrepreneurship, its commitment to home ownership, and in recent years, wider ownership of common stock. There are not many countries in the world where it is as easy for the average person to invest in common stocks, to have a piece of the action, and grow his or her net worth by investing some small part of it in search of a return on investment. This "anyone can be an investor" phenomenon makes the wave of wealth creation in the United States as broad as it is deep. It gives the U.S. economy great strength and a more stable capital foundation than can be found in many other economies of the world where wealth and corporate equity ownership are concentrated in the hands of a small upper class.

The vastly broader distribution of common stock ownership in the United States magnifies the wealth effect, as the benefits of the New Economy extend to more households and create more Investor-Consumers. No doubt, some countries, both developed and developing, will move faster than others toward broader participation in the wealth-building processes in their respective New Economies. Wider stock ownership and an environment of entrepreneurship are not exclusively American. Of course, the word "entrepreneur" is French. One would be hard pressed to find a more entrepreneurial city in the world than Hong Kong, and the former Soviet Bloc countries in Eastern Europe, such as Hungary and Poland, have become increasingly entrepreneurial in their brief lives as free and democratic societies. Opportunities abound for those emerging economies seeking to build a strong foundation for participating in the wealth-building process of the next 20 years.

## THE SOVIET EXPERIMENT

In a global context, the U.S. economic model has already won the ultimate real world "bake-off." During the 1970s and 1980s, the American free-market capital allocation model proved to be superior to the old Soviet-style economy. Although many political analysts point to the

Reagan Star Wars initiative as the crowning blow in the multidecade Cold War between the United States and the Soviet Union, the confrontation was decided fundamentally as a struggle between two economic dogmas. In the end, millions of American consumers who voted daily with both their consumer dollars and their investing dollars were destined to win over a centrally planned Soviet economy, where product development and capital allocation decisions were made by a small cadre of planners moving and rationing rubles in offices that were far removed from the marketplace.

In a very real sense, the Soviet Union was drained by the Cold War military buildup, but its inability to fully participate in the growing Digital Revolution didn't help the Soviet military or its economy. While on the surface the Soviet Union couldn't develop the digital technologies to compete in an increasingly Star Wars-like arms race, it was the lack of a free market-based capital allocation that prevented its best and brightest minds from having the tools and the capital to develop the necessary new technologies to drive productivity growth and wealth creation.

It bears repeating that given the high risks inherent in the development of new technologies and new digitally driven products, the U.S. capital structure and culture of entrepreneurship make the United States ideally tuned for the New Economy. Any economy more centrally planned is likely to be less nimble, less timely, and less efficient in the capital-allocation process. And any economy that does not understand the importance of risk capital and return on investment is likely to be left behind in the generation of both quantity- and quality-based productivity gains.

It is no coincidence that the U.S. economy generated and retained more wealth from the expanding Digital Revolution and its creation of Digital Deflation. It is interesting to note that more recently, Russia has been moving toward a more efficient economy where *capital is not allocated but is instead attracted* to the best opportunities.

## DIGITAL DEFLATION AND THE DOLLAR

Looking forward, the U.S. economy will continue to represent the "model economy" for IT-based wealth creation in the industrialized world. The United States will continue to benefit from benign labor force growth, free flowing and open capital markets, high and rising digital (IT) content, growing Digital Deflation, and surprisingly low inflation. Other countries, no doubt, will release their entrepreneurial potential. But starting from its already high base of existing capital, the U.S. economy is likely to continue to create more wealth than any other single industrialized country. U.S. consumers and investors should also benefit from a strengthening dollar, meaning that they will be able to buy more foreign goods at lower prices.

A strong currency is another wealth-generating benefit of rising Digital Deflation. As improving product quality gets counted and converted into lower inflation—allowing faster economic growth—the dollar should strengthen against the currencies of countries with relatively lower IT content and less Digital Deflation. Currency specialists, take note. The U.S. Government is already beginning to count quality improvement in computers by converting it into the equivalent of about 30 basis points (0.30%) per year of Digital Deflation. This number will only get larger as more products are counted for quality improvement.

Every year that the U.S. economy generates and counts more Digital Deflation than other economies, the United States will likely create a permanent dollar valuation advantage versus other currencies whose underlying economies are creating and counting relatively little Digital Deflation to offset Old Economy inflation. The valuation advantage will be permanent to the extent that foreign currency specialists look forward and will not give another country, which starts to count quality improvement, the chance to reestablish foreign exchange values just because it restates its economic accounting downward for inflation in the past.

For example, when Germany begins to estimate quality improvement for computers, it will likely restate prior years' inflation downward as the United States did in the 1980s. However, currency specialists are likely to regard, say a 0.3% per year downward restatement of inflation as ancient history. Germany's best bet is to try to properly measure quality improvement and Digital Deflation prospectively, which will result in a relatively stronger euro in the future.

More importantly, the proper counting of Digital Deflation by Germany and the other member states of the European Union will enable Europe to conduct a more accommodative monetary policy. This will lift "the Continent" out of its track of unfulfilled economic growth, high unemployment, moderate productivity gains, low growth in real wages, and little generation of real wealth—and better position it to participate in the New Economy. The alternative is for

Germany and other EU members to continue to wage a fierce but fool-ish battle against a nonexistent inflation due to incomplete data. By not counting the steady gains in real value from its own technology-driven industries as good deflation, Europe may continue to overstate inflation and under-nurture its economies. The ironic result might be outright deflation, but of the deleterious cyclical kind caused by overly tight monetary policy.

## GLOBAL PROSPERITY WILL LIFT ALL BOATS

Although there have been many contributors to the successful launch of the Digital Revolution, to date the U.S. economy has had to carry on its back a disproportionately large share of the invention, develop-ment, financing, production, marketing, and sales efforts. This will change for the better. As more countries join the United States, Japan, France, Canada, and Australia in beginning to properly count their annual improvement in the performance and quality of their products and services, it is more likely that they will perceive and appreciate the true value of an expanding, digitally deflating New Economy. With better economic data, monetary and fiscal policy decisions are more likely to be optimized. With more consumers in more countries appreciating continuously improving, faster, better, cheaper new products and services, more countries will participate more fully in the New Economy.

A strong and expanding New Economy worldwide will also stimulate trade and growth in the Old Economy on a global basis. These trends would be particularly beneficial for the Emerging Coun-tries with little capital and a minimal technology base. The opportu-nity is there for *all* countries to participate in the globalization of the New Economy, but much needs to be done. Understandably, not all countries begin with the same foundation, and most countries still need to take the first step.

## NOTES

1. "71st Annual Report," Bank for International Settlements, Basel, June 11, 2001.
2. "The Knowledge-Based Economy: A Set of Facts and Figures," Meeting of the Committee for Scientific and Technological Policy at Ministerial Level, Organisation for Economic Co-operation and Development, June 22–23, 1999.

# 14

## CHAPTER

# Threats and Opportunities: Making the World a Better Place

When one door closes, another opens; but we often look so long and so regretfully upon the closed door that we do not see the one which has opened for us.

*Alexander Graham Bell (1847–1922)*

*Over the next two decades, the Digital Revolution holds the promise of besting the Industrial Revolution. More accurate inflation data will lead to more vigorous economic growth and help reduce budget deficits worldwide. Better data might even lead to a viable solution for the Social Security problem looming in the United States. Monetary policymakers will play a key role in determining whether we slip into years of sluggish growth and possible monetary deflation—or restart the New Economy, with innovation, entrepreneurship, job creation and the rebuilding of wealth lost in the first few years of the new millennium.*

### MAKING THE DIGITAL REVOLUTION BETTER THAN THE INDUSTRIAL REVOLUTION

When I first began putting together the ideas that comprise the Theory of Digital Deflation, I felt that the Digital Revolution of today would prove to be fundamentally different from, and innately superior to, the Industrial Revolution of a century ago. This was because I was focusing on the unusual and powerfully recurring nature of its rapidly improving, digitally driven products. The power of compounding over several decades would be enormous.

In time, however, I began to revise that hypothesis. First, I came to see that the two revolutions actually had a lot in common. Both benefited from major innovation and the resulting extensive periods of rising stock markets and wealth creation. Neither properly accounted for the dramatic increases in the real value of goods and services offered to the American consumer. Both have suffered from policy errors resulting from outmoded and inaccurate economic data, particularly for inflation and productivity.

As for the uniqueness of the products, I realized that digital technologies are no more powerful and no more important today than the inventions of the Industrial Age in their day. Yes, in today's revolution, faster, better, cheaper computers; instantaneous worldwide communication; wonderful new entertainment media; and astounding medical technologies are contributing to a better way of life. But are they really very different from how electricity and the combustion engine improved the quality of life during the Industrial Revolution? Imagine the thrill of getting an Iron Horse for the first time and going 30 miles an hour! Imagine turning on an electric light after a life of illumination by gas or candlelight. These, too, were probably unimaginably dazzling experiences, suggesting a future full of hope and great potential.

In one major respect, however, the Digital Revolution clearly *can* be better than the Industrial Revolution: *It can run longer if the right policies are pursued.* The Digital Age may even last until the next revolution of creativity, innovation, and economic activity, whatever that might be. The promise of the Industrial Revolution was never fully realized, at least not in the 1930s and 1940s. Today, with new and better economic data on the horizon and with fiscal and monetary policymakers becoming more aware of what is driving the New Economy, the Digital Revolution holds the promise of reaching closer to its true potential.

In Chapter 10, I described how the Depression brought the Industrial Revolution to an early and inglorious demise. In hindsight, woefully inadequate economic data, major mistakes in fiscal policy (Smoot-Hawley Tariff), and misguided monetary policy (a 25% reduction in the money supply in an already deflationary economy) slammed the door on that earlier era of entrepreneurship, innovation, and capital investment.

It's tempting to speculate about how different the world would be today if the Depression hadn't happened. One can only wonder how much more value and wealth could have been created, how many wars may not have been fought, and what pain and suffering could have been avoided in the United States and worldwide if the Industrial Revolution had been allowed to play out with a more accommodative monetary policy from the mid-1920s onward. With more vibrant economies worldwide, trade wars might have been averted. With better data and better policies, it is even conceivable that the Industrial Revolution could have extended well into the 1940s and 1950s and maybe overlapped seamlessly with the early years of the Digital Revolution.

As it turned out, we missed a huge opportunity. Instead, it took two decades and a world war for the U.S. economy to shake itself out of a deflationary slump and recover from the policy miscues of the late 1920s and early 1930s.

Today, the U.S. economy is at another crossroad. We are already in a modestly deflationary mode. This would be apparent to all if the economic data properly reflected the 1% to 2% lower inflation from the real annual improvement in digitally driven products and services in both IT and non-IT industries. But this, again, is good news, since Digital Deflation allows monetary policy to accommodate faster GDP growth and the attainment of super full employment.

We must not lose sight of the lessons of Japan's economic predicament. If the U.S. economy is allowed to slip into a full-fledged monetary-based deflationary slump, it may take years for policymakers to extricate the economy and return to a path of innovation and prosperity. Japan's deflationary slump experience has shown us the difficulty of pulling out of a deflationary trap once you have fallen in.

## THE POLITICS OF BETTER DATA

Anyone with a stake in the economy—that is, most of us—knows that in recent years, we've made some mistakes and missed some opportunities. Investors, whose portfolios suffered mightily in the early 2000s, understand by now that monetary policy could have been better, if the data had been better in those years. But equally frustrated are workers concerned about losing their jobs, the millions of unemployed who can't find work, those managers who have had to make job cutback after cutback, an American public perplexed and anxious over the direction of the economy, and policymakers struggling with the return of budget deficits and the looming Social Security and Medicare crises.

What's the solution? First, we simply need better data. The Fed can't do its job right if it's looking at an incomplete picture. The most immediate fiscal policy opportunity is for Congress to vote to allocate more resources to count more accurately the real value being added each year to the economy via faster, better, cheaper digitally driven products and services. This needs to be done as quickly as possible. We have already lost ground that we didn't need to lose.

Although the Consumer Price Index (CPI) is more visible, we should start with fixing the GDP Deflator for a number of reasons. First, errors from undercounting quality improvement are greater in the GDP Deflator than in the CPI, simply because of the higher IT content. Recall that due to the undercounting of a larger amount of quality improvement, the GDP Deflator is estimated in the Digital Deflation models to be overstating inflation by 2% per year, versus a 1% overstatement by the CPI. Also, the GDP Deflator is intended to reflect inflation in the total U.S. economy, so it should be more meaningful to the capital markets than the CPI, which only applies to the two-thirds of the economy that is consumer based. It is also likely, at least initially, that fixing the GDP Deflator should require less political consternation and debate than fixing the CPI.

At a minimum, Congress should commission the equivalent of the Boskin Commission to focus on the GDP Deflator. Ideally, Congress should form a joint task force to work with the White House to develop policies and procedures for a more accurate counting of the improvement in the quality of products and services across the entire economy, not just the consumer sector.

At the same time, more resources should be committed immediately to the already ongoing quest for better data. Conversations with economists at the Bureau of Labor Statistics (BLS) and the Bureau of Economic Analysis (BEA) at the Department of Commerce (DOC) would suggest that a great deal can be done fairly quickly with the addition of a few dozen more economists and analysts and a budget of several million dollars. Eventually, it might take multiples of those totals to properly estimate the quality improvement in many IT and non-IT industries across the entire economy. But we must take further steps soon, particularly in healthcare and communications.

Unfortunately, in recent years, BLS and DOC budgets have gone the other way. Statistical agency budgets have been *cut* by a Congress that has been understandably quite concerned about budget deficits. But if Congress allocates the money needed to obtain more accurate data on quality improvement and inflation, that investment will provide an astronomical return for American society as a whole—and incidentally, make Congress's job far easier over the next several years. With better data, for example, there is even a fair chance that the U.S. government could come closer to funding its entitlement obligations—most notably Social Security and Medicare—as the Baby Boomers retire in the coming decades.

The effort to more accurately count quality improvement in IT and non-IT industries should be a reasonably apolitical and bipartisan activity. Why? Because almost everyone would benefit. What's at stake is a return to conditions much like the 1990s. It is important to realize that better data to reflect quality improvement and Digital Deflation more accurately will result in lower reported rates of inflation, allowing the Federal Reserve to print more money to accommodate stronger economic growth. This will create more jobs, higher incomes, and budget surpluses. Larger surpluses would then provide fiscal policymakers with the financial means to make adjustments to the few groups, such as senior citizens, that may be less advantaged by a burgeoning New Economy.

## FIXING THE THIRD RAIL

Many policymakers in Washington are reluctant to touch the CPI, as it is often viewed as a proverbial "third rail" of politics. Many retirement programs and government wage scales are tied to the CPI through cost of living adjustments, or COLAs. The reality, however, is that the vast majority of Americans would benefit from more accurate inflation indices showing 1% lower reported inflation on the CPI and 2% lower inflation on the GDP Deflator. With faster, more sustained, and more stable economic growth and with declining interest rates, those on wage-scale COLAs would benefit from greater job security in a "super full employment" economy. The unemployment rate could be managed back down to 3% to 4%, and there should be a return to rising real wages, two very visible benefits of the Old and New Economies of the 1990s.

There is one group that will not benefit as much as others when inflation is measured more accurately at lower levels. Senior citizens could be hurt in two ways. First, they are typically consumers of basic Old Economy goods and services that tend to inflate in price as opposed to technology-based New Economy goods and services that tend to deflate in price. However, although the elderly might not be big consumers of flat panel displays or DVD burners, they are likely to more than make up for it by benefiting from accelerating improvements in the quality of medical care.

There is a second way that seniors can be hurt. Retirees who depend heavily upon interest income from Treasury Bills, certificates of deposit, and money market funds will become disadvantaged by a further decline in interest rates. If they did not allocate assets to bonds and even some common stocks in the 1990s, they saw a marked decline in interest income in the decade. It is important to consider that the plunge in interest rate yields on CDs and money market funds may be a relatively long-term phenomenon in an environment of low labor force growth, rising productivity gains, and increasing Digital Deflation.

Some have pointed out that current senior citizens receiving CPI-indexed Social Security benefits have enjoyed disproportionately large upward adjustments to payouts due to the overstatement of the CPI. If Social Security benefits are adjusted up too fast due to an overstated CPI, in effect, wage growth will not be able to make up ground lost each year in funding future benefits for new senior citizens. Essentially, the CPI overstatement adds to the funding gap already being created each year by what one Washington economist attributes to as "the demographic reality that the beneficiary population is growing faster than the working population." He also points out that "the real benefits of new retirees in any given year are always greater than those of the decedents in that same year." In other words, each year, the people retiring had earned more real income than the people passing away, so they are owed more benefits. Also, each year there are more new retirees relative to workers, so the Social Security deficit will grow.

This "time bomb" looming on the horizon was alluded to in a study by Leonard Nakamura, economic adviser at the Philadelphia Fed: "If the Consumer Price Index is overstated, as the Boskin Commission has argued, retirees are enjoying rising real incomes. Indeed, average Social Security benefits have been rising faster than wages—virtually guaranteeing long-run instability."[1]

Unfortunately, it doesn't stop there. The Digital Deflation models suggest that the CPI's overstatement of inflation is even greater than what the Boskin Commission estimated. This would mean that the Social Security Trust Fund's "long-run instability" will be even worse than what economists have suggested. More specifically, the Digital Deflation models estimate that the CPI is overstated by about 1% just for uncounted quality improvement. (The Boskin Report estimated in 1998 that the CPI was overstated by 0.7% to 0.9% for a handful of reasons, including uncounted quality improvement.) This means that Social Security beneficiaries are getting 1% more real value per year than the government has calculated—and therefore more than the Trust Fund can afford.

This is where it gets a little tricky. Many retirees are saying that their market basket of goods is inflating, not deflating. But it is likely that they have not factored in the tremendous gains in healthcare performance and their Digital Deflation, particularly in drugs and in hospital services. What is beginning to become clear is that senior citizens may, in fact, have a very different market basket of goods and services than the average American in the CPI calculation. Perhaps Social Security beneficiaries should have a different inflation index that is more representative of their unique consumption patterns. This would be a logical response for an economy that is steadily bifurcating into an inflating Old Economy and a deflating New Economy.

Following a correction in the CPI for quality improvement as well as for other measurement errors identified in the Boskin Reports, no doubt, some adjustments will have to be made in terms of Social Security (and Medicare) benefits. The good news, of course, is that a stronger economy generating more tax revenues would allow the federal government to target policies to protect seniors—starting by more completely funding the burgeoning retirement and medical needs of an aging, longer-living population. In reality, stronger overall economic growth and growing Digital Deflation may be the only politically attractive path for the U.S. economy to generate enough real wage growth for Social Security taxes to fund long-term Social Security benefits. The *alternatives are to raise taxes or cut benefits.*

How much will taxes have to go up? The Social Security Administration has estimated that the 75-year actuarial shortfall in the Social Security Trust Fund is equal to 1.87% of taxable payroll, and that the annual cost of Social Security will rise from 4.5% of GDP in 2001 to 7.0% in 2076 if there are no new solutions.[2] The greater burden is on workers who already must pay a "Social Security tax (that) began at 2 percent and has been raised more than 20 times, reaching the present 12.4% (of wages and salaries)."[3] Solving the long-term problem by counting inflation more accurately at lower rates today means that Congress may not need to rely completely on further Social Security tax increases or worse—reductions in benefits—to close the funding gap in the future.

At a minimum, we need to count inflation properly, which will allow the Fed to accommodate more rapid economic growth and generate higher Social Security tax revenues. Arguably, in hindsight, we should have been operating at faster growth rates following the 1990s, which would have gotten us started earlier on a path to funding our future retirement obligations. But it's not too late.

Legislation in Washington, D.C., sometimes works in mysterious ways, as reflected in this not very well-known story: Apparently, as Congress contemplated various alternatives to balance the 1997 budget, it actually considered making changes which would have resulted in a *more accurate—and lower—CPI*. While these adjustments would have brought the CPI down closer to the true rate of inflation, ironically, they were being valued by Congress more for their ability to help balance the budget, as they would have reduced cost of living adjustments on government spending programs. In an interesting turn of events, at the last minute, Congressional negotiators asked for an updated assessment of the budget, and found that the stronger-than-expected economy necessitated upward revisions to tax revenues—and the CPI was left intact and overstated. The irony, of course, was that the stronger economy was a result of the New Economy that the CPI was having difficulty measuring.

Our Congress should not let the old politics of an antiquated CPI get in the way of a full-employment New Economy and higher-quality healthcare. It is far better to count the data right and then let the political discussions begin on making necessary adjustments using accurate information. Invariably, better data will lead to better decisions, a stronger economy, and a happier and healthier society. Democracy is a great allocator if it has the right information.

## BETTER HEALTHCARE FROM BETTER DATA

There is another important political consideration, one relating to the quality of life for senior citizens. For an aging population worldwide, it will become increasingly important for technological innovation to continue at the same pace if not accelerate, particularly in the area of healthcare.

The purest form of the Digital Deflation Theory would ascribe higher and rising importance to the improvement in the quality of medical care for senior citizens for whom the benefits are becoming increasingly valuable in terms of improving life expectancy and the quality of life. In fact, in terms of value to the consumer, it is likely that faster and more accurate disease diagnosis, prevention, and therapies will become exponentially more valuable with each passing year for seniors, as well as for Baby Boomers who are rapidly reaching the age of becoming greater consumers of healthcare services. Utilizing advancing digital and other technologies, medical research will get closer to truly "breaking the code" on various cancers, viral infections, and central nervous system disorders such as Alzheimer's and Parkinson's.

Enormous amounts of capital and larger research budgets will be required to follow up on deciphering the human genome and converting that knowledge into bona fide medical products and services, such as "designer drugs" tailored to the specific genetic makeup and side-effect profiles of individual patients. A more prosperous economy and stock market will provide more R&D dollars to speed up medical advances. This may be an important consideration for a demographic segment that may feel, as did one retired 85-year-old CEO, when he said, "I don't have time to buy green bananas!"

What happens to medical advances if inflation continues to be overstated? Inadvertently tight monetary policy will lead to sluggish economic growth, scarce availability of capital and research dollars, fewer pharmaceutical and biologic discoveries, and fewer advances in medical care. Quite clearly, the pace of *advances in medical care in the future* will depend upon the proper measurement of quality improvement and stronger economies *today*.

## MOVING FASTER WITH THE FED

With all the various interests calling on Congress, new legislation can move "glacially slow." The good news, however, is that there is a powerful body that can move very quickly. The Federal Reserve doesn't have to wait the years that it might take for the BLS and the BEA to receive the funding and conduct the studies to count more quality improvement in the economy. The Fed can do its own analysis, make its own quality adjustments to the reported inflation numbers, and translate them relatively quickly into monetary policy decisions.

This is an important point. It is critical that monetary as well as fiscal policymakers not only seek better data, but that they also open their minds to consider new theories and models to better understand the new data and better manage the New Economy. The longer they wait, the more we may fall behind. Time is of the essence.

The real question is to what degree will the Federal Reserve accept the Theory of Digital Deflation—or any part of it? The Fed is appropriately a conservative institution, and for decades, it has been vigilant on the ramparts in the fight against inflation. So, steeped in the tradition of fighting inflation, there may be a fair amount of institutional rigidity and resistance to change. On the positive side, one of the hallmarks of the Greenspan Fed has been its open mind to new ideas as reflected in its multidimensional approach to monetary policy and its willingness to experiment with new economic speed limits in the 1990s.

Again, the great advantage that the Fed has is that it doesn't have to wait for the data to be fixed, which could take several years. If convinced of the logic of the Theory of Digital Deflation, the inaccuracies being built into our inflation numbers, and the changing nature of productivity gains in a deflationary economy, the Fed can move with breathtaking speed.

## HOW MUCH DOES THE FED KNOW?

From the beginning, it was assumed that the Federal Reserve must understand at least some of the beneficial aspects of the Digital Deflation phenomenon. Chairman Greenspan's repeated references to the benefits of structural productivity gains relating to IT implied as much. Yet, policy moves and speeches by Fed governors and regional bank presidents, particularly in the 2002 time period, seemed to suggest otherwise.

Most disconcerting is the fact that the Federal Open Market Committee (FOMC) appeared to believe that the surge in productivity in the early 2000s meant that it didn't have to lower interest rates any further in order to assure a strong enough recovery and to increase employment. This view was reflected in the August 2002 FOMC minutes: "the current accommodative stance of monetary policy, coupled with still-robust underlying growth in productivity, should be sufficient to foster an improving business climate over time."[4]

True, traditional thinking and Old Economy speed limits would suggest that strong productivity gains are associated with periods of strong economic growth. Traditional theories might also conclude that higher interest rates are acceptable or even desirable if productivity growth is accelerating.

With surprisingly strong productivity gains in the early 2000s, why then did the Fed seem to consistently fall short of supplying enough liquidity to the economy? We have already discussed how the undercounting of quality improvement contributed to an overstatement of reported inflation, obscuring deflation in the real economy. This led the Fed to be concerned over inflation that was nonexistent, and to believe that it was therefore sufficiently stimulative when it really wasn't.

In Chapter 10, we also examined how end-product price deflation throughout much of the real economy may have contributed in recent years to a temporary surge in productivity gains that was more a function of headcount reductions that were taken by companies to match falling prices and revenues. These kinds of productivity gains were not nearly as favorable as the healthy kinds of productivity gains found historically in an *inflating*, positive sales growth economy. Productivity gains in an inflationary economy, of course, are what are embedded in the Fed's traditional economic models. So when productivity growth showed unusual strength during the Post '90s economic slowdown, the Fed actually felt compelled to become *less stimulative* than their other indicators, such as employment, might have prescribed.

In addition, strong quality-based productivity gains from the expanding New Economy are fundamentally very different in origin and in their effect on inflation than the quantity-based productivity gains from the Old Economy. Recurring and rapid improvement in the quality and performance of digitally driven products and services create both higher productivity and lower inflation. Recall that the U.S. government is already counting quality-based productivity gains of about 0.3% per year from performance improvements in computers made for final sale, and that this represents much of the heralded surge in productivity in the late 1990s. Recall also that counting this quality improvement equates to Digital Deflation that is reducing overall inflation by 0.3% per year.

The monetary policy response to these New Economy contributions to higher productivity growth and lower inflation should be *greater* stimulus and *lower* interest rates at the margin, not tighter policy and higher interest rates as the Fed appeared to pursue in 1999–2001.

Coming out of the 2001 recession, there was also a fundamental problem with the math. In 2002, productivity growth of about 4% and real GDP growth of about 3% meant that jobs were not being created. They were being lost. Assuming labor hours to be constant, by definition, real GDP growth had to *exceed* productivity growth (real output per person-hour) for the economy to create jobs.

In addition, an economic recovery would be difficult to sustain with 5% to 6% of the labor force remaining unemployed, providing little relief to those still jobless from the recession of 2001. The Fed of the 1990s was willing to let the economy expand despite hurtling through the old traditional speed limits for economic growth and unemployment in particular. Hopefully, it will see that it should make further adjustments to its speed limits in the new decade. The arrival of higher baseline productivity growth presents an opportunity—really a necessity—to *raise* speed limits on economic growth. This is particularly true if it is accompanied by faster, better, cheaper products and increasing Digital Deflation. Certainly, 3% real GDP growth is not fast enough if productivity gains of all kinds are adding up to 3% to 4% per year.

It's easy to fault the Fed for protecting us from a nonexistent enemy—inflation—and for failing to make adjustments for quality improvement in its economic data. But the Fed is not alone in these shortcomings. The vast majority of economists have similarly failed to appreciate the growing importance of the overstatement of inflation due to the undercounting of real quality improvement.

Even those people who are out there creating and generating these quality improvements—the inventors, entrepreneurs and business managers—seem more or less unaware of the collective economic impact of their faster, better, cheaper products on the New Economy. The exception is Intel's Gordon Moore, who seems acutely aware of how the government's data have consistently undermeasured technology's contribution to productivity growth and the economy. His views, insights, and predictions—as well as those of other "Creators of Digital Deflation"—are revealed in the Fireside Chat interviews at the back of the book.

In truth, it is not easy to discern how much the Fed understands about how advancing digital technologies are creating higher-value products and good deflation that are not being counted today. But every year, as the economic data are improved with the addition of new product categories for the measurement of quality improvement, the Fed will better understand the need to become more accommodative. The question is whether the Fed will be willing to act earlier and not wait for the data to be fixed.

## ONE FOOT ON THE BRAKES AND ONE FOOT ON THE GAS

In both the deflationary American Depression of the 1930s and Japan's deflationary slump of the 1990s, monetary policy sat on the sidelines, leaving it up to fiscal policy to do the "heavy lifting." In Japan, monetary policy became ineffective as interest rates approached zero. That left the Japanese government little choice but to rely heavily on fiscal policy. Although it could have elected to cut taxes, it chose to utilize expensive debt-financed public works programs. No doubt, many of these highways and bridges were critical to building a more efficient infrastructure. However, much criticism has been directed at projects that were equivalent to the building of politically motivated and wasteful "bridges to nowhere."

These fiscal measures are reminiscent of the United States in the 1930s, when equally expensive public works programs were instituted to help reemploy America's unemployed. In addition, the advent of World War II mobilized the country for a wartime economy that pushed the economy back to full employment. The focus on winning the war also sowed the early seeds of the Digital Revolution and rejuvenated innovation after over a decade of neglect. Yet, radar, television, and the birth of the semiconductor might have all arrived earlier had monetary and fiscal policies not plunged the economy into a decade of economic stagnation and minimal innovation and entrepreneurship. It took a decade of public works projects plus a costly world war to resurrect the American economy and jumpstart innovation and entrepreneurship that only finally returned in earnest in the 1950s.

In the Post '90s environment of overstated inflation numbers and inadvertently tight monetary policy, the U.S. economy is in a similar situation. In the absence of sufficient monetary stimulus, fiscal policy measures have been mustered up to address the weak economy. The good news is that the current administration is favoring tax cuts to stimulate the economy, rather than expensive and often wasteful public works programs, which obviously haven't worked in Japan. But if monetary policy is too tight, and fiscal policy is moving to a more stimulative mode, it's as if the Fed has its foot on the brakes, while at the same time our fiscal representatives are putting their foot on the gas. That's not very efficient. Obviously, it would be preferable for the Fed to take its foot off the brakes *before* the fiscal foot steps on the gas.

The point is that fiscal and monetary policies need to work together. If the Fed's policies are too restrictive, our legislators will likely feel compelled to overcompensate to make up for that monetary restraint.

## CAPITAL, LABOR, AND TECHNOLOGY

One of the benefits of the Digital Deflation thesis is that it provides a means for quantifying technology as a fundamental economic variable. Just like capital and skilled labor, technology has a cost and a value and can be created, consumed, and employed to create more value. Just as labor can generate labor productivity (output per person-hour) and capital can generate capital productivity (return on capital employed), technology can create technology productivity (higher-quality and better-performing goods and services measured as Digital Deflation and as percentage gains in real output). But historically, in economic terms, technology hasn't been counted very accurately.

The point that technology has not been captured very well in economic statistics is not new. In the footnotes of the quarterly reports on productivity, the Bureau of Labor Statistics itself quite openly refers to many inputs which it does not specifically measure in its productivity data: "Productivity measures describe the relationship between real output and the labor time involved in its production. . . . They do not measure the specific contribution of labor, capital, or any other factor of production. Rather, they reflect the joint effects of many influences, including changes in technology; capital investment; level of output; utilization of capacity, energy, and materials; the organization of production; managerial skill; and the characteristics and effort of the work force."

But as we proceed further into the 21st century, technology becomes far too large a factor *not* to measure accurately, as both an input and an output of our economy. Technology, in fact, has grown so large that by some measures, it is rivaling capital as an economic input. Using GDP accounts, one can identify "wages, salaries, and other labor income" as a proxy for labor input, totaling $6149 billion, or 61.0% of GDP in 2001. Similarly, "consumption of fixed capital," or depreciation and amortization, can be used as a direct proxy for the capital input in the U.S. economy totaling $789 billion, or 7.8% of GDP. But capital costs should also include the annual financial cost of capital, including corporate interest expense ($197 billion in 2001), dividends ($278 billion), and capital gains (estimated $200 billion) for a total of $675 billion, or 6.7% of GDP. Combined, the depreciation and financial cost of capital totaled about $1464 billion, or 14.5% of GDP in 2001.

Technology inputs, on the other hand, are more difficult to identify. The Digital Economy studies of the Department of Commerce estimate information technology industries to have produced output equal to about 8.1% of GDP in 2000. Philadelphia Fed economist Leonard Nakamura has estimated that the U.S. economic data do not measure $1 trillion per year of investment in intangibles: "Historically, in the U.S. national income accounts, only tangible investments in equipment and structures have been included in our measurement of investment. . . . When the inputs that make up intangible investment are measured more accurately, domestic U.S. corporations' investment in intangibles is likely in the range of $700 billion to $1.5 trillion."[5]

The Philadelphia Fed economist went on to identify intangibles yet to be counted as assets, such as "R&D, movie and book production, designs and blueprints, and the advertising associated with the new products introduced." It is reassuring to note that beginning with software in 1999, our U.S. statisticians have already begun to count intangibles as assets rather than only as component costs of another final product.

One of the difficulties in measuring R&D and other intangible technology investments as economic assets or as inputs is that there needs to be a direct and measurable technology-driven output on the other side of the economic equation. In other words, if we are not counting intangible assets being consumed on the input side of the economy, what is it that we are not counting on the other side as output?

This is where Digital Deflation enters into the picture. The rising real value of technology-driven goods and services can be estimated as quality-based real gains in output consistent with reductions in the deflator for each product category. This is already being measured for computers made for final sale today. Recall from Chapter 8 that total counted and uncounted quality improvement totaled about $255 billion, or 2.46% of GDP in 2001. As the government counts more of the uncounted quality improvement for more goods and services across the economy, reported real output will rise. On the input side of the equation, this will allow government statisticians to count an increase in an equivalent amount of currently uncounted "intangible investments" as assets.

This suggestion that Digital Deflation exists to account for a significant part of the undermeasurement of intangibles consumed on the input side of the economy is somewhat theoretical. However, it is highlighted to show that the Theory of Digital Deflation can be accommodated within the current framework of modern economics, and can help us measure technology as an important and growing economic input.

## MANAGING BOOMS AND BUBBLES

There will always be bubbles. They are the natural result of human emotion and excesses and errors in the capital allocation process. It is very critical, however, that policymakers and the public do not confuse the popping of the Y2K and Dot-com Bubbles with the long period of innovation and entrepreneurship that preceded them. It is important to understand that in the 1990s there was an extended period of investment in capital and technology leading to a continuum of true innovation, the delivery of increasing value to consumers, and the creation of real wealth that was shared by a majority of Americans. Surely, a capitalist system that relies on the public ownership of common stock and a tax structure that at least partly encourages stock ownership helped distribute the creation of wealth to a wider base of Americans. Through the wealth effect for consumers and corporations, a significant portion of the increase in wealth was recycled back in the form of fundamentally enhanced demand for goods and services, contributing to an economic expansion that lasted a record 10 years.

In a very real sense, the period of growth and prosperity in the 1990s was also extended by pioneering work in our government's statistical agencies in the more accurate counting of quality improvement for computers made for final sale, reducing reported inflation, and increasing reported productivity.

The 1990s also benefited from a progressive Federal Reserve which let the economy expand when other central banks might have reigned in the expansion based on Old Economy speed limits. Even though the overall economic data did not completely mirror what was happening in the real economy, the Fed of the 1990s perceived that IT was contributing to a New Economy, and it was willing to experiment for a time with letting the expansion run. But in the end, even a progressive Fed could only run for so long on perceptions and instinct without good hard data.

At the turn of the century, the Department of Commerce in a commemorative ceremony pointed to the creation of GDP accounts as the crowning achievement of the statistical agencies in the 20th century. GDP accounts resulted in better fiscal and monetary policies and fewer recessions, allowing us to enjoy in the 1990s the longest expansion in the century.

Today there is an enormous opportunity to more accurately measure the annual improvement in the quality and real value of technology-driven goods and services, resulting in more accurate data on inflation. With new technologies to help managers become more efficient and with better data on inflation, there is every reason to believe that recessions should become less common and less severe than even at the end of the last century. With better data and less volatile economic growth patterns, the challenges of managing booms and bubbles should become considerably less daunting for policymakers and business managers alike, resulting in less pain and suffering—and greater prosperity for all.

## QUALITY IMPROVEMENT AND DEGRADATION

The case has been presented for including more measurements for quality improvement in the government's economic data in ways that will benefit all of us. However, questions can be raised over (1) the consistency of quality improvement over time and (2) whether there are significant cases of quality degradation that should be considered.

On the first question, the annual improvement in digitally driven products and services are not always going to be smooth and linear. End-product innovation, development, and sales ramps can be uneven and subject to economic and capital market cycles. There will be stair-steps and plateaus. Nevertheless, given a healthy and expanding economy, the average annual rate of improvement should remain at a vigorous pace for years into the future. Conversations with several leaders of the Digital Revolution confirmed this view, and several are presented in the Fireside Chat interviews at the end of this book.

To be sure, there will be debate over how much quality improvement is or is not being counted into the economic data. As in past decades, many will question whether we need faster, better, cheaper products and services. But we always seem to want them. Sometimes the technology will lag consumer demand, as in true voice recognition. In many instances, new technologies will lead demand and have to wait a few years for cost declines to bring prices within range of the average consumer. Five years ago, most gurus said that PCs would never get below $1000.

On the second question, there are certainly examples of product or service quality degradation, such as smaller airline seats or longer lines at airports. They too should be included in our further analysis. Who really is in favor of taking two flights through an airline "hub" to get to a destination? "Do you mean I have to do this twice?" Major carriers seem to have overlooked this degradation in service quality—because they don't measure it. They should not be surprised that they are losing market share to "point-to-point" carriers. These are real reductions in quality and value to the consumer. But these examples will be relatively harder to find, and they will not likely suffer from double-digit declines in quality *every year* anywhere near the double-digit rates of annual improvement in the quality and performance of advancing digital technologies.

Also offsetting any undermeasured quality degradations are the many less noticeable gains in quality not addressed in the Digital Deflation models. Despite small rates of annual quality improvement, they are nevertheless important because they comprise large categories in the economy. These include, for example, food, housing, and clothing, which represented 9.8%, 14.2%, and 3.1%, respectively, of GDP in 2001. California grower A.G. Kawamura cites the significant increases in the variety and quality of fresh produce achieved by the farming industry during the last several years. This is just another everyday example of the greater value being offered to consumers that is nowhere counted in the economic data.

## MAKING THE WORLD A BETTER PLACE

While I have placed much of my emphasis in this book on the U.S. economy, American constituents, and domestic policy, I believe strongly that Digital Deflation offers enormous potential for the betterment of people's lives throughout the world. In Chapter 13, I explained the status of individual countries and where they might be headed tomorrow. Let me now explain how the world's economies face a common threat—and opportunity.

Throughout history, some of the biggest policy blunders were the result of misinformation and bad data. Today, huge policy mistakes are being made by central bankers worldwide—huge because inflation is being overstated by 1% to 2% in virtually every economy with a reasonably large IT sector. This is a major reason why fiscal and monetary policymakers in all the major world economies have been struggling to understand why their policies haven't been working. The Victorian interpretation is that we are only paying for our sins and excesses from the dot-com boom. The truth is that with inflation 1% to 2% lower than reports have indicated, in many parts of the world, actual inflation is really close to zero—or even deflationary. Fearful of inflation that is not there, the world's monetary policymakers have been misled into thinking that they have been "accommodative" and have printed enough money to fuel their economies, whereas they have really been inadvertently too tight (and Victorian indeed!).

As long as countries undercount quality improvement and overstate inflation, they will continue to face sluggish economic growth, high unemployment, and enormous unfulfilled potential. They may even be cultivating the genesis of a deflationary trap, for individual industries, if not for their whole economies.

The natural progression of policy responses for these countries would be for their central banks to inadvertently continue to print too little money based on the fiction that inflation is 1% to 2% higher than it really is in a marketplace with rapidly improving goods and services. With nominal interest rates that are too high for transactions to clear the markets of goods and services, and with *real* interest rates actually 1% to 2% higher than generally believed by both borrowers and lenders, those "reluctant economies" worldwide will become (or remain) stagnant, moribund, and well below their potential GDP and potential productivity growth rates.

In those economies constrained by unintentionally tight monetary policies, it will look like people will not need or want to buy faster, better, cheaper computers. Demand will fall short of expectations in many goods and services. There will be hand-wringing over too much capacity in both labor and the capital stock. But a good part of this *excess capacity* will be because there is *underdemand*. Despite being already historically low, interest rates will need to move even lower—at the same time that correctly measured inflation will be moving to record lows. Reluctant economies will be plagued not only by sluggish growth and persistently high unemployment, but also by pressure on corporate profit margins and relatively weak stock markets. Recall that most countries in the European Union (EU), most notably Germany and the UK, did not measure *any* quality improvement in the 1990s.

We must understand that these persistently weak economic conditions may introduce bigger threats. As mentioned earlier, the ultimate risk is that countries or economic trading zones lagging the most will feel even more compelled to protect individual industries and jobs most at peril from slowing aggregate demand as well as from shifting consumer preferences toward rapidly improving New Economy goods and away from inflating Old Economy goods. Some countries may see no alternative but to utilize trade barriers, tax breaks, and other artificial contrivances to protect dying industries. If cool heads do not prevail, the result could be trade wars, which, of course, would doom mankind to repeat history.

However, there is an alternative. That alternative is the creation of more accurate economic data on a *global scale* so that country by country, policymakers will be more inclined to grow their economies with monetary policies that no longer artificially constrain both their naturally deflating New Economies and the nominally inflating Old Economies.

Ideally, there should be a concerted global effort to count quality gains properly. In the spirit of cooperation, the Bureau of Labor Statistics (BLS) and the Bureau of Economic Analysis (BEA) in the United States, Statistics Canada, and statistical agencies in other countries should share methodologies and help others set timetables for more accurately counting the improving real value of products and services worldwide. These efforts should also be apolitical. The benefits would mean faster economic growth globally—with more jobs, rising stock prices, and greater wealth creation—as the rising tide of cross-border trade and investment lifts all boats.

Of course, it will be critical for central bankers worldwide to have open minds to better understand a New Economy that has broken the traditional economic molds. It will also require courage on the part of monetary professionals, who in prior decades were rewarded for fighting inflation, to be open to a new world of rapidly improving product quality and growing Digital Deflation.

We are a lot closer to deflation than most realize, some good and some not so favorable. It is up to governments worldwide to measure more accurately the good deflation being generated by rapidly advancing technologies of all kinds. With other countries joining the effort, more economies worldwide will begin to properly measure the improving quality of products and services as gains in the real value of output and productivity—and as good deflation. If some monetary authorities do not lead, at some point, they will have to follow.

In the United States and in other countries, this may well be one of those rare opportunities where the legislative and executive branches of the government can influence the central banks. They can legislate and implement a more complete measurement of improving product quality and can present the monetary authorities with more accurate inflation data that would show that monetary policy can be more accommodative. In Europe, with interest rates and unemployment already considerably higher than in the United States, and with less quality improvement and Digital Deflation currently being measured, the potential is even greater for producing better economic data and kick-starting their economies. In Japan, with better data to reflect quality improvement from advancing digital technologies, it will be seen that it is even more deflationary than it believes.

As more governments begin to understand the Digital Deflation process, it will become increasingly likely that reported inflation and interest rates will be dropping worldwide. Removing the shackles of Old Economy thinking, global monetary policy can become more expansive, paving the way to faster nominal (and real) economic growth over the next two decades.

The "early adapters" will be those countries that move first to begin to measure and count their faster, better, cheaper technology-driven products and services as higher real output and as good deflation. They will be able to grow their economies, both Old and New, faster than other countries, and they'll be able to do it with deflation in the New Economy offsetting inflation in the Old. With faster economic growth and lower inflation, their currencies should appreciate relative to the "late adapters," attracting capital, boosting stock prices, and creating a true wealth effect for their own Investor-Consumer class, similar to the United States in the 1990s. The most immediate beneficiary could be the European Union, which has further to go in counting quality improvement and Digital Deflation and therefore greater upside potential.

In the United States, the opportunity for creating record amounts of wealth over the next two decades is enormous. The demographic foundation has never been more favorable—with low labor force growth and an absolute need for productivity gains if the real economy is to grow. The outlook for potential productivity growth has never been more promising, with a technology pipeline rich from the entrepreneurial boom and initial investments of the late 1990s. The ongoing Digital Revolution will present enormous opportunities to harness new technologies, unleashing innovation, entrepreneurship, and the delivery of faster, better, cheaper products and services—and greater value—to consumers worldwide. The technologies will be there, with ongoing advances in silicon, software, wireless services, broadband, digital imaging, digital video, new displays, and genomics. The Internet will continue to grow, and there will be important new platforms, such as third generation (3G) wireless cell phone standards and Wi-Fi or 802.11 short-range high-speed wireless communications. There will be new disruptive technologies, such as personalized medicine utilizing each individual's genetic data to identify a proclivity toward a certain disease or to customize therapeutic solutions with fewer side effects.

Encouragingly, in the United States, preliminary conversations with congressional staffers on "the Hill" would suggest that the outlook is quite favorable for a greater focus on seeking better economic data. Congress has a genuine interest on both sides of the aisle in resurrecting the New Economy of the 1990s. A stronger economy, budget surpluses, and a rising stock market can certainly go a long way toward addressing the looming Social Security, Medicare, and private pension plan funding challenges that lie ahead. Importantly, the Department of Labor has a mandate from the White House to improve the accuracy of economic data. Greater funding would accelerate that process immensely.

My belief is that in truly democratic societies, policymakers will try to make the right decisions. With better data to properly measure the improving quality of digitally driven products and services worldwide, policymakers will make *better* decisions, making it more certain that the New Economy will come back to thrive both in the United States and overseas.

Ultimately, a more accurate counting of the growth in the real value of digitally driven goods and services will enable monetary policymakers at key central banks worldwide to pursue above average economic growth *and* maintain price stability. Coupled with fiscal policy reforms to foster capital formation, nominal and real economic growth rates will be elevated, producing a host of economic and social benefits not seen since the 1990s. These would include higher employment levels, growing real wages, declining interest rates, rising stock prices, massive wealth creation, government surpluses, lower crime rates, exciting new consumer products and services, improved healthcare, and generally a higher quality of life.

For those who suffered through supply-demand curves in Economics 101 and feel that economics is a cold or "dismal" science, it is hoped that this book has presented a more human and real life view of how good economics, as well as good or bad economic data, can materially affect a society. By more accurately counting the rapidly improving benefits of the Digital Revolution worldwide, and by then instituting appropriate fiscal and monetary policies, governments in the United States, Europe, Asia, and other parts of the globe can truly make the world a better place.

A century ago, amidst all the innovation, economic growth, and wealth creation of the Industrial Revolution, Alexander Graham Bell, inventor, entrepreneur, and businessman, said that "When one door closes . . . we do not see the one which has opened before us." The door is truly open, presenting a rare opportunity to transform the global economy with a common purpose. This will be accomplished, in part, by creating better and more accurate economic data. The cost of getting the data would be very small relative to the enormous benefits and wealth creation that would result over the next 20 years.

We are at one of the major inflection points in economic history. The Industrial Revolution was brought to an early ending. Let's get it right this time.

## NOTES

1. Nakamura, Leonard, "Is the U.S. Economy Really Growing Too Slowly? Maybe We're Measuring Growth Wrong," Federal Reserve Bank of Philadelphia, *Business Review*, March–April 1997.

2. "The 2002 Annual Report of the Board of Trustees of the Federal Old-Age and Survivors Insurance and Disability Insurance Trust Funds," (ssa.gov), Social Security Administration, March 26, 2002.

3. "Strengthening Social Security and Creating Personal Wealth for All Americans," Report of the President's Council, December 11, 2001.

4. Federal Open Market Committee press release, Federal Reserve, August 13, 2002.

5. Nakamura, Leonard, "Investing in Intangibles: Is a Trillion Dollars Missing from GDP?" Federal Reserve Bank of Philadelphia, *Business Review*, 4th Quarter, 2001.

# Closer to Deflation
# Than You Think

Based on theories developed over many years, this book was largely written in 2000, 2001, and early 2002. Since then our government's statisticians have continued to work diligently to improve our economic data. On August 16, 2002, the Bureau of Labor Statistics (BLS) published a new measure of consumer prices, the C-CPI-U. Although it garnered very little press, the announcement was astounding even to the Bureau. This new inflation series, the "Chained Consumer Price Index for All Urban Consumers," reported that actual inflation for consumers was a whopping 0.8% lower in 2000 when adjusted more accurately for shifting consumer preferences.

The BLS simply added more up-to-date weightings as new products, such as DVD players, grew faster each month than older products in the index. The result was a Chained CPI of only 2.6% compared with the 3.4% that was officially reported for the CPI for 2000. Similarly, the Core CPI (excluding food and energy) for 2000 was measured to have been 0.7% lower at 1.9% for the Core Chained CPI versus 2.6% for the officially reported Core CPI. On a preliminary basis, for the following year, 2001, the BLS estimated a Chained CPI of 1.0% compared with the 1.6% that was officially reported for the CPI. The Core C-CPI-U came in at only 2.0% versus the 2.7% that was officially announced for 2001.

This new C-CPI-U was constructed, according to the BLS, to "reflect any substitution that consumers make across item categories in response to changes in relative prices." This "substitution bias" was one of the four major sources of upward bias to the CPI that the Boskin Commission estimated in 1996 to have collectively overstated the CPI by 1.1%. The substitution bias alone was estimated by the Boskin Commission to have been overstating inflation by 0.4% per year, with the undercounting of new products/quality change overstating the CPI by an additional 0.6%.

Interestingly, with this new C-CPI-U data, the BLS now measures the substitution bias to be overstating the CPI by almost *twice* the rate estimated in the original Boskin Study. It should be pointed out that the substitution effect became even larger as consumers were attracted by the faster improvement in the quality of technology-driven products and services, not just by lower "relative prices."

Now that the substitution bias has been quantified by the BLS, the largest remaining source of error in the CPI is the overstatement from not counting quality improvement. That, of course, is what this book is about. The Digital Deflation model estimates the uncounted quality improvement from digitally driven products and services to be about 1.0% per year on the CPI for 2000, 2001, and 2002. As more Digital Deflation is counted, and as IT becomes a larger part of consumer spending, the overstatement of the CPI from uncounted quality improvement will be seen to be significantly higher than the 0.6% per year overstatement estimated by the Boskin Commission in 1996.

Correcting the official CPI for both the estimated uncounted Digital Deflation from quality improvement, and for the substitution bias, would reduce the CPI from 3.4% to 1.6% in 2000, from 1.6% to 0.0% in 2001, and on a preliminary basis, from 2.4% to 1.0% in 2002. With the GDP Deflator (which is already chain-weighted) also equal to about 0%, 0.2%, and −0.1% in 2000, 2001, and 2002 when adjusted for Digital Deflation, we are already closer to deflation than most people think.

There is now an important opportunity to chain weight the official CPI, as is already being done for the GDP Deflator. In addition to counting more quality improvement and Digital Deflation, this would be an important next step toward "getting the data right" and starting the nation back on a path to prosperity.

# FIRESIDE CHATS

# Interviews with Creators of Digital Deflation

## INTERVIEW WITH GORDON MOORE

*Gordon Moore is cofounder and chairman emeritus of Intel Corporation. He developed the concept that became known as Moore's Law. He was interviewed on November 18, 2000, just before he flew to Sweden to accept posthumous recognition by the Nobel Committee for Intel cofounder, Robert Noyce, for his contribution to science.*

TANAKA: What do you see as Intel's biggest contribution to the New Economy and to the Digital Revolution?

MOORE: I guess it has to be the microprocessor. There have been three major inventions in the semiconductor world over the history of the industry. The first one was the transistor itself. That was a whole new idea that got us going.

TANAKA: And that was basically when?

MOORE: The invention was in 1947. The first transistor appeared in the early 1950s as far as being commercially available. Then the second major invention was the integrated circuit. The integrated circuit was the idea that really got us on the path of low cost. You know, instead of making individual transistors that had to be separately packaged and everything, now we put tens of millions of these things on a chip. The net result is the cost per transistor has gone down something like 10 million-fold.

TANAKA: This is since when?

MOORE: The individual transistors were all we made up until 1961. Transistors today, individual ones, still cost almost as much as a circuit with a million transistors. The idea of building a complete circuit changed the whole economics of electronics. Without that we wouldn't have any of the digital systems we enjoy today. PCs and the like would have been prohibitively expensive. So to me that was the second important contribution. My idea of the third one is the microprocessor. The idea of making a general-purpose computer that could be programmed to any one of an infinite number of different functions. Intel, of course, was formed after the first two, but we did the first microprocessor and are still the leaders in that area.

TANAKA: You developed the concept of Moore's Law. Today, are the numbers of transistors that can be put on a chip accelerating or decelerating? How many years out can you see the number of transistors doubling on a chip?

MOORE: Well, it decelerated a bit when I first wrote the article that's now called Moore's Law in 1965. I predicted a doubling every year for the next 10 years. Something that I never expected to be accurate, but it turned out to be fairly accurate. Then I changed it to doubling every 2 years in 1975 because we lost one of the factors that had really been helping us. We've been on that pretty much ever since. Right now, if anything, we're moving a little bit faster than that, which is amazing. I think I can see it going at least another decade. Then it gets kind of iffy because we're running up against the fact that things are getting so small that the atomic nature of materials is starting to bother us. We get down to where we only have a very few atoms in an area, and the devices don't necessarily behave the same anymore. So that's a really physical barrier that I don't really see yet how we'll get around. But I can see us continuing what we've been doing in the past for at least another decade. Probably sometime between 2010 and 2020 we'll run into the real physical problem.

TANAKA: Then what happens?

MOORE: The worst case is that the rate of progress slows and we only double every 4 or 5 years, instead of every 2. Then we'll make bigger chips and we'll go to other more complex structures that start using the third dimension more than we've used in the past. That will let us keep putting more stuff on a chip.

TANAKA: Other people have talked about brand-new technologies that could figure into the picture. What is your view of such ideas?

MOORE: There are ideas floating around. Personally I'm a skeptic. Maybe I'm just getting too old. I view it the other way around. I think instead of something coming in and replacing our technology, our technology is infiltrating everything else. Essentially the technology we developed for integrated circuits is being used to make things like gene chips now. And there are these microelectromechanical machines or so-called MEMS, little gears and wheels and levers and things that are really exciting. I know a company that makes a little chemical lab on a chip, again with the same technology. You put a drop of blood on it, plug it into a little meter that'll give you a blood analysis in 90 seconds with a half dozen most common things they analyze for.

TANAKA: In other words, there might be other ways to leverage silicon technology?

MOORE: Yes. I think we got kind of a basic technology for making complex microstructures, and I think it's going to be something that sticks around for a very long time. The other things have such a hurdle to get over. You know, people talk of something like quantum computing. Frankly, to me, quantum computing is a good way to show how nonintuitive quantum mechanics is. But to make it a practical computer is a wild leap of faith and nobody even has an idea of how it can be general purpose. They see a class of problems that it could do faster, but I'm skeptical we could ever get to that. I don't see anything coming along that I feel is going to replace our technology in mainstream electronics.

TANAKA: You were saying that Intel has developed a basic technology for making complex microstructures? Do you mean make microstructures like the MEMS or the Biochip?

MOORE: Yes. We build things up layer by layer. The semiconductor on the bottom is almost incidental these days. That's a kind of last layer. The other 20-plus layers are for building the stuff on top of it. These things are phenomenally complex. You can use different materials and still take advantage of this deposition etching combination to build something. It's sort of a three-dimensional structure, whatever you want.

TANAKA: So actually you're saying that the enabling technology gets applied to uses other than, for example, microprocessors or DRAMs? And it goes in a completely different area to then create new productivity-enhancing products?

MOORE: Yes. Absolutely.

TANAKA: What led you to the theory that developed Moore's Law? Did you have any idea that it would be this significant?

MOORE: Well, you know, this was early in the days of integrated circuits and I was given the job of writing an article for *Electronic* magazine for their 35th annual edition. They wanted me to predict what was going to happen in semiconductor components over the next 10 years. So I looked at these first few integrated circuits and saw that they were just about doubling every year in complexity and we were all the way up to 60. I just said, okay, we'll go from 60 to 60,000 in the next 10 years. Just extrapolating that doubling every year.

TANAKA: You were up to only 60 transistors per circuit?

MOORE: Sixty transistors and resistors together was the most complex circuit that was around at that time. That was actually a laboratory device.

TANAKA: This was in what year?

MOORE: 1965. And that was a long extrapolation. Now, I didn't expect it to be accurate, but the point I wanted to get across was that this was going to be the way electronics got cheap. Up until that time, integrated circuits had principally gone into military systems that weren't cost-sensitive. They were expensive to build, but from my position running a laboratory at Fairchild I could see that this was going to continue to change. They were going to get cheaper and cheaper, and that was really the whole point I wanted to get across. We're going to put more stuff on a chip, and because of that electronics are going to get a lot cheaper. One of my colleagues, I think it was Carver Meade from Cal Tech, dubbed that Moore's Law. It used to grind on me and for a long time, I couldn't say it with a straight face. I've outgrown that now.

TANAKA: One of the points I'm exploring is that digital technologies have been undermeasured in terms of economic statistics, as well as underappreciated in the marketplace by economists, technicians, investors, and corporate managements. We're not just talking about semiconductors. Now we have optics, magnetic storage displays, a lot of software—all these things are improving every year, and how do you measure that? What do you think about such a theory? Is it accurate?

MOORE: I think that's a very good point. One of the gripes I've had is that what we've done in our industry essentially doesn't factor into the productivity figures.

TANAKA: Is that right? You've said this?

MOORE: Yes. I've said it wherever I get a forum. The fact that you can buy a 64-megabit DRAM with over 66 million transistors on it for what we used to sell a transistor for doesn't show up in the standard measures of productivity.

TANAKA: Why is that?

MOORE: It's just the way economists measure productivity. No qualitative factor gets in there. The fact is that the computer you buy today, your PC, is 100 times faster than it was 15 years ago. You get a qualitative improvement that doesn't show up. It only shows up if it takes less labor to produce a PC. But the qualitative improvement in the product doesn't show up at all.

TANAKA: What do you think has been technology's biggest disappointment?

MOORE: You know, many things that people thought were going to come earlier have just not arrived. Things like artificial intelligence. I think a lot of us have been disappointed in how slow truly good speech recognition has developed. To me that's going to be a really revolutionary technology when it finally arrives full blown. But it's just taking a heck of a lot longer than I expected—longer than I think that a lot of the people who are even doing it expected.

TANAKA: When do you think that might be? It seems as if we're close.

MOORE: Well, we're close to doing some of the simple things. But I want a speech system that can understand when I say too, if I mean *to*, or *too*, or *two*, by understanding in context. Once it understands what you're saying in context, it seems to me you can have an intelligent conversation with your computer. It'll really be understanding language then, and that's going to change dramatically how things are done. A lot more people will be able to participate. It'll be a lot easier to interact. I don't know how far away from that we are. I think it'll happen during this century, but I don't know if it's 5 years or 50 years. You can do a halfway job of dictation now, but you've got to do a lot of correcting of the words. It recognizes word by word rather than by sentence and context, and that's the big difference I'm looking for.

TANAKA: What do you think might be the "Next Big Thing" or the next biggest surprise from digital technology?

MOORE: The trouble is I can never predict the surprises that usually turn out to be the most important things. To give you an idea of my ability to see some of these things, if you had asked me in 1980, I still probably would have missed the significance of the PC. In 1990 I would have missed the significance of the Internet. I don't know what I'm going to miss in 2000, but I'm sure it's equally big.

TANAKA: But there's something out there?

MOORE: I think so. There are a lot of things going on, and it evidently wasn't the e-business for the consumer. That was a big miss. But something is going to happen that's going to have a real impact on how technology gets applied and where does the biggest bang occur, but I don't know what it's going to be. I think as we keep changing these things, making them more powerful and cheaper, eventually it becomes a qualitative change instead of just a quantitative change.

TANAKA: I'm not sure exactly what you mean.

MOORE: I mean that you do things completely differently rather than just do old things faster. There may not be an obvious breakpoint in the technology, your "something new" coming along technologically, but just for the fact that you have all this additional capability that someone can tackle problems from a completely different direction.

TANAKA: So in other words, it would be even more difficult for the government to measure the future technologies, as they become more qualitative?

MOORE: That's true also, but it'll at least change the way we do things. It's very hard to predict where the things of the biggest bang are going to come from. At least it's hard for me to predict.

TANAKA: How would you like to see yourself and Intel described in the history books for posterity?

MOORE: For me, it would be for my role in founding and growing Intel. Because Intel, at least based on its history so far, is really changing the direction of electronics. You know, we did all the early memory chips first and we did the microprocessor. And memory and microprocessors have become the driving force of the industry, certainly for the last 30 years. Communication chips are getting increasingly important, but not to that level of importance yet.

TANAKA: What do you think the government should do now and in the future to really help the digital industry and to maximize the value of these products for society?

MOORE: The first thing you have to do is to preserve a good environment to start and run companies. The government sets a lot of the rules in place and these ought to be things that work well for industry. This includes securities regulations, tax regulations, all kinds of things. Beyond that the government increasingly had the role dumped on it of being the supporter of basic research. For a variety of reasons companies have backed away from that. The Bell Labs of the world are shadows of what they used to be. I think that this is a phenomenal investment for the country long term and something that just isn't going to get done otherwise. So I feel very strongly there that the government has a major role.

TANAKA: Why doesn't private industry take greater interest or commit the assets?

MOORE: One of the principal reasons is that it's very difficult for a company to capture the fruits of its own research. First, you're never quite sure what's going to come out of a research program. And you can't plan the time scale. So it'll either come out at a time when the particular company is supportive and can use it, or in an area where the company is not interested or active. The net result is it becomes part of the common good. The research is generally widely published and it runs a lot faster if everybody interacts. What we need is just a lot of that information becoming available, and then we have the entrepreneurial system in the United States that seems to be able to take advantage of new ideas. I think we're way ahead if we can keep that moving rapidly.

## INTERVIEW WITH RICHARD S. HILL

*Richard S. Hill is chairman and CEO of Novellus Systems, Inc., a leading provider of equipment for depositing conductive and insulating films on semiconductor devices. He was interviewed by telephone on October 16, 2000.*

TANAKA: How far out can you see Novellus, semiconductor equipment companies, and the semiconductor industry in general continuing to double the performance of semiconductors according to Moore's Law or at any other rate?

HILL: The way I look at it is for at least the next 20 years we ought to be able to continue at half the costs or double the performance every 18 to 24 months. It's going to happen in a little bit different way. I think up until this point it's been totally performance increases, and I don't think that's going to be the case anymore. I think it's going to be probably 50% from performance increases. I think that performance isn't going to continue to double every 18 months. I think it's going to go to more like a 36-month or a 4-year double, and I think there's going to be tremendous pressure on costs over the next 20 years. I think costs are going to come down dramatically.

TANAKA: How will those costs come down?

HILL: I think processing technology is going to start to change. You see it with the advent of copper. With the lower temperature process, you're using an electrofill process to put down copper. It doesn't get much lower relative to energy consumption. As opposed to huge PVD (physical vapor deposition) machines you're eliminating very, very high cost equipment. When you look at the cost to make an integrated circuit (IC), the actual raw material cost in the product itself is a relatively nominal number. Everything revolves around the processing of that material and everything over the next 20 years is going to be the optimization of the processing of that material.

TANAKA: Do you think it can continue at that rate for 20 years?

HILL: Yes, for 20 years.

TANAKA: Are you basing that on faith or do you actually know the technologies today?

HILL: Well no, I think if you look at some of the changes in technology, some things are evolving with optics and lower [energy] consumption. I see the extendibility of copper for at least 10 years. I absolutely guarantee the extendibility for 10 years, and beyond that the question is how do we put optical connections on integrated circuits. I think that's the next wave. I think you're going to see two things that will emerge in the next, I'd say, 5 years that will really change integrated circuits design. One is going to be a radio frequency [RF] clock distribution. I don't think you're going to run a clock around a device anymore. I think you're going to have an RF transmission in the IC itself.

TANAKA: How does that work?

HILL: Today you have a clock signal that's got "clock skew" as it runs around a chip with delays in different areas. Now, imagine if you have an RF [signal] that was broadcasting a perfectly tuned clock and it's broadcast across the entire surface of the chip.

TANAKA: Basically as a timer?

HILL: As a timer. So now you get rid of clock skew, which is one of the biggest inhibitors of increasing speed.

TANAKA: That could come in how many years?

HILL: It could be in active use in 5 years.

TANAKA: And what's the second one?

HILL: The second one will actually be optical lines, a fiber-optic kind of chip.

TANAKA: Is that within 5 years but not in volume?

HILL: That's probably within 10 years.

TANAKA: Is this a process that would replace deposition?

HILL: I think I'd look at it a different way. If you really look at what Applied Materials and Novellus do, they put down dielectrics [insulators] and they put down metal [conductors]. Well, what are you going to see on an optical device? You're going to see that the oxides are nothing more than glass, which is going to become the "run," and the metal is going to become the reflector for the mirrors. Imagine inverting a device from having metal as the conductor to having the oxide become the conductor.

TANAKA: But what then acts as a switch in that kind of a model?

HILL: Well, you've got to have detectors and emitters.

TANAKA: But what replaces the actual semiconductor switch?

HILL: The first step you have is a combination of photo optics as well as integrated circuit technology on the device, plus traditional technology. You'll probably see a fiber-optic clock circuit that would be a photo detector. You would have a fiber-optic cable that goes to every one of those photo detectors and it would be strobing the clocks in the device. Then the rest of the circuit would be electrical with the normal wiring and the normal CMOS [complementary metal-oxide semiconductor] transistors. Ultimately one could conceive or intellectualize the ability to have nothing but photo optic cells as transistors and you have a light on and you have a light off and that's the switch—photosensitive transistors.

TANAKA: In this kind of a model how difficult is it for Novellus to make the transition?

HILL: The reality is that making optics or making integrated circuits is a deposition and etch type of business. Your traditional companies will just evolve equipment to meet the demands of the market. I don't think you'll see new companies emerge. I think one of the things you're going to see is atomic layer deposition. In order to make these things happen, you're going to have to have an effective and commercial means of doing atomic layer deposition. That's one of the limiters today. For the accuracy required to be able to make these photo optic devices repeatedly, the equipment is not there yet. If you look at the way you make transistors today, in a traditional semiconductor you manufacture the semiconductor and you produce at high quality a good number of devices. In photo optics, there is a statistical anomaly that takes place that allows you to get the right thickness of a material to get a photo detector or a photo emitter of the right frequency. We don't do that with integrated circuit technology today. Our control is not good enough at the fiber-optic level yet or for optical components to produce them reliably and with high yield.

TANAKA: Changing topics a bit. When do you think the Digital Revolution began and when will it end?

HILL: I think the Digital Revolution really began probably after the invention of the [digital] calculator in 1968. The first digital calculators and digital watches came out in that time period.

TANAKA: When do you think it might end?

HILL: I don't think it's going to end in the next 20 years. I think the whole world is going to go so digital that it's analog. If you look at a digital signal and compare it to two analog signals with a DC level on each end, as you go faster and faster the transition is always analog. If you look at the rise time of any device, that's an analog function. As you go faster and faster and you get 1 gigahertz, 2 gigahertz, 4 gigahertz, 8 gigahertz, 10 gigahertz—the next thing you know, you go back to analog. You're so fast that all you're dealing with is the rise time in the circuits. The performance of your device is going to be a function of the analog performance—the rise time of the device.

TANAKA: You're saying that just because of physics, the analog part of the digital components will become more important?

HILL: Right.

TANAKA: What does that mean for product design, and does that mean there's a wall that we will hit?

HILL: There is a wall and it's dictated by delays, prop delays.

TANAKA: But could it limit the Digital Revolution?

HILL: Well, I don't think so. Not in my lifetime.

TANAKA: What do you think will be the Next Big Thing, either in your industry or in the digital economy? Could there be anything as big as the Internet coming down the pike?

HILL: I think one of the biggest things coming down the pike is the elimination of the telephone system as you know it today. Within 5 years, you won't have a normal handset in your house. You'll communicate with a video image across the Internet.

Today you get on the line and you have voice and data. You dial up to Europe and it costs you a buck a minute, and in 5 years it will cost you nothing but your access charge to call Europe. By the way, it won't be just voice and data. It'll be video data as well. Your phone will be a small video camera that's looking at you, with a microphone. The world is going to an appliance model—wireless communication appliances. You don't want to be tethered to a line. The bottom line is that in order to really be untethered you've got to reduce power consumption. The faster you make a circuit, the higher the power consumption unless you lower the battery voltage. We're getting down to where you've got the limits of transistor technology to be able to have the kind of noise immunity you're going to want to have. People are going to make trade-offs in design, in power, in order to be untethered. So I don't see the compatibility between pushing the Pentium processor and untethering the world and then trying to push it down to a Celeron-type product by getting the cost out of the device. It's not only cost you've got to get out of the device, you've got to get power out of the device because its battery operated. You get the power out of the device by slowing the speed. The faster you switch the CMOS device, the higher the power consumption. By not switching it, CMOS draws very little power, so in the idle mode it's fine.

TANAKA: So the solution would be to not use anything more than a Pentium?

HILL: Or use something much less than a Pentium. Why use a gigahertz processor if you can get by with a 100 megahertz processor? By the way, the ability to make the 100 megahertz processor a tenth of the size is available. So now you consume less area and you reduce weight.

TANAKA: Will they be using the Internet or other platforms besides the Internet?

HILL: The Internet will be one vehicle. But let's talk about Microsoft Office. I think the concept of Microsoft Office will be dead.

TANAKA: Do you mean because of the ASP (application service provider) model?

HILL: Yes, because of the ASP model. And because you need a word processor and you need a spreadsheet to type a deal. But you're going to have an entry system with a small compute power and the majority of that is going to be centralized. The Windows operating system isn't going to be the vehicle.

TANAKA: What about the Intels of the world and your other major customers? Does that change the way they operate and can those guys continue to thrive?

HILL: They've got to change. There's no question.

TANAKA: Are economists measuring correctly the output of your company and others in the semiconductor industry?

HILL: I don't know that they measure our output. The reality is that semiconductors have contributed in a major way to increases in productivity, largely through the application of digital electronics, and to the efficiency of routine operations. That will continue for some time to come. One of the things that you've seen here most recently is that there is a tremendous amount of wealth that has gone out of the economy, especially in the United States with the fall of the market. That loss of wealth is going to ripple into consumer demand. We're not talking about the CEO of Marimba who went from net worth of $143 million to $13 million overnight. We're talking about the 100 or 200 engineers that were working for her, who went from $3 million market valuation to $300,000. It's going to change buying patterns, and it's going to put some pressure on consumer spending that's going to ripple back to slow this whole train down. I think that's what the Fed wants to do and that's what the Fed is doing. We're going to get back on a curve where I think the market is not going to be trying to look so far out in advance and price earnings ratios will be coming back in line. But make no mistake. Semiconductors will still grow at 15% a year, will still be profitable, and will be a major growth industry for the next 20 years.

## INTERVIEW WITH DOUG J. DUNN

*Doug J. Dunn is president, chief executive officer, and chairman of the board of management of ASML Holding N.V. of Veldhoven, The Netherlands, the worldwide leader of advanced lithography equipment critical for the manufacture of semicon-*

*ductors. Mr. Dunn was interviewed by telephone on September 22, 2000, and in person in New York on October 10, 2000, and updated on December 18, 2002.*

TANAKA: What has ASML contributed to this New Economy, to the Digital Revolution?

DUNN: ASML's contribution has been to innovate lithography into a viable low-cost, high-volume production technology in the shortest possible time. Other people can make the same imaging, but we get the imaging and the volume through at the earliest in the game.

TANAKA: How much have your products contributed to price and performance over the past 5 or 10 years, and is the pace accelerating or slowing down?

DUNN: The stock answer will be Gordon Moore's Law, which he developed 30 years ago. Now, we're in the process of making it reality. The lithography systems ASML have developed lead Moore's Law. We actually give more capability in packing density, in cost reduction, and in volume efficiencies—and outpace Gordon Moore's law.

TANAKA: In terms of time, or at a faster pace?

DUNN: In terms of timing—the migration of technology nodes. Think about it—it goes 0.25, 0.20. 0.18, 0.15 micron [line widths]. The semiconductor technology nodes—those are the heartbeats we have to live by. And in a way that heartbeat is the function of Moore's Law. You can get to 0.10, which is the complex node in 2002, with a development tool and play around with it, or you can get there with a production tool and make millions of them. We're the latter. We get to the next technology node more quickly than anyone else, which allows you to create chips with greater complexity and capacity. Since volume throughput is our claim, our hallmark, the cost also comes down at a rate equal to or greater than Moore's Law. So we get the increase in capacity and the lower cost and we get there first.

TANAKA: Would you agree that lithography is the gating factor?

DUNN: There's no doubt that lithography is the gating element. I don't say that because I work for ASML. I'd say that no matter whom I worked for, and my colleagues will totally support that. If you want to follow Moore's Law or beat it, the first thing you start to be concerned about is lithography. Once you've got the lithography, by and large, other things are relatively simple.

TANAKA: How long can you keep this rate up? Some of your charts go out to 2010 and maybe further than that?

DUNN: You see the charts go to 2010 because the longer chart won't fit on the screen. Looking out 5 years is an act of faith. You have history to base your views on. I would say right now that silicon as a basic technology has a lifetime measured in decades and that the ability to innovate in the manufacture of semiconductors in better implementation, better lithography, and better action will continue to be equal to Moore's Law. Therefore, we see no reason why lithography shouldn't play its key part in upholding Moore's Law for the next—within my horizons—15 years. After that, I just don't know. There are techniques being developed right now that will take you beyond conventional processing technology. That's why I have a lot of faith that bright engineers who are much younger than I will continue to uphold Moore's Law for a long, long time in the future. Although I can't see beyond 5 years of the engineering solutions, I'm sure that in the next 5 years bright young minds will have solved those problems and taken us beyond that—just as they always did in the past. I've been around 30 years. Every 5 years there is a problem and bright young engineers have come through and blown it away and taken us forward again. So here we are now resolving images down to 0.10 micron.

TANAKA: How would you define when this New Economy or this Digital Revolution, started? When was the defining moment?

DUNN: There are various break points you can look at. You might say the original microprocessor, and I would put that claim to Intel. However, others have claimed it before them, but I would say that would be an Intel step 25 to 30 years ago. It's not a function of a product like the microprocessor. It is more a function of complexity. Because it is a bit like a function of the human brain. We are what we are because we have sufficient neurons and network connections to get over critical mass. One difference between us and monkeys is that they have got good brains also, but there is just not just enough critical mass there. It's the same with the Digital Revolution. To do things digitally requires a lot of density and packing of components. So the world had to wait until human beings were invented and they invented semiconductors. Then they invented integrated circuits, then they invented about 0.25 micron processing. Then you got above the 10 to 20 million transistors on a chip capability, and then you got the Digital Revolution started.

TANAKA: You're saying it is not just a function of having microprocessors or semiconductors. It is a function of having the density and having human beings invent products with that technology.

DUNN: I think personally it is the density of the chip. You can have a wonderful microprocessor and it is no good. When you can get a microprocessor and other parts of the system that operate in the digital domain, you take in analog and transform it digitally, then you've got a Digital Revolution. It starts with PCs, CD players—they were the first consumer digital products—DVDs, digital boxes, and digital televisions. It's all a function of component density. Some of these things could have been invented 20 years ago, but it would have taken a machine as big as my office to have achieved the function.

TANAKA: Do you see an end to the Digital Revolution and its advances?

DUNN: The good news, for me and my kids, and maybe society, is that I don't see an end to it. It is like a marathon—the next mile is always tougher than the last mile. But we keep running marathons and keep doing the extra mile. But I see no reason why it should come to an end. Maybe sometime in the next 15-year horizon there will be a slowdown using existing silicon and what we know of today. But by then we will have developed some new compounds and new processing. We can already talk about molecular electronics and bioelectronics. I would predict no end, although we can see some changes in the way we achieve this—for example, the compression of feature sizes and the escalation of capacity.

TANAKA: Are you seeing an end at some point to the semiconductor process?

DUNN: Maybe in 15 years' time we're going to go through sometime in which other competing technologies will start to come alongside silicon and take off. It could be that in 25 to 50 years from now it is no longer a silicon-dominated industry. It is dominated by something else.

TANAKA: So it could be really that long—25 to 50 years?

DUNN: Think of the installed base of silicon. Think of the fabs that are being built right now. Think of the 5 billion square inches of silicon that was produced last year. That is a lot of football fields, right? I think that economically this industry can't die. It powers so much of the world. It is going to have a huge flywheel effect, a huge momentum. Fifteen years will go by and silicon will rule—no contest. In 15 years new things may build up and silicon will start to slow down. In 45 to 50 years perhaps we will depend not on silicon, but on something else. I think you're talking long term.

TANAKA: How do you see the Internet changing?

DUNN: I think the Internet will be changing shape and form through the next 200 years, and it will become more pervasive. What we have today will be just a mechanical thing compared to what we will have in the future. We will all have fiber [optics] to the home, blinding speeds of data access, and better-organized data.

TANAKA: What will be the Next Big Thing? We've had the microprocessor, the Internet, lots of big things that are driving this New Economy.

DUNN: If you look at more mundane things, we see them divided into PC-centric, entertainment-centric, communications-centric, and productivity. We still see those as separate things because integration levels still don't allow us to do a good combination of all those in a matchbox size appliance. You may think we do it in things like Psion organizers, but they're not really that sophisticated. I think in a few years' time we will see a tremendous merging of things which will again make a breakthrough, such as the PC and the Internet. And like the monkey made a breakthrough to a human being once he got over critical size, there will be a breakthrough, and I think it is that convergence. I think we will no longer think in discrete products. I will have an appliance on me, or embedded in me, or close to me, that will essentially allow me to do anything: download video, surf the Web, talk to my wife, program my microwave oven from 1000 miles away, and switch on my car engine. This will be something that will be really user friendly.

So the next breakthrough has to be an escalation of integration to give the performance and user interface. Right now we're all struggling to use our PCs and VCRs. The interface is lousy. I spent half an hour programming my VCR for the Olympics. I don't do it very often. You get integration at a certain level. I will say to my house, record tonight's Women's 80 meters semifinal. I will relax and sit back and watch it. That requires a degree of integration. I can do it in English, and even though my tape recorder is in Spanish, it will still understand it. I think user interface is the next breakthrough. We're all stalled by user interface. My typing is terrible. When you get that breakthrough, when you can record by thought, or by voice, you blow away more barriers and allow much greater user friendliness. That will give rise to the next blaze forward.

TANAKA: Does it mean more demand for semiconductors, too?

DUNN: It will consume hundreds of square miles of silicon.

TANAKA: What is the outlook for Europe? Many people say that Europe has a greater global view than the United States does, but that the United States is driving and leading the Digital Revolution.

DUNN: I'm not sure that I would agree.

TANAKA: I wasn't sure if you would agree on who's driving the Digital Revolution, but what is the outlook for Europe in the next 5 to 10 years as the Digital Revolution spreads and becomes more of a global phenomenon? You have mentioned how Europeans are using cell phones at a higher penetration rate than the United States. So you're actually ahead of the United States in usage. Yet many people would say the investments are in the United States because Silicon Valley is in the United States. What do you think is the correct view? How will it change?

DUNN: I'd argue your original premise that the Digital Revolution was spawned in the USA. It was not. I might tell you the PC was spawned here [in the United States] and maybe we give the full praise for that to the U.S. But look at two of the arms a bit. While the U.S. was still making analog telephones for the U.S. market the size and the weight of the brick, Europe had come together, formed the standard code GSM, which is now the prevalent standard in 75 countries worldwide. The European markets blossomed quickly with a single European standard, and the European phone manufacturers, Ericsson, Nokia, Siemens, and Alcatel, along with some others, now own the mobile phone business.

TANAKA: And what was the other one?

DUNN: If you look carefully at entertainment, the first digital entertainment was the CD player, right? You look at where the CD standards were formed. It was a European–Japanese axis. It was actually Phillips and Sony that formed the CD, who gave birth to the concept, developed the algorithms, and the patents, and they receive the royalty income from all people who make CD players to this day. Then if you look at the advances beyond the CD and look at DVD, the same situation applies.

There's nothing the U.S. has developed in the consumer digital arena that I can think of, quite frankly. If you look at digital applications for consumers, apart from media entertainment like DVD and CD, if you look at digital cameras, name a U.S. manufacturer in the formative stage of the digital camera revolution. Kodak hired a semiconductor guy to do it and what happened? It failed. Right? Sony is going great guns with camcorders and digital cameras. Europe doesn't have the same success there, but certainly the digital entertainment arena was driven by Europe. The U.S. ruled supreme in the analog set-top boxes. If you look at digital set-top boxes, however, the early ones were digital TV and the digital set-top box came out of Europe. I would contest your point that America is the only bastion for digital products. Of the three arenas, they only have the PC to claim to their fame. The digital telephone and the digital consumer products are Japanese and European.

So let's look to the future now. Look at the drivers that are going to propel the next killer products after the conventional application, which is firstly a voice transmission. Now, it is data that will become video, and versions of GSM will be the carrier. It will become the third generation technology, but that's merely like an application development. Look at Europe. What Europe has that makes it culturally strong, but difficult to communicate, are different languages. All Europeans want to communicate. So if you look at the next killer applications for digital product, it's going to be in the translation area where certainly computing power or digital transformation power will be utilized. Not just for phone activation, which we have today. And by the way, the first voice-activated digital telephone was built by a non-American company called Phillips in the Netherlands. So moving on European companies like Phillips and others—and IBM also figures in here—have taken that a stage further into voice-activated systems and also voice translation into text. So now you can buy from IBM, originally from Phillips . . . software, which you speak into and it will perform the text translation—not very good yet but getting better. And of course voice synthesis is fairly easy, so anyone can create voice synthesis.

TANAKA: Voice synthesis?

DUNN: When you have voice input and voice output and recognition of the meaning of the voice input, you very quickly are going to come to things like direct online language translation. That's because you've got voice going in, you've got translation, and you've got voice coming out. We can do both ends. It's the middle that's the difficult bit. So increased complexity of digital products will allow that.

TANAKA: How far away is true voice recognition and voice translation?

DUNN: Voice recognition as far as I'm concerned is here now. Voice synthesis is here now. It's not long before you can say to your washing machine, "I've got some dirty white shirts here, wash them please," and then your washer does them. It's voice activated. The next thing is voice translation so you can speak in English and see the output in Dutch. Europe has a greater need and therefore I would suggest that Europe is going to lead. Europe will play a strong role in the use of voice rather than keyboard for data input and ultimately in data analysis, data output, and direct online translation. So the next killer products are going to be voice-activated, voice-responsive, and direct online translation. I suspect Europe will play a strong role in that. The underlying algorithms for speech recognition activation were first developed for commercial use in Europe. If you want to go back to the origins, I would point out that the first computational systems were developed in Europe in the Second World War. The computational engines and the first computational algorithms, Boolean algebra, were developed by George Boole, a European.

TANAKA: What are the limits on software and can it continue to compound in performance? How much software do you use in your products, and isn't software becoming more of the value of your equipment? Is that a value to the customer?

DUNN: Let's take a simple example—advanced television. It's been around for 60 years now. There are about 5 megabytes of software in advanced television. Ten years ago it was probably zero, or maybe a few hundred bytes doing simple tasks. So even the simple analog product television has got a lot of software. There is more in digital television. I'm just showing the way in which software has permeated all things that we have. If you look at any analog television program, or [digital] products made by a manufacturer that have been delayed, I can guarantee you that software code has been one of the main sources of the delay. It is an issue, and one of the things that we have to face up to with software is that right now it's still very much a hand-crafted technology. People sit down and write code. There are now sophisticated techniques by which you can do structured software and reusable software, but honestly the tools are so complex and difficult and the time pressure so great that it's very rare that any [product development] program can afford the luxury, the time, to force its engineers to write software in a structured way. So you get code which is from the heart and written in long-hand, and then when you do the next generation product you can't reuse it because it's not written in a modular and reusable way.

We have to go through two stages of software development. The first is to structure our own handwritten code into modular, reusable software so we can reuse portions of it—where memory is free and processing power is free—then you can be more liberal with the amount of code that you write. The second stage will be automated techniques to write software. Some of us remember when all integrated circuits, known as ICs, were laid out by hand. We also remember the day in which the first automatic place and route software came that took that chore away from a human being. Initially it was not as compact as a hand-laid one. Now you could never lay out a 25 million-transistor chip by hand. It's got to be automatic to route it and lay out. The same with software. There will be technology developed that will take out the manual creation process of software and make it more automated.

TANAKA: In other words, you're thinking software can continue to be developed and improved along with hardware, that it can improve for the next 10 to 15 years along with the semiconductor?

DUNN: Absolutely. I would argue it's lagging behind partly because we haven't yet become skilled and scripted in the approach and also because we haven't got tools that can do it automatically. Computer design is here, but computer-aided software development is still a pipe dream by and large and that's the next breakthrough.

TANAKA: How important is software in terms of value to your customer?

DUNN: In our products there's kind of hidden software. People buy the machines as a tool together with the software inside it. Until we come along and say we can increase the throughput by 10%, how do you do that? Certainly the value of software takes on a different meaning. You cannot differentiate the value of the software from the machine itself. It's such an intrinsic part of it.

## INTERVIEW WITH MICHAEL DELL

*Michael Dell is chairman of Dell Computer, the worldwide leader in personal computers with rising shares in servers, storage, and other digital devices and services. Mr. Dell was interviewed in New York on April 4, 2002, and by e-mail.*

TANAKA: How would you define the New Economy?

DELL: The New Economy is about tools that bring people and processes closer together. It's about connectivity, efficiency, speed, and global relationships. The New Economy is ultimately about greater productivity.

TANAKA: I began doing research for this book thinking that the Technology (Digital) Revolution is superior to the Industrial Revolution of some 100 years ago. What do you think and why?

DELL: The Technology Revolution is standing on the shoulders of the Industrial Revolution. It was the rise of industry that gave us the capabilities to produce all of the technologies we enjoy today: semiconductors, photonics, genomics, etc. Digital technologies have dramatically changed the world—and will continue to do so for a long time to come—but we still owe a debt to what came before.

TANAKA: What has been Dell Computer's role in the Digital Revolution and how do you see it changing in the future?

DELL: Dell's contributions to the Digital Revolution have been in our approach to business. The Direct Model is a simple concept—providing the latest technology directly to the end user without any of the friction historically found in most industries. But there's much more to it than that. Through direct relationships with customers, we're able to listen to what they tell us they want and satisfy their needs more precisely, more quickly, and more efficiently than anyone else. Dell has served to bring the latest technology to great numbers of people, tailored to their needs, directly. And I don't see that fundamentally changing at all . . . just improving.

TANAKA: There were doubters and critics, but it appears that you have been able to successfully transplant the Dell Direct Model to Europe, the Middle East, and Africa, and more recently into Asia. What is the potential for the Digital Revolution in these overseas economies? Are there limits?

DELL: The customer benefits of the Direct Model aren't dependent on specific languages or geographies. And we've seen Direct take root around the world. But the Digital Revolution offers the same kinds of benefits—speed, efficiency, value, and ultimately greater productivity. Individuals and economies worldwide will continue to look for digital solutions for advancement. There isn't just great potential for the Digital Revolution to continue around the world, it's inevitable. And we're seeing it every day.

TANAKA: What do you believe might be the Next Big Thing or things after the Internet? When might they appear?

DELL: The possibilities associated with the Internet have barely been tapped. So I don't think the Internet's time in the spotlight is coming to a close quite yet. But the combination of multiple technologies creates enormous possibilities in terms of new industries. The intersection of technology and biology is one exciting example. The Next Big Thing will likely come as a complement to the Internet, not in place of it. But at Dell, we tend to spend most of our time focused on how we can best serve customers right now, instead of prognosticating too much about the future.

TANAKA: What do you believe is the biggest bottleneck or threat to the New Economy?

DELL: I don't think there is any credible threat to the New Economy. After all, the New Economy is about greater productivity and I expect that trend will continue. Many dot-com businesses went away over the past couple years . . . but the Internet and the productivity it offers is still alive and well. There will always be bottlenecks to that productivity. One bottleneck in the near term is broadband connectivity. But bottlenecks just expose the opportunity to reach the next level of success.

TANAKA: What do you think the government's role should be, if any, regarding the Digital Revolution or the New Economy of the next one or two decades?

DELL: The success of the New Economy requires freedom to build new relationships. Governments are often the gatekeepers of that freedom. From the deployment of broadband to ensuring open markets unburdened by tariffs, governments worldwide must create an environment where the New Economy can thrive.

## INTERVIEW WITH IRWIN JACOBS

*Dr. Irwin Jacobs is chairman and CEO of Qualcomm Inc., the leader in wireless communications protocols and software, including advanced CDMA (code division multiple access) and position location technologies. Mr. Jacobs was interviewed on October 24, 2000, and provided revisions in June 2003.*

TANAKA: I'm writing a book about how technology is contributing to the economy, and I'm focusing on the technology drivers as well as the enablers and beneficiaries of the Digital Revolution. A lot of people talk about silicon and Moore's Law, and I think one area that is undercounted is software. I believe that the key technologies that are employed in wireless communications, including CDMA, are a form of software really. During my last trip out we talked about how much cell phones add in terms of performance on an annual basis or on every upgrade cycle. That is one measure of how technology is improving. I was wondering how Qualcomm has contributed to the Digital Revolution and the New Economy and how it might in the future?

JACOBS: Well, the best focus on wireless technology improvement, one that is enabled by Moore's Law and by great strides in software, is the development and deployment of CDMA. The latest versions of CDMA support affordable, wide area, broadband wireless access. Applications and content supported by such access are increasingly major drivers of the economy, improving efficiency for business, services, education, and entertainment through a growing body of applications and increased use of the Internet. Most of us now carry devices we refer to as "cell phones" but which are increasingly powerful computers, always connected to the Internet, many with digital cameras and precise position location capability through use of global position system (GPS) satellite signals. We have developed a system called BREW that allows software developers anywhere in the world to develop new applications that, after test and certification, can be made available by mobile operators for download to their cell phones whenever desired by their customers. One application may allow a current local map to be displayed on the phone along with directions to desired businesses such as restaurants.

TANAKA: You're saying the driver would be CDMA?

JACOBS: Yes, CDMA economically supports many users with high-data-rate, "always-on" connections to the net, wherever they may be, encouraging entrepreneurs to supply a broad range of new capabilities. Users are increasingly attracted to these services, and are willing to pay for downloading new capabilities and content. The operator bills the customer based on a cost negotiated with the developer, and we facilitate payments to the developers.

TANAKA: How much more performance would go into 3G (third generation) CDMA, relative to 2G (second generation)? How much technical performance in features and functions would you get with 3G, and how much more value would that offer to the customer?

JACOBS: Third generation wireless has been developed to support efficient voice, video, and broadband data delivery to cell phones. CDMA is the technology of choice. The first version to become commercial, now supporting over 45 million subscribers, is CDMA2000 1x technology. Providing almost a doubling of voice capacity and an increase in the peak rate of data transmission from 14.4 Kbps [thousand bits per second] for second generation (2G) to 153 Kbps. Deployment is now proceeding on CDMA2000 1x EV-DO with a peak rate of 2.4 megabits per second. A high data rate provides a noticeably better user experience for many applications, but, more important, by reducing the time required to service each user, more users are able to be supported, and thus the cost of delivering packets is reduced.

TANAKA: Can we quantify that? For example, does it allow four times the usage of spectrum? Does it allow three times more convenience?

JACOBS: It's always a little hard to be precise because of the many factors involved, but 1x EV-DO technology should provide more than an order of magnitude improvement in the economics of data delivery compared to 2G.

TANAKA: "Order of magnitude" meaning 10 times?

JACOBS: Right. Each base station can support more than 10 times the number of data subscribers while providing a better user experience.

TANAKA: That's the base station economics, and then the burst rate improvement is how much?

JACOBS: Second generation systems are either 9.6 or 14.4 Kbps. Some operators have installed 2.5 generation CDMA, which supports data rates of 64 Kbps. CDMA2000 1x EV-DO supports a peak rate of 2.4 Mbps [million bits per second], a data rate improvement of over 2 orders of magnitude.

TANAKA: That's a phenomenal improvement in burst rate. So in terms of what the consumer sees, this is partly why the government doesn't really measure you guys very well.

JACOBS: Right.

TANAKA: It's hard to measure. What does the consumer see? Does he get a 10 times improvement in value or . . .

JACOBS: Again, it's the same thing that's driving people at home these days to switch over to broadband access, DSL, or cable. Early phone line modems supported perhaps 2.4 Kbps, then increased to 9.6, 14.4, 28.8, and 56.6 kilobits per second. Users continually want a higher data rate because it makes existing applications easier to use and enables new applications such as streaming audio and video. Once you get up to 2.4 megabits per second, most applications run very well, and the cost to use them is greatly reduced.

TANAKA: Could the consumer get as much as a 10 times improvement in economics, in other words, a 90% drop in costs?

JACOBS: As the cost to the operator drops an order of magnitude, then after early expenses have been amortized, prices charged to users drop, encouraging more users and more use per user, allowing the price charged by operators to drop further. I expect the cost of broadband wireless service to become quite competitive with broadband wired services while providing greater convenience with mobility. As noted earlier, Moore's Law is allowing the portable device that we are increasingly finding to be indispensible to become more and more powerful as well as compact and lightweight and with long battery life. In the next few years, we will be carrying around a device with the capabilities of today's desktop and with an "always on" connection to the Internet. What it doesn't have is a large keypad or display, but when you walk into hotels, offices, homes, or other fixed locations, you will often be able to automatically connect wirelessly to different types of peripheral devices.

TANAKA: Yes, people pull out their portable keyboard and plug it into their Palm Pilot.

JACOBS: There are a variety of compact peripherals becoming available, supporting convenient use of tremendous computing power and "always on, always available" connection to the Internet. You are always connected to the world. With reliable authentication, so that you can prove who you are, mobile commerce and the ability to access confidential information become convenient. So cell phones will be broadly used for entertainment, for education, for business, and in many new ways that are yet to become clear.

TANAKA: And if you look ahead say 10 or maybe even 20 years, do you think this rate of improvement will slow down? What rate of improvement do you see?

JACOBS: That's always hard to say. I suspect that the communication capabilities and the cost of using mobile devices will continue to come down so that, probably much before the 20-year period, the costs of connecting anywhere in the world will be very small. Long distance costs will have essentially gone away. Much of what we'll be able to do will depend on software developers and content providers, with servers anywhere in the world. Software and services for mobile devices impacting on our lives in many ways will be an exciting business for at least a decade.

TANAKA: How much of the value you deliver, do you think, is software?

JACOBS: Well, we call ourselves a chip supplier, but an important part of what we supply with the chip is the software—not only to enable basic functionality, but now software to do voice recognition, and software to do position location, software to do the audio and video decoding, so you can listen to downloaded music and view video clips. But the fact that you're also connected to the net allows many other entrepreneurs to deliver other services on the net, services that we will all be making use of in the future.

TANAKA: In other words, application software by hooking up to the net?

JACOBS: That's correct. You'll have applications that are both hosted on the net or downloaded to your portable device, your cell phone. Voice recognition will probably always be somewhat divided. With a server on the net, you can have some very large vocabulary stored, as well as a lot of information about syntax, grammar, etc., that allows you to do a much better job of voice recognition of continuous speech. In the handset you'll have more limited capability, and they'll just work hand in glove.

TANAKA: Have you thought in terms of when this Digital Revolution began and when it might end?

JACOBS: Along with Professor Jack Wozencraft, we wrote a textbook on digital communications that was published back in 1965, so it goes back a long way.

TANAKA: What was the book called?

JACOBS: *Principles of Communication Engineering.* People had been looking at digital technology and information theory, a very theoretical subject at the time, and in that book we try to point out that digital communications and processing would become very practical. Then the next big step in digital communications was the Arpanet, developed in the early '70s. At my first company, called Linkabit, I was in charge of a program to extend the Arpanet to Europe by satellite. Robert Kahn, one of the key contributors who, together with Vince Cerf, developed the Internet protocol, and I visited Europe and spoke with a number of the phone companies there, but was unable to interest them in packet communications. We did get several universities and research labs involved. That was an interesting extension of the Arpanet, which later became the Internet.

TANAKA: I didn't realize you were that involved early on. That's fabulous. What came before that?

JACOBS: I mentioned our communications textbook. An important part of information theory, based on seminal work by Claude Shannon, also provides a theoretic foundation for "source coding," now used to represent voice and video efficiently as sequences of bits in an efficient fashion and with acceptably low distortion.

TANAKA: So in other words, you're defining the beginning of this Digital Revolution in terms of when you went to coding and using bits for communication.

JACOBS: That's right. The ability to communicate efficiently with digital techniques and the Arpanet digital protocol that afforded the ability to code and network voice, pictures, movies, whatever, all that really began to fall into place in the '60s and '70s. Well, the very first birth of this was back in Claude Shannon's book that came out at the end of World War II, in 1948, I think.

TANAKA: When do you think the Digital Revolution will end?

JACOBS: Well, I keep telling people here that there's always another decade of excitement, and each year that decade slips out one more year. So I don't see an end coming in the near term.

TANAKA: In other words, you keep pushing out the next 10 years.

JACOBS: Right, a year at a time.

TANAKA: What do you think might be the Next Big Thing?

JACOBS:  Not just one Big Thing, but rather the ready availability of the latest in applications and content that enrich our education, entertainment, commerce, business, medical, and health needs and do so conveniently, inexpensively, and individually tailored.

TANAKA:  I guess you're saying that there are going to be software apps that we don't even know about today.

JACOBS:  Applications we can access on our mobile devices will just get better and more easy to use and therefore available to more people.

TANAKA:  That's great. I was wondering if there was anything that you could cite as an example of how fast things have evolved in terms of digital technologies. Just an example of productivity or how fast things change.

JACOBS:  We had very large numbers of employees throughout the life of Linkabit—illustrators, writers, a high ratio of secretaries. We have many fewer at Qualcomm, since we accomplish many of these functions ourselves with less effort and more accuracy and in a shorter time. With e-mail, companies today can be more horizontally organized with rapid communication across management levels and functions. All of this greatly benefits productivity.

TANAKA:  It's interesting that you mention this because an important message in my research is that productivity didn't appear when it was supposed to 10 to 20 years ago.

JACOBS:  Right. Everybody kept questioning it, but it was definitely moving ahead.

TANAKA:  So you think it just wasn't being measured?

JACOBS:  It was hard to measure. Just in the time between forming Linkabit and forming Qualcomm, the changes have been dramatic for productivity. The way we give courses and train people has changed. A lot of us are now up on the Internet. To make a presentation, you used to have to send all the materials out to an outsource group, and then it took several days, came back incorrect, and it was really hard to get the whole thing straight. Now you just do it yourself. In fact, these days, of course, I take along a laptop, and the night before I give the talk I edit it and arrange it.

TANAKA:  Qualcomm is clearly one of the primary enablers of the Digital Revolution. Thank you very much for speaking with me.

## INTERVIEW WITH STEPHEN FODOR

*Stephen P. A. Fodor, Ph.D., is founder, chairman, and CEO of Affymetrix, Inc., a leading provider of genetic analysis systems. Dr. Fodor's interview was conducted by telephone on December 11, 2000, and was updated in December 2002. The Affymetrix*

*proprietary GeneChip platform utilizes ongoing advancements in semiconductor fab-*
*rication technologies to make DNA microarrays and gene analysis increasingly af-*
*fordable and productive. The surface of the GeneChip array or "biochip" contains*
*billions of single strands of DNA known as probes that are approximately 25 DNA*
*"letters" long. Currently, a set of two GeneChip arrays contains probes for over*
*33,000 genes available through public databases. To use the array, RNA is extracted*
*from a sample (blood or biopsy tissue), prepared, and then allowed to hybridize with*
*the chip. The sample RNA binds strongly to the matching chip-bound probes. A laser*
*scanner is then used to read the pattern of genes present in the sample. As an example,*
*one can compare the genes that are only found in breast cancer tissue when compared*
*to normal breast tissue, and can use these unique genes as markers for breast cancer.*

TANAKA: I was wondering how your use of digital technologies has improved productivity for Affymetrix and for the performance of your
GeneChip product.

FODOR: The real enhancement is that it is allowing people to ask questions
that could never be asked before—highly parallel questions about the entire
genome.

TANAKA: And how do you measure the value of that?

FODOR: The biotech world is characterized by discovery, so new high-
throughput tools or technologies would allow you to make quantum jumps
in discovery, and therefore increase productivity. It is not quite like a
straight manufacturing field, where you know the consumer market and
make predictions like "we want to have a five-fold increase in output or a
three-fold drop in price." It's much more than that. Here is this vast, unknown area of biology that has been dumped on our lap after 5 billion years
of evolution. How do we solve some of the intricate puzzles that are contained in it?

TANAKA: What are these technologies, these various digital technologies, doing to allow you to do what you couldn't do before?

FODOR: I think that what the digital technologies are doing, particularly for
the genome and for drug discovery, are allowing you to take a whole new
systems' approach to problem solving. There is a big difference between the
digital technologies that allow you to keep track of samples, such as computers, robotics, or high-throughput screening and the idea of applying digital technologies and DNA chips to study the entire human genome. I think
those are two very separate things, and I just want to contrast those two.

TANAKA: Please do.

FODOR: Imagine that I have a pharmaceutical company and I can do experiments using microtiter trays. I am going to keep track of each sample and

each receptor that I am studying with a computer. That is probably a more classical increase in productivity by application of high-tech to pharmaceutical research.

I think we are now undergoing a paradigm shift that says we are going to simultaneously look at 33,000 genes across the human genome and will do this by modeling all gene interactions with the aid of digital technology in order to try to understand all the molecular pathways. So, I am no longer looking at one molecular pathway or one receptor at a time. I will be looking at the entire system and trying to deconvolute the whole circuitry of the cell. This effort has been really spurred on by the human genome. Once we have all the components of the cell, how do we apply technology, digital technology, and DNA chips in order to understand the basic molecular circuitry of life?

TANAKA: But how does that work? How do these new technologies come into play?

FODOR: It is important to point out that the genome is really big. For example, computer technology itself has become efficient at organizing lots of data. The genome has three billion base pairs per genome, and we have barely sequenced the first one. The genome is at the magnitude where it starts to push the limits even for some of the most current computer technology. What has been missing up until now, I think, has been the other piece, the piece that allows you to experimentally do something with that information, and that is what these chips allow you to do.

TANAKA: What do these biochips allow you to do experimentally?

FODOR: The biochip in terms of information content is "phase matched" with the human genome. It allows you to study perturbations of the human genome on the same scale as the genome itself. So as an example, a previous researcher would look at the expression of BRCA1 in cancer and then try to understand cancer. That is like trying to understand an automobile engine by going in and looking at the fuel pump. You can't do it. It's just not enough. If I was investigating an automobile and all I had was a core centimeter field of view, I would never understand it. But, if I can take a full-blown picture of the auto and have a way to take all the parts apart and keep track of all of them and in addition be able to make perturbations and understand how those perturbations change the whole system, I can understand that system. You need to have tools that are matched with that level of information of the system you are trying to study.

TANAKA: You are saying, using the car analogy, that you would be able to look at all of the parts of a car at the same time?

FODOR: Exactly. So now a researcher can say, "I think BRCA1 is important and I want to watch its behavior, but I am also watching over those other 30,000 genes so I am sure not to miss anything else."

TANAKA: How many genes will you be looking at? How many are out there?

FODOR: I think in the near term, over the next 10 to 20 years, there is absolutely no doubt in my mind the answer to that question is going to be the *whole genome*.

TANAKA: How many genes is that?

FODOR: Well, there are anywhere from 30,000 to 120,000 genes, depending on who you believe, and exactly what you call *a gene.*

TANAKA: So with 30,000 to 120,000 genes in the human genome, how many can you look at now in one chip?

FODOR: We have a set of chips that looks at over 33,000 genes simultaneously—the entire known human genome. And that is not limited in any fundamental way. That will just keep increasing. As more information is known about the genome, we will come out with new revisions with a higher density. The chips have plenty of processing future in terms of capacity, but what I might point out is that the genes themselves only constitute around 4% to 5% of the total human genome. There is an enormous amount of data in the human genome, and we have no idea of its purpose.

TANAKA: What's the other 95%?

FODOR: Not much is known about it. Since some of the regions between genes are conserved from organism to organism, that suggests that they are biologically important, although no one is quite clear as to their function. Some of these are gene enhancers and probably regulate transcription at some level. That will all be investigated. It all stems from the question you asked me, of how many genes people will be looking at. I believe that it is a monumental accomplishment to say that we have sequenced the first genome. It is as if we had cracked open an undiscovered tomb or a pyramid and walked inside, and there was writing all over the walls, but we had no idea how to decipher its language. Going back to the car analogy, what people are currently doing is somewhat like pulling a spark plug and seeing what happens. They try to perturb the system by knocking out a gene. That does not necessarily tell you the fundamental principles of how the entire system works. It just tells you how to break it and sometimes, by trial and error, how to fix it. That's kind of where we are on the genome.

TANAKA: By introducing the GeneChip microarray, how much time do you think that this technology has saved the industry and researchers?

FODOR: An order of magnitude. If you didn't have a convenient format to do this in, such as the microarray technology, you would have had a couple of monumental and expensive efforts funded by federal agencies that would have attempted to do a couple genome-like experiments. It would have been tens of millions of dollars just to try and do a few experiments. Now, what is going to happen is that the genome will be available to anyone. The vision for the technology is that within 5 to 10 years you will be able to do this kind of research in an undergraduate course. It is a huge difference. How do you measure that? I am not sure.

The second way to think about this is how this technology will then screen multiple genomes. To get the first human genome required 10 years of funding, a lot of technology development, and brute force. There was the competition between Celera and the U.S. government's Human Genome Project to sequence the genome, and people spent probably close to a billion dollars. Now, scientists, using a new generation of our arrays with up to 60 million probes each, have completed the screening of 50 genomes to discover common human genetic variations. This could be accomplished in an extremely cost-effective way because once you know the genetic sequence, all you have to do is print out the arrays.

TANAKA: Will you screen individual genomes for 50 different people?

FODOR: Yes, individual genomes. Of course, after you do the next 50, it is going to be just a matter of time before the next 5000 are completed.

TANAKA: And scientists have done this in 1 year?

FODOR: Perlegen Sciences, an affiliate of Affymetrix, took approximately 1 year to screen 50 genomes. And, with future shrink of these biochips and the amount of information density that we will be able to cram onto them over time, this will just get easier and easier. The full genome systems approach is going to be the rule rather than the exception.

TANAKA: What was the cost of a full genome analysis by Perlegen?

FODOR: The first 50 genomes cost approximately 100 million dollars.

TANAKA: Basically, 2 million dollars a genome. What would it cost in 5 years?

FODOR: I don't know. But I think that the path is clearly set in that we will be doing whole genome analysis, and I think you will see two flavors of these over the next 5 or 10 years. First, there will be this continued expansion on the so-called gene expression area where researchers will be looking at the genes and asking which genes are involved in specific functions. If there are 100,000 genes, researchers will be able to look at all 100,000 genes simultaneously. Second, we'll be trying to understand the diversity of the genome in total and its association with health.

TANAKA: By diversity you mean from one person to the next?

FODOR: Yes.

TANAKA: So, you will be comparing genome to genome?

FODOR: There are two major fields unfolding. Right now people are really interested in looking at the 33,000 genes and their function. We only know the function of about 10,000 of them. What is the so-called molecular circuitry of the cell? When a cell goes from one type of cell and transforms into another type of cell, what is the circuitry that is turned on and expressed?

The second field is trying to discover why we are different, given that we all have the same set of genes. To answer that, we need to study the diversity question. We need to do a base-to-base comparison throughout the genome and understand the differences between two people.

TANAKA: So even though we may understand the circuitry of the cell, we also want to understand, if we have the same genes, why are they acting differently?

FODOR: That's right. It is all part of the structure of the human genome. Currently though, no one understands the global structure of the human genome.

TANAKA: So even though people are saying we have mapped the human genome, all they are really saying is that we have mapped what we think are the important genes in the genome, but we don't know much about the stuff in between.

FODOR: Yes. We are probably within 90% of knowing where most of the genes are on the genome. We do not yet understand a lot about the concerted expression of these genes. For example, when you go from an egg to a fully developed person, you go from one cell into billions of different cells, each of them expressing different parts of the genome. That whole symphony of how genes are turned on and how the circuitry works is still unknown. Moreover, the whole symphony has to be studied in different diseases and different states, under different drugs, etc.

TANAKA: Could this have been considered without digital technology?

FODOR: No. Additionally, new technologies are yet to be invented.

TANAKA: If you look at the technologies you have now, particularly the GeneChip microarray, how many more years do you think you will continue to make the chip "faster, better, cheaper"? Are there any physical or scientific limits to improving the biochip 5, 10, or 20 years from now?

FODOR: I think that in our case, the roadmap is very clear. It is a question of market size, adoption, and investment. Technically, there are some fantastic things we can do, but you have to justify those technical advances based on people absorbing and adopting those technical advances. I think that the technical improvements for the genome, for example, the microarray, are going to be dictated by the ability of the scientific community to understand its value. Let me give you an example. We currently sell chips with 500,000 probes on them. Three to five years ago people could not conduct experiments on 500,000 unique pieces of DNA at the same time. They did a couple at a time. Now all of a sudden, they are faced with 500,000 simultaneous assays. There are many questions that stem out of these technical innovations, such as, how do we do the experiments? How do we understand the experiments? How do we handle the data? That is where these other digital technologies come in, the advances in computers, storage devices, and so on. You need all the ancillary support around this technology so that the researcher can keep up with the amount of experimental results. If we weren't limited by having this kind of information support structure, there is no technical reason that would prevent us from increasing the information density on the chips. In the next 5, 10 years we could increase it by a factor of 10 and maybe even by a factor of 100!

TANAKA: Could you increase the density on a GeneChip by 100 times?

FODOR: Yes, by going from your current feature size of 18 microns down to 2 microns, you increase the information density by more than a factor of 100. At a 2-micron size, you get a factor of 10 in each dimension of resolution, or a factor of 10 squared, which is 100 times more genetic information. So, every chip we would make at 2 microns would contain the same information as 100 of today's chips. The question is: how will the community absorb that? I certainly think that over the next 5 to 10 years we will go into higher and higher resolution. The technical path is clear. We will be focused on providing the entire technical solution to people, and this will allow them to take advantage of that sort of processing power.

TANAKA: There are analogies in the PC industry during the last 10 years. Everything came up around the PC. The software, support, storage, networking, and access to the Internet—all of these things, developed along with the advances in computing. I have been looking at the basic drivers, the silicon, the software. You are taking the same digital technologies and applying them to a completely different area, genomics—and the public does not yet really appreciate it. You are on a Moore's Law type of price-performance curve on silicon, and taking advantage of other advances in magnetic storage and software. Are you thinking that you can keep doing this for 5 to 10 years?

FODOR: Actually, I see we could probably do this for the next 25 to 30 years. I actually think that it will be at least that long before people have a really good understanding of what is happening throughout the entire human genome. We will make a lot of advances over the next 10 years, but I think that 15 to 20 years from now it will be commonplace to be doing whole genome analysis at the undergraduate level for, of course, simple organisms.

TANAKA: What does this mean for society? What will it mean for healthcare, how we do things, how we live, and the quality of life?

FODOR: I hope that what will happen is that people are going to begin to appreciate the diversity of human beings. Ultimately, I think that will help people. We will get away from this sort of medieval point of view about some superiority of ethnics and background, etc. What we will see is that everybody's genome is quite similar, and hopefully that will help people accept each other better. And, the areas where we differ in our genome will hopefully help us understand ourselves a lot better. In terms of healthcare, we will be able to dive into the molecular basis of life. We will be able to understand much more about this information molecule that actually codes for our life, it is both the program and the information storage device.

TANAKA: What is the program?

FODOR: The DNA is the program of life and it also stores the information for life. You have this massive calculation going on via the DNA and the calculation is evolution.

TANAKA: Are you talking in terms of evolution over several generations?

FODOR: Yes, I think that over time we will be more focused on that issue. We've got this molecule of life, DNA. It is constantly evolving or adding diversity from generation to generation. I just think it is a fantastic thing. I believe that people will begin to understand and appreciate the commonality among us in terms of genetic sequences. Obviously, as soon as we understand what is happening at the DNA level, we will be able to address our needs in terms of healthcare and other things.

TANAKA: To change the focus a bit, I'm trying to relate this to the broad reality of the economy. I'm trying to estimate what is not being measured in GDP accounts. In other words, what improvements to the economy and to the value of the products and services you provide are not being captured by the economic statistics?

FODOR: I generally don't think about things in that way. I think about the new opportunities that the whole field opens up. But to me, the real benefit here is that you are really opening up new fields and you are looking at human diversity, by understanding the circuitry of the cell, and the DNA itself and its language and the massive calculations that this molecule is performing through evolution. Those are going to have further implications in terms of novel things, whether it's "DNA computers" or different ways to think about information storage or processing. I do not know how you measure all those things. It is a self-sustaining cycle. As you innovate and get into these new concepts, you need to put good business practices behind them because it is ultimately how you finance these new things. To me, that's the real value to the economy.

TANAKA: What should the government do, or should it do anything, to help the Genomic Revolution?

FODOR: That is a good question. The government has done a pretty good job, I think, in terms of the genome community. One of the big questions was in terms of people patenting the genome, and I think the government has done a pretty good job in making sure that there is broad public access to the sequence of the genome, but I think there needs to be more stringent requirements on genomic patents. I think that is very, very important. It is like having the Internet as a globally accessible tool. Maybe you should be able to build commerce off of it. If the Internet, the interstate highway system, the national communications systems, telephone lines, and the infrastructure of power going to everybody's home are national priorities, I would argue that there is also national priority in the human genome. I think that this is the appropriate level for government involvement—to make sure that these fundamental fountains of information are put in place so that we can expand commerce on top of it.

TANAKA: Creating a common fundamental understanding?

FODOR: Yes, fundamental understanding and fundamental data. The human genome is very much like having a public database so that people can develop commerce off it, very much like the Internet. You want to have it as the backbone on which commerce can be built. That sort of prevents people from locking it up legally. Can you imagine if the government had allowed a company to come in and patent and own the human genome? Think about how that would stifle research and the economy.

TANAKA: I think what we're talking about sounds like a whole new area of science that's opening up. This is important to society, but how important is it to the economy?

FODOR: It has to be important, but again, there is the question of adoption. For example, how long will it take for perfume or cosmetic companies to get very interested in looking at genetic profiles to understand how they should market to different individuals? Will General Foods be interested in looking at genetic variations and who likes to eat what kinds of food? Will Kawasaki be interested in who has "risk-taking genes" to sell them motorcycles? Or will people be very interested in their ethnic roots?

I think there are three levels of how this will play out. There are *serious issues* like healthcare, which I think is the driving force right now and shows no sign of letting up. There are *lifestyle issues* that will also grow, like the genetics of choice. Do I have the right variety of enzymes to biosynthesize all the vitamins I need? Should I be eating some different health foods? What is my metabolism like? Do I like these perfumes or those perfumes, these foods or those foods? May I eat these things without consequence? Those are all genetic lifestyle decisions. The third is just fun or *knowledge-based*. What is my family heritage or the history of mankind? That is the benefit of where we are with genetics. I think there is just a fantastic set of opportunities that are going to come upon us, we just need to pick those opportunities based on people's wants.

TANAKA: Do you have to pick the ones that are commercially desirable right now?

FODOR: You bet. But the general solution to healthcare problems has to wait for our understanding of the genome itself. If you can come up with technologies that allow people to do what they can't do any other way, that's the real win.

TANAKA: This is interesting because economic accounting can be fairly rigid. It doesn't account very well for products or services that are brand new.

FODOR: That is my point exactly. That is part of the problem with the way of normal economic analysis. I've experienced this. Ten years ago, I would have diagnostic companies come into Affymetrix and say, "Why are you going to develop these chips that can look at 100,000 pieces of DNA simultaneously? I can do everything I need to do with eight." Everybody was looking at a handful of cystic fibrosis mutations, or they were thinking about doing a simple diagnostic on sickle-cell anemia. The problem is that the market wasn't there. You develop these technologies, but you also have to develop the market.

TANAKA: But my point is this: economists are trying to measure the economy and are looking at products that have been sold for years.

FODOR: They are making a fundamental assumption that the market for X exists and they are trying to figure out how to better fill that market need. That's fundamentally different, I think, from new technology innovations which allow a breakout scenario for a whole new area. Three or four years ago, people would ask us, "How big is the gene expression market going to be and do you think it's a 50 million dollar a year opportunity?" In 2001 we reported over 200 million dollars in revenue. Now I think people are very comfortable saying that in 5 years it will be over a billion dollar market. What has happened is that an enabling technology has come along that has opened a new field that allows people to do things that they could never do before. Now it has become a necessity to do these experiments in order to be competitive in the life sciences.

TANAKA: Has it become a necessity?

FODOR: It has become a necessity. You cannot be competitive in life sciences research and the world of drug discovery without doing these experiments. That's really what's happened. Four years ago when I would go to scientific symposiums and people would talk about genetic research, some professor would get up and present work that his graduates did for the last 4 years, and he'd look at eight genes in two or three different tumor types. The poor kids had spent 4 years doing this, and in the next talk I'd get up there and talk about looking at 10,000 genes simultaneously. It was that much of a paradigm shift, practically overnight.

TANAKA: I understand that you developed the first biochip. That was when?

FODOR: We developed our first prototype in 1989 and first started distributing the product to collaborators in 1994. Now we have an installed base of over 740 GeneChip systems worldwide. In a matter of a few years, it has gone from almost obscurity to a fundamental technique in modern life sciences.

TANAKA: This is exciting. I've talked to a lot of people who are service providers, users, and enablers of the Digital Revolution, but you're talking about a whole new market that is just beginning. Who knows how big it is going to get, but genetics could be the Next Big Thing.

FODOR: I think genetics is going to be a big deal. People are going to think about how to make money off of it so that it can be a major driver in the economy. But, in the long term, what is the advantage of this technology? Looking out 50 to 100 years, people will really want us to be investing in technology so we better understand ourselves and our health, from healthcare issues to lifestyle issues to common knowledge interest issues. I think the investment in these technologies is going to increase dramatically. What the timing is, I don't know. I also don't know how fast society can adopt it and embrace it. However, I have certainly seen, firsthand, how fast it can happen, and it has been a complete transformation.

*A special thanks to Gordon Moore, Rick Hill, Doug Dunn, Michael Dell, Irwin Jacobs, and Stephen Fodor for taking time out of their busy schedules to help me understand and validate the concept of Digital Deflation and how rapidly improving technologies will drive the economy of the future.*

*—Graham Tanaka*

## Tanaka Capital Management P/E Conversion Table

| S&P: 500 Composite, P/E Ratio 4-Qtr. Future Earnings (1955–2000) | | | | S&P: 500 Composite, P/E Ratio* 4-Qtr. Future Earnings (2Q1985–2Q2001) | | | |
|---|---|---|---|---|---|---|---|
| GDP Deflator | P/E | GDP Deflator | P/E | 10-Yr Treasury Rate | P/E | 10-Yr Treasury Rate | P/E |
| 0.1% | 52.4 | 3.3% | 13.8 | 0.1% | 1846.0 | 3.3% | 34.2 |
| 0.2% | 40.2 | 3.4% | 13.7 | 0.2% | 837.3 | 3.4% | 33.1 |
| 0.3% | 34.5 | 3.5% | 13.5 | 0.3% | 527.3 | 3.5% | 32.0 |
| 0.4% | 30.9 | 3.6% | 13.4 | 0.4% | 379.8 | 3.6% | 31.0 |
| 0.5% | 28.4 | 3.7% | 13.2 | 0.5% | 294.5 | 3.7% | 30.0 |
| 0.6% | 26.5 | 3.8% | 13.1 | 0.6% | 239.2 | 3.8% | 29.1 |
| 0.7% | 24.9 | 3.9% | 13.0 | 0.7% | 200.6 | 3.9% | 28.3 |
| 0.8% | 23.7 | 4.0% | 12.8 | 0.8% | 172.3 | 4.0% | 27.5 |
| 0.9% | 22.7 | 4.1% | 12.7 | 0.9% | 150.6 | 4.1% | 26.7 |
| 1.0% | 21.8 | 4.2% | 12.6 | 1.0% | 133.6 | 4.2% | 26.0 |
| 1.1% | 21.0 | 4.3% | 12.5 | 1.1% | 119.8 | 4.3% | 25.3 |
| 1.2% | 20.3 | 4.4% | 12.4 | 1.2% | 108.5 | 4.4% | 24.7 |
| 1.3% | 19.7 | 4.5% | 12.3 | 1.3% | 99.0 | 4.5% | 24.0 |
| 1.4% | 19.2 | 4.6% | 12.2 | 1.4% | 91.0 | 4.6% | 23.4 |
| 1.5% | 18.7 | 4.7% | 12.1 | 1.5% | 84.1 | 4.7% | 22.9 |
| 1.6% | 18.2 | 4.8% | 12.0 | 1.6% | 78.1 | 4.8% | 22.3 |
| 1.7% | 17.8 | 4.9% | 11.9 | 1.7% | 72.9 | 4.9% | 21.8 |
| 1.8% | 17.4 | 5.0% | 11.8 | 1.8% | 68.3 | 5.0% | 21.3 |
| 1.9% | 17.0 | 5.1% | 11.7 | 1.9% | 64.2 | 5.1% | 20.8 |
| 2.0% | 16.7 | 5.2% | 11.6 | 2.0% | 60.6 | 5.2% | 20.4 |
| 2.1% | 16.4 | 5.3% | 11.5 | 2.1% | 57.3 | 5.3% | 19.9 |
| 2.2% | 16.1 | 5.4% | 11.5 | 2.2% | 54.3 | 5.4% | 19.5 |
| 2.3% | 15.9 | 5.5% | 11.4 | 2.3% | 51.7 | 5.5% | 19.1 |
| 2.4% | 15.6 | 6.0% | 11.0 | 2.4% | 49.2 | 6.0% | 17.3 |
| 2.5% | 15.4 | 6.5% | 10.7 | 2.5% | 47.0 | 6.5% | 15.8 |
| 2.6% | 15.1 | 7.0% | 10.4 | 2.6% | 44.9 | 7.0% | 14.5 |
| 2.7% | 14.9 | 7.5% | 10.1 | 2.7% | 43.0 | 7.5% | 13.4 |
| 2.8% | 14.7 | 8.0% | 9.9 | 2.8% | 41.3 | 8.0% | 12.5 |
| 2.9% | 14.5 | 8.5% | 9.6 | 2.9% | 39.7 | 8.5% | 11.6 |
| 3.0% | 14.3 | 9.0% | 9.4 | 3.0% | 38.2 | 9.0% | 10.9 |
| 3.1% | 14.1 | 9.5% | 9.2 | 3.1% | 36.8 | 9.5% | 10.2 |
| 3.2% | 14.0 | 10.0% | 9.1 | 3.2% | 35.4 | 10.0% | 9.7 |

\* Often Referred to as the "Fed Model."

$y=3.7646x^{(-.03811)}$

$r^2=.5184$

$r= -.72$

$y=.6994x^{(-1.1405)}$

$r^2=.7038$

$r= -.84$

Sources: Bureau of Labor Statistics; Federal Reserve; Tanaka Capital Management, Inc.

## Household Tangible, Net Financial, and Equity-Like Assets as Percentage of Net Worth

Consumer's Tangible – Financial Assets Shifts

| | (1) | (2) | (3) | (4) | (5) | (6) | (7) | (8) | (9) | (10) | (11) |
|---|---|---|---|---|---|---|---|---|---|---|---|
| | | | | | Assets as % of Net Worth | | | | | | |
| | Net | | Tangible Assets | | | Financial Assets | | | | Liabilities | Net Financial |
| | Worth | Inflation | Total | Housing | Total | Common | Mutual | Com. Stk. | Liquid | as % of | Assets |
| | ($Bil.) | (CPI) | Tangible | & Land | Financial | Stocks | Funds | & M Fund | Assets | Net Worth | (5) - (10) |
| 1950 | $1,044 | 1.10 % | 36.6 % | 23.4 % | 70.7 % | 12.3 % | 0.3 % | 12.6 % | 11.9 % | 7.3 % | 63.4 % |
| 1951 | 1,145 | 7.95 | 37.1 | 23.7 | 70.3 | 13.2 | 0.3 | 13.5 | 11.6 | 7.4 | 62.9 |
| 1952 | 1,195 | 2.32 | 38.4 | 24.7 | 69.8 | 12.6 | 0.3 | 13.0 | 11.9 | 8.1 | 61.6 |
| 1953 | 1,230 | 0.78 | 39.7 | 25.7 | 69.3 | 11.9 | 0.3 | 12.2 | 12.4 | 8.9 | 60.3 |
| 1954 | 1,325 | 0.31 | 38.9 | 25.5 | 70.3 | 15.0 | 0.5 | 15.5 | 12.3 | 9.2 | 61.1 |
| 1955 | 1,435 | -0.22 | 39.0 | 25.6 | 71.0 | 17.3 | 0.5 | 17.8 | 12.0 | 10.0 | 61.0 |
| 1956 | 1,532 | 1.43 | 39.3 | 25.8 | 71.0 | 17.7 | 0.6 | 18.3 | 12.0 | 10.4 | 60.7 |
| 1957 | 1,566 | 3.40 | 40.7 | 26.7 | 70.2 | 15.6 | 0.6 | 16.2 | 12.4 | 10.9 | 59.3 |
| 1958 | 1,711 | 2.70 | 38.8 | 25.7 | 71.9 | 18.8 | 0.8 | 19.6 | 12.3 | 10.7 | 61.2 |
| 1959 | 1,802 | 1.01 | 38.7 | 25.8 | 72.7 | 19.8 | 0.9 | 20.7 | 12.4 | 11.4 | 61.3 |
| 1960 | 1,866 | 1.46 | 39.1 | 26.1 | 72.9 | 19.3 | 0.9 | 20.2 | 12.7 | 12.0 | 60.9 |
| 1961 | 2,024 | 0.99 | 37.6 | 25.3 | 74.3 | 21.9 | 1.1 | 23.0 | 12.6 | 11.9 | 62.4 |
| 1962 | 2,079 | 1.23 | 38.3 | 25.7 | 74.4 | 20.7 | 1.0 | 21.7 | 13.5 | 12.7 | 61.7 |
| 1963 | 2,184 | 1.29 | 38.1 | 25.4 | 75.3 | 21.5 | 1.1 | 22.7 | 14.2 | 13.4 | 61.9 |
| 1964 | 2,353 | 1.31 | 37.2 | 24.7 | 76.4 | 23.1 | 1.2 | 24.3 | 14.4 | 13.6 | 62.8 |
| 1965 | 2,536 | 1.64 | 36.3 | 23.9 | 77.5 | 24.3 | 1.4 | 25.6 | 14.7 | 13.8 | 63.7 |
| 1966 | 2,611 | 3.01 | 38.1 | 24.9 | 76.2 | 21.0 | 1.3 | 22.3 | 15.1 | 14.3 | 61.9 |
| 1967 | 2,905 | 2.69 | 36.6 | 23.6 | 77.1 | 23.5 | 1.5 | 25.0 | 15.1 | 13.7 | 63.4 |
| 1968 | 3,262 | 4.24 | 36.4 | 23.6 | 76.8 | 25.0 | 1.5 | 26.5 | 14.7 | 13.3 | 63.6 |
| 1969 | 3,304 | 5.43 | 39.2 | 25.2 | 74.8 | 17.8 | 1.3 | 19.0 | 14.6 | 14.0 | 60.8 |
| 1970 | 3,464 | 5.89 | 39.7 | 25.3 | 74.1 | 16.5 | 1.2 | 17.7 | 15.4 | 13.8 | 60.3 |
| 1971 | 3,834 | 4.23 | 39.1 | 25.0 | 74.6 | 17.0 | 1.3 | 18.2 | 15.9 | 13.7 | 60.9 |
| 1972 | 4,382 | 3.27 | 38.7 | 25.1 | 74.7 | 18.6 | 1.2 | 19.7 | 15.8 | 13.4 | 61.3 |
| 1973 | 4,548 | 6.24 | 42.2 | 27.5 | 72.2 | 13.1 | 0.9 | 14.0 | 16.7 | 14.4 | 57.8 |
| 1974 | 4,576 | 10.99 | 44.5 | 27.6 | 71.1 | 8.2 | 0.6 | 8.8 | 18.0 | 15.5 | 55.5 |
| 1975 | 5,200 | 9.19 | 43.3 | 27.2 | 71.4 | 9.6 | 0.7 | 10.3 | 17.3 | 14.7 | 56.7 |
| 1976 | 5,852 | 5.78 | 42.8 | 27.2 | 71.9 | 10.9 | 0.6 | 11.5 | 17.3 | 14.7 | 57.2 |
| 1977 | 6,386 | 6.47 | 45.5 | 29.6 | 70.0 | 8.5 | 0.6 | 9.1 | 17.6 | 15.5 | 54.5 |
| 1978 | 7,214 | 7.61 | 46.6 | 30.7 | 69.4 | 7.6 | 0.5 | 8.1 | 17.2 | 16.0 | 53.4 |
| 1979 | 8,325 | 11.22 | 46.9 | 31.3 | 69.0 | 8.1 | 0.5 | 8.6 | 16.3 | 15.9 | 53.1 |
| 1980 | 9,533 | 13.53 | 46.0 | 30.9 | 69.3 | 9.2 | 0.5 | 9.7 | 15.9 | 15.3 | 54.0 |
| 1981 | 10,305 | 10.40 | 47.0 | 32.0 | 68.2 | 7.6 | 0.5 | 8.0 | 16.6 | 15.2 | 53.0 |
| 1982 | 11,074 | 6.19 | 45.8 | 31.1 | 69.0 | 7.5 | 0.5 | 8.0 | 16.9 | 14.8 | 54.2 |
| 1983 | 11,946 | 3.16 | 44.6 | 30.2 | 70.6 | 7.8 | 0.7 | 8.6 | 17.2 | 15.2 | 55.4 |
| 1984 | 12,839 | 4.73 | 45.7 | 31.3 | 70.1 | 6.7 | 0.8 | 7.5 | 18.2 | 15.8 | 54.3 |
| 1985 | 14,350 | 3.53 | 45.8 | 32.0 | 70.8 | 7.4 | 1.4 | 8.8 | 17.3 | 16.6 | 54.2 |
| 1986 | 15,794 | 1.95 | 45.5 | 31.9 | 71.3 | 8.4 | 2.1 | 10.5 | 17.2 | 16.7 | 54.5 |
| 1987 | 16,808 | 3.67 | 46.2 | 32.5 | 71.0 | 7.8 | 2.3 | 10.0 | 17.0 | 17.2 | 53.8 |
| 1988 | 18,379 | 4.07 | 45.9 | 32.4 | 71.4 | 8.6 | 2.2 | 10.8 | 16.6 | 17.3 | 54.1 |
| 1989 | 20,175 | 4.80 | 45.2 | 32.2 | 71.9 | 9.6 | 2.3 | 11.9 | 15.9 | 17.2 | 54.8 |
| 1990 | 20,508 | 5.42 | 45.5 | 32.2 | 72.8 | 8.7 | 2.2 | 10.9 | 15.9 | 18.3 | 54.5 |
| 1991 | 21,915 | 4.24 | 43.1 | 30.6 | 75.0 | 11.6 | 2.6 | 14.2 | 14.8 | 18.1 | 56.9 |
| 1992 | 22,775 | 3.04 | 42.5 | 30.5 | 75.7 | 12.6 | 3.1 | 15.7 | 14.2 | 18.2 | 57.5 |
| 1993 | 23,928 | 2.96 | 41.4 | 29.7 | 77.0 | 13.6 | 4.0 | 17.6 | 13.2 | 18.4 | 58.6 |
| 1994 | 24,611 | 2.61 | 41.6 | 29.6 | 77.6 | 12.6 | 4.0 | 16.6 | 12.7 | 19.2 | 58.4 |
| 1995 | 27,343 | 2.82 | 39.1 | 27.9 | 79.5 | 15.3 | 4.2 | 19.5 | 12.1 | 18.6 | 60.9 |
| 1996 | 29,853 | 2.92 | 37.5 | 26.8 | 80.8 | 16.3 | 5.0 | 21.3 | 11.6 | 18.2 | 62.5 |
| 1997 | 33,589 | 2.34 | 35.5 | 25.5 | 81.8 | 18.5 | 5.8 | 24.3 | 10.8 | 17.4 | 64.5 |
| 1998 | 37,019 | 1.55 | 34.6 | 24.9 | 82.5 | 19.4 | 6.4 | 25.8 | 10.8 | 17.1 | 65.4 |
| 1999 | 42,031 | 2.18 | 32.8 | 23.8 | 83.7 | 22.0 | 7.4 | 29.4 | 9.9 | 16.5 | 67.2 |
| 2000 | 40,995 | 3.40 | 36.8 | 29.8 | 81.5 | 17.8 | 7.5 | 25.3 | 10.9 | 18.2 | 63.2 |
| 2001 | 39,883 | 1.60 | 40.8 | 33.2 | 79.4 | 14.8 | 7.4 | 22.2 | 12.2 | 20.2 | 59.2 |

Sources: Federal Reserve Flow of Funds; Tanaka Capital Management, Inc.

## Decades of Growth in Equity-Like Assets

| | End of Decade Asset Values ($Bil.) | | | | % Growth in Decade | | |
|---|---|---|---|---|---|---|---|
| | 1989 | 1999 | 2009[E] | 2019[E] | 1989–1999 | 1999–2009 | 2009–2019 |
| Annual Total Return on S&P 500 | — | — | — | — | 19.0%/yr. | 11.3% | 9.5% |
| S&P 500 Total Return For Decade | — | — | — | — | 469% | 192% | 147% |
| Corporate Equities | $1,946 | $9,240 | $23,403 | $50,908 | 375% | 153% | 118% |
| Mutual Fund Shares | $463 | $3,106 | $10,357 | $28,894 | 571% | 233% | 179% |
| Pension Fund Reserves | $3,221 | $9,041 | $15,722 | $24,629 | 181% | 74% | 57% |
| Equity in Non-Corporate Business | $3,203 | $4,736 | $5,663 | $6,513 | 48% | 20% | 15% |
| Bank Personal Trusts | $541 | $1,130 | $1,633 | $2,191 | 109% | 45% | 34% |
| Total Equity-Like Assets | $9,374 | $27,253 | $56,777 | $113,134 | 191% | 108% | 99% |

Sources: Federal Reserve Flow of Funds; Tanaka Capital Management, Inc.

# APPENDIX D

## Wealth Models Using 3.00% Real Rate on 10-Year Treasury (vs. 3.90% in CBO projections and in all prior models)

| | 1ST DECADE (2000–2009) | | | | 2ND DECADE (2010–2019) | | | |
|---|---|---|---|---|---|---|---|---|
| | CASE (A) | CASE (B) | CASE (C) | CASE (D) | CASE (A) | CASE (B) | CASE (C) | CASE (D) |
| % Digital Deflation Counted by End of Decade | 100% | 75% | 50% | 0% | 100% | 75% | 50% | 0% |
| % Conversion of Productivity to Profits As % GDP | 75% | 75% | 75% | 75% | 75% | 75% | 75% | 75% |
| **DIGITAL DEFLATION & PRODUCTIVITY MODELS:** | | | | | | | | |
| Adjusted Digital Deflation Counted by the End of the Decade (a) | 2.8% | 2.1% | 1.4% | 0.0% | 3.7% | 2.8% | 1.9% | 0.0% |
| CBO's Productivity Growth Projections | 2.5% | 2.5% | 2.5% | 2.5% | 2.5% | 2.5% | 2.5% | 2.5% |
| Quality-Based Productivity Gains fr. Digital Deflation (a) | 2.8% | 2.1% | 1.4% | 0.0% | 3.7% | 2.8% | 1.9% | 0.0% |
| Quantity-Based Productivity Gains fr. Rising IT Cap. Ex.(a) | 0.4% | 0.4% | 0.4% | 0.4% | 1.1% | 1.1% | 1.1% | 1.1% |
| Total Counted Productivity Adjusted for Rising IT & Digital Deflation (a) | 5.7% | 5.0% | 4.3% | 2.9% | 7.3% | 6.4% | 5.5% | 3.6% |
| **STOCK MARKET MODEL:** | | | | | | | | |
| % Chg. in S&P 500 EPS/Yr. | 8.9% | 8.9% | 8.9% | 8.9% | 6.5% | 6.5% | 6.5% | 6.5% |
| GDP Deflator Adj. For Rising IT and Digital Deflation (a) | -1.17% | -0.47% | 0.23% | 1.63% | -2.30% | -1.37% | -0.43% | 1.44% |
| 10-year Treasury Bond Yield Adj. for Rising IT & Digital Deflation (a) | 1.83% | 2.53% | 3.23% | 4.63% | 0.70% | 1.64% | 2.57% | 4.44% |
| P/E Ratio in Last Year of Decade | 67.1 | 46.3 | 35.1 | 23.3 | 200.6 | 76.2 | 45.5 | 24.4 |
| % Chg. in P/E Ratio/Yr.(CAGR) using 10-Yr. Treas. Model | 11.05% | 7.03% | 4.09% | -0.10% | 11.58% | 5.11% | 2.64% | 0.48% |
| Nominal Return on Comm. Stocks (S&P 500) CAGR | 22.0% | 17.6% | 14.4% | 9.9% | 19.7% | 12.8% | 10.1% | 7.8% |
| Real Return on Comm. Stocks (CAGR) | 20.5% | 15.8% | 12.3% | 7.2% | 18.7% | 11.4% | 8.4% | 5.3% |
| **WEALTH MODEL:** | | | | | | | | |
| Incr. In Nominal Net Worth per Decade ($Tril.) | $101 | $67 | $48 | $28 | $461 | $153 | $85 | $43 |
| % Incr. In Nominal Net Worth per Decade | 242% | 159% | 114% | 67% | 321% | 141% | 94% | 61% |
| % Incr. In Inflation (CPI) per Decade | 16% | 20% | 23% | 30% | 10% | 14% | 19% | 28% |
| % Incr. In Real Net Worth per Decade | 193% | 117% | 74% | 29% | 283% | 111% | 64% | 26% |

(a) Rate in last year of decade.
Source: Tanaka Capital Management, Inc.

# REFERENCES

"Aging America Poses Unprecedented Challenge." National Institutes of Health, May 20, 1996.

"A Spanner in the Productivity Miracle." *The Economist*, August 11, 2001.

"A Wealth Effect." *EconSouth* 2(2), Federal Reserve of Atlanta, Q2 2000.

"Banking and Monetary Statistics 1941–1970." Board of Governors of the Federal Reserve System.

"Defense Technology Objectives." U.S. Department of Defense, 1998, *www.mcint .com/milnet/pentagon/dto/intro*.

"Digital Economy 2000." Economics and Statistics Administration, U.S. Department of Commerce, June 2000.

"Digital Economy 2002." Economics and Statistics Administration, U.S. Department of Commerce, February 2002.

"Drop in Death Rates for Diseases Treated with Pharmaceuticals, 1965–1996." *Pharmaceutical Industry Profile 2000*, Pharmaceutical Research and Manufacturers of America.

"Economic Report of the President." The White House, January 2001.

"Economic Report of the President." The White House, January 2002.

"Fed Officials Say Policy on Mark, Little Deflation Risk." Reuters, *Investor's Business Daily*, August 22, 2002.

"Fedpoint 49: The Money Supply." Federal Reserve Bank of New York, September 2000.

"GDP: One of the Great Inventions of the 20th Century." *Survey of Current Business*, January 2000.

"Has the United States Entered a New Era in Productivity Growth?" *The Budget and Economic Outlook: Fiscal Years 2001–2010*, Congressional Budget Office, January 2000.

"Hedonic Pricing Method." Ecosystem Valuation, *www.ecosystemvaluation.org*.

"How The Bubbles Burst." *Investor's Business Daily*, March 15, 2001.

"Measurement Issues in the Consumer Price Index." Bureau of Labor Statistics, U.S. Department of Labor, June 1997.

"National Defense Budget Estimates for FY 2000." U.S. Department of Defense, 2000.

"Prescription Drug Expenditures in 2000: The Upward Trend Continues." National Institute for Health Care Management, May 2001.

"Preventing Deflation: Lessons from Japan's Experience in the 1990s." International Finance Discussion Papers, Board of Governors of the Federal Reserve System, June 2002.

"71st Annual Report." Bank for International Settlements, Basel, June 11, 2001.

"Strengthening Social Security and Creating Personal Wealth for All Americans." Report of the President's Commission, December 11, 2001.

" 'Strained Silicon' Speeds Electrons and Rewrites Moore's Law." IBM, Armonk, N.Y., June 8, 2001.

"The Budget and Economic Outlook: An Update." Congressional Budget Office, July 2000.

"The Budget and Economic Outlook: Fiscal Years 2002–2011." Congressional Budget Office, January 2001.

"The Budget and Economic Outlook: An Update." Congressional Budget Office, August 2001.

"The Budget and Economic Outlook: Fiscal Years 2003–2012." Congressional Budget Office, January 2002.

"The Emerging Digital Economy." Economics and Statistics Administration, U.S. Department of Commerce, 1998.

"The Emerging Digital Economy II." Economics and Statistics Administration, U.S. Department of Commerce, June 1999.

"The Knowledge-Based Economy: A Set of Facts and Figures." OECD, June 1999.

"Updated Response to the Recommendations of the Advisory Commission to Study the Consumer Price Index." Bureau of Labor Statistics, U.S. Department of Labor, June 1998.

"U.S. Productivity Growth 1995–2000." McKinsey Global Institute, October 2001.

"Value of Medicines." *APMA Facts Book—1999–2000*," APMA, Australia.

Abelson, Alan. "Irrational Adulation," *Barron's*, July 22, 2002.

Ahmed, Shaghil; Levin, Andrew; and Wilson, Beth Anne. "Recent U.S. Macroeconomic Stability: Good Policies, Good Practices, or Good Luck?" Federal Reserve Board, 2002.

Aizcorbe, Ana; Corrado, Carol; and Doms, Mark. "Constructing Price and Quantity Indexes for High Technology Goods," Division of Research and Statistics, Federal Reserve Board, July 26, 2000.

Altman, Daniel. "Is Economic Double Dip Lurking on the Horizon?" *The New York Times*, July 29, 2002.

Altman, Lawrence K., M.D. "Cancer Doctors See New Era of Optimism," *The New York Times*, May 22, 2001.

Angell, Wayne, "Greenspan's Deflation." *The Wall Street Journal*, October 29, 2002.

Angell, Wayne; Ryding, John; Hardy, Melanie; DeQuadros, Conrad. "Productivity Is a Good Thing After All," Bear, Stearns & Co., July 3, 2000.

Bartley, Robert L. "Meanderings on Money." *The Wall Street Journal*, May 20, 2002.

Bartley, Robert L. "The Anti-Keynes: Do Surpluses Stimulate?" *The Wall Street Journal*, February 25, 2002.

Berry, Kate. "One Less Tax-Time Headache: Software to Download Data," *The New York Times*, October 16, 2000.

Boskin, Michael J.; Dulberger, Ellen R.; Gordon Robert J.; Griliches, Zvi; and Jorgenson, Dale. "Final Report of the Advisory Commission to Study the Consumer Price Index," Committee on Finance, United States Senate, William V. Roth, Jr., Chairman, December 4, 1996.

Boskin, Michael J.; Dulberger, Ellen R.; Gordon, Robert J.; and Jorgenson, Dale. "Consumer Price Index, Update of Boskin Commission's Estimate of Bias." Report to the Ranking Minority Member, Committee on Finance, U.S. Senate, General Accounting Office, February 2000.

Bosworth, Barry P. and Triplett, Jack E. "Numbers Matter: The U.S. Statistical System and a Rapidly Changing Economy," Policy Brief, The Brookings Institute, July 2000.

Bosworth, Barry P. and Triplett, Jack E. "The Adequacy of Data for Analyzing and Forecasting the High-Tech Sector," Brookings Workshop on Economic Measurement, October 12, 2001.

Browning, E.S. "Where Is the Love? It Isn't Oozing From Stocks." *The Wall Street Journal*, December 24, 2001.

*Business Week* editorial. "Are We Headed for a Tech-led Recession?" *Business Week*, October 9, 2000.

*Business Week* editorial. "The 21st Century Corporation," *Business Week*, August 28, 2000.

Chelena, Joe. "Using a Hedonic Model to Adjust Prices of Personal Computers in the Consumer Price Index for Changes in Quality," Bureau of Labor Statistics, July 16, 1997.

Clark, Don. "Intel to Unveil Tiny New Transistors," *The Wall Street Journal*, August 13, 2002.

Colecchia, Alessandra and Schreyer, Paul. "ICT Investment and Economic Growth in the 1990s: Is the United States a Unique Case?" OECD, October 25, 2001.

Cooper, James C. and Madigan, Kathleen. "It's Productivity to the Rescue! Superstrong Gains Rule Out Higher Interest Rates Anytime Soon," *Business Week*, August 28, 2000.

Corrado, Carol. "Industrial Production and Capacity Utilization: The 2000 Annual Revision," *Federal Reserve Bulletin*, March 2001.

Crippen, Dan L. et al. "The Long-Term Budget Outlook," Congressional Budget Office, October 2000.

Davies, Gavyn. "Productivity and the Digital Revolution," *Global Economics Weekly*, Goldman Sachs, June 14, 2000.

Davies, Gavyn; Martin Brookes, Neil Williams. "Technology, the Internet, and the New Global Economy," Goldman Sachs, March 17, 2000.

Davis, Bob. "Upbeat Regional Fed Presidents Damp Rate-Cut Expectations," *The Wall Street Journal*, August 22, 2002.

DeLong, J. Bradford, and Summers, Lawrence H. "The 'New Economy': Background, Historical Perspective, Questions, and Speculations," *Economic Review*, 4Q 2001, Federal Reserve Bank of Kansas City.

Doms, Mark, and Forman, Christopher. "Prices for Local Area Network Equipment," Workshop on Communications Output and Productivity, Brookings Institution, February 23, 2001.

Dudley, William C. "Bubble Trouble for the Federal Reserve," *Barron's*, July 22, 2002.

Epstein, Gene. "The Median Is the Message for the CPI," *Barron's*, October 23, 2000.

Fixler, Dennis; Fortuna, Charles; Greenlees, John; Lane, Walter. "The Use of Hedonic Regressions to Handle Quality Change: The Experience in the U.S. CPI," Bureau of Labor Statistics, Fifth Meeting of the International Working Group on Price Indices, Reykjavik, Iceland, August 1999.

Freudenheim, Milt. "Decrease in Chronic Illness Bodes Well for Medicare Costs," *The New York Times*, May 8, 2001.

Gibson, Sharon. "Announcement—BLS to Use Geometric Mean Formula for Calculating Most Basic Indexes Starting in January 1999," Bureau of Labor Statistics, May 8, 1998.

Gibson, Sharon. "Consumer Price Indexes: Frequently Asked Questions," Bureau of Labor Statistics, April 18, 2000.

Gibson, Sharon. "Future Schedule for Expenditure Weight Updates in the Consumer Price Index," Bureau of Labor Statistics, January 19, 1999.

Gibson, Sharon. "How BLS Measures Changes in Consumer Prices," Bureau of Labor Statistics, June 29, 2000.

Gibson, Sharon. "How BLS Measures Price Change for Cellular Telephone Service in the Consumer Price Index," Bureau of Labor Statistics, January 31, 2001.

Gibson, Sharon. "Measuring Price Change for Medical Care in the CPI," Bureau of Labor Statistics, July 7, 1998.

Gibson, Sharon. "The Treatment of Mandated Pollution Control Measures in the CPI," Bureau of Labor Statistics, October 16, 1998.

Gibson, Sharon. "Using a Hedonic Model to Adjust Television Prices in the Consumer Price Index for Changes in Quality," Bureau of Labor Statistics, August 3, 1998.

Gilpin, Kenneth N. "If the Fed Cuts Rates, Will History Again Be Kind to Stocks?" *The New York Times*, March 17, 2001.

Greenspan, Alan. "Challenges for Monetary Policymakers," 18th Annual Conference: Monetary Policy in the New Economy, Cato Institute, Washington, D.C., October 19, 2000.

Greenspan, Alan. "Current Fiscal Issues," Before the Committee on the Budget, U.S. House of Representatives, March 2, 2001.

Greenspan, Alan. "Current Fiscal Issues," Before the Committee on the Budget, U.S. House of Representatives, September 12, 2002.

Greenspan, Alan. "Economic Developments," Before the Economic Club of New York, May 24, 2001.

Greenspan, Alan. "Evolving Fiscal Challenges," Before the Committee on the Budget, U.S. Senate, January 25, 2001.

Greenspan, Alan. "Federal Reserve Board's Semiannual Monetary Policy Report to the Congress," Before the Committee on Banking, Housing and Urban Affairs, U.S. Senate, February 13, 2001.

Greenspan, Alan. "Federal Reserve Board's Semiannual Monetary Policy Report to the Congress," Before the Committee on Financial Services, U.S. House of Representatives, July 18, 2001.

Greenspan, Alan. "Federal Reserve Board's Semiannual Monetary Policy Report to the Congress," Before the Committee on Banking, Housing and Urban Affairs, U.S. Senate, March 7, 2002.

Greenspan, Alan. "Federal Reserve Board's Semiannual Monetary Policy Report to the Congress," Before the Committee on Banking, Housing and Urban Affairs, U.S. Senate, July 16, 2002.

Greenspan, Alan. "Monetary Policy and Economic Outlook," Before the Joint Economic Committee, U.S. House of Representatives, October 17, 2001.

Greenspan, Alan. "Opening Remarks at a Symposium Sponsored by the Federal Reserve Bank of Kansas City at Jackson Hole, Wyoming," August 31, 2001.

Greenspan, Alan. "Social Security," at the Abraham Lincoln Award Ceremony of the Union League of Philadelphia, December 6, 1996.

Greenspan, Alan. "Structural Change in the New Economy," at the National Governors' Association, July 2000.

Greenspan, Alan. "Structural Changes in the Economy and Financial Markets," at the America's Community Bankers Conference, New York, December 5, 2000.

Greenspan, Alan. "The Challenge of Central Banking in a Democratic Society," at the Annual Dinner and Francis Boyer Lecture of the American Enterprise Institute for Public Policy Research, December 5, 1996.

Greenspan, Alan. "The Challenge of Measuring and Modeling a Dynamic Economy," at the Washington Economic Policy Conference of the National Association for Business Economics, March 27, 2001.

Greenspan, Alan. "The Federal Reserve's Report on Monetary Policy," before the Committee on Banking and Financial Services, U.S. House of Representatives, July 25, 2000.

Greenspan, Alan. "The State of the Economy," Before the Committee on the Budget, U.S. Senate, January 24, 2002.

Greenspan, Alan. "The U.S. Economy," Before the Independent Community Bankers of America, March 13, 2002.

Grimm, Bruce T. "Price Indexes for Selected Semiconductors, 1974–96," *Survey of Current Business*, February 1998.

Guinto, Joseph. "Can We Measure The New Economy with Archaic Data?" *Investor'sBusiness Daily*, March 30, 2001.

Guinto, Joseph. "Just How New Is 'New' Economy? We've Seen It All Before—In 1915," *Investor's Business Daily*, May 5, 2000.

Guinto, Joseph. "Soaring Productivity Shows New Economy Still With Us," *Investor's Business Daily*, June 21, 2002.

Guinto, Joseph. "Will Congress' Spending Appetite Keep Growing with the Surplus?" *Investor's Business Daily*, February 5, 2001.

Hall, Robert; Feldstein, Martin; Bernanke, Ben; Frankel, Jeffrey; Gordon, Robert; and Zarnowitz, Victor. "The NBER's Recession Dating Procedure," National Bureau of Economic Research, May 8, 2002.

Harris, Maury. "Patents, Productivity, Inflation, and an Unchanged Monetary Policy." Paine Weber, August 10, 2000.

Hassett, Kevin. "Rx for the Economy," *The Wall Street Journal*, May 16, 2001.

Higgins, Sean. "Medicare's Pending Collapse Could Dwarf Social Security." *Investor's Business Daily*, May 14, 2002.

Hokenson, Richard F. "A Long Wave of Productivity," Donaldson, Lufkin & Jenrette.

Holdway, Michael. "Quality-Adjusting Computer Prices in the Producer Price Index: An Overview," Bureau of Labor Statistics, November 27, 2000.

Holdway, Michael, and Gerduk, Irwin B. "PPI Quality Improvement Initiative: Responses to New Item Bias in IT Equipment," Bureau of Labor Statistics, October 2001.

Hooper, Peter, and Dinmore, Trevor. "The U.S. Productivity Boom. What's Behind It? Why Will It Last?" *Global Markets Research*, Deutsche Bank, September 5, 2000.

Hyman, Ed. "Swings in Consumer Spending: The NASDAQ Is Now Almost Four Times More Important Than Income," ISI Group, January 16, 2001.

Ip, Greg. "Greenspan Expresses Optimism As Productivity Keeps Growing," *The Wall Street Journal*, May 13, 2002.

Ip, Greg. "The Rise and Fall of Intangible Assets Leads to Shorter Company Life Spans," *The Wall Street Journal*, April 4, 2002.

Ip, Greg, and Schlesinger, Jacob M. "Did Greenspan Push His Optimism About the New Economy Too Far?" *The Wall Street Journal*, December 28, 2001.

Jaffe, Greg. "In the New Military, Technology May Alter Chain of Command," *The New York Times*, March 30, 2001.

Jorgenson, Dale W.; Ho, Mun S.; and Stiroh, Kevin J. "Projecting Productivity Growth: Lessons from the U.S. Growth Resurgence," Federal Reserve Bank of Atlanta, December 31, 2001.

Jorgenson, Dale W., and Stiroh, Kevin. "Raising the Speed Limit: U.S. Economic Growth in the Information Age," Federal Reserve Bank of New York, May 1, 2000.

Kerschner, Edward, and Geraghty, Michael. "Explanation of the Comparative Values Models," UBS Warburg, November 2000.

Kerschner, Edward, and Geraghty, Michael. "More Affluent Than Ever," Paine Webber, September 8, 2000.

Kokoski, Mary; Waehrer, Keith; and Rozaklis, Patricia. "Using Hedonic Methods for Quality Adjustment in the CPI: The Consumer Audio Products Component," Bureau of Labor Statistics, November 17, 1999.

Koretz, Gene. "Productivity: All Signs Are Go, Fed Investment Feeds Fed Optimism," *Business Week*, September 25, 2000.

Kudlow, Lawrence. "It's Productivity, Stupid," Schroeders, June 1, 2000.

Kudlow, Lawrence. "It Wasn't a Bubble," Kudlow & Co., November 28, 2001.

Kudlow, Lawrence. "Productivity Is the Key," Kudlow & Co., May 10, 2002.

Landefeld, J. Steven, and Fraumeni, Barbara M. "Measuring the New Economy," *Survey of Current Business*, March 2001.

Landefeld, J. Steven, and Grimm, Bruce T. "A Note on the Impact of Hedonics and Computers on Real GDP," *Survey of Current Business*, December 2000.

Liegey, Paul R. "Apparel Price Indexes: Effects of Hedonic Adjustment," *Monthly Labor Review*, Bureau of Labor Statistics, May 1994.

Liegey, Paul R. "Developing an Hedonic Regression Model For DVD Players in the U.S. CPI," Bureau of Labor Statistics, June 16, 2000.

Liegey, Paul R. "Hedonic Quality Adjustment Methods for Microwave Ovens in the U.S. CPI," Bureau of Labor Statistics, August 25, 2000.

Linden, Fabian. "The Boom Next Time," *The New York Times*, May 2, 1982.

Ludvigson, Sydney; Steindel, Charles. "How Important Is the Stock Market Effect on Consumption?" Federal Reserve Bank of New York, July 1999.

Lum, Sherlene K.S.; Moyer, Brian C.; and Yuskavage, Robert E.. "Improved Estimates of Gross Product by Industry for 1947–98," *Survey of Current Business*, June 2000.

Maddison, Angus. *Monitoring the World Economy 1820–1992*, Development Centre of the O.E.C.D., Paris, 1995.

Maki, Dean M.; Palumbo, Michael G. "Disentangling the Wealth Effect: A Cohort Analysis of Household Saving in the 1990s," Federal Reserve Board, April 2001.

Mandel, Michael J. "Restating the '90s," *Business Week*, April 1, 2002.

Manton, Kenneth G., and Gu, Xi Liang. "Changes in the Prevalence of Chronic Disability in the United States Black and Nonblack Population Above Age 65 from 1982 to 1999," *PNAS Early Edition*, 2001.

McTeer, Robert D. "Believe Your Eyes. The New Economy Is Real," *The Wall Street Journal*, November 18, 1999.

McTeer, Robert D., Jr. et.al. "The New Paradigm," Federal Reserve Bank of Dallas, 1999 Annual Report.

Mesenbourg, Thomas L.. "Measuring Electronic Business: Definitions, Underlying Concepts, and Measurement Plans," U.S. Census Bureau.

Milne, George M., Jr.. "Health Care Innovation," *Going Global*, Council on Competitiveness, 1998.

Morgenson, Gretchen. "How Did They Value Stocks? Count the Absurd Ways," *The New York Times*, March 18, 2001.

Morgenson, Gretchen. "Nightmare on Wall Street: A Tightfisted Consumer," *The New York Times*, April 4, 2001.

Moulton, Brent R., and Seskin, Eugene P. "A Preview of the 1999 Comprehensive Revision of the National Income and Product Accounts," *Survey of Current Business*, October 1999.

Moulton, Brent R.; Parker, Robert P.; and Seskin, Eugene P. "A Preview of the 1999 Comprehensive Revision of the National Income and Product Accounts: Definitional and Classificational Changes," *Survey of Current Business*, August 1999.

Moylan, Carol. "Estimation of Software in the U.S. National Accounts: New Developments," Organisation for Economic Co-operation and Development, September 24, 2001.

Nakamura, Leonard. "Economics and the New Economy: The Invisible Hand Meets Creative Destruction." *Business Review*, Federal Reserve Bank of Philadelphia, July–August 2000.

Nakamura, Leonard. "Intangibles: What Put the New in the New Economy?" *Business Review*, Federal Reserve Bank of Philadelphia, July–August 1999.

Nakamura, Leonard. "Investing in Intangibles: Is a Trillion Dollars Missing from GDP?" *Business Review*, Federal Reserve Bank of Philadelphia, Q4 2001.

Nakamura, Leonard. "Is the U.S. Economy Really Growing Too Slowly? Maybe We're Measuring Growth Wrong," *Business Review*, Federal Reserve Bank of Philadelphia, March–April 1997.

Nakamura, Leonard. "What Is the U.S. Gross Investment in Intangibles? (At Least) One Trillion Dollars a Year!" Working Papers, Federal Reserve Bank of Philadelphia, October 2001.

Oliner, Stephen D., and Sichel, Daniel E. "The Resurgence of Growth Information Technology: The Story?" Federal Reserve, March 2000.

Parker, Robert; Grimm, Bruce, et.al. "Recognition of Business and Government Expenditures for Software as Investment: Methodology and Quantitative Impacts, 1959–98," Bureau of Economic Analysis, Department of Commerce, 1999.

Pear, Robert. "Spending on Prescription Drugs Increases by Almost 19 Percent," *The New York Times*, May 8, 2001.

Prado, Antonio. "Economists Say Internet Boom Pales Next To Industrial Age," *Investor's Business Daily*, January 11, 2001.

Prud'homme, Marc, and Yu, Kam. "Trends in Internet Access Prices," Brookings Institution, February 2001.

Raisch, Dennis W. "Understanding Quality-Adjusted Life Years and Their Application to Pharmacoeconomic Research," *Pub Med*, National Library of Medicine, July–August 2000.

Reese, Mike. "Hedonic Quality Adjustment Methods for College Textbooks in the U.S. CPI," Bureau of Labor Statistics, November 2, 2000.

Robbins, Robert. "Major Market Moves Follow Inflation," Robinson-Humphrey Company, 1987.

Schlesinger, Jacob M. "Fed Signals Rise in Productivity Estimate," *The Wall Street Journal*, August 26, 2000.

Schlesinger, Jacob M. "Puzzled Investors Ask: Will the Real Economy Please Step Forward?" *The Wall Street Journal*, March 22, 2000.

Seskin, Eugene P. "Improved Estimates of the National Income and Product Accounts for 1959–98: Results of the Comprehensive Revision," *Survey of Current Business*, December 1999.

Sharpe, Steven A. "Reexamining Stock Valuation and Inflation: The Implications of Analysts' Earnings Forecasts," Federal Reserve Board Division of Research and Statistics, July 2000.

Shepler, Nicole. "Developing a Hedonic Regression Model for Camcorders in the U.S. CPI," Bureau of Labor Statistics, February 25, 2000.

Shepler, Nicole. "Developing a Hedonic Regression Model for Refrigerators in the U.S. CPI," Bureau of Labor Statistics, August 18, 2000.

Sichel, Dan. "Government Plans for Improving Real Output for the High-Tech Sector," Brookings Workshop on Economic Measurement, October 12, 2001.

Smith, Greg. "12 Month Forward P/E Ratio vs. 10-Yr. Treasury," Prudential Securities, May 2001.

Starr-McCluer, Martha. "Stock Market Wealth and Consumer Spending," Federal Reserve Board of Governors, April 1998.

Stevenson, Richard W. "Surplus Estimate Hits $5.6 Trillion," *The New York Times*, January 31, 2001.

Stewart, Kenneth J. "The Experimental CPI Using Geometric Means (CPI-U-XG)," Bureau of Labor Statistics, September 1, 1998.

Stewart, Kenneth J., and Reed, Stephen B. "Consumer Price Index Research Series Using Current Methods, 1978–98," *Monthly Labor Review*, Bureau of Labor Statistics, June 1999.

Tanaka, Graham Y. "As Deflation Rears Its Head, Fed Must Cut Interest Rates," *Investor's Business Daily*, Op-Ed, March 18, 2003.

Tanaka, Graham Y. "Demographics and the Stock Market," *MT&A Outlook*, July 1982.

Tanaka, Graham Y. "Demographics, Productivity, and the Return on Common Stocks," *MT&A Outlook*, December 1983.

Tanaka, Graham Y. "Digital Deflation and the Stock Market," Presented to the O'Rourke Invitational, Melrose, South Carolina, December 3, 1999.

Tanaka, Graham Y. "Disinflation, Consumer Spending, and a Healthy Surge in Financial Assets," *MT&A Outlook*, May 1983.

Tanaka, Graham Y. "The Economy In Transition and High Real Rates," *MT&A Outlook*, March 1982.

Tanaka, Graham Y. "Monetarists, Supply Siders, and Inflation Expectations," *MT&A Outlook*, April 1984.

Tanaka, Graham Y. "Oil Price Drop—Hidden Surprises," *MT&A Outlook*, February 1986.

Tanaka, Graham Y. "The Ongoing Revaluation of Financial Assets," *MT&A Outlook*, June 1984.

Tanaka, Graham Y. "Productivity and Profitability," *MT&A Outlook*, February 1983.

Tanaka, Graham Y. "Why the Best Is Yet to Come," *MT&A Outlook*, October 1982.

Thompson, William. "Developing a Hedonic Regression Model for VCR's in the U.S. CPI," June 19, 2000.

Uchitelle, Louis. "Deepening Wrinkles in the New Economy," *The New York Times*, October 17, 2001.

Uchitelle, Louis. "This Time the Fed Is Boxed In on Rates," *The New York Times*, June 16, 2002.

Uchitelle, Louis. "Wild Card of the Recovery: Inflation," *The New York Times*, March 17, 2002.

Varian, Hal R. "Productivity and Profitability: An Odd Couple in an Odd Recession," *The New York Times*, June 6, 2002.

Wasshausen, David. "Computer Price in the National Accounts," National Income and Wealth Division, Bureau of Economic Analysis, U.S. Department of Commerce, April 2000.

Wessel, David. "The Wealth Effect Goes into Reverse," *The Wall Street Journal*, May 24, 2001.

Xie, Andy. "It Ain't IT That's Roaring Back," *Greater China Monthly*, Morgan Stanley Dean Witter, July 3, 2001.

Yardeni, Edward. "Productivity Trends." Deutsche Banc., Alex. Brown, February 12, 2001.

Yuskavage, Robert E. "Measurement of Business and Professional Services in BEA's Gross Product Originating Series," Brookings Program on Output and Productivity Measurement in the Service Sector, May 14, 1999.

# INDEX

Affymetrix, 380–391
Angell, Wayne, 67
ASML, contribution to New Economy, 368
ASP (Application Service Provider) model, 367
AT&T, 22, 23

Baby Boomers
  inflation and, 133
  labor force and, 12, 14, 69, 70–73
  parents of, 54–55
  Politics of Need and, 290
  Working Women and, 11
BEA (Bureau of Economic Analysis), Congressional funds for, 292
Bell, Alexander Graham, 331, 353
Berra, Yogi, 74
"Better Tools: Improving the Accuracy and Timeliness of Economic Statistics," 293
Biochip, development of, 391
Blaylock, Paul, 22
BLS (Bureau of Labor Statistics)
  Boskin Report and, 20, 21
  computer quality measured by, 111
  congressional funds for, 292
  PPI and, 111
  software adjustment by, 115
Bond market
  downward turn in, 312
  interest rates and, 223
Boskin, Michael J., 19
Boskin Report, 19, 20, 21, 355
Browning, E. S., 299
Budget deficit
  Bush, George, and reduction of, 69
  1990s and reduction of, 76
  record levels of 1980s, 67
Budget surpluses, New Economy and, 2, 294–295
Bull market (1982–2000), 241
Bureau of Economic Analysis, 162
Bureau of Labor Statistics. See BLS
Bush, George, budget deficit reduction by, 69

Bush, George W., 91, 283
Business fixed investment, IP Equipment and Software, 141
Business objects, 310

Capital investment, labor substituted for, 70
Capital spending, rising, 124
Capital spending-productivity model, 140–142, 151–156
Carter, Jimmy
  inflation and, 60
  Volcker, Paul, appointment by, 62
CAT scans, 169
CBO (Congressional Budget Office)
  CPI's flat growth projected by, 127, 212
  goal of, 298
  long term estimates, 231
  real interest rates forecast by, 223
  "rule of thumb," 295
  10-year surplus predicted by, 294
C-CPI-U ("Chained Consumer Price Index for All Urban Consumers"), 355
CDMA (code division multiple access), 376
Cellular phones
  CPI and, 117
  Digital Deflation Theory and, 83
  quality improvement and, 21–22
China, Digital Revolution in, 322
Cisco, 148
Clarke, Arthur C., 35
Clinton Administration
  Internet study requested by, 157
  technology appreciated by, 78
Clinton, Bill, 77, 78
Communications, as non-quality-adjusted IT category, 117, 165
Communications hardware, as percentage of Digital Deflation, 167
Computer quality improvement, productivity and, 112–113
Computer services, as non-quality-adjusted IT category, 163

Computers
  Digital Deflation and, 45
  GDP and, 44
Consumer spending
  "Disinflation, Consumer Spending,
     and a Healthy Surge in Financial
     Assets" and, 93
  net worth/disposable income, rela-
     tionship to, 93
Consumers
  digital technology, effect on, 24–25
  hedonics and, 82
  quality improvement passed to, 151
Cook, Scott, 164
Cost-cutting deflation, Digital Deflation
     v., 34
CPI (consumer price index), 4
  adjusted for Digital Deflation, 212
  Boskin Report on, 19
  cellular phone service in, 117
  chained, 355
  Digital Deflation model, 173–177, 213
  GDP Deflator and, 213–215
  net worth and, 178
  1960s/early 1970s and, 55
  P/E ratios and, 19
  as proverbial "third rail," 335
  quality improvement aspect of, 21
  upward bias in, 19
  youngest segment of work force and,
     131
Crime
  New Economy and decline of, 288, 289
  and unemployment, 288, 289

Defense Department, and inflation, 172
Deflation
  closeness to/reality of, 350–351
  cyclical, 264
  digital technology's effect on, 28, 82–83
  equals quality improvement, 110
  Industrialization, 264
  Japan and, 9, 275–277, 278
  lower interest rates and, 239
  naturally created, 101
  New Economy/expanding, 238
  quality improvement and, 28

Deflation (cont.)
  undercounting of, 50
  United States and, 9, 275
Degradation in service, examples of, 122
Dell Computer
  product price elasticity curves and, 149
  role in Digital Revolution, 375–376
Dell, Michael, interview with, 374–376
Demographic Theory of Economics, 15,
     16, 64, 67, 70, 252
  labor force growth and, 134
Demographic-GDP models, 137
Demographic-Inflation model, 131–134
Demographic-Productivity model,
     135–136
  adjusted for unmeasured Digital De-
     flation, 136–137
Demographics
  foundation for wealth, 203
  impact of, 69, 70
  inflation-accelerating, 204
  negative aspect of, 295–298
  1970s/1980s forces of, 80
"Demographics and the Stock Market,"
     12, 72, 203
Demographic-Stock Market model,
     134–135
  common stock v. labor force growth
     in, 135
Department of Commerce. See DOC
     studies
Depression, 9, 58, 260–265, 332, 343
Digital calculator, as start of Digital Rev-
     olution, 365
Digital Deflation
  adjusting wealth for, 202–203
  beneficiaries of, 300
  boosts in P/E ratios, 218
  cell phone example and, 83
  communications contribution to, 118
  computers in, 45
  cost-cutting deflation v., 34
  CPI divergence, 213
  creators of, 300
  definition of, 32–34, 83, 194
  digital drivers and, 114
  Digital Revolution's relation to, 32

Digital Deflation (*cont.*)
  GDP Deflator model, 231
  GDP relation to, 43, 44, 47
  government measurement of, 110–112
  hedonics and, 321
  home ownership and, 242
  intermediate goods and, 157
  laws of, 41–43
  medical care services and, 120
  New Economy companies creating, 108
  production v. value in, 83
  quality v. quantity in, 84
  redefines the New Economy, 100–103
  strongest form of, 122
  and uncounted healthcare services, 168
  unmeasured, 157, 159
  wealth multipliers, 206–207
Digital democracy, 316
Digital drivers, Digital Revolution
    driven by, 35, 37
Digital Economy 2000 study, 143
  DOC revised IT estimates in, 158
Digital Revolution
  benefits of, 8, 25, 31
  China/Japan and, 320
  contributors to, 291
  deceleration of, 265
  Digital Deflation's relation to, 32
  and economic growth, 260
  going global, 192
  Industrial Revolution compared to,
    40–41, 332
  politics and, 332
  quality improvement and, 84
  return of, 95
  semiconductor/driver of, 35–37
  wealth creation from, 316
Digital technology
  advancements, ongoing in, 38, 82
  consumer's benefits from, 24–25, 82
  deflation affected by, 28
  GDP's (gross domestic product) rela-
    tion to, 28–29
  performance lift for military, 171
  replacing analog products/pro-
    cesses/services, 308
  wealth creation and, 206

Disaggregation, 128, 256
Disintermediation, 77
DNA computers, 388
DOC (Department of Commerce) stud-
    ies, 47, 79
  "Digital Economy 2000" and, 158
Dollar, Digital Deflation and, 328
Dot-com Bubble, 3, 204, 206, 346
Dow Jones Industrial Average, 14, 72, 253
  New Economy companies in, 303
Duell, Charles H., 31
Dunn, Doug J.
  interview with, 367–374
  and start of New Economy/Digital
    Revolution, 369

Earnings yield, 224
EBITDA (earnings before interest, taxes,
    depreciation, and amortization), 4
Economic growth, scenarios for, 193
Economic models, variety of, 53–54
Economics, classical, high-technology
    capital investments and, 125
Employment, superfull, 284
Empty calories, 148–151
Entrepreneurship, U.S. encouragement
    of, 326
Equities, importance of, 218–219
Equity-like assets, growth in, 240, 394
eToys, 311
Europe
  Digital Revolution and, 371–372
  wealth creation in, 323
European Monetary Union, 325

Faster, better, cheaper, 21–25, 102, 196
Federal Open Market Committee, 278
Federal Reserve
  in the 1990s, 281
  acceptance of Digital Deflation, 340
  Act of 1913, 261
  BLS numbers and, 156
  deflation and, 281
  gradualist approach of, 91
  inflation and, 9, 255, 256
  interest rate actions of, 258
  need for updated data, 293

Federal Reserve (*cont.*)
  Old Economy numbers and, 265
  over/undercreation of liquidity, 259
  recession of 2001 and, 258
  Regulation Q and, 76
  restricts monetary policy, 257
  speed limits, 255, 266, 268–273
Federal Reserve Board, fudge factor of,
    266
Fed model, 224
Fiscal restraint, Clinton, Bill, and, 78
Fodor, Stephen, interview with, 381–391
FOMC (Federal Reserve Open Market
    Committee), zero interest rates and,
    273
Ford, Gerald, inflation and, 60
Friedman, Milton, 60
Full employment economy, benefits of,
    284
Gates, Bill, 40
GDP (gross domestic product)
  computers and, 44, 50
  corporate profit margins as percent of,
    229
  GPO's differences with, 48
  growth rate speed limit, 268–269
  by Industry, 157
  Information Processing and Software,
    category of, 44
  Internet and, 117
  IT and, 47, 153
  monetarism and, 61
  P/E ratio curves and, 227
  productivity growth and, 18, 141
  stock market and, 137
GDP Deflator, 44
  adjusted for Digital Deflation, 210–212
  applied to final goods sold, 161
  CBO projections and, 210, 231
  CPI and, 213–215
  deflation's contribution toward, 44
  Digital Deflation Model, 159–161, 173
  reducing of, 159, 212
  software and, 116
GeneChip microarray, 384, 386, 387
General Electric, 99, 103–104
Germany, Digital Deflation and, 329

Getty, J. Paul, 315
Gore, Al, 91
Government
  Digital Deflation not measured by, 86
  hedonic models used by, 27
  most likely scenario, 248
  1990s and paying down debt by, 75
  100%/75%/50%/0% quality improve-
    ment uncounted by, 215–217, 245,
    251
  quality improvement measured by,
    26
  undercounting quantity-based pro-
    ductivity, 125
  upside scenario, 245, 247
  value not reported by, 86
GPO (gross product originating by in-
    dustry)
  GDP's differences, 48
  Information Technology Producing
    Industries within, 48
  IT/non-IT categories of, 49
GPO Deflator, accuracy of, 49
GPS (Global Positioning System) satel-
    lite signals, 377
Graham, Benjamin, 218
Great Depression, 9, 58
  factors leading to, 264
  and Industrial Revolution, 260
  Smoot-Hawley Tariff and, 58–59
Greenspan, Alan, 68, 87, 93, 99, 255
  speech on Banking, Housing and Ur-
    ban affairs, 125
  technology mentioned by, 266
Gretzky, Wayne, 129
Gross Domestic Product. *See* GDP (gross
    domestic product)
Gross Product Originating by Industry.
    *See* GPO
Grove, Andy, 23

*Hamlet* (Shakespeare), 11
Healthcare
  better data and, 338–339
  deterioration in, 119
  parties involved in, 169
  quality improvement in, 119, 168, 170

Healthcare (*cont.*)
  technological innovation and, 338
  uncounted Digital Deflation and, 168
Hedonic models
  of France/Finland, 324
  quality improvement estimates via, 27
Hill, Richard S., interview with, 363–367
Home ownership, 242
Housing
  declining inflation and, 238
  soaring prices for, 280
Human genome, and DNA chips/digital technologies, 382
Human Genome Project, 120, 385
Hyman, Ed, wealth effect and, 93
Hyperinflation
  financial decimation by, 71
  (late)1970s and, 59–60
  underlying source of, 72

IBM, 110, 309
Immelt, Jeff, 280
Industrial Revolution
  Digital Revolution compared to, 40–41, 260, 332
  economic growth and, 260
Inflation
  around the world, 349
  Baby Boomer's effect on, 133
  Defense Department and, 172
  demographics and, 132, 133–134
  expected drop in, 223
  Federal Reserve and, 256
  labor force's growth and, 14, 133
  overstatement of, 86
  rise of, 14, 58, 208
  speed limit, 269–270
  wage gains and, 286
  wealth and low, 207
  zero/near zero, 208–210, 241
Information Processing Equipment and Software, as percent of GDP, 44, 142, 143, 210
Information technology. *See* IT
Intel, 23, 148, 209
  business model, 151

Intel (*cont.*)
  contribution to New Economy/Digital Revolution, 357
Interest rate(s)
  bond market and, 223
  decline of, 1
  Digital Deflation's lowering of, 243
  disintermediation/rising, 275
  double-digit, 14
  fluctuation of, 62
  speed limits, 270–271
Internet
  based supply chains, 292
  boom, 304–306
  Bubble, 313
  changing shape of, 370
  companies leveraging, 308
  investors use of, 92
  New Economy not, 3, 306
  phenomenon of, 39
  price-earning ratios and, 195
  slowdown of, 80
  U.S. economy and, 47
Investing
  in New Economy, 306–307
  real-world, 299
Investor-Consumer, 95–96, 183–185, 198, 214, 244
Ireland, as technology player, 323
Irrational exuberance, 93
IT (information technology)
  above average growth rates in, 196
  capital spending on, 4, 6, 7, 127, 233
  GDP and, 47, 153
  labor productivity and, 5, 141
  military use of, 171
  New Economy and, 3, 4, 77–78
  non-quality adjusted categories of, 163
  quality improvement and, 48
  upward spending trajectory for, 233, 234

Jacobs, Irwin, interview with, 376–381
Japan
  above average productivity gains in, 318, 320
  deflationary slump in, 275–277, 278

Japan (*cont.*)
　U.S. economy in relation to, 9, 275, 343
　zero inflation/interest rates in, 276
Jobs, loss of, 90

Key Performance Attributes, 33, 115,
　122, 168–169
Keynesian economics, 56, 60, 61, 69, 76
Keynes, John Maynard, 98
Kudlow, Larry, 67

Labor force
　age relation to, 15
　Baby Boomers/working women and,
　　12, 14, 69, 70
　effects of changes in, 132
　growth of, 12, 133
　inflation's relation to, 14, 133
　1990's decline in, 75
　productivity disconnect, 136
　shortage in, 72
　stock market/relation to, 16
Labor productivity, IT and, 5
Life expectancy trends, 296
Lost components, 49, 51, 161

Maddison, Angus, 263
Management, underpromise/overdeliv-
　ers, 311
Market price rule theories, late 1980s
　and, 67–69
McTeer, Bob, 5
Medical care services, Digital Deflation
　and, 120
Medical science, advances in, 296
Medicare/Medicaid, CBO's projections
　for, 296
Melnyk, Eugene, 170
Microsoft, 23, 106, 148, 194
Military quality improvement, 171
Monetarism, 60–62
　definition of, 61
　GDP and, 61
Monetary policy
　and American Depression/Japan's de-
　　flationary slump, 343
　response to New Economy contribu-
　　tions, 341

Monetary Policy (*cont.*)
　tightening of, 294
　undercounting Digital Deflation and,
　　256
Money supply, speed limits, 270
Moore, Gordon, 35, 342
　interview with, 357–367
Moore's Law, 35–36, 156, 363, 368
　development of, 358, 359–360
　Intel and, 309
　Meade, Carver, and, 360

NABE (National Association for Busi-
　ness Economics), lobbying for fund-
　ing, 293
NAIRU (non-accelerated inflation rate
　of unemployment), 76, 269
Nakamura, Leonard, 345
NASDAQ
　1929-like decline of, 3
　crash of 2000–2002, 310
Net financial assets, 177–181
Net worth
　CPI and, 178
　household tangible, financial, equity-
　　like assets and, 393
New Economy
　better data for, 292–294
　budget surpluses and, 2, 294–295
　communication's contribution to,
　　118
　Companies, 102, 108, 150, 191, 233,
　　300
　consumers benefits in, 121
　contributors to, 291
　crime's decline in, 288, 289
　definition of, 3, 11, 98–103
　demographic foundation for, 130
　disaggregation into, 128
　entrepreneurship, 315–316
　expanded in 2000–2002, 281
　gains share/profit from Old Economy,
　　107–108
　government measurement of, 142
　Internet and, 3, 80
　investing wisely in, 306–307
　IT and, 3, 4, 77–78
　Old Economy analysis, 301

New Economy (*cont.*)
old economy companies in, 103–105
productivity lifted by, 108–109
productivity-profit enigma, 146–148
quality improvements, consumers
and, 148
and rise in P/E ratios, 199, 230
stock (equity) financing and, 135
stock market model, 219–224, 231, 252
stock market projections, 236, 253
value-to-wealth virtuous circle of,
199
wealth creation in, 239, 299
New Economy companies
non-tech, 307
Old Economy companies v., 301–304
strong balance sheets of, 310
Next Big Thing, 39–40, 352, 361, 366, 370,
375, 380, 391
Nextel Communications, 22
1920s/1930s
learning from, 265
1990s compared to, 4, 262
shrinking money supply in, 263
1950s/1960s, economic models of,
54–55
(late) 1960s/early 1970s, CPI during,
55
1970s, late
demographic forces of, 80
hyperinflation in, 59–60
1980s
demographic forces of, 80
productivity decline in, 78
stock market, soaring in, 12
Volcker, Paul, 62
1980s, early, 64, 67
budget deficit/record levels in, 67
inflation peaked in, 71
supply-side economics in, 64, 67
(late) 1980s, market price rule theories
in, 67–69
1990s
corporate sector, benefits during, 75
Demographic Theory of Economics in,
16
Digital Deflation and, 81
Federal Reserve and, 5, 281

1990s (*cont.*)
gain in real wealth, 201
high P/E in, 222
inflation's decline in, 4, 8, 74
inflation's overstatement in, 81
IT and, 5
labor, scarcity of in, 75
New Economy and, 1, 2, 3, 4
productivity decline in, 78, 81
productivity surge/late, 284
real world experience of, 301
record long expansion, 151–152
rise in productivity growth, 127
social services, demand reduced in,
285
stock market, soaring in, 12, 220,
222
technology investments in, 77–78, 79
Nixon, Richard M., 56–58
Nonaccelerated inflation rate of unemployment. *See* NAIRU
Novellus Systems, 363

OECD (Organization for Economic Co-
operation and Development), 317
productivity gains/IT content by
country in, 319
Oil price, speed limits, 272–273
Old Economy
approach to fighting inflation, 281
Companies and New Economy,
102–105, 300–306
disaggregation into, 128
group, 299–300
prices paid/provider costs in, 121
removing shackles of, 351
share/profit loss to New Economy,
107–108
Olson, Ken, 40
120% rule of thumb, for productivity,
145–146
OPEC, price increases/1973, by, 59
Optical chip, 364
Over 3.0% Productivity Rule, 146

PCs (personal computers)
growing sales of, 150
quality improvement in, 23–24

P/E ratio(s)
  10-year treasury model v., 227
  CPI and, 19
  Digital Deflation boosted by, 218
  earnings yield and, 224
  fair value, 226
  forecasts, 228–229
  inflation v., 224
  interest rate models v., 224, 227
  investment valuation discipline and,
    311
  on S&P 500, 229
  value creation, 109
  wealth/fair value, 217
  zero inflation and, 267
Personalized medicine, 40, 339, 352, 389
Pfizer, 309
Pharmaceuticals, unmeasured increases
    in performance of, 170
Phillips curve, NAIRU and, 76
Politics of Need, 12, 13, 283
  Baby Boomers and, 290
  jobs, creation of and, 70
Popular Mechanics, 40
Post '90s, 278–281, 306, 343
Potential productivity, 139–140
Poverty, in New Economy, 283–286
PPI (Producer Price Index), BLS and, 111
Price elasticity of demand, 149
Price-Performance Curve, 38
"Prices for Local Area Network Equip-
    ment, " 167
Productivity
  declining, 124
  gains in a deflationary economy, 278
  government undermeasurement of,
    142–143
  information technology and, 141
  labor force disconnect, 136
  120% rule of thumb and, 145–146
  potential, 139–140
  profit margin models and, 143–145
  rising, 206
"Productivity and Profitability," 145, 146
Productivity decline, in 1980s/1990s, 78
Productivity growth
  corporate profitability and, 144–145,
    231

Productivity growth (cont.)
  Digital Revolution's contribution to,
    85
  formula for, 18
  GDP and, 18
  New Economy and, 19
  Over 3.0% Productivity Rule and, 146
  projections for next decade, 287
  quality-based improvements and, 84,
    85, 86
  second upward boost to, 127
  2000 and, 89–90
  undermeasurement of, 86
Productivity paradox, 6
Productivity Revolution, 126–128
Product-Performance Curve, 173
Prosperity
  global, 330
  new era of, 98, 312–314

Qualcomm, 376–381
Quality improvement
  absence of data in, 126
  cell phone example of, 21–22
  CPI affected by, 21
  deflation and, 28
  degradation and, 347–348
  Digital Revolution's effect on, 84
  equals deflation, 110
  GDP affected by, 26
  government measurement of, 26, 292
  information technology expansion
    and, 48
  undermeasurement of, 27–28, 50, 126
  value and digitally driven, 194–196
Quality IQ™ (Quality Improvement
    Quotient), 172
  Digital Deflation test and, 307–308
Quality v. quantity, Digital Deflation
    and, 84
Quality-based productivity gains, from
    Digital Deflation, 234
Quantity-based productivity gains, IT
    capital expenditures and, 234

R&D (research and development)
  importance of, 106
  medical advances and, 339

R&D (research and development) (*cont.*)
  new product pipeline, 309
  product performance, quality v. quantity and, 126
  return on investment for, 172
Reagan, Ronald, 62, 64, 67
Real bond rate, importance of, 223, 229, 248–252
Real interest rates, 257, 270–271
Real wages, and productivity gains, 286, 288
Recession
  of 1980, 62
  of 2001, 7, 294
  consumer discounting of, 92
  in New Economy, 257
Regulation Q
  Federal Reserve and, 76
  1980s phaseout of, 76
"The Resurgence of Growth in the Late 1990's: Is Information Technology the Story?", 152
RF (radio frequency) clock distribution, 364

Semiconductors
  as digital performance multipliers, 162
  Digital Revolution driven by, 35–37
  good deflation and, 49–50
  quality improvement, uncounted, from, 49–50
Senior Citizens, inflationary effect on, 335–336
Service sector
  Digital Deflation and, 123
  supply chain, 122–124
  undermeasurement of, 120
Silicon Valley, 87
Smoot-Hawley Tariff, Great Depression and, 58–59, 260
Social Security
  CBO's projections for, 296
  CPI and, 336
  funding of, 192
  looming challenge of, 298
  privatization of, 96
  raising taxes for, 337

Software
  BLS and, 115–116
  GDP deflator for, 116
  as non-quality-adjusted IT category, 164
  quality-based productivity gains of, 165
  quality improvements in, 115–116
Solow, Robert, 6
Soviet Union, Digital Revolution in, 328
S&P 500, P/E ratio and, 229
Statistics Canada, DOC's counterpart, 166
Step-down parallel pricing, 149
Stock market
  "anyone can be an investor" phenomenon and, 327
  corporate profits and, 139
  extended, meteoric rise of, 183
  labor force/relation to, 16, 134
  New Economy model of, 219–224
  New Economy stocks and, 304
  1987 crash of, 68
  1980s/1990s soaring, 12
  Old Economy stocks and, 304
  and real GDP, 137
  record high valuations and, 195
Structural productivity, gains in, 109–110
Substitution Bias, 355–356
Supply-side economics, 64, 67

Tanaka Capital Management
  IT Capital Spending regression model, 155
  IT Contribution to Productivity regression model, 155
  P/E conversion tables, 392
Tangible assets
  growth of, 242
  lower interest rates and, 243
Tangible-Net Financial Asset Model, 177–181
Technology
  accurate measurements of, 344
  biggest disappointment of, 361
  Clinton Administration's appreciation of, 78
  constant advances in, 285
  leveraging silicon, 359

Technology (*cont.*)
   third economic input, as, 344
   upgrades to, 87
   value of, 32
Telephone system, elimination of, 366
Third Generation technology, 377
Total Cost of Delivery, 124
Total Cost of Ownership, 123–124
"Trends in Internet Access Prices," 166
Tucker, Sophie, 191
Twain, Mark, 53
21st century, next two decades
   corporate profit margins in, 237
   Dow Jones Industrial Average, S&P
      500 in, 254
   household net worth in, 239
   low interest rates in, 240
The 2020 Vision, 191–193
2000–2002, economic slowdown during,
   96
2000
   capital spending/technology before, 89
   Digital Revolution/politics in, 91
   economic slowdown after, 94
   productivity growth of, 89

Underdemand, 349
Unemployment, crime rate and, 288,
   289
Unemployment rate, 2
   speed limit, 269
United States
   deflation and, 9
   Internet's effect on, 47
U.S. Treasury bonds
   downward trend of, 249
   and Federal Reserve, 274
   as key benchmark, 248
   possible drop in yields, 250
   and Reagan Revolution, 249

Valery, Paul, 1
Value creation
   two more decades of, 196–197
   and wealth creation, 198

Voice recognition/translation, 373
Volcker, Paul, 62–66

Wage gains, 286
Wage/price controls, internal disruption
   from, 57, 58–59
Wal-mart, 105
Watson, Thomas, 40
Wealth
   creation over next two decades, 236,
      237–239
   Creation Table, 246
   demographic foundation for generat-
      ing, 203–204, 206
   Digital Deflation adjusted for,
      202–203
   fair value P/E and, 217
   low inflation and, 207
   measuring, 200
   models using 3.00% real rate/10-year
      Treasury, 395
   in New Economy, 283–286
   outcomes of creating, 245
   scenarios of future, 215–217
Wealth effect, 92–95
   corporate, 95, 186–189
   for Investor-Consumers, 181–
      185
   realized capital gains, 185
   speed limit, 273
Welch, Jack, 99, 103–104
Working Women, 12–14, 70
Wozencraft, Jack, 380

Y2K, 3, 88, 90, 186
   capital spending spike, 313

Zero-bound nominal rate, 274
Zero growth, 72
Zero inflation, 208–210
   P/E ratios and, 267
Zero interest rates
   FOMC and, 273
   "running out of room" at, 273
Zero-bound nominal rate, 274

# A C K N O W L E D G M E N T S

I wish to thank my family and friends, who provided help and encouragement during the long journey toward writing this book. Special thanks to Marsha Brown, my administrative assistant at Tanaka Capital Management, who was there to help in innumerable ways, as well as to Bob Grant, Vicky McCann, Donna Conti, Mike Brady, Hans Wiemann, Charles Burmaster, Steve Albert, Dmitriy Perelstein, and Liam Nolan, who helped enormously.

In the editing process, I'd especially like to thank friend and author Mike Norden, whose wisdom and instant e-mails improved and accelerated the writing process; my editors, Stephen Isaacs, Jeffrey Cruikshanks, and Scott Kurtz; my publisher, Philip Ruppel; and those readers who contributed many valuable suggestions: my wife, Molly Fergusson, David Fox, Bruce Graham, Craig J. Hoffman, Seth Lukash, Daniel Mackell, Joseph J. Minarik, William J. Nolan, Mike O'Rourke, and Thomas R. Schwarz. Thanks also to my professor of economic forecasting, William Dunkelberg, who provided invaluable advice and historic perspective; to Charles Dill, Bart Schuldman, and Scott Stooker for their encouragement; and to my brother, Greg, and my sister, Tina Tanaka Urata, who inspired me by writing their own books.

I apologize that we were not able to include all interviews, but I'd like to express my appreciation to the many people whose interviews helped me better understand Digital Deflation. Thank you, Jim Balsillie, Carol Ben-Maimon, Paul Blaylock, Edward H. Braun, Jeff Cianci, Dr. Michael Clain, Scott D. Cook, Michael Dell, Doug J. Dunn, Steve Fodor, Ed Gerck, Dr. Marc D. Grodman, Dr. William Haseltine, Peter Haynes, Richard Hill, John Hilton, Irwin Jacobs, Dr. Gary Kalan, John Kreitler, Ira Lampert, Dr. Robert Longnecker, Doug Marsh, Eugene Melnyk, George M. Milne, Jr., Gordon Moore, James C. Morgan, Dr. Jeff Ranta, Gary Reiner, Jack Saltich, Christopher Sebes, Albert E. Sisto, Donna Smith, Eric Steiner, Michael Wales, Dr. Francis Walsh, Barry Weinstein, Pamela Wickham, and Thomas Williams.

I am particularly indebted to many economists, analysts, and career professionals of our government who answered my questions, provided valuable insight, and gave me great confidence that our country is in good hands with people who are at the top of their profession, very knowledgeable and dedicated to making the world a better place. It would have been more difficult to develop the Theory of Digital Deflation without the prior work of people like David Henry, Michael Holdway, David Wasshausen, Bruce T. Grimm, and others who have already contributed to improving the quality of our economic data. I am also appreciative of the time and insight provided by many other good people of the Bureau of Labor Statistics, the Department of Commerce, the Federal Reserve and the Congressional staff, including: Chris Amin, David Barry, Patricia Buckley, Curt Bursani, Elaine

Cardenas, Joe Chelena, Sandra Cooke, Jim Farrington, Mike Harper, Brent Hill, Patrick Jackman, Tom Kahn, John Kitchen, Deborah Kline, Paul Lally, Virginia Mannering, Brent R. Moulton, Brian Moyer, Carol Moylan, Fred Murkel, Leonard Nakamura, Lois Orr, Lee Price, Mike Reese, Todd Reese, Larry Rosenblum, Eugene P. Seskin, Nicole Shepler, Daniel E. Sichel, Robert Shapiro, Bill Thomas, and Frankie Valez.

Thanks also to economists Wayne Angell, Ed Hyman, Larry Kudlow, and Ed Yardeni for their sage advice and to Conrad DeQuadros, Melanie Hardy, Lisa Kirschner, and Kurt Walters for providing data digitally.

If I have missed anyone, it is truly unintended. Opinions and conclusions are entirely mine and not necessarily reflective of the above people. This book was an enormous undertaking, but if it helps our government to improve its data and policies, we may have all contributed to better times ahead. Many thanks!

# ABOUT THE AUTHOR

Graham Y. Tanaka is the President, Chief Investment Officer, and Chief Economist of Tanaka Capital Management, Inc. and TANAKA Funds, Inc. He first studied demographics, inflation, and interest rates as a housing and real estate analyst at Morgan Guaranty Trust and first developed expertise as a technology analyst at Fiduciary Trust Company of New York. He was among the first Japanese American Registered Investment Advisors in the United States and is a Chartered Financial Analyst (CFA) and member of the Electronic Analysts Group. Tanaka Capital Management, founded by Mr. Tanaka in 1986, manages investment portfolios for pension funds, foundations, and high net worth individuals, as well as the TANAKA Growth Fund for the general investing public. Tanaka Capital was ranked by Nelson's as the #1 Mid-cap U.S. Equity Manager and the tenth best money manager for All Styles of U.S. Equity Managers for the fourth quarter of 2002. Mr. Tanaka has appeared on CNBC, Fox News, Bloomberg Television, TV Tokyo, *Wall Street Journal Weekend Report*, and TheStreet.com and has been published in *Investors Business Daily* and quoted in a variety of newspapers and magazines. He serves on the Board of Directors of Trans-Act Technologies, Inc., the Board of Trustees for the Japanese American National Museum and the National Center for the Preservation of Democracy, and the Council of Governors of the East West Players. He holds A.B.-Sc.B. degrees from Brown University and an M.B.A. from Stanford University.